TIME AND INTIMACY: A NEW SCIENCE OF PERSONAL RELATIONSHIPS

LEA's Series on Personal Relationships
Steve Duck, Series Editor

TIME AND INTIMACY: A NEW SCIENCE OF PERSONAL RELATIONSHIPS

JOEL B. BENNETT
Texas Christian University

2000

LAWRENCE ERLBAUM ASSOCIATES, PUBLISHERS
Mahwah, New Jersey   London

The author and publisher collaborated in preparing the final camera copy for this work and together they share responsibility for consistency and correctness of typographical style. This arrangement helps to make publication of this kind of scholarship possible.

Grateful acknowledgment is made to the following for permission to reprint previously published material: Excerpt from "Revising Prose (3rd Ed.)" by Richard A. Lanham © 1992. Reprinted by permission from *Allyn & Bacon, Simon & Schuster Education Group* ◆ Excerpts from "Time, Self and Social Being" by Patrick Baert © 1992. Reprinted by permission from *Ashgate Publishing Limited* ◆ Excerpts from "Intimate Relations" by Murray S. Davis © 1973. Reprinted by permission from *The Free Press* and *Murray S. Davis* ◆ Excerpt from "Stopping the Clock" by Michele Ritterman, which first appeared in *The Family Therapy Networker* and is copied here with permission. ◆ Excerpts from "Love Cycles" by Winifred B. Cutler © 1995. Reprinted by permission from *Random House, Inc.* ◆ Excerpts and Figure 11.3 from "A Theory of Social Interaction" by Jonathan H. Turner. Reprinted with the permission of the publishers, *Stanford University Press* © 1988 by the Board of Trustees of the Leland Stanford Junior University. ◆ "Love Line" by Libby Stephens © 1996. Reprinted by permission from *Utne Reader*. Note. Policy at Lawrence Erlbaum Associates is to obtain permission for copying excerpts from a single source that exceeds 200 words. Grateful acknowledgement is made to the many different publishers that have also contributed extracts of less than 200 words.

Lawrence Erlbaum Associates, Inc., Publishers
10 Industrial Avenue
Mahwah, New Jersey 07430

Cover design by Kathryn Houghtaling Lacey

Library of Congress Cataloging-in-Publication Data

Bennett, Joel B.
    Time and Intimacy : a new science of personal relationships / Joel B. Bennett.
        p. cm. – (LEA's series on personal relationships)
    Includes bibliographical references and indexes.
    ISBN 0-8058-3679-9 (alk. paper) – ISBN 0-8058-3680-2 (pbk. : alk. paper)
    1. Intimacy (Psychology) 2. Time. 3. Interpersonal relations. I. Title II. Series.

    BF575.I5 B45 2000
    158.2—dc21   00-041106

Books published by Lawrence Erlbaum Associates are printed on acid-free paper, and their bindings are chosen for strength and durability.

Printed in the United States of America
10   9   8   7   6   5   4   3   2   1

Contents

LIST OF RESEARCH REFLECTIONS

Series Editor's Foreword

Steve Duck
University of Iowa

This series on personal relationships from Lawrence Erlbaum Associates is intended to review the progress in the academic work on relationships in respect to a broad array of issues and does so in an accessible manner that also illustrates its practical value. This series will also include books intended to pass on the accumulated scholarship to the next generation of students and to those who deal with relationship issues in the broader world beyond the academy. It will thus comprise not only monographs and other academic resources exemplifying the multidisciplinary nature of this area, but also textbooks suitable for use in the growing numbers of courses on relationships.

The series provides a comprehensive and current survey of theory and research in personal relationships through the careful analysis of the problems encountered, and solved, yet it also considers the systematic application of that work in a practical context. These resources are intended to be not only comprehensive assessments of progress on particular topics, but also significant influences on the future directions and development of the study of personal relationships. Although each volume is focused and centered, authors attempt to place the respective topics in the broader context of other research on relationships and within a range of wider disciplinary traditions. The series thus not only offers incisive and forward-looking reviews, but also demonstrates the broader theoretical implications of relationships for the range of disciplines from which the research originates.

Series volumes include original studies, reviews of relevant theory and research, and new theories oriented toward the understanding of personal relationships both in themselves and within the context of broader theories of family process, social psychology, and communication. Reflecting the diverse composition of personal relationship study, readers in numerous disciplines—social psychology, communication, sociology, family studies, developmental psychology, clinical psychology, personality, counseling, women's studies, gerontology, and others—will find valuable and insightful perspectives in the series.

Apart from the academic scholars who research the dynamics and processes of relationships, there are many other people whose work takes them up against the operation of relationships in the real world. For such people as nurses, the police, teachers, therapists, lawyers, drug and alcohol counselors, marital counselors, and those who take care of the elderly, a number of issues routinely arise concerning the ways in which relationships affect the people whom they

ix

serve. Examples are the role of loneliness in illness and the ways to circumvent it, the complex impact of the temporal structure of daily life on expectations about the appropriateness of behaviors in a given relationship, the role of playground unpopularity on a child's learning, the issues involved in dealing with the relational side of chronic illness, the management of conflict in marriage, the establishment of good rapport between physicians and seriously ill patients, the support of the bereaved, and the correction of violent styles of behavior in dating or marriage. Each is a problem that may confront some of the aforementioned professionals as part of their daily concerns. Each demonstrates the far-reaching influences of relationship processes on much else in life that is presently theorized independently of relationship considerations.

The present volume is a particularly interesting example of the philosophy of the series. The book is about the interweaving of notions of time and relationships. It is an extremely original work not simply born of the latest empirical research articles, but a deeply structured and innovative rethinking of previous approaches to time, both philosophical, organizational, psychological, and sociological. Not only does the author show an impressive range of knowledge about a disparate set of research findings and theories from a broad set of scholarly disciplines, but his own application of their scholarship to the conceptual and practical issues of temporal structuring in social and relational lives is unique. The book is also written in a form that intertwines the scholarly work with the real-life experiences of the author in compelling ways that make it accessible and involving as well as theoretically challenging and deep.

Because this book is innovative and exciting in its conceptual style and in its structure, is academically fascinating, and is a particularly well-written volume, it is likely to revolutionize the ways in which researchers think about time in relationships. As such, it will be used as a reference for many people in the field. I also believe that its evocative style of reporting human experience makes it a volume that will have appeal outside the offices of researchers alone and therefore that many people who do not normally read academic books will find that it has something direct and compelling to say to them also.

Love's not Time's fool, though rosy lips and cheeks
Within his bending sickle's compass come:
Love alters not with his brief hours and weeks,
But bears it out even to the edge of doom.

—William Shakespeare (from *Sonnet CXVI*)

But time has stood still, since we've been apart.

—Hank Williams (from "I Can't Stop Loving You")

Preface

SINCE THE 1970s, there has been a marked flourish of writing and research on the topics of personal relationships and intimacy. In addition to the thousands of magazine articles and popular books on love and intimacy, scientists have examined a broad array of phenomena, ranging from analysis of love and styles of romantic attachment to genetic influences on marital success. I believe that all this activity represents humanity's search for a new way of living in and understanding—a new model of—close relationships. Although our knowledge is growing, many research efforts are misguided and trivial. There is more to the study of intimacy than can be addressed by current scientific models (Berscheid & Reis, 1998). Both reductionistic and quantitative, these models fail to address both the deeper, spiritual aspects of intimate meaning and the importance of time, growth, and change that is woven into this meaning. These models suffer from several limitations. First, they do not address the future or the possible evolution of close relationships. Almost by definition, research focuses on data, identifying what is, "the given," and tries to discover probabilities, regularities, and laws. There is room for new models that explore the possibility that relationships can be more than what we imagine they could be (see Levine & Levine, 1996). Second, most research on relationships is based on an outdated or classical (Newtonian) conception of time that ignores the dynamic and complex nature of intimacy. Third, trying to mimic the methods of the physical sciences, the social science of personal relationships has nearly divorced itself from a wellspring of previous knowledge and wisdom about intimacy. Such wisdom lies in the humanities (poetry and literature), in philosophy, and in spiritual or religious texts. This book attempts to redress the scientific paradigm and catalyze a broader, transdisciplinary exploration of how human relationships engender and awaken intimacy and how time shapes this awakening. I hope it benefits anyone who is seeking new ways of understanding personal relationships of all types.

Because it deals with time, this book may also help those who wish to recapture the meaning of intimacy in a hurried world. In fact, recent social trends suggest that those of us who are the most starved for intimacy are also likely to be those most starved for time. As a society, we have been taught, and have bought the wholesale illusion, that time is scarce (Rechtschaffen, 1996). We have fallen into a consensual trance, fascinated by information and the "media"; that is, the digitized, video-graphic, telemediated, and virtual world. Gradually and without much notice, we have cultivated an insatiable hunger for as much information as possible in the shortest possible amount of time. A central point of this book is that such hunger belies a deeply thwarted need for intimacy. The fascination with media and the hunger or search for information is a direct externalization of a deeper, forgotten, soulful longing to feel connected.

To some degree, this fascination originated as a result of the postmodern compression of our sense of time (Gleick, 1999). To the degree that we hunger for the perfect temporal "byte" of information, we forget about the inner journey, about community, about each other, and about eternity.

The recent expansion of both popular (consumer-oriented) and academic "knowledge" about intimacy is an outgrowth of our thwarted need for intimacy. That is, the soulful need for intimacy, as a result of its diversion to the exterior of the information-glutted world, presses for satiety in every aspect of modern culture (popular media, religion, and even academia). On the one hand, we want to know more about what we have lost. On the other hand, we want to reshape the meaning of intimacy in a way that fits with a newly evolving, telemediated, and hurried society. In response and in some ways, the science of intimacy holds out a promise. We can learn from ancient texts, myths, and stories about meeting, about love, and about the soul's journey. The logic of science teaches that we could also discover a new image. I take up the task of outlining and sketching some possible images.

THE TIME-INTIMACY EQUATION

This book is about the time-intimacy equation, which has four different forms. The most popular or pedestrian states that real intimacy requires an investment of time. We believe that in order for genuine intimacy to develop within a relationship, two individuals must be willing to give or spend time with each other. This first form of the equation generally assumes that intimacy is equated with some reciprocal exchange of self-disclosure, vulnerability, or sexuality. Most research on time and intimacy deals with this form of the equation (Derlega, Metts, Petronio, & Margulis, 1993).

A second form of this equation states that deeper experiences of intimacy entail some transcendence of the temporal world. Throughout history, individuals—lovers as well as poets and mystics from all religious traditions—have described an essential quality of timelessness woven into their experience of the beloved. This quality plays a significant role even within our more typical encounters or "ordinary" relationships. Many difficulties in relationships stem from a lack of the sense of the beloved, from one or both partner's attachment to their own time-limited viewpoint, ego, or personality. From a spiritual or transpersonal view, this personality is a false sense of self that may be distinguished from our authentic self or essence (Almaas, 1987; Tart, 1987). This essence is a pure sense of our uniqueness that is covered over through socialization and enculturation processes. As we shall see, the intimate experience is not merely about disclosure and sexuality; it stimulates the timeless, whole, and compassionate aspects of our essential self. In fact, research suggests that one's sense of self expands through intimate relations (Aron & Aron, 1996).

A third form of the equation states that sensitivity to natural temporal qualities—such as cycles, rhythms, periods of coming together and going apart—defines the capacity for intimacy. As we tune into and live according to natural cycles and rhythms, we feel connection and continuity with life and others. This temporal sensitivity pertains to a wide array of phenomena, from the ability of counselors to follow and encourage their client's natural cycle of healing, to the ability of mediators to "read" a system of marital conflict (Sillars & Wilmot, 1994). It is in the language of sensuality and sexual dialogue where we see this equation most often. That is, lovers intuitively recognize different temporal signatures, for example, when they hold, stroke, squeeze, and glide. Whereas this third form of the equation has been central in discussions by anthropologists (Hall, 1983), philosophers (Buber, 1958/1970), feminists (Kristeva, 1981), and Native American writers (Allen, 1986), it has yet to be incorporated into any scientific or psychological understanding of personal relationships.

The fourth form is perhaps the most difficult to understand. The human experience of time in all of its personal aspects—from talking with an acquaintance, to social schedules, to the sense of mortality—is influenced by how we prioritize intimacy and negotiate time together with others. That is, our social relations, especially those we consider the most intimate, define time in a most existential and personal manner. In fact, research indicates that intimacy, love, and the sense of belonging are directly related to biological longevity or mortality (Ornish, 1998). We also feel that time passes more quickly when absorbed in pleasurable or intimate contact. An old cartoon shows Albert Einstein talking with the "ordinary man" who is trying to understand relativity theory (in Priestly, 1964, p. 68). The man says: "Your theory is this—supposing I were to sit next to a pretty girl for half an hour it would seem like half a minute. . . . But if I were to sit on a hot stove for two seconds then it would seem like two hours."

We may experience the fourth equation most poignantly when we wait for, or are kept waiting for, an intimate other or when we redeem the past through forgiveness. Our closest relationships often challenge us to develop the virtues of sobriety, patience, humility, and equanimity; attitudes that require a deeper relationship to time. Also, when we resume contact with someone once close to us (e.g., an old lover or friend), it may feel like we are resuming from where we left off. Time has not passed at all. We glimpse that time has to do with our state of being with others. In fact, as many who are dying look back at their life, they often attend to how they loved and how they related to others with whom they were closest (Levine, 1982). This is scrutinized more so than their works, the progress they made, or their achievements.

ISSUES ADDRESSED (AND NOT ADDRESSED)

While collecting research for this book, I discerned several issues that relate to the time-intimacy equation. First, psychologists mostly define intimacy as a behavioral or communication skill (cf. "responsiveness to disclosure"; Reis &

Shaver, 1988). This skill is important, but intimacy should not be equated only with action and competence. It also entails psychic qualities like presence, patience, or a sense of wholeness. For example, presence underlies the attitude of regard, cherishing, or attentiveness that appears to make couples happy. Of course, intimacy entails skill, such as the capacity to embrace the many kinds of changes (such as in feelings) that occur over time. However, this skill requires an awareness of the qualities of intimacy as well as behavior. My focus is more on the dynamic experience of intimacy; I only touch on different aspects of behavioral skill. Thus, this is not a "how to" book but I believe it has implications for understanding how to cultivate intimacy.

Second, more than in any other point in history, modern popular culture has given increased attention to intimacy. At the same time, technological changes occurring within our fast-paced society shape and color our experience of community, privacy, and intimacy. People find and maintain relationships through newspaper "Want Ads," the Internet, cellular phones, and telephone pagers. In fact, a significant amount of research is currently exploring how to make computers and the

> *We need to stop
> RUNNING out of
> time and learn how to
> DANCE with time.*

Internet more sensitive and responsive to the moods of their users (cf. "affective computing," MIT Media Lab, 1999; also see "telepresence," e.g., Microsoft, 1999). While helpful, such technology can create a false sense of connection and the motivation for this "felt sense" may come to displace the original motive for face-to-face, real-time interaction. In fact, a growing number of Internet users develop personal problems because of addictive relationships formed on the Internet (Yang, 2000; Young, 1998). Any viable understanding of intimacy must contend with these technological issues. Thus, this book examines our "taken for granted" views on both time and intimacy, and shows how these assumptions constrain our experiences of both. Seekers of intimacy as well as their counselors or therapists may benefit from a broader understanding of intimacy.

Third, we live in a hurried society where many feel that we are "running out of time." Time management courses and workshops teach us how to squeeze more time in but do not really improve intimacy. (See Rechtschaffen, 1996, on alternatives to time management that show how we can slow down and reorient to the present moment.) Similarly, the fragmentation of this fast-paced society can result in feelings of alienation, apathy, and loneliness (all symptoms of the lack of intimacy) as well as addiction (the need to get high quick). To address the pervasive trends toward busyness and addiction, we need to stop "running out of time" and instead learn how to dance with time. This book explores the vital steps in how couples dance with time.

Fourth, there is a peculiar split in the audience interested in personal relationships and their improvement. Books written for researchers are of little interest to lovers. The "how to" books of lovers either lack scientific value or they can be criticized as lacking scientific evidence for the effectiveness of methods they describe. Yet, they are in abundance and growing. My informal search on the Internet provided one list of over 5,000 different books and audiocassettes! (Amazon.com, 1999). In short, there is little common ground or a language for dialogue between the scientist and the lover. This book seeks to build a link between the scientific and the personal/experiential languages of intimacy.

Finally, consider the issue of our own personal purpose, our reason for being, or our spirituality—as persons and as intimates. Spirituality may be the necessary ingredient to a happy and enduring relationship. Consider those who have fallen in love, who make the deep vow "until death do us part," and who have sensed timelessness in the eyes of their beloved. Researchers who study relationships often neglect this spirituality even though—as the epigram quotes by Shakespeare and Hank Williams tell—timelessness is an important part of the experience of love. A recent review of research on close relationships has few references concerning spirituality (Berscheid & Reis, 1998). Social scientists appear to be lagging behind scientists in biology and physics (e.g., Barlow, 1997; Crick, 1994) who have come to new understandings about time and about the intimate connections revealed in nature. The chapters of this book follow the lead of these writers and show how any complete analysis of intimacy must consider the way two individuals learn to move beyond time and their own mortality.

Recent research shows how some of these issues are interrelated. In their book, Robinson and Godbey (1997) drew several conclusions from over three decades of research. First, they found that Americans have generally shown increases in their perceptions of feeling more rushed, with less time to do the things they need to do. Paradoxically, Americans actually have more leisure time available to them than they did 30 years ago. This is one way our need for intimacy has been thwarted: We have outpaced ourselves so much that we have forgotten how to stop. Second, Americans spend less of their free or leisure time in direct, face-to-face informal socializing with others (visiting others, dinner) or participating in involuntary organizations (clubs, political, religious). At the same time, there has been a marked increase in television use or media-related leisure activities (Putnam, 1995). In a 1985 study, 11 percent of free time was in home communication versus 38 percent watching television (even though the latter is not necessarily satisfying). Our time experiencing others is less "media-free," less direct, less somatic.

In explaining these results, Robinson and Godbey (1997) concluded:

> Many people have developed dysfunctional attitudes toward time as an infinitely expandable resource. . . . As numerous scholars have observed, two modes of human consciousness exist. One perceives reality as separate objects existing in three-dimensional space and linear time. The other, which may be called spiritual, holistic, or transpersonal, views reality

as a series of relationships among all things that is part of some universal consciousness. People who subscribe to the first mode typically lead ego-centered, competitive, goal-oriented lives. . . . Such a consciousness is related to how time is viewed and the extent to which pace of life is an issue. Those who cannot derive satisfaction from ordinary activities of everyday life will always be rushed to construct another basis of satisfaction. (pp. 304–307)

But how much control do we have over these attitudes in a culture that rewards swiftness, speed, and anything that is faster (*rapid* transit, *fast* food, *fast* company; see Gleick, 1999)? Hochschild's (1997) intensive study of couples and families showed that people have very little control and argued that only collective, national action may help us get out of the "time prisons" in which we live. Hochschild revealed how many families have given up intimacy and time at home because of the intense workaholic standards imposed by the workplace. Importantly, our mental health has deteriorated because of these standards and the lack of time for intimacy. In one study, Simon (1997) asked 40 full-time employed parents to describe in their own words what "being a spouse (parent and worker) personally means to you?" Simon examined the open-ended responses and their relation to a separate measure of psychological distress. Paradoxically, the strongest correlate of distress was a spousal role that provided companionship and intimacy ("sharing your life. . . a special bond"). That is, relationships often fall short of the "companion ideal" and the resulting lack of meaning is a significant source of distress. In addition, individuals, particularly females, were distressed when their work identity meant a lack of time and energy for children and spouse. Simon's findings suggest that we may be happier if we do not expect too much companionship and intimacy and we do not view our roles as giving time for our family. We may be more satisfied if we forget about time and intimacy altogether.

> *Science can either contribute to or solve the problems of time and intimacy.*

But apathy is not the solution. Rather, we (social scientists included) must thoroughly examine our culturally and economically shaped assumptions about time, and how these influence personal habits that limit intimacy. We have been taught that intimacy means sexuality, closeness, and disclosure, and that time means money. But intimacy is not only about having sex, or feeling good about each other. Intimacy is not a goal we achieve by attaining these outcomes. It is more about process than outcome, more about mutual meaning, stopping, holding, waiting, wondering, listening, moving through time with another, being present through changing feelings and situations, and a sense of participating in a common story. We think "it takes time" to appreciate these things, but time actually expands when we cherish and appreciate. I believe that scientists need to study the pauses, the waiting, the listening. I believe that a new appreciation will come from a scientific (and non-Newtonian) understanding of the role of time and temporality in intimacy and human relationships. We need a language that might help us see our own biases, our limited perspectives (of time) that prevent a more whole perception of intimacy.

HOW TO USE THIS BOOK

I have formatted this book so it may be read in different ways and for different purposes. Although it is not a "how to" book, it may serve as a reference guide for various types of readers, including academics, scientists, students, counselors, and those with a general interest in relationships. Beyond a reference resource, the book may help them to better notice and broaden their "inner" sense of intimacy, their ways of thinking about and observing intimacy, and how they use and think about time within human relationships. To foster this, I propose seven models, which I describe and elaborate on through the main text. Each of these models attempts to encourage a new image of personal relationships, one that I hope will foster understanding of the transpersonal or spiritual side of intimacy. In addition, several chapters explore new ideas about marriage and time, and about how insensitivity to time creates blocks to intimacy. Many of these ideas are abstract and highly conceptual. There are illustrations at various points, using either a fictional couple or my own personal experiences. I also borrow statements from questionnaires that researchers have used to study psychological factors relevant to time and personal relationships. These are boxed and highlighted as 18 distinct **RESEARCH REFLECTIONS** and I encourage readers to assess whether the statements apply to their own experiences. An appendix also reviews these reflections together so readers can think about how a transpersonal science of intimacy might actually test hypotheses about the time and intimacy equation.

> *This book seeks to build a bridge between common everyday understandings, the humanities, and the sciences.*

This book seeks to stimulate new ways of thinking about relationships and specifically about the role of time in them. Some or even much of what I have to say is speculative or synthetic; I do not focus on new research as much as try to present things in a new light. That is, I merge, compare, and contrast empirical knowledge with philosophical and even older metaphysical ideas. At the same time, I only sketch ways in which the different models may be related or how they may be tested. These topics may be of primary interest to researchers in the study of personal relationships, but my hope is that they will be useful to couples' therapists and to students from different disciplines who seek to set up a dialogue about the journey of intimacy.

Because it reviews some basic ideas in the study of personal relationships—methodology, theory, and research studies—this book may also serve as a supplement or reference guide to graduate courses on personal relationships, social psychology, and marital or family studies. Here, readers might be interested in chapter 7 as well as sections labeled "Research Notes" in chapters 4 and 6. Because the topics I discuss shuttle back and forth between philosophy, science, and spirituality, this book may also be used to develop an interdisciplinary course that seeks to bridge the humanities and the sciences.

I hope this book will help renovate existing research models. I am not suggesting that the ideas presented should replace or even guide existing research programs, but that the perspectives offered bring some new light to these programs. The field of personal relationship research focuses on different topics (e.g., attraction, mate selection, love, relationship cognition, self-disclosure). As a result, it paints a somewhat fragmented and disconnected image. Given the issues outlined here, the time seems right to work toward a new, more holistic, and integrated science. For this reason, the beginning (epigram) page at the start of the primary chapters (2 through 8) contains my "thoughts on a new science."

Finally, although I focus on intimacy in close, personal relationships, I believe the processes described have some application to intimacy as it occurs in other types of relationships: that is, in friendship, religion/church, family (parent–child), counseling (therapist-client), education (student–teacher/mentor), and work (supervisor–employee). In fact, for some the transpersonal experience of intimacy might occur in only one of these relationship types. I encourage the reader to consider how ideas in this book apply (and perhaps do not apply) to these types.

ACKNOWLEDGMENTS

I have benefited from the conversations and support of many over the ten years that it took to complete this book. Special recognition goes to Steve Duck for his early encouragement and continuous commitment throughout the various twists and turns of this project. Joseph E. McGrath, Richard Archer, and Ted Huston also provided helpful encouragement during the early phases. I have also been fortunate to have colleagues—Randy Cornelius, Andrea Birch, and Karen Prager—who read through some version of the manuscript and provided many helpful tips. Along the way, different friends—especially Duane Piety and George Daughtery—listened and provided needed intellectual support to help me flesh out ideas. More recently, the format and readability of the manuscript has benefited from technical support provided by Jim Dodson, Janna M. Franzwa, and Nancy J. Bartosek. Thanks guys! I also wish to thank Jan Bennett, Sandhya Rao and Shawn Reynolds for helping out with indexing.

The above acknowledgements reflect my gratitude to those who helped me with my ideas and their communication to others. Special recognition goes to Lawrence Erlbaum Associates, Inc. and Linda Bathgate for making these ideas a printed reality.

I am also grateful to those teachers along the path who either aided in my spiritual growth or bolstered my confidence enough to find the way to express the "deeper" idea. These teachers have included Michele Katz, Robert C. Neville, Oscar Ichazo, Richard J. Davidson, Jack Kornfeld, Janet Taylor Spence, and Anne Wilson Schaef.

I do not think I could write, and complete, a book about intimacy without having actually had some experience of it. For their love and guidance, I thank my mother, Jane Shapiro Bennett (1931-1977), and my father, Gerald Stanley Bennett. I am most grateful to my wife Jan for her love, patience, and companionship.

The couple is a place where we can make a deal to learn our most intimate lessons on the spiritual path. Learning how to live in the couple is healing for the consciousness of all humanity. The crisis of the couple is the crisis of society.

—Oscar Ichazo (founder of Arica® Institute,
a school for the development of consciousness)

Men and women need each other more than ever as partners in facing an increasingly demanding and accelerated pace of life.

—Gail Sheehy (author, political journalist,
and contributing editor to *Vanity Fair*)

1

Introduction

LIKE UNSEEN hands, many "clocks"—social, psychological, and communicative—guide the course and development of personal relationships. In the field of sociology, researchers have discovered that the way individuals follow "social clock" norms can bear on later developments in life. Our age at different transition points in the life of our closest relationships (first sexual intercourse, first marriage, first child) may be "early" or "late" compared to the average age, and so may influence the nature of those relationships (e.g., Helson, Mitchell, & Moane, 1984). Psychologists have discovered that different social motives may be influenced by early childhood experiences in our families and, in turn, shape how we behave with those with which we choose to seek intimacy. Sometimes our need for intimacy ("I want to be close with someone") may be stronger or weaker than the need for stability ("I like things to run smoothly and in ways I can predict") or the need for change ("I want to have new and exciting experiences"). Communication scientists as well, studying the moment-to-moment behavior of married couples, have discovered sequences of interaction that take on a life of their own. Some couples "lock in" to cycles of interaction, and others have rhythms of communication that are less predictable but nonetheless determine the character of the couple. These clocks work together, a weave of temporal forces, to shape every challenge and opportunity for intimacy and closeness.

Despite the importance of these clocks, relationships—in their most intimate form—move through and even beyond time. In a sort of paradoxical way, when we experience deeply knowing and caring for another, we sense that relationships are not merely temporal, not strictly bound to age, personal need, or chains of events. This book seeks to bridge these two ways of understanding relationships—one temporal and one transcendent of time. It seeks to show that the weave of time that impels relationships is a precious weave that can be known through science as well as direct experience.

ORIENTATION AND DEFINITIONS: GRASPING AT COMPLEXITY

This book provides seven different ways (in seven corresponding chapters) of understanding intimacy in a more process-oriented or time-sensitive manner. By "process-oriented" I mean that intimacy is not just some goal to achieve or reach—that is, an outcome, a state, phase, or feeling. This goal is often implied when we talk about sexual union, closeness in just being together, an exchange

3

of secrets, or new levels of disclosure. Intimacy can occur just as much, if not more, between, before, or after these occurrences. It is a process of interacting with another in ways that are sensitive to change and nuance. By "sensitive to time" I mean that anyone who thinks about intimate relationships—be it their own or others—can appreciate or be mindful of the effect that time has on such relationships.

This temporal sensitivity has been developing in widely different areas of science. For example, in theoretical biology, Bornstein (1989) wrote about life cycle development in animal and human neurobiology, defining 14 distinct features of "sensitive periods" of development (e.g., hours for ducklings to imprint, days for a bird to learn a song, months to ensure sexual normalcy in monkeys). Certain features demarcate the temporal profile of the sensitive period. These include dating or when the event begins, the rise and decay in terms of setting event and time, the duration or temporal window of susceptibility, and the asymptote (whether the sensitive period is shaped more like a peak or a plateau). In addition, there are temporal aspects to the mechanisms of change, which stimulate the sensitive period, and to the consequences of the sensitive period (e.g., outcome and duration of outcome). Research on "sensitive periods" in personal relationships might benefit from this biological nomenclature.

In counseling psychology, Zhu and Pierce (1995) argued that certain time-limited forms of counseling could be more efficient if sensitive to issues such as client's learning curve, and probability of relapse. A client's need for counseling is often not a linear function of time. Zhu and Pierce provided the example of "relapse-sensitive" scheduling in recovery from smoking cessation, with sessions scheduled 0, 1, 3, 7, 14, and 30 days after quitting rather than on a weekly basis. In the field of ecology, researchers are discovering that farming and land management practices are also more efficient when sensitive to the natural cycles of seasons, animal grazing, and crop cycles (Savory, 1988). This view of ecosystem management, called holistic resource management, views people and the environment as a whole.

These examples teach us something about intimacy. Whether biologist, counselor, farmer, or ecologist, they all benefit from a greater appreciation of the temporal complexities within the systems in which they work. By listening to these temporal shapes, the system teaches them how to respond better. In fact, by not imposing their own preconceived temporal framework (e.g., schedules for feeding, mating, crop rotation, counseling), they actually come to participate or interact more with these systems and help them to thrive. After years of studying the relationship between marital interaction and divorce, Gottman (1994b) reached a similar conclusion about how to best conduct therapy with distressed couples. He suggested "Minimal Marital Therapy," where counselors provide couples with repetitive practice of a small set of communication skills and "then hope that a self-guided and self-correcting system takes over after that" (p. 434).

Gottman's research shows that sensitivity to temporal process in intimate relations requires an appreciation of complexity. I believe that for such appreciation, more than one model or definition is required. The scientific tendency toward "the best explanation" or "single guiding theory" may reify a reductionistic, mechanistic, or formulaic viewpoint that is not process-oriented. For this reason, and because this book seeks to stimulate new ideas, I do not provide a single definition of either intimacy or time. However, it may help to know something about how other writers and researchers have defined intimacy and time.

DEFINING INTIMACY

> The word intimacy is derived from the Latin *intimus,* meaning inner or inmost. To be intimate with another is to have access to, and to comprehend, his/her inmost character. In most Romance languages the root word for intimate refers to the interior or inmost quality of a person. The Spanish, *intimo,* for example means familiar, conversant, closely acquainted. In Italian, *intimo* signifies internal, close in friendship and familiar, whereas the French *intime* conveys deep, secret, close, confidential. In German *innig* means heartfelt, sincere, cordial, ardent, fervent. (R. E. Sexton and V. S. Sexton, 1982, p. 1)

As Sexton and Sexton suggested, there is a common thread through different definitions of intimacy—an awareness of the innermost character of another person—but there are some differences as well. As Prager (1995) pointed out, an ultimate definition of intimacy is unattainable, partly because it is a "fuzzy" concept, meaning that it is characterized by "a *shifting* template of features rather than a clearly bounded set" (p. 13, italics added). In fact, it is this shifting, dynamic—what I call *catalytic*—quality of intimacy that escapes most definitions of intimacy. There is something about the intimate experience that moves us in ways that cannot be neatly defined. Because intimacy is about discovery, it is an "open-system" concept that defies complete definition. Following Prager, this book views intimacy as a superordinate construct, and as multidimensional; it means different things at different times. For scientists, understanding intimacy is a discipline requiring good conceptual tools, careful observation, and an ability to shift from "a clearly bounded set." Intimacy may not be reducible to a specific set of behaviors that occur when two are together, or to cognitions, beliefs, and attitudes about those behaviors. Rather, intimacy occurs as certain catalytic qualities of experience are discovered when individuals participate in knowing another as they know themselves. These catalytic qualities (described in detail in chap. 2) constitute the intimate experience.

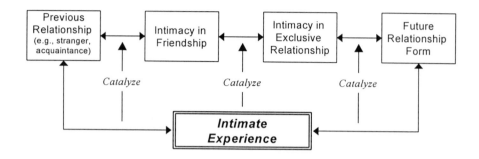

FIG. 1.1. Operational concepts of intimacy.

Measuring Intimacy

Having stated the difficulty in defining intimacy, it helps to present some ways in which scientists have actually measured it. I present three approaches here and the interested reader may consult Prager (1995, Table 2.2) for a list of more than 40 different measures assessing some aspect of intimacy or intimate relationships. Tzeng (1993) also provided a number of actual scales and showed how they are related and distinct from scales that assess love. Each of the following approaches also show how intimacy is alternatively defined as an attitude, a relationship, and as an experiential state. People can experience attitudes and initiate behaviors toward friends that make those friendships more intimate than others (Sharabany, 1994). As those friendships become more intimate, they may turn into more exclusive, partner, marital, or sexual relationships (Garthoeffner, Henry, & Robinson, 1993). Sometime in the development of this intimate bond, individuals may experience a deep personal sense of intimacy (Register & Henley, 1992) that either leads to the intimate friendship or exclusive relationship, shifts the nature of the relationship, or to some other possibility. Thus, intimacy may be experienced as a state, as a process, as a quality of a relationship, or as all three at different times. Figure 1.1 integrates these different operational conceptions of intimacy.

Thus, we may experience intimacy as part of or within a variety of relationship forms (a previous relationship, a friendship, an exclusive or sexually committed relationship). The experience of intimacy may even give the relationship its form and distinguish it from other relationships. Conversely, different relationship forms can stimulate, shape, and mellow the intimate experience. It is also possible that the intimate experience is a critical catalyzer that moves a relationship from one form to another. An intimate experience may move an acquaintance relationship to an intimate friendship, or an intimate friendship may become exclusively sexual through some intimate experience. The following research reflection shows ways in which scientists have tried to capture these different aspects of intimacy. With these and other research reflections, consider whether the questionnaire statements apply to you.

RESEARCH **REFLECTION** 1

Intimacy in Friendship

Sharabany (1994) developed the *Intimate Friendship Scale* to study intimacy in the friendships of children and preadolescents, but the items also apply to adult friendships. This scale has eight different dimensions. The following is a list of the major factors and some exemplary or paraphrased items.

Frankness and spontaneity: I feel free to talk with him or her about anything.
Sensitivity and knowing: I can tell when he or she is worried about something.
Attachment: I like him or I feel close to him or her.
Exclusiveness: The most exciting things happen when we are alone together.
Giving and sharing: I offer him or her the use of my things.
Imposition: I am sure he'll (she'll) help me whenever I ask.
Common activities: I like doing things with him or her.
Trust and loyalty: I know that whatever I tell him or her is kept a secret.

Interpersonal Relationships

It is important to point out that not all relationships are intimate and that not all intimate experience occurs in a relationship. Individuals may be married for years and not feel any intimacy, and many people experience intimacy only in solitude or through nature. Interestingly, the features measured by Sharabany overlap with various qualities measured in a more general assessment of adult interpersonal relationships. Garthoeffner et al. (1993) tested the reliability and validity of the Interpersonal Relationship Scale, first developed by Guerney (1977). Whereas it does not refer to the psychological construct of interpersonal intimacy, any individual who experiences most of the factors described in this scale could be experiencing intimacy. The following is a list of the major factors from this scale and some exemplary items:

Trust: There are times when my partner cannot be trusted. (Reverse scored)
Self-Disclosure: I tell my partner some things of which I am very ashamed.
Genuineness: My partner is truly sincere in his/her promises.
Empathy: I feel my partner misinterprets what I say. (Reverse scored)
Comfort: I seek my partner's attention when I am facing troubles.
Communication: I can accept my partner even when we disagree.

There are some subtle but noticeable differences with the previous measure. There may be differences in how intimacy is experienced in childhood, adolescence, and adulthood. I encourage those interested in understanding developmental aspects of intimacy to read Prager's (1995) thorough analysis of intimacy across the life span.

Continued

Intimate Experience

The features listed in both of the aforementioned measures contribute to the overall quality of interpersonal relationships. However, these features—captured and represented by questionnaire wording—may not convey the unique, deeply personal or phenomenological aspects of intimate experience. To do this, Register and Henley (1992) asked people what they meant by intimacy without imposing prefabricated questionnaire items. They discovered seven different themes that made up the central structure of each narrative of intimacy. The following lists these themes and some exemplary or paraphrased reports from the people in Register and Henley's study:

Nonverbal communication (difficult to convey in words)

- A touch of the hand, the meeting of our eyes conveyed our intimacy better than a thousand words.
- Words did not seem adequate for what we had between us.

Presence (a noticeable existence of the presence or "spirit" of another within one)

- I can feel her presence, somewhere within me, and it gives me great pleasure to do so.
- He was just "there" for me and I have been "here" for him.

Time (a keen awareness of the concept of time)

- I believe that the intimacy was for each day and renewed for each day after.
- It's about experiencing a complete day with each other.

Boundary (the removal of boundaries between people)

- I had a cool and distant exterior, but here was a boyfriend chipping away at my defenses.
- The walls had crumbled that had, for many years, been built between us.

Body (body awareness and bodily touching)

- It felt like a combination of butterflies in my stomach, complete muscular relaxation, and a weight off my shoulders.
- Holding hands, arms around waists, sitting together with legs intertwined.

Destiny and surprise (the experience is both unusual and very natural, destined)

- It was so spontaneous and unordinary, but so right, like we were meant to happen.
- I should have been surprised but it rang a bell somewhere inside of me.

Transformation (creating something new through movement or merging)

- You have this sense that she and I are not separate, we have become one, a whole, Unity.
- I was becoming something different with her, and it was a deeper revelation of who I was.

Features of this list—presence, destiny, and transformation—all speak to the spiritual or transpersonal nature of intimate experience and to the fact that, through such experience, individuals (self-concepts) are somehow moved or changed. The list also shows how time is important, a finding consistent with the phenomenological study of intimacy (see McAdams, 1989).

DEFINING TIME

Today, time is a commodity, bought, sold, packaged and rationed. Vacation time, sick time, time off for good behavior, time valued at a market rate (minimum wage), time over which no one has control, nor even any input. One's life is now neatly compartmentalized into work and leisure, youth and age, public and private—and all viewed as seemingly predetermined.

Actually, it's completely arbitrary. (Ventura, 1995, p. 10)

This previous quote shows how much culture plays a role in how people, arbitrarily it seems, define time. But the effects of these cultural definitions on our personal consciousness are far from arbitrary. As the time-intimacy equation described in the preface pointed out, definitions of time are also definitions of intimacy. For example, Allen (1986) wrote about the tribal or ceremonial time of Native American culture, where human existence and nature move together in a dynamic equilibrium, as in ceremonial dances, and there is no separation of the individual out of the context of this dance. Native American time is woven through stories and tales that keep individuals connected to the tribe or community. There is a sense of timelessness or, what Allen called "achronicity." She distinguished this from the chronological time of Western industrialists:

Chronological time structuring is useful in promoting and supporting an industrial time sense. The idea that everything has a starting point and an ending point reflects accurately the process by which industry produces goods. Western industrialists engage in time-motion studies hoping to enhance profits. Chronological organization also supports allied Western beliefs that the individual is separate from the environment, that man is separate from God, that life is an isolated business, and that the person who controls the events around him is a hero. (p. 149)

Although a chronological view of time has its place and serves an important function (e.g., control, prediction), it clearly differs from other cultural views. According to Allen (1986), "Indian time rests on a perception of the individual as part of an entire gestalt in which fittingness is not a matter of how gear teeth mesh with each other but rather how the person meshes with the revolving of the seasons, the land, and the mythic reality that shapes all life into significance" (p. 154).

Such cultural definitions of time—as well as scientific and philosophical definitions—are pertinent to the study of intimacy. Scientific research on daily biological rhythms and longer term hormonal clocks help in the understanding of a wide variety of relationship phenomena, from changes in mood to the psychological changes that come with aging. Even new understandings about time in quantum physics (e.g., complexity theory, chaos theory) have been applied to analyses of relationships as systems (Vallacher & Nowak, 1994; Ward, 1995). Philosophical and cultural conceptions of time as well, both Eastern and Western, especially contribute to our understanding of spiritual or transpersonal intimacy.

Clearly, definitions of time may be cultural, scientific, and philosophical. Moreover, some definitions of time are compatible with the spiritual dimension of intimacy. These distinctions are derived from McGrath and Kelly (1986) and Slife (1993). Both described the dominant view of time in Western lay culture, that is, the classical, or "Newtonian," view. Newtonian time is objective, absolute, successive, unidirectional, and divisible into units. McGrath and Kelly distinguished this view from three subcultural variations. These are the "new physics" or Einsteinian view, the "new biology," organismic or transactional view, and a mystical or Eastern view. McGrath and Kelly pointed out how the Newtonian view has dominated our sociocultural understanding of time through clocks, calendars, and schedules. It has also dominated psychological understanding of time (Slife, 1993). A central hypothesis of this book is that this dominant view may have helped to bring about social conditions antagonistic to intimacy. This dominant view has also helped prevent researchers from considering the importance of the spiritual or contextual dimensions of intimacy.

> *The classical, Newtonian view of time has helped bring about social conditions antagonistic to intimacy.*

One reason that this classical, Western view of time seems antithetical to a richer understanding of intimacy lies in the root meanings of the word time:

> The Latin word *tempus* comes from the Greek *tempo*. The early meaning of tempo was that of anything that has been cut out or marked off, such as the parts of the heaven marked off by the motion of the sun along its path. Hence the meaning of *tempo* and *tempus* as a period, season, or time. The association of the act of cutting with the word *tempus* survives in the English word "template," meaning a thin plate that has been cut out to serve as a guide in mechanical work. (Fraser, 1987, p. xiii)

Thus, time—as defined in original Western thought—does not connote flow, wholeness, or context, but rather interval, separateness, and division. Interestingly, Fraser (1987) pointed out that the word *templum*, from the Greek, meant an area marked off to observe omens and foresee the works of the gods that came from the heavens. This was a place (i.e., a temple) to contemplate (from *contemplatio)* the meaning of these omens. Perhaps the Greeks recognized that in order to "cut" the heavens, they also had to pay some respect for them as a whole.

Alternatives to Classical, Newtonian Time

> *Absolute, true and mathematical time, of itself, and from its own nature, flows equably and without relation to anything external.*
> — Sir Isaac Newton

Einsteinian. There are several aspects to this new physics view of time. First, time has a quality of "complementarity" or "transposability"; it varies in ways similar to how energy varies between wave and pulse formations in quantum physics. That is, time is indivisible, but it sometimes behaves one way (like it can be separated into discrete quantum parts) and sometimes another (like one whole and continuous wave). Importantly, these different forms can never be perceived simultaneously. This particle-wave distinction serves as an analogy for understanding transpersonal intimacy. Hines (1996) explained that human consciousness only is able to know something about parts, rather than everything about the whole. He argues that the "quantum wave function is to material science as Spirit is to spiritual science; everpresent, filling all space, guiding each part of creation, imperceptible by the senses, the unmoved mover" (p. 200). Thus, as separate individuals we know intimacy through our sensory contact with "parts" of experience (e.g., with another in the moment), but these parts—at another complementary or transposable level—reflect a continuous transpersonal whole.

In the Einsteinian view, time is also relative, or determined by the viewpoint of the observer. It is also uniform, irreversible, and "unidirectional in its flow (as in thermodynamics' "arrow of time" that yields ever-increasing entropy)" (McGrath & Kelly, 1986, p. 32). Finally, it cannot be separated out of a unitary spacetime continuum. Each of these qualities suggests there can be no single, permanent, or unitary definition of time for two individuals; each person experiences it differently. However, as two individuals communicate, or share their separate experience of space and time together, they can start to see beyond their own viewpoint (i.e., transpersonal) and they may be able to glimpse aspects of time as defined in the new physics.

Transactional ("Organismic Holism"). The new biology, as described by Kelly and McGrath, "pays special attention to periodic or cyclical phenomena in living systems at various levels (cells, organisms, species, etc.), and to the mutual entrainment of these oscillatory processes" (p. 33). Time is divisible into critical transition points (e.g., birth, metamorphosis), and it is phasic in how it flows. Because of the developmental basis of biological systems, time has a spiral-like quality—passing in phases from critical transition to critical transition—as the system differentiates, matures, and disintegrates.

This transactional view is quite similar to another alternative conception of time called organismic holism (Slife, 1993). Slife developed this view in response to the limitations of the Newtonian view for explanations in various areas of psychology (e.g., personality theory, cognitive psychology). The principle of holism states that the qualities of entities are not entities in themselves but in the relations among the entities. Moreover, as these entities change, "they change as a whole, and therefore change in quality, *discontinuously*" (p. 242). An emergent property of the whole can occur that is not deducible from the original condition of the individual entities.

Thus, time has a gestalt quality that is derived from the relations among parts. Like a hologram, the smallest part (or moment), may reflect the meaning of the whole (or entire duration). Unlike the Newtonian or Einsteinian view, the time of organismic holism also has the potential for discontinuous change and it cannot be reducible into separate or divisible parts.

Both of these views, the transactional and organismic holism, are relevant for intimacy. The intimate experience—as described previously (Register & Henley, 1992)—contains unity, surprise, destiny, and transformation. These somatic aspects of experience are less easily explained by classical physics. As partners experience their boundaries diminish, they are in a sense experiencing a wholeness that transcends their separate sense of self. As they experience surprise, they are experiencing discontinuity. And, as they experience destiny, they may have a sense of that spiral-like quality of time that moves them through critical transitions.

Eastern Mysticism. In this view, time is illusory, reversible, determined by observation, has duration, and is recurrent. Unlike the other views presented, time is completely experiential and any measure of it is completely illusionary. In Buddhism particularly, there is no such thing as an entity that exists for any period and no beginning or end of time. Rather, there are just moments of experience that arise and pass away. This is the Buddhist doctrine of impermanence, insight into which brings enlightenment. Many forms of Eastern mysticism explain that there is a higher state of consciousness in which time and space dissolve into nothingness. The temporal or material world is an obstacle or veil to this higher state. This obstacle is overcome only by detaching from the senses and one's own sense of self or ego. Interestingly, many of these traditions describe that the spiritual seeker "comes alive by dying" to this self and ego. In other words, all personal history and personal memory of self (interests, opinions, attitudes, and beliefs) are hindrances to experiencing God or a supreme being.

The mystical traditions of Sufism and Christianity often describe this being as "the beloved" or "bridegroom." Here, spiritual enlightenment equates with spiritual union (communion) with some divine presence (spirit). In terms of transpersonal intimacy, the path of spiritual development involves surrender, devotion, humility, and watchfulness for those vices that make one "undeserving" of the beloved. There are some parallels with human relationships. Many aspects of mystical time manifest through the trials of a committed relationship. For example, through forgiveness, we experience how time is reversible: A previous hurt is cleared and memory of the past is changed. We may also experience time's recurrence as we face the same difficulties over and over again until there is some transforming insight or surrender.

Hermeneutic Temporality. This is Slife's adaptation of time as defined in phenomenology, existentialism, and hermeneutics. Again, time is dynamic and variable and has no "objective" being. Following the philosophy of Heidegger (1962), Slife explained that humans are not separable from the world as something that exists "outside" their skin, but are "beings-in-the-world" and are inseparably linked to one another, as parts of the same entity. Heidegger called this "deeply contextual entity" *Dasein*. Time does not exist apart from *Dasein*, and is defined by our living with each other. As such, time is not linear or flowing in a certain direction; it is not a quantity, but rather is lived in the present moment. Unlike Newtonian time, which is some independent measure that is free of context (past and future) and can be imposed on context, hermeneutic temporality is never free of context. Slife explained:

> In hermeneutic temporality . . . each moment is filled with temporal context. In this sense, *Dasein* can change quite radically as the context itself changes. This is true even of temporal dimensions. Newton's conception leaves the past "dead" and immutable, while it constrains the present and future because of their consistent "flow" with one another. Temporality, on the other hand, permits all dimensions of time to affect one another (e.g., the "future" affecting the "past"). The past is not dead and gone but part of the living present and future. Our memories are not "stored" and "objective" entities but living parts of ourselves in the present. (p. 260)

Unlike previous views of time, hermeneutics speaks directly to how individuals relate to one another in the present. In fact, through mutual embracing of the temporal context (*Dasein*) we come to understand one another and our own being as well. The transpersonal theme is clear. There is always the sense of "the possible" and all events that occur are interpreted (translated) according to the view of the interpreter. Our world is continually constructed through this interpretation and this construction is open-ended. Our task is to engage the world (with others) in as authentic a way as possible. This requires treating others not as "objects" (to be manipulated, imposed on) but, like us, as "subjective" beings with whom we share. Thus, hermeneutic temporality (like mystical time) is, by definition, transpersonal. There is no self that can be separated from the Other one seeks to know. In mysticism, that Other is some supreme being. In hermeneutics, that Other can be our neighbor or intimate partner.

A NOTE ON METAPHOR

Hopefully, the previous review of definitions helps pave the way for a new understanding of time, intimacy, and their relation to one another. Because of the limits of definitions, metaphors can often create a more accurate sense of the complexity of intimacy. In this and subsequent chapters, many different metaphors are used to help in this understanding. (Readers interested in the fast-growing science of metaphor analysis should consult Cameron and Low (1999).) Different questionnaire items are also used, like those on intimacy in this chapter, to give readers a concrete sense of the concepts discussed. Both of these approaches—metaphor and questionnaires, are combined in the Time Metaphor

Test (Knapp & Garbutt, 1958). This test was developed as a projective technique—a psychological measure—to assess how individuals feel about the aesthetic appropriateness of a list of metaphors. Twenty-five metaphors were selected to represent a variety of poetic allusions to time. Knapp and Garbutt simply asked how much the metaphor evoked a satisfying image of time. A few of these metaphors are presented below, along with some of my own. You may wish to create your own metaphor. In reviewing metaphors, you may get a sense of the rich and varied aspects of how time and intimacy relate. Perhaps by nurturing this "inner" sense, we can moderate that hunger for information and that rush for more time that keeps us from intimacy.

RESEARCH **REFLECTION** 2

THE TIME METAPHOR TEST

Time is an aspect of experience that we are aware of in different ways. Within our close relationships, we also experience time in unique and different ways. From the following list of phrases, select those that evoke a satisfying image of time for you, as you experience both time in general and in your relationship as well. Consider which metaphors evoke different views of time (Einsteinian, Transactional, Mystical, or Hermeneutic). Use this sentence stem, and check off the metaphor that is most satisfying to you.

Time (*in my close relationship*) is like:

- ❑ a road leading over a hill.
- ❑ an old man with a staff.
- ❑ a speeding train.
- ❑ a tapestry being woven on a loom.
- ❑ the Rock of Gibralter.
- ❑ a string of beads.
- ❑ a stairway leading upward.
- ❑ moving through a maze.
- ❑ a merry-go-round.
- ❑ a roller-coaster ride.

(Adapted from Knapp & Garbutt, 1958)

OUTLINE OF BOOK

The chapters that follow provide seven different images of intimacy. These may be called elaborate ideas, conceptual models, or cognitive frameworks. Figure 1.2 provides a thumbnail sketch of each model.

Two Primary Themes

Inspection of Fig. 1.2 reveals two integrating ideas or themes that connect each model with the other. These ideas form the backbone of the book. The first theme is *transpersonal intimacy*. In a basic sense transpersonal means "extending or going beyond the personal or individual." Because intimacy always involves an Other, it requires going beyond the individual as a separate self. Transpersonal also means extending or going beyond time; that is, individuals who "know" another at a deep level often feel a sense of connection that is timeless. Box 1.1 (pp. 18-20) offers some other ideas about the science of transpersonal psychology.

Each of the first five models addresses this transpersonal theme directly. The fifth model also provides a transition between this explicit transpersonal view and a more rigorous empirical view of personal relationships. As Fig. 1.2 suggests, this transition is based on drawing parallels between scientists and lovers as seekers of knowledge. I suggest that scientists (e.g., psychologists and sociologists) who investigate personal relationships cannot ignore the spiritual dimension of intimacy, especially as they become more "sensitive to time."

This transition between the spiritual and scientific pivots on the second main theme of the book: Relationships create and evolve in overlapping contexts of time. The different clocks mentioned at the beginning of this chapter—sociological, psychological, and communicative—represent forces that shape these contexts of time. Specifically, many different time frames are woven together and are created by the coming together of two individuals into a relationship. These *temporal contexts* include everything from the long-term evolutionary cycles we have learned as a species (e.g., about mating) to the short-term biological changes (heart rate) that occur in a 10 second exchange between two partners. Everything that changes in a relationship can be framed in a context, including interactions, situations, phases, life stages, relationship stages, hormonal cycles, historical changes (e.g., in courtship norms), and changes in personal growth or maturity.

Although couples evolve across many contexts, certain ones are of particular relevance for understanding intimacy. These are interactions (communication sequences), situations (exchanges or transactions), and phases (transitions in the history of the relationship). The first three models provide a transpersonal perspective on each of these temporal contexts. The first model views all interactions as containing elements that either constrain or facilitate intimacy. The second model describes four types of intimate situations. The third model shows how couples' movement through phases of time actually reflects deeper (metaphysical) aspects of time in nature.

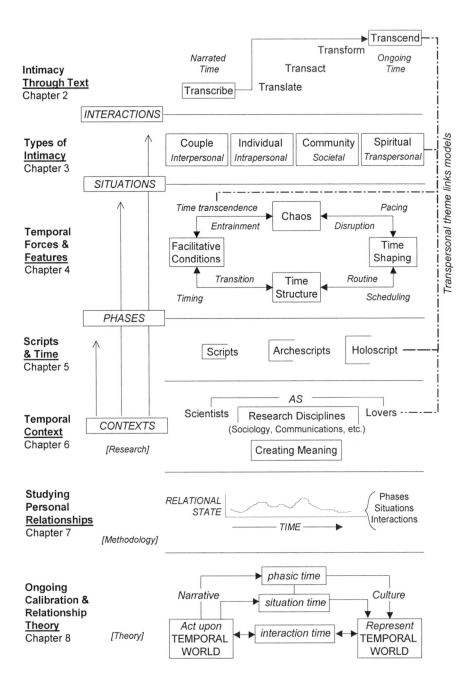

FIG. 1.2. Overview of seven models (and transpersonal and contextual themes).

Seven Models

Intimacy Through Text (Model 1). This model argues that all human interaction is an example of text, or of textual form. Partners can only grow in intimacy if they see this form for what it is—that is, if they listen and communicate, whether it is to each other or through a counselor, advisor, or mediator. The main mode of contact is communication, and communication requires interaction, translation, and application. For example, advice columns and self-help books are only helpful if people translate what they read in terms of their own lives and apply what they learn when they interact with others. During the first few years of the relationship, Donna read one self-help book after another. They made her feel good and reassured, but the relationship did not change until she applied what she read in a way that worked. All guidance really has to come face to face with the dynamics of intimacy. This first model uses the metaphor of text and argues that intimacy is like a journey through text.

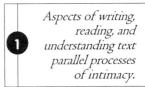

Aspects of writing, reading, and understanding text parallel processes of intimacy.

The word "through" here has a double meaning. It is a journey through in that as we "read" each other, as we get to know each other over time and situations, we may find intimacy. This is like readers who gradually shape an image of a character or hero as they go from page to page and chapter to chapter. But, like Alice *through* the looking glass, there is another meaning for the word. We also must go through the text and leave it behind if we are to enter the world of another and find that a partner is more than a mirror, such that the relationship is alive, dynamic, and continually changing. In this way, an intimate other is never like a character in a book because we do not live with fictional characters or they with us; nor do these characters live with the pressing changes of life. This first model offers the metaphor of text and shows how it can be helpful, but also examines its limitations.

This model is introduced first to remind readers that the map is not the territory, and the finger pointing at the moon is not the moon. All images and models can only partially reflect reality. The time of text is never the time of life, except that good fiction makes it seem so. It is also a call to anyone who would read *about* intimacy to know the pitfalls of doing so. As noted earlier, there has been an enormous amount of publications devoted to either understanding relationships or helping couples: self-help books, research articles, and popular magazines. In fact, the growth of such popularity in these books has a parallel with two other phenomena in our culture: the use of the computer for online correspondence (the Internet), and the parade of all forms of human relationship in the daily television talk shows. Both of these speak to what I call "virtual intimacy" (cf. *parasocial attachment*; Cole & Leets, 1999).

BOX 1.1. WHAT IS TRANSPERSONAL SCIENCE?

There are at least three ways to understand transpersonal science. First, it may be viewed as a new branch of either psychological or religious science that seeks to address some of the blind spots and shortcomings of both psychology and religion. This view is represented in the work of Abraham Maslow and the Association of Humanistic Psychology (visit their Web site at www.ahpweb.org). Second, it can be considered as a recent development in the old meaning of "psychology" as the philosophy of human potential. This is sometimes known as "The Fourth Way" created by the Russian mystic G.I. Gurdjieff and philosopher P.D. Ouspensky (visit the Web site of the school of "The Fourth Way" at www.geocities.com/Tokyo/1236). Third, transpersonal science may be seen as an academic field of psychology, which has its own organization of scholars, an academic journal, and the goal of combining experiential and scientific understandings of spirituality (visit their web site at http://www.igc.org/atp). The human experience of intimacy, especially its transpersonal aspects, can be systematically explored and rightly understood within each of these views of transpersonal science.

Maslow. Maslow (1976) described the need for a new science that can ask the same questions about values and spirituality that religions have asked, but also provide answers that avoid some of the shortcomings of fundamentalist religion and orthodox science. Maslow suggested that such a science is needed for three reasons. First, we have "seen that science can be dangerous to human ends and that scientists can become monsters as long as science is conceived to be akin to a chess game, an end in itself, with arbitrary rules, whose only purpose is to explore the existent, and which makes the fatal blunder of excluding subjective experience" (p. 16). In short, science, by neglecting values, human potential, and subjectivity, can be blind and amoral.

Second, Maslow argued that orthodox religion can lead to "dichotomizing life into the transcendent and the secular-profane" (p. 33), whereby deep, mystical experiences somehow threaten the organized, ritualized, legalistic aspects of organizational religion. For these religions may promote a conformity to "thoughtless, habitual, reflex-like, absent-minded, automatic responses" (p. 34) where "familiarization and repetition produces a lowering of the intensity and richness of consciousness, even though it also produces preference, security, comfort, etc." (p. 34). In short, mystical or "peak" experiences of transpersonal intimacy do not fit into the conventional religious organization, even though sharing of them may help bring vitality and renewal to the organization.

Third, orthodox science (as well as many religions) by stressing rational knowledge and logic, "leave out too much that is precious to most human beings" (p. 40).

Continued

BOX 1.1 Continued   "They make no place in their systems for the mysterious, the unknown, the unknowable, the dangerous-to-know, or the ineffable. . . . The inexact, the illogical, the metaphorical, the mythic, the symbolic, the contradictory or conflicted, the ambiguous, the ambivalent are all considered to be 'lower' or 'not good,' i.e., something to be 'improved' toward pure rationality and thought" (p. 41). In short, both science and religion have de-valued aspects of "inner" experience that do not fit a rational model.

Ouspensky. Transpersonal psychology is both an academic discipline and a personal path of self-transformation, wisdom, and understanding. As a path, it brings together thinking from various spiritual disciplines and mystical aspects of religion. In some ways, transpersonal psychology is the oldest as well as a forgotten branch of modern psychological science, its roots lying in philosophy; that is, in yoga, Sufi teachings, studies of "the mysteries" in Egypt and Ancient Greece, and in Christian mysticism (Ouspensky, 1973).

Ouspensky's distinction between modern scientific psychology and this original psychology should help clarify the purpose of this book. He wrote that all psychological systems and doctrines can be divided into two categories:

> First: systems which study man *as they find him, or such as they suppose or imagine him to be.* . . . Second: systems which study man not from the point of view of what he is, or what seems to be, but from the point of view of what he may become; that is, from the point of view of his *possible evolution.* (Ouspensky, 1973, p. 6)

As a study of transpersonal science, this book points to the possible evolution of intimacy, to the possible evolution of our consciousness of time, and to how the two evolutionary paths may be related.

Ouspensky's and Maslow's ideas may be considered as only one line of thought within the broad discipline of transpersonal psychology (see also Almaas, 1986, 1987; Davison, 1995; Moore, 1991; Tart, 1987, 1992; Wilber, 1979). As a brief introduction to this field of study, Boucouvalas' (1980) definition and Metzner's (1980) descriptions of self-transformation are summarized next.

Transpersonal Psychology. As an academic field, transpersonal psychology seeks to understand the total human being and the role of humanity with the purpose of improving human consciousness, facilitating spiritual awakening, enhancing the quality of life, and transforming society so that it functions more harmoniously. Transpersonal psychologists study a number of topics, including spiritual potential, extraordinary human experiences (e.g., alternative healing, mystical union, ESP), methods for "inner" psychological work, convergence between Eastern spiritual disciplines and Western psychology, and the development of theories and concepts related to "ultimate" human values. Transpersonal therapists/educators assume that every individual (relationship) has the capacity for achieving far beyond what they now think is possible and are generally not restricted to a single set of techniques or models for facilitating transpersonal goals. The field seeks to balance relations between self-discovery and social responsibility.

Continued

BOX 1.1 Continued   Many transpersonal psychologists believe that the
evolution of human consciousness and society depends on the evolution
and transformation of individuals (and couples). Metzner described
classical metaphors that have been used by many spiritual traditions to
capture the process through which consciousness is transformed.
Examination of these metaphors reveals two interesting facts. First, they
are similar to the metaphors and images that lovers and poets have used
for centuries to describe their own experiences of intimacy and love.
Second, they suggest that time is discontinuous and nonlinear; that
transformation requires a shift or marked change from one state to
another.

- *From* DREAM-SLEEP *to* AWAKENING
- *From* IMPRISONMENT *to* LIBERATION
- *From* FRAGMENTATION *to* WHOLENESS
- *From* SEPARATION *to* ONENESS
- *From* BEING ON A JOURNEY *to* ARRIVING AT THE DESTINATION
- *From* BEING IN EXILE *to* COMING HOME
- *From* SEED *to* FLOWERING TREE
- *From* DEATH *to* REBIRTH

A growing number of people only know each other through the Internet.
There has been an increase in television shows for viewers who fulfill
voyeuristic motives by listening to others talk about the tragedies and
dysfunction in their own searches for and lack of intimacy. The computer can be
helpful for those who seek out like-minded people to discuss common interests
and, over time, such mutuality may expand into intimacy. But many people are
using the computer to have their intimacy needs met as well. One purpose of this
first model is to introduce a framework for understanding and exploring this
phenomenon of virtual intimacy (see Box 1.2). At which point in a computer
correspondence—a purely textual base—does the interaction of two individuals
take on the quality that could be called intimacy? Can it ever do so? Does the
lack of face-to-face interaction across different situations place a limit on
intimacy? Can Internet users transcend these limits? These questions are
beginning to be addressed and, in fact, some believe that the construction of
"alternate relaities" in cyberspace might mimic transpersonal states of
consciousness (Gackenbach, 1998). Thus, text—whether in book form or in
cyberspace—may be a helpful metaphor for understanding intimacy.

More specifically, the text-as-metaphor model shows how, in any given
moment of human contact, the quality of intimate continuity or ongoingness is
experienced in one of five different levels. Across each stage, intimacy becomes
more dynamic and interactive and time itself is experienced as less static. In the
first stage, authors take their experience and transcribe it for another to see.   Time

is completely narrated and so filtered and controlled by one individual. There is no interaction and no continuity, only a sequence of events as transcribed by one individual and interpreted by another. In the second and subsequent stages, time becomes more important and intimacy less virtual. For example, face-to-face encounters create a common memory, a collection of images and feelings that are unique in being mutually shared by two intimates. Using the textual metaphor, the first model explores several catalytic qualities of intimacy (e.g., waking up, sensitivity, wholeness, continuity) and some blocks to the direct experience of intimacy.

BOX 1.2. Virtual Intimacy, Television, and the Internet

> Frank Jones, a 34-year-old New York City man, actually believed he was married to Janet Jackson; last July he was sentenced to two years in prison for sending the singer desperate, threatening letters ("Well, Janet," began one, "you have reason to fear "). Joseph Mallon of Philadelphia not only believed the Pretenders' Chrissie Hyde was his wife but took her to court because she refused to recognize it. The suit was dismissed. Margaret Ray, the nutty David Letterman stalker, broke into Dave's house for the eighth time last summer, after being arrested repeatedly already (once for driving his $80,000 sports car and introducing herself as Mrs. David Letterman). All because Letterman, Ray has said, became "the dominant figure in my life." (Hochman, 1994, p. 34)

Examples of fans who become obsessed with the lives of celebrities, who "fall in love" with them, range from the sweet to the bizarre and delusional. Hochman argued that "to some fans, the fictional characters they see on the screen seem a lot more real than the friends and family they're watching with." Celebrities hire security consultants to screen their fan mail for "signs of dangerous fixations." One such consultant said, "It's a very manageable form of intimacy. You don't have to extend yourself or make yourself vulnerable to have a relationship with Dolly Parton."

These virtual relationships appear to come about through several processes. First, fans often have accessibility to repeated (voyeuristic) viewing of their star. With recording capabilities, they can listen to and watch performances over and over again; in short, they can control how often they want to be "in the presence" of their virtual partner. The technology of the modern entertainment industry is another factor. The television, video, or cinematic image of the star itself tends to convey a sense of visual closeness that evokes an emotional response. A third factor—the popularity of celebrity journalism—is explained by Rubin (cited by Hochman, also see Rubin, 1998). He argues that characters on the screen take on a social presence and that fans perpetuate the illusion of this presence by "mentally participating in the exploits of the character, talking back to the person on the screen, reading newspaper or magazine stories about a favorite performer, writing fan letters or attending local appearances trying to meet a TV celebrity" (p. 34). Fans can elaborate on their ideas and impressions of the celebrity on a continuous basis, and with such a variety of media so as to create a sense of ongoing connection to them.

Continued

BOX 1.2 Continued

The phenomena of virtual relationships speaks to the issue of time and intimacy. I believe it is symptomatic of the lack of (and the deep need for) real-time, ongoing relationships. Celebrity magazines such as *People*, *Us*, the entertainment sections of newspapers, and popular tabloids are havens for people to live vicariously through the rich and the famous and the tumultuous and chaotic successes and failures of others. The sense of privacy—a key aspect of intimacy—has eroded for many in our society and people find it only by imagining it, i.e., they have virtual intimacy with another.

In real-life relationships, people do not have as much control over the time of the give and take, the time for intimacy, to develop. As these virtual relationships appear to attest, the drive to have this reciprocity is so strong that it erupts into obsessive fantasy (or possibly Internet addiction, Young, 1998). But intimacy—true intimacy—occurs in the flow of interaction, in conversation, in dancing and meeting with another, in allowing one to see each other's weaknesses, and in going through different situations, different transitions, different phases of life together. Real relationship entails disruption, chaos, failures in timing, interruptions; and the willingness of both partners to correct for these difficulties. There is no messiness or real changing together in virtual relationships.

No matter how much television we watch or how much we know about another through the Internet, we cannot have intimacy without participation. Information is not intimation, except as it is imagined so. As one star consultant says in Hochman's article, "If you turn your TV around, all you'll find is dust and wires, not people. Television and movies are not windows on the world. The only window on the world is a window" (p. 37).

Types and Phases of Intimacy (Model 2). The second model considers four different situations of intimacy and the role of time in each. The first type is couple intimacy. The remainder are *intrapersonal* intimacy, when one learns about oneself; *transpersonal* intimacy, when one embraces the spiritual aspects of life; and *societal* intimacy, when community develops between many individuals and these individuals create a social network and sometimes give to a larger social cause. Time is different in each of these types, and the four combined make up a metaphorical melody that can either have harmony or disharmony. In self-learning or individuation, time has a very personal signature; as we grow, we become familiar with our own daily and seasonal rhythms, highlights of our own history, significant transitions, and life cycles.

In spiritual or transpersonal intimacy, the idea of eternity and the ability to transcend the temporal world becomes important. Many philosophical and religious books are devoted to these topics and the related ideas of salvation, atonement, the afterlife, and reincarnation. Time also differs in community relations. Social networks have their own cycles in which groups and couples come together and go apart; plans, activities, and projects are executed, and organizations develop, flourish, and decay. The business literature and the study of organizational behavior provide some examples of this community time.

These include the life cycles of work organizations and team development (see Tuckman, 1965; Quinn, 1996).

This second model also suggests that these four types of intimacy become important in different periods of a person's life. In some periods people focus on self-development, sometimes on a relationship with one other person, sometimes on a spiritual journey, and sometimes on community. In this second model, time also has a phase-like quality. Jay and Donna enjoy their time together, but they find that the social networks they have with others

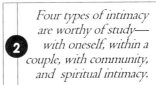

Four types of intimacy are worthy of study—with oneself, within a couple, with community, and spiritual intimacy.

enrich them. Jay takes religion more seriously and goes to church on a regular basis; Donna stays home. When Donna is at home, she takes walks and enjoys a special solitude, which is spirituality for her. As a couple, they find they have intimacy at different times and in different ways. An older couple, Wayne and Sally, like to take long, mostly silent, walks together, followed by dinner with friends. This helps them find and balance solitude, couple time, and social time.

Temporal Forces and Features (Model 3). The third model defines the main temporal features of all relationships. The focus of the chapter is more on time than on intimacy and on developing a language or grammar for time. The model shows that different temporal features and relationship phases arise as a function of fundamental, perhaps cosmic, temporal forces.

The four temporal forces are: *time shaping*, which is the way the couple acts to structure time together and apart; *chaos*, or the ways in which events, either internal or external to the relationship system, cause changes, developments, or regressions in that system; *facilitative (nurturing) conditions*, which are those conditions that foster or nurture intimacy within the relationship; and *structure or form*, which are the ways in which relationships take on one form (e.g., marriage) versus another (e.g., cohabitation), or enter into one particular phase or stage (e.g., courtship) versus another (e.g., raising children). These four forces may also be thought of as functions or elements. The metaphor of sailing can help in understanding them.

Sailing requires working with the wind, water currents, charting courses, and knowing and operating the sails, rudder, and other features of the boat. *Time shaping* is like charting courses and planning routes. *Chaos* is like the weather and changes in the wind that are not entirely predictable but that must continually be monitored and responded to. *Facilitative conditions* refer to the confluence of conditions, when all the elements—wind, sailing techniques, the condition of the boat, relations between the crew—work together to create successful, moment-to-moment, sailing. *Structure or form* relates to the boat itself, the crew roles, and the rules of sailing. Like sailing, relationships require rules, responsiveness to chaos, some forethought or plans, and the right conditions.

The four temporal forces also relate to each other in active and receptive ways. Eight temporal features define these relationships. First, couples shape time through the active processes of *scheduling* and *pacing*. For example, Jay asks Donna to go out with him to a new movie. In order to make the 7:30 show, they are going to have to rush through dinner. They decide instead to have a leisurely meal and catch the later show. Second, couples experience aspects of chaos through the active processes of *perturbation (disruption)* and *time transcendence*. At dinner, Jay and Donna get into an argument about which movie to go and see. This disrupts their meal but, after listening to each other, they find time to be close and enjoy each other so much that they forget about the time and are almost late to the second show.

Third, couples become sensitive to facilitative conditions through the active processes of *rhythm entrainment* (synchronizing their personal rhythms) and through *transitions* (together witnessing life's changes). Because they stay out late, Donna has to sleep late Sunday morning and this upsets her schedule for the day. She and Jay end up feeling sleepy and hungry at different times; they are "out of synch." They compromise by taking a nap together, which puts them back in rhythm with each other. This also refreshes them so they can make the transition to Monday morning better.

Finally, couples actively structure their relationship through *routines* and *timing*. The Monday morning routine requires using the right amount of water for the shower so that they both have enough hot water. Also, it's Jay's job to make toast so that it's ready (and not burnt) just as Donna is getting her bag for work. After years of working out this routine, Jay and Donna have timed it just right so that they can enjoy breakfast together and not be late for work.

Each of these eight temporal features is also passive to the four temporal functions. For example, *time transcendence* is an essential spiritual aspect of intimacy that can be shared by couples. Its most common expression occurs in the feeling of falling in love. In its active form, time transcendence is an attitude and a choice to fully embrace the chaos, the ups and downs, of life together. The idea of living life to its fullest is as applicable to couples' growth in love as it is to an individual's gradual awakening. But time

> *Different relationship processes and phases arise as a function of* **3** *fundamental, perhaps cosmic temporal forces.*

transcendence also becomes passive in the form of surrendering, of learning patience, of listening, discerning, and waiting for those conditions that nurture the relationship. This process of listening and surrendering itself becomes the path of intimacy.

In a related way, the more mundane task of *scheduling* has both an active and passive form. Actively, couples use it to shape their time together. Passively, scheduling is subjected to, or constrained by, the relationship structure or form. A committed marriage with children has more schedule limitations than a casual dating relationship. Similarly, *perturbation* or *disruption* is the typical way chaos becomes active in a relationship. However, without the potential of disruption or of continually reacting to whatever was happening in the situation, there would be less need for time shaping. Thus, *disruption* makes time shaping a passive process, whereas *scheduling* makes time shaping an active process. This third model describes these temporal features and how they work together and attempts to construct a comprehensive and cohesive temporal grammar for intimate relationships.

This model, and the preceding two models, are interrelated in several ways. The primary thread running throughout them and the fourth model is that time transcendence and intimacy are interconnected. A basic assumption underlies these ideas, namely, that individuals have the capacity to both embrace and transcend time through a greater sensitivity to the process of relating. This process applies to scientists, as they relate to their work, as well as to all people in their search for intimacy. As a thread that runs through all chapters, this assumption provides the transpersonal theme of the book. We can transcend text as a static metaphor of relationships and come to continually discover our friends and lovers (Model 1). We can experience intimacy in solitude and spirituality as well as in its interpersonal forms (Model 2). We can learn to nurture intimacy at the same time we embrace the messy, difficult, and chaotic aspects of relationships (Model 3). The fourth model extends this transpersonal theme as well.

Scripts, Archescripts, and Holoscripts (Model 4). The fourth model examines time and intimacy via the concept of psychological scripts. It highlights the importance of stories, myths, and dreams; which are all forms that reveal relationship scripts that are hidden to us. The model is a synthesis of ideas previously described by others and it seeks to bridge the gap between depth psychology and more recent developments in the study of cognition within personal relationships (Berscheid, 1994). In transactional analysis (Berne, 1964, 1976), unconscious scripts about parent, adult, and child states that make up their personality guide individuals through relationships. In archetypal theory (Jung, 1972), individuals have various unconscious images of their own masculine and feminine aspects, as well as of creative, childlike, darker, and other aspects of their personality. In holonomic theory (Argüelles, 1988; Schaef, 1992), individuals, relationships, societies, and humanity both embody and reflect certain cosmic principles that operate throughout the universe.

The fourth model distinguishes between the relatively unconscious, but directly accessible, *scripts* that individuals develop about intimate relationships, and the largely unconscious *archescripts* developed through human evolution. These archescripts contain intimations about how to relate to others, as well as about the sequences, time lines, and transitions that are found in the course of such relating. The model distinguishes these archescripts from a universal *holoscript* that embodies certain principles, often labeled as masculine and feminine. Masculine principles are stereotypically expressed as logical, active, creative, and forming qualities, whereas feminine principles are stereotypically expressed as emotional, passive, receptive, changeable, and erotic qualities. The holoscript is like a great story or cosmic myth that can be found in some form in all cultures.

The idea of script is most commonly known through the interpretations, distortions, and translations that occur when men and women perceive their opposite sex partner. When Jay works out at the club and talks about sports, Donna feels that all he is interested in is his selfish desire for self-improvement and hanging out with his buddies. When Donna likes to spend all her time at home, Jay feels that she lacks vitality and is not very entertaining. As a result of their frustration with each other, they end up playing out their scripts in transactional games. Jay plays the "Please Be Nice" and "Nobody Understands Me" games whenever Donna confronts him about his excessive exercising. Donna plays the "I Need You" and "What If?!" games whenever she is home alone and fantasizes about having a partner who can meet her needs. Caught up in these scripts, both partners are reacting to each other instead of seeing beneath the surface.

> *The scripts we use to navigate intimacy are informed by our childhoods, by human evolution, and by ancient cosmologies.* **4**

Jay is able to get past his fears (of being misunderstood) when he starts to recognize that Donna has a legitimate need for closeness. One day he feels very lonely because of distance between them and recognizes that he too has a need for closeness. Donna is able to loosen her obsessive need for Jay and her fantasizing about the future when she starts to recognize that she has a pressing need to get out in the world and have some fun. One day she feels too depressed and sluggish because she has been opposing Jay rather than meeting him. She takes the initiative in asking him to go out dancing.

This transformation, from staying stuck in scripts to being intimate, requires that both partners recognize aspects of the self other than what is obvious. Jay becomes more sensitive and Donna becomes creative in taking the initiative. These qualities may be seen as coming from the archescripts, or deeper aspects of the partner's personality. It is a core paradox of intimacy that their conflict provided the initial stimulus for Jay and Donna's deepening. At the even deeper holoscript level, the tension or contracted quality of their relating, feelings of distance, the subsequent working through their feelings, and the return to closeness, reflect universal principles of contraction and expansion, activity and receptivity.

The fourth model has links with the previous models and the model to be described in chapter 8. For example, scripts are a dynamic form of text (Model 1) and they are also elements in any narrative or story the couple has about their relationship (Model 8). Where the first model describes text as a metaphor and a medium for intimacy, the fourth model shows how text, in the form of script, becomes an active cognitive process for couples.

The holoscript also has relationships to the temporal factors discussed in the third model. Time shaping and structure may be viewed as the more active, creative, or masculine temporal forces, and chaos and facilitative conditions are viewed as the more passive, receptive, or feminine temporal forces. We can understand and experience these principles through stories, whether read or heard, or seen in a theatrical play or cinematic movie. Donna likes the movie *Gone with the Wind* because it shows her how strong and defiant a woman can be. This helps her to be more assertive with Jay. Jay likes the movie *The Wizard of Oz* because it is fun and every time he watches it, he recognizes different parts of himself in the courageous lion, the intelligent scarecrow, and the sensitive tin-man. This helps him to be more balanced in the way he relates to Donna.

The first four models deal with the process-oriented aspects of relationships and the role of time in intimacy. They show how couples go through stages in entering real time together (Model 1); how intimacy emerges in different types of time—personal, relational, societal, and spiritual (Model 2); how time has different features—such as pacing and routine—within relationships (Model 3); and the ways in which we cognitively and psychically organize time through learned, innate, and cosmic scripts (Model 4). Each model provides limited perspectives of both intimacy and time. Importantly, they all focus on time rather than the study of time or *changefullness* (temporality) or the scientific study of intimacy. The next model (introduced in chap. 6) introduces what we know about relationships through the scientific or empirical perspective from different academic disciplines. The fields of psychology, biology, sociology, communication studies, anthropology, and marital studies each provide information on temporality and intimacy. These separate disciplines have been recently integrated into a single interdisciplinary field devoted solely to the study of personal relationships. This field has not, however, specifically examined the role of time in such relationships. The fifth model begins to address this area.

Temporal Context: From Lovers to Scientists (Model 5). Temporal context is the central idea of the fifth model. *Temporal context* has several meanings. It refers to the ways in which people frame or construe time or temporality when they think about human relationships. More broadly, it refers to the dynamic weaving of events, interactions, situations, and phases that comprise those relationships.

As an example of the importance of context, consider Donna's changing view of spending time with another couple, Bill and Liz. Donna knew that whenever she and Jay went over to their friends' home, Jay liked to spend time talking with Bill. At first, Donna felt that Jay neglected her and she was forced to socialize with Liz. For Donna, the situation "spending time with Liz and Bill" really meant that Jay would spend time with Bill and she would feel frustrated. After their first fight about this issue, Donna decided she had better things to do than to go with Jay. So he went alone. Because Liz liked Donna, she began to make overtures and eventually invited her out to lunch, socializing with her independently of "the boys." A friendship developed and now Donna gladly accompanies Jay when they visit Bill and Liz. Donna has even initiated inviting them over as a couple. The situation "spending time with Liz and Bill" is now a context for friendship and fun rather than neglect and frustration. Another way of describing Donna's new view is to say she now sees the situation in context. This context is temporal because the future and the past have a new meaning. For example, what was earlier seen as a hassle is now thought of as "the good old days."

Temporal context differs from the related ideas of text and script. Script refers to the mentally organized action sequences individuals rely on when interacting with intimate others. Individuals use scripts to guide their behaviors when getting to know and when relating to their intimate other. In contrast, individuals use temporal context to help them understand both their partner and the relationship as a whole, a relationship with a past, a present, and future. Although scripts are guides for action, temporal context is more of a cognitive framework or schema that can be used to think about all the actions in a relationship. In one sense, scripts work from the inside out, whereas temporal context weaves the inside and outside worlds together into a meaningful whole. In the previous example, Donna may have had a "You Don't Care About Me!" script and Jay a "Can't a Guy Have Any Fun?!" script that helped shape their first interpretations of the situation. These ego scripts were driving their views of the situation. The whole context changed after Liz and Donna became friendly. As a result, the ego scripts were no longer necessary or helpful.

> *Intimacy—and the meaning it brings—is a dynamic weaving of the events, interactions, situations, and phases of human relationship.* **5**

Text and context also differ in important ways. Text is a medium through which we seek to know the other person. As we find intimacy, we no longer need text to the same degree. For this reason, text always operates as a tool for becoming more fully centered in the present moment with another. It is a means to an end. In contrast, context is the way we organize the present in reference to some other point in the remembered past or the imagined future. Context is an end in itself that keeps on changing.

To understand the difference between text and context, recall the earlier metaphor of sailing that was used to explain the four temporal forces. In this metaphor, text is like the navigator's chart, a map or plan for using, exploring, and enjoying. Maps, however, are of most help when used in context—that is, when we need to get somewhere. In order to use the map (a written/drawn document), we have to relate it to the real world; we have to find some reference point, like the North Star or some landmark, to gauge where we have come from and where we are going. A compass is an example of a tool that contextualizes.

Charts are only helpful if we apply them to the territory we traverse. Context helps us put the text to use. Once we use and understand a text, it can be put away and so frees up our time for the journey. If we lose the map or fail to remember our course, the context provides other references for us. Early on, Donna would usually feel apprehensive and anxious whenever she heard Jay say "I'm going over to see Bill, I'll see you later." As text, Jay's statement had a singular meaning for Donna; it meant she would be neglected. With changes in their relationship, the statement now has different meanings at different times. If it follows a fight, Donna thinks Jay is abandoning her. If it follows Donna's saying that she is meeting Liz for dinner, then Donna knows that "I'll see you" shows Jay's excitement. Most importantly, as they have grown together, Donna now knows that the statement may mean more than one thing. She has become able to revise her original interpretation and create a new meaning for the statement, a meaning based in the new context rather than in her old fears. These comparisons between context, text, and script can be summarized. Where script guides behavior, context guides understanding; where text serves as a medium for intimacy, context serves as a gauge or reference point for continual relating.

The fifth model begins by showing how both lovers and scientists engage in similar processes in their search for knowledge. Whereas lovers seek to know their lover or beloved, scientists seek to know some phenomenon or natural process. There may be fundamental differences in these "knowings," but both do involve thought processes, cognition, and understanding. Thinking helps furnish the context for understanding sequences, events, and situations. Scientists have already done a great deal of such thinking about relationships. The fifth model integrates ideas about temporal context drawn from different academic disciplines, primarily communication studies and sociology but other fields as well.

Methodological Time in the Study of Personal Relationships (Model 6). Many temporal contexts are woven into relationships. However, as already noted, three appear central and have been given the most attention in the interdisciplinary field of personal relationships (PRs): **sequences** that make up and define an **interaction**, **exchanges** that occur within and define a **situation**, and **transitions** that signal and define relationship **phases**. The sixth model focuses on these contexts and shows how interactions are often embedded within or contextualized by situations, and how situations are embedded within phases. Unlike previous models, this one is oriented more toward the study and science of PRs and to the methods scientists use to study time in PRs. Thus, the model consists of a temporal scale that could be used to both design and evaluate research studies in terms of how sensitive these studies are to temporal aspects of relationships.

There are aspects of this sixth model that deal with the specific measurement of time as we more typically understand time in our daily lives; that is, seconds, minutes, hours, days, weeks, months, and years. These units of linear time are discussed for the first time in the book, as they make up most scientific descriptions of PRs. Any statement made about PRs implies some temporal context and some temporal unit. For example, take the following description: "Jay and Donna had a nice quiet evening at home until Donna mentioned she was quitting her job."

Research methods in the study of personal relationships vary in how sensitive they are to the real-time, ongoing dynamics of intimacy. **6**

The phrase "a nice quiet evening" is comprised of hours and several *situations*: dinner, washing dishes, talking about the day, watching television. Donna's comment about "quitting her job" takes seconds or minutes that represent part of an interaction. Jay's response of concern and frustration is one part of the interaction, to be followed by Donna's explanation as the other part. The phrase "quitting a job" refers to the preceding long period, in which Donna was employed, possibly years. This period comprised one *phase* of their relationship, now to be terminated and also signaling a new phase. The term "until" also implies a change in the couple's situation.

The language of temporal units and contexts may be more useful to scientists of PRs than to individuals seeking intimacy. However, because the study of PRs is quite new, it is possible that research into them can eventually be useful. In any science, there is basic research and the subsequent application of research by practitioners. For PRs, we usually think that such practitioners are marriage therapists or counselors. However, as stated earlier, the ultimate users of these ideas may be couples themselves. Thus, whereas the sixth model is written for students of the science of PRs, it is designed for such students to become more cognizant of temporal aspects of PRs. I hope the model encourages students to conduct research that is more temporally sensitive and so has a greater chance of application in the real-world, ongoing dynamics of PRs (see Kelly & McGrath, 1988; Werner & Haggard, 1985).

Ongoing Calibration and PR Theory (Model 7). The scientific field of PRs contains numerous models and theories that attempt to directly or indirectly incorporate time. In developing the seventh model, a sample of these theories is reviewed through the lens of temporal context (developed in the previous chapters). The last model attempts to synthesize these previous theories and delineate the interconnection between couple interactions, the situations they define, and the phases of their relationship.

The central idea of this final model is that couples are continuously calibrating their relationship over time. At an implicit, automatic, and often unconscious level, they are constantly gauging temporal context and using it as a reference point. Again, the metaphor of sailing may help. When the wind changes, the crew makes changes in the sail and the rudder. When greater speed is required or the boat enters shallow water, then other changes must be made. In relationships, such calibrations occur because couples learned both how to perceive, read, or represent their temporal world and because they also know how to take action and respond to their temporal world. For example, when Jay and Donna first met, Jay was more of a morning person and Donna was more of an evening person. Jay was not willing to give up his morning workout by staying up late with Donna. In order to spend time together, they had to make accommodations in their daily routine. These accommodations were a gradual process whereby both partners began playing a more central role in each other's lives. In this example, the temporal world consisted of disparities in their sleep-waking cycle.

Couples act on their temporal world through joint action and through joint communication. Two previously discussed ideas are relevant here: Time shaping (Model 3) and the ways in which couples talk about and define their relationship using text (Model 1) and scripts (Model 4). In this last model, couples are seen as allocating time (scheduling, time budgeting) on an ongoing basis through the medium of interactive sequences. Whether or not they agree to do things together, whether or not they agree to spend time on certain things, or if they miss, keep, or are late for appointments; all have an influence over the roles and situations that make up their relationship. On days when Jay gets up early to exercise, Donna is more likely to clean the kitchen and have time for spiritual reflection.

Also, couples are seen as causing changes in their relationship through how they talk about it and mutually define and redefine it. These mutual definitions serve as narratives that, in effect, transform the relationship and bring about transitions and new phases (see Sternberg, 1999). As Donna feels that she does more of the house cleaning and she confronts Jay about it. They have a talk and a more equitable solution is reached.

Partners also represent their temporal world through the way their culture and their own unconscious defines time. Previously discussed ideas are relevant here: the different structures or forms that relationships can take (time structure, Model 3), and the rules people use (sociology, in Model 5) and roles they assume (archescripts, Model 4) for interpreting sequences of interactions. For example, the culture provides certain guidelines concerning the appropriate age to start dating and get married and the appropriate length of time between dating, engagement, and marriage. Some couples get married early, some are engaged for years before consummating

Couples continuously calibrate their relation over time and theory can reveal a time-sensitive view of this ongoing process.

their commitment with a wedding. In this way, phases of the relationship are partially shaped by culture. In certain situations, individuals assume more masculine or feminine roles because these allow for easier relating. For example, when dating, males are stereotypically more likely to initiate, whereas females may like to be pursued. In this way, couples adapt roles that provide a map for when to act a certain way in a certain situation. The situation helps them to define the sequences of exchanges they should make.

Overall, there is an ongoing dynamic relation between the way couples *act on* and the way they *perceive* their temporal world. Their talks—and the scripts they use—cause new phases to develop that, in turn, bring about new situations. These new situations require revising ways of seeing and doing things that, in turn, requires them to coordinate through time allocation. All of this is partially affected by the length of the relationship—how long and how well they know each other—or the couple's current phase of commitment. As they are able to navigate their new situation, the couple also finds new and different things to talk about that, in turn transform their relationship. Couples participate in a never-ending cycle in which different relational aspects are constantly organized, disorganized, and reorganized. This is why temporal context is dynamic, changing, and more "alive" than static and fixed.

I . . . admired your poetry for years, & to feel that you liked to write to me & be written to was a pleasure & a pride, as I used to tell you I am sure. . . . & then your letters were not like other letters. . . . as I must not tell you again. And you influenced me, in a way in which no one else did. For instance, by two or three halfwords you made me see you, & other people had delivered orations on the same subject quite without effect. I surprised everybody in this house by consenting to see you—Then, when you came, . . . you never went away—I mean I had a sense of your presence constantly.

—Elizabeth Barrett
(in a letter to Robert Browning, dated 23 February, 1846)

Dearest, my soul drank thy letter this forenoon, and has been conscious of it ever since, in the midst of business and noise and all sorts of wearisome babble. How dreamlike it makes all my external life, this continual thought and deepest, inmostest musing upon thee! . . . Thou makest me a disembodied spirit; and with the eye of a spirit, I look on all worldly things—and this it [is] that separates thy husband from those who seem to be his fellows—therefore is he "among them, but not of them."

—Nathaniel Hawthorne
(in a letter to Sophia Amelia Peabody, dated 6 April, 1840)

THOUGHTS ON A NEW SCIENCE

- That in every encounter with another the information exchanged could be used to transmute the relationship into a deeper meeting.

- A mutual understanding exists—a moral and spiritual code— where we recognize the steps we can take from the illusion of separateness to the reality of unity.

- That we allow each other to take these steps in our own time and in our own way, both in our separate and shared journeys.

- That science helps us to identify these steps and how to take them.

2

Intimacy as a Journey Through This Text: Time and Change From Transcription to Transcendence

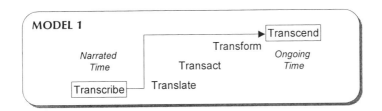

Strangers often have an easier time revealing crucial secrets to each other than acquaintances do. Strangers do not have to contend with the discrepancy between their secret and their surface characteristics. Unlike acquaintances, each stranger *has not yet had time* to construct the public image of the other, which the latter's secrets would normally contradict. (M. S. Davis, 1973; pp. 119-120, italics added)

IN WRITING, it is possible to move beyond the surface, to intimate as well as inform, to touch as well as make a point. Words, nested well within a story or poem, reach us through some fathomed coincidence of feeling, and through a deeper listening and coloring of that feeling (see letters by Barrett and Hawthorne on p. 33). If we listen in a suspended way, reading can move us— bring us to expectancy, insight, catharsis—in ways similar to the experiences shared in each other's presence. Intimacy, by its nature, does not conform to a single type of text or narrative; it is more about secrets than surface, more about openness and uncertainty than about closure and definition. Intimacy shifts the quality of an interaction; it bridges levels of meaning to make the impersonal more personal and close the distance. The meanings conveyed through both conversation and writing become intimate if we cue or reveal that the messages are offered to a specific *you,* whom we wish to know and whom we hope to know us.

Thus, information is not intimation. Information, facts, and the mere sending of signals are not intimacy, no matter how much of them we give to one another. As such, the operations—the analysis and synthesis—of scholars are typically not intimate. Similarly, our technological, postmodern, computerized, consumer-oriented world contains loads of information. Nevertheless, intimacy requires quality, not quantity—a shift in the level of understanding not an accumulation of data. It has been difficult for me—more through academic prose than metaphor or poetry—to convey the allusive, dynamic, and multilevel quality of intimacy. I wrote this chapter at different levels to capture these different qualities of intimacy.

First, the main text describes my experience of writing to *you* about the topic of intimacy. It reveals my (until now, secret) struggle to write *about* intimacy with the question: "How can I write about intimacy to someone I am not necessarily intimate with?" On one hand, the abstract, scientific prose would not touch on *qualities* we experience in intimacy. On the other hand, to write about my personal experience with intimacy runs the risk of appearing presumptuous, intrusive, or irrelevant. There is a dilemma here similar to the one we face when exploring whether (and at what degree) to become intimate with others. In conversation—especially with strangers—we may balance how much the focus is topical and distant versus more personal or revelatory. Scientists call this "privacy regulation." In a sort of parallel fashion, the main text of this chapter balances two explorations: It explores the edge of the "my writing ⇆ your reading" process (as an imperfect vehicle or metaphor for

---

✍ PARTICIPATE IN THIS EXPERIMENT ON SELF-DISCLOSURE (PART 1) ✍

Read the following list of topics and choose three that you would be willing to share with me (either talk about or write about). That is, before reading any further in the chapter, stop for a moment and consider whether you would be willing to right now let me (i.e., a stranger) know something about you.

From the following list choose those three that you would be the most willing to discuss (i.e., the most interesting for you). That is, put a "1" next to the topic you might feel most willing to discuss, a "2" next to the topic you are a little bit less willing to discuss, and so on. If you wish to make this a dynamic experiment (and get more out of the chapter), actually write a paragraph disclosing something about yourself on each topic. To make it even more dynamic, write the paragraph and send it to me by mail or over the Internet now before reading further (my address appears in "About the Author" at the back of the book). I will return to Part 2 of this experiment at the end of the chapter (don't peek ahead).

1. _____ How I feel about mercy killings.
2. _____ Times I have felt lonely.
3. _____ Lies that I have told my parents.
4. _____ My feelings about whether there is a conflict between religious and scientific beliefs.
5. _____ Whom I most admire.
6. _____ How I really feel about the people I work for or work with.
7. _____ As a child, what I thought I wanted to be when I grew up.

imitating intimacy). That is, it explores the question: Can you and I ever become intimate through this book, were we never to meet in person? And it explores the first of seven models for studying time and intimacy. To help, I highlight this model in a separate Figure (see Fig. 2.1 and accompanying Box 2.1 on page 46-50). I recommend first reading through this main text of the chapter.

I support these two explorations in the main text with supplemental text. First, I disclose some about myself (italicized font). I hope this will enrich two main hypotheses of this chapter: First, text can *mimic* the real-time, collaborative process of intimate discovery, and second, this mimesis can be useful for understanding more about the nature, the qualities, and the structure of intimate experience. I believe that a more serious understanding of this mimesis is necessary in our increasingly *virtual* society (i.e., the Internet, and televised, telephoned, and otherwise mediated or "removed" correspondence). We know each other more through this mediated or "tele-" (i.e., television, telephone, etc.) world (from the Greek *tele* meaning at a distance) and less directly. In response, this chapter introduces a model of the "trans-" (as in translate, transact) world (from the Latin *trans* meaning across or to move across). Such a world is more about closeness, about meeting, about touching.

Second, I apply philosophy and psychology to highlight 11 key catalytic qualities (metaphors) of intimacy (boxed and typed in smaller font at the bottom of the page). These metaphors show intimacy as taking time, as intrinsic wholeness, as ongoingness, continuity of connection, as sensitivity to context, as a capacity to change, as a willingness to interrupt, to listen, to translate; and intimacy as waking up, as the process of making meaning for or validating the other, as romanticism. Each quality shows that *intimacy is a process of discovery with another.* These qualities change or catalyze the relationship. This supplementary text provides historical background for a transpersonal science of intimacy in that it links previous writing with current hypotheses.

PERSONAL DISCLOSURE

> *I walk out of my home shortly after dawn. Bluffs and farmland surround the valley. From my doorway, I can see a small field across the paved two-lane, which backs up to a curved row of trees along the creek. Behind the creek lies a glen, and then a cornfield raises gently up to the distinctive, tree-filled bluffs about half a mile away. On this morning, a heavy mist shrouds the whole scene; the valley is unusually quiet for summer. The birds rest.*
>
> *I take a few steps and hear a short, subtle sound from the road ahead. A full-sized buck stands there, still and silent, eyeing me steadily. For a few breaths, we are present to each other. Just now, gliding from behind and directly above me breathes a great blue heron. Before I inhale, again she sails about ten feet over me in the direction of the buck and into the fog. The buck quietly saunters off. The mist folds in upon the two paths the creatures have just made. I stand alone, alive with awe and gratitude; grateful to witness this crossing, for the connection I felt to life. Tears well up in my soul and eyes.*

IS THIS "OUR" TEXT?

Self-transformation is precisely what life is, and human relationships, which are an extract of life, are the most changeable of all, rising and falling from minute to minute, and lovers are those in whose relationship and contact no one moment resembles another.

—Rainer Maria Rilke

The fragment of a life, however typical, is not the ample of an even web: promises may not be kept, and an ardent outset may be followed by a declension, latent powers may find their long-awaited opportunity; a past error may urge a grand retrieval.

—George Eliot

Is it possible that this could ever be *our* text, *our* story? No sooner do my words leave me than they—in some way—hope to find you. However, this is writing and reading, not intimacy. Intimacy is a special story; it is a journey that arrives in the present, a mutual exploration that continually shapes and discovers a relationship. The fixed nature of text on a page can only mirror the changing nature of an intimate relationship. However, as a mirror, I think it has a lot to teach us. I do not know exactly whether you will receive, listen to, or process these words, just as I cannot control the perception of those with whom I

Quality 1   TIME FOR INTIMACY

Intimacy requires relaxing into the moment in direct contact with another. This is not to say that we need to have more time to also have intimate experience. Neither time or relationships are things—material or otherwise—capable of being possessed, although everyday speech suggests differently with use of such phrases as "I don't have enough time" and "I have a relationship with Mary." This emphasis on "having" can influence one's worldview, or entire approach to life (cf. Fromm, 1976). This way of thinking underlies the fast-paced, future orientation of most modern consumerist, marketing cultures.

Other writers in the field of personal relationships (Duck, 1994; Scanzoni, Polonko, Teachman, & Thompson, 1989) explain how our language tends to "reify" relationships as entities, as things capable of being possessed. We do the same thing with time. Some individuals need to *have* time so much they develop a trait of "time urgency" (Landy, Rastegary, Thayer, & Colvin, 1991). Young (1988) coined the phrase "time famine" to describe modern economies where an emphasis on production leads workers ever hungering after more time to do everything. Servan-Schreiber (1988), in his discussion of the overworked individual, explained how we "deprive ourselves of a large part of our time" through "time thieves" or "time stealers" (e.g., external thieves include unexpected visitors, errands; internal thieves include scattered interests, indecisiveness). He explained:

> The lack of time also constitutes a convenient stronghold for avoiding others and warding off intimacy. For some persons, two elements in the life

experience intimacy. I lack the full and living context of your life, your reasons for reading, your way of seeing things, your private world. Moreover, what you learn or discern now may be different tomorrow or on re-reading. In fiction, the course of a good story (as the journey of intimacy) is filled with surprise, twists, and delayed arrivals. However, in a book on concepts, such changes can appear deviant or distracting. You may want an explanation, an organized explication. My attempt to use text to mimic intimacy, this text—our (author to reader) story—may alienate you. I can let you know my purpose: to provide a deeper understanding of how time is such a crucial aspect of relationships.

When I first thought of writing about intimacy for academics and fellow researchers in the scientific field of personal relationships, I did not expect to include my personal experiences. But my personal experiences like the one I experienced that misty morning, told me that intimacy was a process. The more research I read, the more I needed to keep returning to my personal experiences. They reminded me to see and feel my relationships in all their changing complexity: private as well as the public, cyclical as well as linear, and chaotic as well as ordered. I slowly realized that reports emphasizing research summaries and statistics perpetuate a nonintimate view of the world by either deleting personal disclosure or treating it as less than serious ("The Official Style"; Lanham, 1992). By slowing down and taking in the scenery that morning, I entered a state of presence, of "being with," of intimacy.

of a couple become threatening over time: sexuality and communication. . . . For sexuality, the overworked life may be a cause as well as a pretext . . . the office where the lights are on very late often shelters someone who has found good reasons for not going home. And when he does, his "tension," will justify his hardly saying a thing during supper and then his going to bed as soon after that as he can. (p. 63)

Fassel's (1990) description of workaholism—the norm in modern society—lists lack of intimacy as a key characteristic; she described the adverse effects and stresses families experience who have workaholic members. Hoschhild's (1997) ethnographic study convincingly shows how work is consuming greater portions of families' lives (i.e., "the Taylorized or Total Quality family"). She showed how even "family-friendly" workplaces produce "time-poor parents who dreamed of being time-millionaires" (p. 235). Moore-Ede (1993) described how our society has been "outpaced by our own technology" in developing the "round-the-clock" workplace. He convincingly documented the costs (in terms of health, economy, and human life) of this pace. Many writers have implied a relation between this culturally dictated lack of time ("time famine," "time prison") and the erosion of intimacy in modern life (e.g., Fromm, 1976; Laing, 1967; May, 1969). Like Fromm, I believe individuals can free themselves from this cultural bind. I think we must re-examine how we think, talk, and act regarding time and intimacy. I think we need to slow down, like when we take the time to read rather than watch TV.

I also discovered that research has not addressed different forms of intimate experience. Although I experienced some core aspects of intimacy that morning (i.e., participation, presence, beauty), my encounter with the deer and the heron was more fleeting than enduring and more *personal* than *relational*. This personal experience of intimacy with nature differs from the relational experience of intimacy with another person, but they are both important. In fact, when I talk with others, I find their experience of intimacy often tends to be less in interaction with people and more with nature, art (movies), animals, and within solitude. For many, intimacy, whether it is with nature, with others, or with oneself is often ephemeral. We find it when we can and often this is when we are alone. The breakdown of community, the fragmentation of society, and the fast-paced, "time-starved" habits of *Homo Faber* (i.e., humanity as producer, fabricator) leaves many with a constricted sense of time for intimacy (see Quality 1).

Before continuing, you may want to assess whether you have any time for intimacy. On the one hand, you may often feel too pressed for time and have a sense of urgency about your life. On the other hand, you may have no urgency at all and consider yourself a procrastinator. If urgent, you may not take the time to slow down and experience the qualities of intimacy described in this chapter. If you are a procrastinator, then you may lack the ability to use your time to bring more intimacy into your life. In addition, you may be overly or hedonistically oriented toward the present, only experiencing life in terms of the pleasure it can give. It may help to understand your own orientation toward time and to reflect on how this keeps you from experiencing more intimacy in your life. The following research reflection contains a brief survey on three different dimensions of personality.

| RESEARCH | REFLECTION | 3 |

WHAT IS YOUR PSYCHOLOGICAL ORIENTATION TOWARD TIME?

Psychologists have developed questionnaires that tap personality differences in time urgency (Landy et. al., 1991) or time press (Zimbardo, 1985), procrastination (Lay, 1986; Wessman, 1973), and present-hedonistic time orientation (Zimbardo, 1985). Consider these examples:

Time Urgency	Procrastination	Present-Hedonistic Time Orientation
☐ I glance at my watch or the clock frequently during the day.	☐ I rarely begin or finish a task on time.	☐ I take risks to put excitement in my life.
☐ I rush from one activity or meeting to another.	☐ I usually put off until tomorrow what I could really get done today.	☐ I get drunk at parties; I think it's fun to gamble.

The Changing Nature of Relationships:
The Essence of Intimacy

Another thing that destroys intimacy is the lack of change. We're afraid of change. Intimacy needs change. It's changing, everything in it is in a state of change, and you can't expect others to remain the same; they're going to change too.

—Leo Buscaglia

I first began thinking about time and personal relationships as a graduate student researching the topic of love and power in romantic relationships. I came across research on topics such as the time of year that young couples break up, the sequence individuals follow in disclosing private information when getting acquainted, and how feelings of ambivalence and conflict seem to change at different stages of a relationship. As I read, I grew increasingly uncomfortable with theories, models, and statistical reports that quantify and summarize relationship patterns. The scientific emphasis on prediction and control as a way of understanding relationships contrasted with the more random, unpredictable qualities I experienced in my life.

I discovered that scientific research on personal relationships was often not directly or immediately helpful to me. It was, and still is, exciting to study the fascinating and myriad patterns through which two individuals navigate and define their relating. But the research was missing something essential to my own personal experience of relationship. I sensed it had to do with time and with the ever changing and essentially dynamic nature of personal relationships, with something that I called "ongoingness" (see Quality 2).

One dictionary definition of intimate is intrinsic, essential. "How could something intrinsic be measured?" I thought. Science only measures "extrinsics": objectifiable, material phenomena. Because they take (time-limited) snapshots of some feature of behavior or self-report, experiments seemed to miss this ongoing quality. Even studies that follow a couple over weeks, months, or years (i.e., longitudinal studies) still isolate specifics. Scientists know that we can only look for laws with the methods and the time we have. Scientific methods determine or shape what can be studied. This methodological determinism gives both license to the scientific enterprise and a sense of futility: We can never measure the whole of phenomena (see Quality 3).

My concern was that the essential aspects of intimacy are processual, ongoing. They included an inspired sense of connection to an "Other," with a "connected knowing," with an ongoing empathic dialogue that somehow transcended particular times and particular spaces. Intimacy seemed immanently intersubjective, your experience and my experience together—"I–Thou" rather than "I–It"—and so involved spontaneity, flow, and unpredictability. How could methods, based on prediction and impersonal procedure, get at these intrinsic aspects, this essence?

The analogy of a snapshot helped to illustrate my discontent. How fascinating and beautiful it is to watch a flock of birds in mid-flight as they traverse a patch of sky? Paying close attention, one can see the birds continually shift their positions relative to each other. At one moment, the front flyer will dip down and to the side and others will glide from back to front or side to middle. There is no taking of each other's position. The whole pattern keeps shifting. A photograph of the flock could not convey the context of this changing pattern. A series of photographs could not show this either. A movie could convey ongoingness, but to be articulate the camera would have to keep parallel with the flock; the changing terrain under the migration would make such "followability" difficult.

The analogy of visually "capturing" a shifting flock of birds demonstrates that sophisticated research methods can track and document aspects of phenomena that are impossible with unaided perception. For example, through playback of film records I could track particular birds and examine the position and time of different shifts and thereby detect rhythmic patterns within the overall migration. Although such records are very helpful for quantification and analysis, these methods do not assess my experience of fascination and beauty. They do not reveal what Keller (1983) called a "connected knowing," a "feel for the organism," that is, intimacy (see Quality 4).

This analogy has stayed with me and I believe it still, albeit to a lesser degree, portrays the issue of ongoingness and the limits of scientific method to investigate the

---

Quality 2   INTIMACY AS ONGOINGNESS

There are many scientific models that view relationships as processes. Communication theories (Berlo, 1960), models of intimacy (Reis & Shaver, 1988), and theories of relationship development (Conville, 1991) each indicate that relationships depend upon time and upon partners' movement through time. Such movement may be from moment to moment (as in communication), from one psychological state to another (as in feeling validated in intimacy), or from one relationship stage to another (as in getting engaged). Process typically refers to the movement between these different periods of time (Duck & Sants, 1983).

I mean to distinguish this view of process (or "mere process") from ongoingness. Ongoingness captures a sense of the organic, ever-changing flow of intimacy that is comprised in the togetherness of various time frames. That is, relationships are ongoing in that they simultaneously are changing across moments, across psychological states, and across relational stages. As such, this ongoing process should not be confused with continuity in relationship or with a sense of continuity. In fact, intimacy involves a discontinuity, a shift in a relational state. These time frames and relational states cannot be separated from each other without destroying a sense of intimacy. Neville (1993), in his metaphysical discussion of time, described the togetherness of time's modes—present, past, and future. The metaphor that

changing nature of relationships. Like my experience that misty morning, intimacy is a dynamic phenomena that arises, lasts, and passes away in many contexts of time (i.e., temporal contexts) that I, simultaneously, cannot control, account for, or measure but that I can sense or experience (see Quality 5).

TYPES OF CHANGE AND INTIMACY

To live is to change time into experience
—Caleb Gattegno

Change is central to this sense of ongoingness and it is an inherent feature of all human relationships. On the one hand, too much routine can erode the spontaneous aspect of intimacy. On the other hand, too much unpredictability can diminish our sense of continuity. Each human relationship, permeated with rhythms of order and chaos, is unique precisely because it is continually subject to laws of change. It is possible to understand these laws.

My experience with the heron and the buck is a good place to begin. It was simple and profound. It demonstrates how some form of intimacy is possible without actual ongoing dialogue, without extended periods that characterize the complex and mundane personal relationship. By using my encounter as a comparison point, it is possible to describe this *mundane complexity.* Figure 2.1 outlines different types of change and describes the continuum of comparisons I am about to make. This figure

time "flows" recognizes that these modes are mutually conditioned. "No one mode by itself constitutes temporal flow, not the coming-into-being of present timeliness, nor the objective fixity of the past, nor the subjunctive formal patterns of the future. . . . If the dynamic moving present were not real, there would be no flow, only arbitrary stopping points on a cinema film of states of actuality or possibility" (Neville, 1993, pp. 103-104). Just as the temporal modes are intrinsically connected, so too are the various temporal contexts (i.e., moment to moment, state to state, and stage to stage) of relationships. Just as we have a real sense that time flows, so too, when we are intimate, we feel the flow (not just the process) of relationship.

The various models presented in this book—in this and later chapters—each rest on the assumption that ongoingness is an inherent aspect of intimacy. Each model attempts to show how partners gain a sense of this flow. Intimacy is a "taking notice" at all points in time, not just when the relationship disintegrates (Conville, 1991). Clearly, many couples need "wake up calls" before they make an effort to be intimate. I believe that when we have a sense of the big picture, when we are able to embrace various temporal contexts, when we see relationships as a "precious weave," then we enter into a deeper intimacy with others. Conversely, intimacy entails having glimpses of this ongoingness. This is what makes relationships a spiritual discipline (McBee, 1994).

shows how you and I—with our language ability and empathy—can approach ongoingness through the text.

Figure 2.1 (p. 46) depicts five different types of changes that occur in the process of communication: transcription, translation, transaction, transformation, and transcendence. I am suggesting a parallel between how these changes occur while reading (col. 1) with how they are experienced in an actual ongoing encounter (Action: col. 2) and am using the metaphor of the text to make this parallel. Suppose you do not understand a sequence of words that I write. You may feel confused, go back and re-read, or review the surrounding words and sentences until you feel some understanding or give up. Now recall hearing a person tell you something you did not understand. Your look of confusion may cause the person to use gestures, tones, and expressions. That is, you give signals that tell the other—if that person is sensitive to receive it— that he or she is not making sense. The static medium of text differs from the dynamic one of conversation, but re-framing in conversation has some parallel with re-reading (reviewing) in text.

I am also suggesting that time itself is experienced differently within the five types of changes I outline, whether you are interacting with a text (i.e., me now) or a person (col. 3). Intimacy involves meeting and sharing experience, something impossible with written words alone. In order for us to meet, we need a meeting

---

Quality 3   INTIMACY AS WHOLENESS

The words "measure" and "intimate" have meanings that coincide when we take intimate to mean intrinsic, essential. Bohm (1980) viewed classical notions of measurement as contributing to a fragmentary view of the world and society. Tracing the etymological roots and original meanings of the word "measure," Bohm described how, for the Ancient Greeks:

> To keep everything in its right measure was regarded as one of the essentials of a good life. . . . In this regard, measure was not looked on in its modern sense as being primarily some sort of comparison of an object with an external standard or unit. Rather, this later procedure was regarded as a kind of outward display of a deeper "inner measure," which played an essential role in everything. . . . When something went beyond its proper measure . . . this meant that it was inwardly out of harmony, so that it was bound to lose its integrity and break up into fragments. (p. 20, italics added)

Bohm showed how the words for "medicine" (mederi), "moderation," and "meditation" are based on the same Latin root as measure. The definition of intimate as intrinsic, essential, is similar to these ancient notions of (inner) measure as referring to some whole, and essential aspect of life. Bohm's view of quantum mechanics implies that nature functions as a whole; whereas this wholeness is immeasurable, we can still have knowledge (i.e., intimacy) that is itself in flux with this wholeness, and not split off from reality. In the new physics that Bohm described, time is always relative to the observer—something we project onto a multidimensional reality—and not merely some fixed, external standard that we use to measure the progression of events, such as our lives, our work, or our

ground or common medium to talk about our experience (col. 4 and 5). As I write I experience different types of changes in different ways (col. 4) and I hypothesize what your experience is as you read (col. 5). Again, I shall refer to my experience with nature to elucidate these different types of change.

In fact, different changes had occurred in the crossing of paths that morning: Change within the encounter itself, change within the environment, and change within me. The encounter began with my consciousness of the buck and ended when he left; it was an indentation that changed the stream of that day's events. The heron cut a path in the mist and the buck left hoof prints. The encounter itself also consists of change: the speed of the heron, the saunter of the buck, the flexion of surprise in my posture. And as I acutely felt more connected to my surrounding environment, I too changed from the experience.

By speaking about this as an event or encounter, I make it some "thing" that arises in time, has duration, and then passes away. I feel very uncomfortable as I continue to write about my experience. Something essential gets lost in this transcription of an intimate, emotional experience that often only poetry can convey or awaken. Telling you about my experience of intimacy will not give you the same changing sensation as would poetry. (*continued on p. 50*)

---

relationships. I believe that the process of scientific knowing, which we will return to in chapter 6, entails a "feeling for the organism" (Keller, 1983), where these temporal standards are played with, relaxed, and ultimately transcended.

This quantum view of scientific measurement contrasts with the classical, mechanistic view that separates the observer from the observed. Subjective experiencers, with their biases, are clearly distinct from the objective reality to be measured with unbiased instrumentation. The scientist applies measurement "as an explorer bent on discovery" of formal, atemporal laws. As such, "nature" or "the world" can only be known in parts. Compare Bohm's holistic view with these philosophers writing about laws in science:

> But scientific inquiry is always specific and limited. We do not study "the world," but some special and usually very restricted portion or aspect of it. . . . Beliefs about the world as a *whole* are not involved, therefore, but only beliefs about the specific subject-matter of inquiry. (Kaplan, 1964, p. 123, italics added)

> Nature is not a gigantic formalizable system. In order to formalize it, we have to make some assumptions which cut out some parts. We then lose the total connectivity. And what we get is a superb metaphor, but it is not a system which can embrace the *whole* of nature. (Bronowski, 1978, p. 80, italics added)

In human relationships, intimacy, the process of knowing, has a quality of unity or wholeness that appears lacking in the classical scientific knowing described in the previous quotes. The subject–object distinction is relaxed and flexible in human intimacy as well as in the new physics. The "lesson of modern physics is that the subject (perceiving apparatus) and object (reality measured) form one seamless whole" (Yankelovich & Barrett, 1970, p. 203).

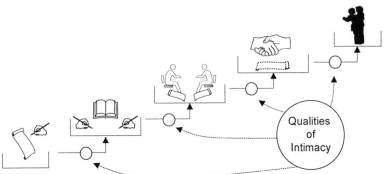

FIG. 2.1 The qualities of intimacy catalyze movement from one experience to another.

	TYPE OF CHANGE	ACTION	NATURE OF TIME	EXPERIENCE & METAPHOR
Transcription	I write down what I think I know to tell you	**EXPRESSION** I tell you (or project) my experience	Time is narrated; self as text is in foreground, other is interpreted, not present	I intend coherence, you understand Text that separates
Translation	I clarify what you may not understand	**CORRESPONDENCE** You tell me what you heard or understood	Time is sequence: action-reaction; self and text in foreground, other is receiver only	I revise to help you understand The Inter-subjective text
Transaction	You read what I write (say) as I intend and respond	**COLLABORATION** We both share our own meanings and find mutual ground	Time is continuous overlap between self & other as both sender & receiver (text is medium)	We experience meaning, and follow the meaning The Occasion
Transformation	The text fades and is replaced by fluid meeting	**CO-CREATION** We are both changed from sharing as we go	Time is continuous and discontinuous; Time _is the relation_ among events experienced together (organismic holism)	We experience meeting and empathy The Weave
Transcendence	The I that is We (self – boundaries dissolve)	Embodying the above (and seeking to express it again)	Time is illusory; simultaneous awareness of impermanence & eternal qualities	We experience flow, presence, synchronicity The Dance

Time in Text & Action: Change and Experience (Accompanies FIG 2.1)

BOX 2.1. Time in Text and Action (Model 1)

Figure 2.1 may help to clarify the ideas discussed in this chapter. There is a distinction between each of the five levels of text-dependence, with the experience of transcription being most text-dependent and that of transcendence being least text-dependent. These are not developmental levels, where we must experience one stage before another. Rather, they are moments where two individuals can meet each other depending upon the degree to which they are free from using text to meet. This nondependence on text is an alchemical process. No matter what we are presented with in experience, we have the capacity to transmute it into something deeper. That is, as we experience intimacy in a moment of transcription, we are moved to translate. Similarly, we may transcend as we experience intimacy in a moment of transformation. This is also a map for comparing real-time interaction (i.e., transaction) with reading and writing (i.e., transcription) and with a deep ongoing sense of unity with another (i.e., transcendence).

As the figure shows, each level of text-dependence is represented as one of five figures. A circle represents the qualities of intimacy discussed elsewhere in this chapter (e.g., ongoingess, validation). As hypothesized in chapter 1, intimacy has catalytic qualities that can transform relationships and experiences of relationship (see Fig. 1.1). Thus, the arrows coming from the circle in Fig. 2.1 convey that these qualities facilitate movement from one level to another. The images representing each level are meant to convey the increasing depth of subsequent levels. Thus, transcription is symbolized by the solitary act of transcribing while a couple dancing represents transcendence. The bottom of Fig. 2.1 and the following sections explain each level in more detail.

Transcription. There are two meanings to the term *transcription*, depending on the way script is defined. To transcribe may simply mean to copy or duplicate what I have in my mind either through writing or through talk. As such, I simply record and transfer the meanings I perceive into the public domain. However, I may not be completely conscious of the meanings I perceive or my intentions in transferring or copying them. In this latter instance, the unconscious script may get projected or placed over events like a film or screen is placed between things.

In both meanings, my action is to express the script through narration; as such, the text of my narrative is a static and linear representation of my thoughts. The text (my recollections from memory, my interpretations of meaning) separates us, but if I am coherent (if the text has sufficient meaning) and you understand me, then we share a common medium.

An example of transcription gone awry occurs in the motion picture *Network* (Dir. Lumet, 1976) that satirizes how television producers distort reality with their scripts. One of the main characters, whose job is to program television shows that will be popular and receive high ratings, becomes so obsessed with achieving the right script that she becomes progressively callous. She suggests the assassination of a television host in order to bring back higher ratings for the network. At one point in the story, her lover leaves her because she has lost the capacity for intimacy. Before leaving, he confronts her with how she treats him like a character in her own personal script, without considering that he is a

Continued

BOX 2.1 Continued

human being with needs that are real and separate from hers. The movie painfully shows how—left to itself—transcription can be a destructive force in private interaction and the public media.

TRANSLATION. Translation occurs either following or in anticipation of the moment when I receive negative feedback on the intended coherence of my transcription; that is, you did not understand me. At this point, I clarify what you may not understand by corresponding with you. You tell me what you heard and we both enter a sequence of action and reaction.

Now the text only partially separates us because, to the degree that I revise on the basis of feedback from you and to the degree that you *review* my revisions, we actually begin to create a text together. The text is no longer a repository of my own subjective narration, it includes your subjective views as well. It becomes intersubjective.

Translation is an essential part of any relationship. For each misunderstanding or miscommunication, translation is required if partners care to understand what happened. In order to maintain close relationships, issues of jealousy and the suspicion of infidelity require the correction of misunderstandings. Couples may break up when one partner's requests for clarification about the suspected betrayal are only met with silence or avoidance. By showing no willingness to clarify the situation, the suspect is essentially saying that the text (what happened) should not be reviewed or revised for the benefit of the other. In contrast, the partner who either admits to a breach and asks forgiveness or who honestly shares details begins a sequence where the other can both describe and allay any fears or regrets they may have (see Staske, 1999, and endnote 1 of this chapter). Both partners are reviewing what happened. They may be doing it one at a time, but they both honor the situation together.

TRANSACTION. At the moment where you read what I write just as I intended it, there is no longer any need to stop for clarification, revision, or translation. We both share a common meaning; instead of corresponding in a sequence of "back and forth" (messages sent → messages received → response made → response received), we now collaborate in a continuous interaction. Your meaning and my meaning are both important and acted on.

At this point, time is no longer fixed in the sequence of the narration but is shaped by the interaction of shared meanings. The text begins to recede and our actions—the occasion of creating meaning together—becomes the salient focus of our time together. I sense that I am being meaningful and you have a deeper experience of me. My messages are more than just coherent, no longer in need of review; rather, you experience followability of me and soften awareness of any mediating text.

The key difference between translation and transaction lies in the emergence of a shared and collaborated occasion as opposed to a reviewing of shared text. Communication is happening continuously in real time rather than in a piecemeal, give-and-take sequence. Many romance stories are essentially about the promise of a shift from sequence to continuity. The main characters experience several, often chance, encounters with each other where

Continued

BOX 2.1 Continued

they are thrown together in a single situation. The plot revolves around the possibility that these situations will evolve into something more permanent—a future that the couple creates together—typically at the end of the story. Also, couples who build a home or family together—coordinating schedules with work and children—cannot do so very efficiently on the basis of translation only. They carry out transactions continuously (i.e., who will make dinner, who will pay the rent, who will take Johnny to soccer practice). Only when agreements break down the couples have to step back and translate to clear up miscommunications.

TRANSFORMATION. At this moment, there is no longer any effort required to express and to understand, or to transact and create meaning. Meaning is a given. "We just have an understanding." Our sharing is no longer based on text or dependent on symbolic interchange. Our whole relationship has changed as a function of just being with time together. Our relationship is not about two separate selves who have collaborated on some event (task, conversation, project); rather through our joint creativity, through creation, we are moved, inspired, enlivened, and altered. Our common medium is not only a single occasion of meaning, but a weaving of occasions. We are a meeting, we empathize with each other. We may still be aware of our separateness (e.g., "you are you and I am me"), but this is enriching rather than threatening; it gives variety and unpredictability to the dance.

Just as couples must understand each other in order to carry out a transaction, so must they meet each other in order to be transformed. Transformation comes in several ways: as commitment, consummation, falling in love, deciding to change a habit for the relationship, or in finally seeing some truth about the other or the relationship. Each of these leads to a change in the nature of the relationship itself. The story of Pygmalion—depicted in the modern motion pictures of *My Fair Lady* (Dir. Cukor, 1964), *Educating Rita* (Dir. Gilbert, 1983), and *To Sir With Love* (Dir. Clavell, 1967) tells how a teacher's love for his student transforms her character. The children's story of *The Velveteen Rabbit* (Bianco, 1981) describes how love can transform something fictional into something real, just as Pinocchio's love for his father made him a real boy, or Beauty's love for the Beast returned him to his true prince state. Although the changes in these stories occur to individuals or characters, they occur through intimacy and, as such, change the relationship as well.

TRANSCENDENCE. At this moment, there is no longer some entity that can be called a relationship or partnership (a thing separate from other events as a unity unto itself). In joining, our unity reflects the Unity of all things. All metaphors fall away as being imperfect screens of this deeper sense. We are not separate actors, but participants in (and embodying) the ongoingness of time's flow (cf. Neville, 1993).

We have moved from simply being with the passage of time to gaining insight into the impermanence (the ongoing dissipation, dissolution) of our being. As such, all is experienced as flow. There is nothing to maintain, nothing to communicate, and nothing to do. We do not even have to be together (i.e., in each other's physical presence) anymore. Instead, our common medium is to join together in a dance, a celebration of unity as events arise and pass

Continued

BOX 2.1 Continued

away. Transcendence allows us to transmute whatever arises and experience it as love (e.g., compassion, kindness, joy, care).

Transaction is to transformation as transformation is to transcendence. Two individuals are not only changed from sharing together, but the change has a discontinuous quality that somehow allows the individuals to rise above the routine, mundane, or difficult conditions of their shared lives. I read the story of a Jewish couple who spent many months hiding in an attic in Amsterdam during Nazi Germany (Berman & Weiss, 1978). Their love for each other allowed them to enjoy life even in the direst circumstances. It is helpful to distinguish this transcendent, interpersonal intimacy—that arises within and infuses an ongoing and committed relationship—from a transcendent, intrapersonal intimacy—that may be stimulated by a brief romance or affair.

A recently popular American novella and film *The Bridges of Madison County* describes how, through a brief adulterous affair with a traveling photographer, a farm wife finds a renewed sense of life that allows her to go beyond routine housewife chores. In writing down the rich emotional details of her four-day affair in several journals, she is able to transcend the monotony faced on a daily basis. In a sense, she experiences a discontinuity with the stream of events in her routine life. Her transcendence, however, is limited, unrequited, and poignant, as she never achieves a similar depth for the remainder of her life with her husband. This may be contrasted with the transcendence that Elizabeth Barrett and Nathaniel Hawthorne's letters reveal in the epigrams that begin this chapter. Both describe an ongoing experience that is born out of, shared within, and strengthens a committed relationship.

In fact, the more I write about it, the more ordinary it becomes; the special, sublime, and spontaneous features begin to fade. Memory, in this sense, separates you and I. We do not have a shared past. We do not have a common memory from which to move into the present. Perhaps I just do not want to talk about change, but prefer to share my experience. This desire for, and the act of, communication points to a difference between *personal* (or intrapersonal) and *relational* (or interpersonal) intimacy and to a different kind of change than considered in my account of the deer and heron. Our personal relationships can include an ongoing, mutual influence between two individuals. We talk to others, listen, and express feelings in a collaborative give and take ("I hope you'll agree with me after I tell you my feelings about it"). We have access to and can verbalize our inner experiences ("That's not how I feel!"). We can modify our gestures and phrasing in response to others and across situations. Thus, we change how we speak from listening to each other ("Could you put that in a different way?"). Our memories of previous encounters, our expectations, habits, and feelings guide us along. Thus, we change from building, reviewing, and sometimes editing a common history with each other ("That's not how I remember it"). An extended collaboration is possible because we share a common language with words that denote experiences we can verify and compare ("Remember the time when you thought I hated you?") (see Quality 6).

Have you ever "felt close" to an animal, perhaps a pet you own or once owned? What is this feeling of closeness? How does it differ from any feelings you may have for a person? *Personal* intimacy involves one's own feelings of closeness, union, transcendence, or warmth. These can occur with a person, an animal, with nature, or while reading, listening to music, or watching a movie. In contrast, *relational* intimacy involves verbal feedback about the inner experience of the other. It involves an ongoing give and take that requires verbal memory, a common history, and the constant opportunity to re-evaluate and check out the meaning of what has been communicated. Both types of intimacy are important and both are necessary in a relationship. Even personal intimacy involves an experience over time that can develop and change the meaning of a previous event. We can see a movie or read a book two, three, or many times and have a very different understanding each time. We can see nature with new eyes; it can even "speak" to us.

PERSONAL DISCLOSURE

> *Years pass. It is time for me to leave my home in the bluffs. The deer paths twist through the red sumac. Rows of brittle corn husks and roots have cracked in the snow, under my skis. The dance of fireflies has played against the garden sky. There is the creekside and it's burdock and nettle. There is the chorus of crows, the duet of owls, the solo whippoorwill.*
>
> *Now I pack my things and either give away or sell some belongings. I go for last walks. I go to my prayer place in the slope of a glen. And, as I do these things, the hawk sees. Every morning he circles my house and sings that high pitch of his. Softly but proudly he cuts the summer quiet. He has done this for four, five days now and never in a row before. So high up too. I like to think that he may be saying good-bye.*

THE DIFFERENCES BETWEEN READING AND MEETING

You and I are not in each other's presence; you can stop reading, look away, yawn. You and I are temporally remote, independent from any real-time collaboration, from ongoing dialogue (See Box 2.2, "The Mimetics of Philemics" on pp. 66-70). Thus, my personal encounters with nature are similar to "my writing-your reading" because you are not giving me any feedback, *at this time*, to indicate whether you understand, agree with, or are bored. I have merely transcribed my experience and have no *ongoing* sense of your response. I do not know whether you care, whether you have ever sensed the same things I did with nature, or whether—right now—you want me to make a point or yield an insight. Even if you wanted to compare your views with mine, then you could not interrupt me (see Quality 7).

You may not know exactly what I am saying here. You are putting some trust in me and I simply may not be communicating to you. Were you to ask me to explain further, I could paraphrase or *translate* my experience in a form that conveyed the meaning until some point in time when you understood (at least until I thought you understood). But presently you cannot do this; you cannot respond, give me feedback in real time, tell me to paraphrase, to recode, or elaborate; in short to translate. There is a difference between the self-corrective act of writing down my experience (transcription) and the responsive act of rewording it because you have asked me to (translation). This is a difference between "literary time" and a sequence of correspondence. In correspondence, we both place our subjective interpretations on our own and each other's text. In this way, the text is *intersubjective.* Because we each recognize that there is an "other" involved, we work on the text. I revise for you and you review (go over what you do not understand) for me. The distinction between a virtual relationship (refer to Box 1.2), in which we only imagine intimacy with another, and a real relationship, in which we mutually create a context for intimacy, begins with translation (see Quality 8).

In our everyday interactions, we often do not need to translate our words in any constant manner. We help their meaning through hand gestures, facial expressions, body postures. Meaning is continually transferred and interactions

---

Quality 4   CONTINUOUS & CONNECTED KNOWING

An empathy, a knowing of the other, that transcends time characterizes the intimate relationship. Belenky, Clinchy, Goldbreger, and Tarule (1986), in their study of women's ways of knowing, distinguished between two epistemologies: a separate knowing, based on impersonal procedures for establishing truth, and a connected knowing, where truth emerges through care and empathy (also see Keller, 1985). McAdams (1989), in his study of the intimacy motive, distinguished common themes in imaginative stories written under conditions arousing the intimacy motive. One theme was the tendency for relationships to transcend the usual limitations of time and/or space. Similarly, Oden (1974) described intimate relationships as having contracts with no "specific terminus:" "The intimate relationship would be offended by the thought that it should have a designated end" (p. 13).

Buber (1970) wrote extensively on the I–Thou experience, describing how intimacy can neither be impersonal nor specifically temporal:

> When I confront a human being as my Thou and speak the basic word I–Thou to him . . . he is no longer He or She, a dot in the world grid of space and time, nor a condition to be experienced and described, a loose bundle of named qualities. (p. 59)

Some might argue that philosophical or epistemological premises—such as Oden's or Buber's—are not particularly helpful for the measurement of intimacy. However, as described in chapter 1, even researchers in the field of personal relationships have had difficulty forging such definitions.

flow because we have a well-learned (and somewhat unconscious and automatic) system of both verbal and nonverbal feedback mechanisms. In this sense, meaning is more of a social act than an individual thinking process. Thus, there is another difference here: between translation (responding to clarification requests) and real-time, ongoing transaction (reciprocal exchanges). In transaction, time is not just a series of instants—a sequence of actions and reactions—but a more continuous interaction. We begin to collaborate in a shared experience. We construct a common memory, a common meaning, and even a common emotion. For example, Staske (1999), in a detailed analysis of couple's talking to each other about jealousy, showed how the use of certain phrases and intonations was associated with a collaborated construction of emotion.[1]

In transaction, the emphasis moves away from meaning; the quality of translation is defined by the accurate portrayal (rendering, interpreting, conveyance) of meaning. In transaction, the emphasis is on action—on collaboration, moving with, meeting, co-creation. We both have made sense to each other (meaning) and so are now able to follow along (followability). The distinction between *personal* intimacy and *relational* intimacy begins with transaction.

Quality 5   SENSITIVITY TO CONTEXT

Context is a key term in later chapters. The analogy presented here as a continuum—snapshot, series of photographs, a movie, an ongoing documentary—reveals comparatively longer durations of study. Longer durations also mean broader contexts of time when a particular element (e.g., the distance between two birds) is situated in a particular frame. The element means different things within different contexts.

Hermeneutics, or the study of interpretation, stresses the importance of knowing context when interpreting data and of being sensitive to the biases and limitations of one's own perspective when studying text. Many psychologists advocate a longitudinal approach (favoring the movie over the photograph) in the study of persons and personal relationships. This provides a way of better testing causal theories of change (e.g., Huston & Robins, 1982), but also for increasing our contextual sensitivity (see Meichenbaum, 1988). As argued by Wakefield (1988), however, the relationship between empiricism and hermeneutics is complex, and the study of interpretation is distinct from the study of cause and change. My point here (and developed later) is that intimacy involves both meaning and change together; relationships take on meaning through change. Because these meanings are essentially empathic, connected, and visceral, they have historically been more difficult for empiricists and hermeneuts than for phenomenologists. One purpose of this book is to present a model of temporal context that integrates these approaches to knowledge.

The other day I was with a friend who has recently divorced. He has been feeling depressed and, for over a year, rarely reached out or initiated calling others for support. On this day, he received a phone call from his son who had recently left to live with his mother who herself had moved over a thousand miles away to live with her new lover. After this call my friend asked me to sit with him as he began to sob, to let out his grief, to release feelings of pain that he had held in for so long. I felt honored to witness his releasing: every few minutes a wave of grief would move through his body followed by deep sobbing and tears. We talked little but he did say how good it felt to cry and how much he felt a spiritual connection, a sense of a "higher power," through crying and releasing.

After about an hour, he looked at me and our eyes met. I felt very touched by his willingness to stay with himself and to move through his grief. Then I felt a mixture of anxiety and empathy as we looked into each other's eyes. He then spoke:

"I feel safe and I trust you, Joel."

I leaned forward to listen better but, in my body I felt a tendency to contract, to not really let in what he was saying.

"I have always felt that way," he took a breath as another tear came across his cheek onto the pillow, from the beginning I have felt that sense . . . that . . . that I could trust you."

Part of me was delighted to hear this, for I had reached out to him in the past but had stopped because I was afraid of being too giving when there was not some reciprocity. Another part of me started to contract, to pull away. I looked away and started to feel a tenderness in my chest, a crying inside.

Almost as if reading my mind, he continued, "I know that you had been reaching out to me and that I just have not been available." He did not say he was sorry. His tone was caring and apologetic. I felt tears—of joy and pain—begin to form. And then I realized something. This was intimacy. I was really listening to him and he really knew it! This was something that I craved, searched for, and read about. This wasn't something I could predict or control and here it was, and my body, my chest would not let in the love I was feeling in my heart and throat. There was some block in my chest at my ribs; a few minutes later I too, was crying. Eventually, we both felt affirmed through our acknowledgment of each other.

Change that comes from a continual transaction between two individuals—between my friend and me—differs qualitatively from the changes that occurred in my encounter with nature. There is give-and-take, an affirmation, a feeling of being seen that is reciprocated in the moment and sustained. Our whole relationship with others can change in the process of transaction, when we listen, empathize, and are willing to be vulnerable. This type of change is a *transformation*. It is not merely a change from one state to another state (e.g., from feeling distant to feeling close), but a change in the way we behave, a change in the whole process of our transactions. Transpersonal intimacy begins with just such a transformation; the process of meeting each other becomes an end in itself, we embrace time together and become our own story. We play and we create (see Quality 9).

Textual Time and Intimacy

Time becomes human to the extent that it is articulated through a narrative mode, and narrative attains its full meaning when it becomes a condition of temporal experience.

—Paul Ricouer

Human beings are most aptly designated **Homo Narrans** . . . *they are essentially storytellers.*

—Walter R. Fisher

You and I are remotely associated through this text. This is a monologue; we are not interacting together now. Our remote association is as different from an ongoing conversation as is the study of a personal relationship different from the ongoing relationship itself. Yet, as the aforementioned quote from Ricouer indicates, there is something about narration—even about this monologue—that makes time human, that affords us an intimate part in the evolution of a story. In a vicarious sense, reading and writing can transform our relationship even though we may never meet. This especially happens in creative writing and poetry, where your interpretation, your structuring of my words is reflexive (i.e., you imagine, reflect, and participate from your own life) and empathic (i.e., you put yourself in my shoes). It can also happen here if we both suspend judgment, if I do not assume too authoritative a tone, and if my character—my personality—can somehow come across to you.

| Quality 6 | THE CAPACITY TO CHANGE |

Malone and Malone (1987) distinguished between the intimate experience and the intimate dyad, which parallels the current distinction between intrapersonal and interpersonal. The intimate experience "is the sense of being in touch with our real selves" (p. 19), which can happen with nature, within our ordinary routine, and with others. The intimate dyad "is our term for the experience between two persons that produces the feelings of intimacy" (p. 152). The Malones wrote that experiential pairing is a subset of the personal form of intimacy; we can experience intimacy outside of pairing with another person; but they suggested that pairing is exceptional. "The importance of intimacy is that it provides us with experience in our pairing that not only allows us, but usually demands and compels us, to change" (p. 169).

Therefore, I believe we can mimic a process of intimacy through written communication. In this regard, it is important to note that linear narrative has served as a critical metaphor in the scientific psychology of relationships. For example, individuals do have scripts for how to behave in their encounters with others (see chap. 5) and our memories of close relationships can be sequenced much like the chapters of a novel.[2] But again, the ongoing reciprocity, the mutual exchange and interdependence that proceeds when two interact in time, is something more than just text. Recently, some authors have been suggesting a different metaphor, that of the "dance," to better capture this ongoing, interdependent quality of relationships.[3] According to Gergen (1988):

> People must be more than texts . . . forms of action are what they are, not symbols or emanations, and people are responsive to other's words and actions. Specifically, we can shift from an emphasis on the text and its reader, or the single action and reaction, to more extended patterns of interdependence. In this sense my conduct is neither a response or a stimulus, but an integer in an extended pattern of which both of us are part. . . . This relational account views the interpretive process not as the act of the single individual attempting to locate the inner region of the other, but as a process of mutual collaboration. The metaphor of the dance or the game replaces that of the text. (pp. 49-51)

Quality 7   CAPACITY & WILLINGNESS TO INTERRUPT

Even if you do not understand me, chances are that you would use your own knowledge structures and expectations to revise what it was you thought I was saying (without ever telling me). This assumptive or "top-down" approach is distinct from a "bottom-up" strategy where you might ask for clarification. Kellerman and Sleight (1989) suggested that top-down repairs are more likely because they are more efficient and permit both you and I to "save face." But intimacy is less about efficiency than about empathy and presence in a shared world of action and sensation. The very point I am making—that, in reading, you cannot ask for clarification (re-translation)—presumes that you would ask for it were we together in real-time conversation. A certain degree of intimacy occurs when you can relax "face-saving" routines and formalities. Intimacy can occur when you interrupt, seek clarification, and talk concurrently with me (i.e., "impose" as in Sharabany's, 1994, Intimate Friendship Scale, see chap. 1). It occurs when strangeness enters into our familiarity (cf. Malone & Malone, 1987, chap. 9); that is, when you show me that you care enough to let me know that you do not know, that you disagree, and that you want to know (cf. Laing's concept of "confirmation," 1969). The capacity to interrupt hearkens back to hermeneutic temporality (Slife, 1993; see chap. 1) and it foreshadows discussion in chapter 4 about perturbation. That is, the willingness to enter into the moment and processes of disruption are integral to the intimate experience of time.

Much research has examined interaction rules and rituals that help keep our everyday communications running smoothly without the need for translation. Leeds-Hurwitz (1989) provided a comprehensive review of communication in everyday life, and Goffman (1959, 1967, 1974) is a seminal source.

Again, the critical difference between textual time and the real time of an ongoing relationship lies in *mutual* collaboration, trans*action*, the ability to transform *together* through our *actions*. Ultimately, intimacy depends on both you and I in time, on translation and understanding, on mutual collaboration. And because it is unpredictable, intimacy is also a mutual creation. Were we to talk and to know each other, we would continually negotiate meanings in our encounter. We just do not meet and immediately "know" each other. Miscommunication, misunderstanding, blunt interruption, disjuncture, conflict, and upset: All could be reinterpreted, reformulated in the context of further interaction. This is the kind of change that comes definitively and only from communication. A human communication system is a collaborative dance that continually calibrates itself, which must correct itself if the dance is to continue. It becomes a creative dance when we go beyond merely trying to understand each other, when we value each other's humanness and embrace the unexpected. In this way, true intimacy stretches our sense of self and may even transform us (see Quality 10).

Quality 8   CAPACITY & WILLINGNESS TO TRANSLATE

That interactions are well-learned may make them rhetorically efficient but not philemically effective. We may both guess we understand each other when we never really do. This, of course, is not intimacy. In fact, intimacy deteriorates when interactions become habitual and automatic. For example, Gottman (1979) has found that couples in distressed marriages exhibit sequential patterns of interaction that are more predictable than the patterns of happy couples. Communication breakdowns are not due to failures in translation as much as to assumptions that translation is not necessary (Laing, Phillipson, & Lee, 1966; Watzlawick, 1976, chap. 1). We develop routines and assume the other sees things the way we do. To find out otherwise can be threatening; more information can lead to uncertainty and anxiety (Berlo, 1960), and over time we develop overlearned routines that are both self-confirming and mindless (Langer, 1989). In fact, social conflict escalates when two parties selectively perceive the other in ways that confirm their original beliefs; no effort is made at translation (Pruitt & Rubin, 1986).

Effective communication requires learning how to listen, reflect, and reframe messages (Carkhuff, 1983). This ability to listen—which is distinctively non-habitual—is an important aspect of intimacy.

Listening is never easy. It involves overcoming the habitual tendency to roadblock. It requires a certain maturity, a certain self-transcendence, an openness to understand values and points of view very different from our own. When we really listen, our own ideas and values are sometimes altered. To listen well means to be vulnerable. (Bolton, 1979, p. 111)

BLOCKS TO THE PRESENT: COLLUSION AND ROMANCE

> There are those who believe they are already free of the past and that what they see in their partner as faults are realities independent of their own distorting judgments . . . if a partner does something provoking, depressing, irritating, saddening, the other has by definition participated by interpreting in this way—even though not responding outwardly and perhaps believing as well that he or she did nothing to set up the situation initially. Although participation is sometimes outward, taking place before or after the incident, it is *always* mental, and it is *always* a choice. (Prather & Prather, 1988, pp. 123-126)

There are at least two ways in which we keep ourselves from the present ongoingness of relationship; the first is a mutual decision not to do so (collusion), and the second is solipsistic (romantic illusion). Participation in the reality of another human being is fundamental to intimacy. To fully participate when one reads a text requires a certain amount of effort, choice, and absorption; so too it is with participation in an ongoing relationship. When participation becomes automatic and taken for granted—when it involves blaming or automatically projecting one's romantic fantasies onto another—it then becomes dysfunctional. When both partners do this, they are not really living in an ongoing, real-time relationship. They are exhibiting the antithesis of intimacy; they are colluding.[4]

Collusion. Collusion is mutual deception, a choice made by both partners to protect each other from the truth. It often takes the form: "I'll protect your ego if you protect mine." Intimacy can occur when we interrupt these deceptive scripts with empathy and honesty. Schmalz wrote about AIDS (Acquired

---

Quality 9   INTIMACY AS WAKING UP

McAdams (1985) defined the intimacy motive as a "recurrent preference or readiness for *warm, close and communicative exchange with other*—an interpersonal interaction perceived as an end in itself rather than a means to another end" (p. 87). Relationships are not intimate when they are transacted toward some particular end. When intimate, they become transformative, a *process* unlike the more sequential nature of transactions. Whereas transactions are necessary for intimacy, they are not sufficient; a shift to a process orientation is also involved.

This transformation is like that described by Watzlawick, Weakland, and Fisch (1974) as second-order change. In first-order change a system changes from state to state; in second-order change, the whole way the system behaves changes. Watzlawick et al. explained:

> To exemplify this distinction in more behavioral terms: a person having a nightmare can do many things *in* his dream—run, hide, fight, scream, jump off a cliff, etc.—but no change from any one of these

Immune Deficiency Syndrome) for the *New York Times,* interviewing individuals who have the disease. Schmalz himself had AIDS and could often cut through the deception with his own candor:

> "When I interviewed Hattoy in Los Angeles, he said to me that he really had come to deal with it very well," Mr. Schmalz recalled recently. "I said, 'Bullshit. I know what it's like. I know what it's like to wake up in the middle of the night and think you're dying, and I don't want to hear this, that it's not difficult for you. I don't believe it.' Then he broke down—he cried, and he said, 'I know I'm going to die of AIDS.' And then he looked at me and said, 'Aren't you?' And it was just such a dagger into my heart, you know, because, yeah, the answer is yes." (from *The New Yorker* magazine, October 5, 1992, p. 63)

There are aspects of communication—pace, rhythm, and timing of disclosures—that generally do not emerge in reading. However, these aspects can become salient when you really participate. The text can mimic a dance if writer and reader do their best to stay in step with each other, if you stay honest with yourself while reading. Otherwise, you and I could be colluding as well—both of us thinking that I know what I'm talking about. I may be gloating in my ability to use words and you are interpreting them in such a manner as to confirm your preexisting beliefs.

Intimacy is transformative because it requires a level of honesty such that individuals do not hide behind pretense, face-saving devices, or protection of each other's sense of self. It is possible to collude as long as there is no transformation. In fact, real change can threaten the pretense and cause relational (marital) systems to dissolve. "Changing is, indeed, a form of betrayal. It asserts one partner's essential *differentness* from the vision in the other

> behaviors to another would ever terminate the nightmare. *We shall henceforth refer to this kind of change as first-order.* The one way *out* of a dream involves a change from dreaming to waking. Waking, obviously, is no longer a part of the dream, but a change to an altogether different state. *This kind of change will from now on be referred to as second-order change.* (p. 11; original italics)

In one sense, intimacy is a "waking-up," a recurrent challenge to redefine our identity in the stories we create with others. This fits with Brown and Rogers' (1992) view of the "self" as a discursive process fashioned out of interaction with others: "Self-disclosure is not an *im*-mediate, mimetic *re*-presentation of some underlying entity (self/personality), but a mediated, presentational, discursive construction" (p. 156). Self-disclosure is itself transforming in a way that merely effective communication cannot be.

partner's head. This is why, in collusive marital systems, one spouse's effort to change will generally be blocked by the other or met with a rapid compensatory move directed toward restoring the system's customary equilibrium and balance" (Scarf, 1987, p. 334). This quote highlights the importance of understanding intimacy as a process, involving an openness to change that ongoing collusion cannot support.

We may often act "as if" we know what the other is about. For example, in conversation, we act as if we understand what has been said in hopes that subsequent information will help us to "fill in the blanks." Regarding intimacy—

Quality 10   VALIDATION: CREATING MEANING FOR THE OTHER

The possibility of intimacy through reading can be approached in three ways. The first, reviewed in Box 2.2 ("The Mimetics of Philemics" on pp. 66-70), explores ways in which the process of communicating in real time, face-to-face relationships is both similar and different from the processes of reading someone's prose. The second involves examining the way that text or narratives are imbued with a temporal dimension (Ricouer, 1984/1985), and then showing parallels with the temporal process of intimacy. The third requires examining how certain styles of writing are more involving or absorbing than others (Lanham, 1992). The second and third are explored here.

Time and Narrative. Ricouer's (1984, 1985) extensive and complex analysis of time and narrative, primarily applied to fiction and history, can be paralleled with a process view of intimacy (Reis & Shaver, 1988). He distinguished three types of mimesis between narration and time that can only be sketched here. Mimesis$_1$ refers to the narrators representing time—mostly implicitly—through the representation of action and suffering (emplotment), the symbols used, and the structuration of text. If I follow Ricouer accurately, this first step in narration involves somehow representing the timing or flow of events through a stylistic weaving of plot and action, giving special meaning to certain events and not others. Mimesis$_2$ refers to "the kingdom of the as if," to the fact that a story has "followability," that it can be lived by the reader. This second step involves some perspective taking; the narrator asks "to what degree can the reader follow along the various (and often implicit) time frames I am using?" Mimesis$_3$ "marks the intersection of the world of the text and the world of the hearer or reader." This third step is one of closure and reciprocity; readers bring their own schema and actually interface with the schema of the author. Readers complete the work through reading: "the act of reading is thus the operator that joins mimesis$_3$ to mimesis$_2$."

Ricouer discussed how mimesis helps readers feel a sense of order in an otherwise chaotic world, and how they can recover meaning and life through a work of art. There is a "relation of the time of narration to the time of life through narrated time":

> Here Goethe's meditation comes to the fore: life in itself does not represent a whole. Nature can produce living things but these are indifferent (*gleichgültig*). Art can produce only dead things, but they

knowing another—we may act "as if" we know because we sense there is still so much more to discover. Alternatively, we may act "as if" because we do not want to know, to "rock the boat" of our seemingly stable image of the other. This pretense of knowing seems to help when we do not fully understand or missed something about another, but it often means that we do not take the time to translate and transact. In a related way, we often collude when we read, reaching for the meanings of words, continually positing contexts that help that meaning. As Michael (1989) pointed out:

> Look closely at an idea, a sentence, the components of a description or a definition: Each gradually evaporates into metaphors and metametaphors.

> are meaningful. Yes, this is the horizon of thinking: drawing narrated time out of indifference by means of the narrative. (vol. 2, p. 80)

This discussion of narrative and time in literature parallels the process of validation in intimacy. For Reis and Shaver (1988), intimacy is a process of feeling validated and cared for; it involves fostering the other's self-insight and personal growth. This process is not unlike what happens at the interface of reader and author in Ricouer's mimesis$_3$: where meaning is created for the reader. Reis and Shaver outlined a recurrent, serial process where each partner (a) self-discloses, (b) filters the other's disclosure through an interpretive filter, and (c) responds; each partner's motives, fears, and goals influence their disclosures and interpretations. The validation of each other's self that emerges in this process can also be equated with the empathic identification with a character/narrator that may be the first stage in effective bibliotherapy (Shrodes & Russell, 1950; also see Box 2.2, point 4).

Revising Prose. In his book on revising prose, Lanham (1992) described how a certain form of writing, what he calls "The Official Style," contains a dominance of nouns and an atrophy of verbs and values "stasis over action." People do not write in plain English anymore. Writing has become impersonal, bureaucratic. Lanham presented a method for revising prose to make it more personal, more social, and more alive. Like the process of revision in writing, when I am intimate with another, I too, must become personal, revealing, active. My words are not intended just to represent my experience, but to somehow meet you in your experience, that is, to "occasion" with you. This requires revision. Lanham explained:

> Revision aims to "clear up" the *person*, to present a self more coherent, more in control. A mind thinking, not a mind asleep. It aims, that is, not to denature the human relationship that prose sets up but to enhance and to enrich it. It tries not to squeeze out the expression of personality but to make such expression possible, not to squeeze out *all record of a particular occasion and its human relationships* but to make them maximally clear. . . . Human beings, we need to remind ourselves here, are social beings. Our reality is a social reality. Our identity draws its felt life from our relation to other people. We become uneasy if, *for extended periods of time*, we neither hear nor see other people. We feel uneasy with The Official Style for the same reason. It has no human voice, no face, no personality behind it. (pp. 110–113, italics added)

> Words, whether about the self or the "real" world, are unavoidably murky, sloppy, and incomplete. Meanings branch interminably and disappear into the gloom. Nevertheless, we act—and I believe it is beneficial to so act *some* of the time—as if words really do describe, as if we know what we are talking about: Both presenter and recipient collude in this pretense. (p. 43)

Thus, collusion or acting "as if" we know may help some of the time. To be truly present, however, we must make the effort to participate beyond pre-existing scripts and schemas.

The Limits and Hope of Romance. We live in a culture that is fascinated with and literally consumed by one relational form: romance. We talk about celebrities' romances, we vicariously live romances through movies and soap operas, and we listen to popular musicians whose main theme is romantic. As a culture, we devote much time and finances on imagining and fantasizing about

---

Quality 11 INTIMACY AS REALISTIC (VS. ESCAPIST) ROMANTICISM

The Romantic plot-novel, argued Branden (1980), gave its characters more choice and free will than did pre-Romantic literature in which characters' fates were governed by "fortuitous external circumstances." Although romantic literature has been criticized for its escapism, the romantic theme—with its assumption that we can choose our future, that we have a "deep interior" or core self (cf. Gergen, 1992)—is woven into much of our culture. Branden revised this notion of romanticism by discussing a *realistic romanticism,* which means seeing one's partner as they are instead of as some fantasy of who we want them to be. Essentially, *realistic romanticism* involves mutual self-disclosure, communicating emotions, and intimacy.

Bergmann (1987) placed romanticism in the context of the history of love as it has been defined in literature, poetry, and psychoanalysis. He suggested that narcissistic love and romantic love have similar origins in medieval literature (cf. Kearney, 1988, p. 188). Both Branden's history of romantic love and Bergmann's literary analysis demonstrate how much romanticism is defined by self-absorption and projection of one's own image of the beloved. Kearney's historical analysis of imagination supported this view:

> The romantic imagination could not possibly deliver on its promises. . . . Indeed Wordsworth provides one of the exemplary metaphors for the romantic imagination in straits, when he writes of the poet withdrawing from the hostile world to the "watchtower" of his solitary spirit. Henceforth, it seemed, the creative imagination could only survive as a recluse. It could continue to form *images*; but it could no longer hope to transform *reality*. Romantic fiction could not be translated into fact. (p. 185)

It could be argued that romanticism is not merely about projection and imagination, that it contains the seeds for intimacy and relatedness in modern

the possibility of romance. It is important to see romanticism for what it is. Whereas intimacy emphasizes the present (knowing), romance often emphasizes the future (hoping).

These emphases suggest links between our views of time, relationship, and narrative. We tend to believe that solely romantic relationships "never last"; that true romance is fleeting. We view relationships as progressing into and out of a romantic phase. In fact, Western notions of romance, intertwined with the history of the novel and the "love story," conditions us to think of relationships as linear. For example, we think of relationships as progressing in stages (e.g., courtship – engagement – marriage), and as typically following certain gender stereotyped scripts (e.g., males are usually the initiators in a courtship). As is evident from an increase in both the divorce rate and in alternative forms of relationship (e.g., serial monogamy, cohabitation, and stepfamilies), this linear view jars with social reality. Our cultural heritage,

culture. Gergen suggested that modernism has eroded important aspects of relating that were born in the age of romanticism: sensitivity, sincerity, and intimacy. "Because of romanticism we can trust in moral values and an ultimate significance to the human venture. . . . If love as intimate communion, intrinsic worth, creative inspiration, moral values and passionate expression were all scratched from our vocabularies, life for many would be a pallid affair indeed" (Gergen, 1992, p. 27).

By definition, romanticism is about value and meaning; and through meaning it can lead us to encounter, to meeting, and to the ongoingness of intimacy. But the shift from romantic love to intimacy is a shift from transaction to transformation, from collaboration to creation. When confronted with the change and ongoingness of intimacy, romanticism reaches its limits. According to Brickman (1987):

> Love is in a sense seeing something as ideal that is not ideal. The primal dissonance that accompanies romantic passion is therefore the pursuit of an impossibility, the placing upon a partner of hopes and dreams and fantasies that cannot possibly be fulfilled. The partner that would be required to fulfill them would have to be ideal and unchanging, and real partners are not only not ideal, they do not like being idealized. Furthermore, they change, they grow old, and ultimately they die. The objects of love are not permanent, but romantic passion commits itself to permanence. (p. 80)

Through time, intimacy may involve an ongoing calibration of reality with imagination. We may learn to distill the virtues of romance (sensitivity, disclosure, inspiration, passion) from the self-absorbing images and ideals (e.g., of permanence) that interfere with honest perception and reality.

steeped in its emphasis on narrative linearity (and the romantic promise), has wedded us more to the clock than to each other, and has given us romantic ideals that have more to do with imagination than with intimacy. On one hand, it is important to recognize how romance can limit intimacy. On the other hand, the passion, fantasy, and magic of romance can sometimes stimulate intimacy (see Quality 11).

CONCLUSION

Time and human relationships define a dance, a changing puzzle pattern, a metamorphosis, a rhapsody, a flowering, a weave. In my own personal, close relationships, these changes are often hard, even impossible, to see. I think this inability to understand how time and relationship interlace is true for most couples. This inability becomes most poignant or has the most impact on our emotions when our relationships change, whether that change seems predictable or unpredictable. Whether or not we like it, it is in the nature of human relationships to change. Whether or not we intend to, these changes often depend on our own actions or lack of action. Whether we realize it or not, these changes are opportunities to experience the qualities of intimacy described in this chapter (e.g., taking time out).

A paradox here is central to the dance. How, on the one hand, can we relate to change without becoming over-controlling, trying to shape the outcome or soften the pain? On the other hand, how do we give up control without being overwhelmed by insecurity and anxiety in the face of flux? Partnerships that continue over any length of time find answers to this paradox. It may be an individual answer, such as becoming too urgent about time or, conversely, becoming a procrastinator. It might not be a healthy answer, as in the case of the couple who collude—who never argue, who hide feelings for fear of conflict and future change. Alternatively, the healthy dance that flows and invigorates, keeps us in the present—noticing and responding—even in the midst of change. It keeps us moving from transcription to transaction and so on. We are not too pressed for time, or putting things off. The text is not fixed, the dance is improvised, the seasons are filled with hints and surprises, the puzzle never gets finished, and the rhapsody continually shifts in meter and tone.

As we shall see, change is only one place where time and relationship intersect. Partners have biological rhythms (e.g., sleep, hormonal cycles) that may or may not overlap or that may affect daily, weekly, and monthly schedules. There are also rhythms and sequences in our communication. I sometimes interrupt my partner and she smiles and nods for me to go ahead or there may be a moment of silence at (what has become) a blunder. There are also phases where couples come together and go apart and phases where cohabitation, marriage, childbirth, or separations keep partners connected to wider spans of time. Still, these cycles and phases are not the whole picture or the whole dance.

The remainder of this book attempts to glimpse the whole picture. To do this, different metaphors (e.g., weaving, dance, story, kaleidoscope, flowering) are required at different times. The same is true with our different views of time: Sometimes time seems independent of us, sometimes we use it, sometimes it is in us, and sometimes it all depends on how we feel. This chapter uses this very text as a metaphor for change. Through my self-disclosure and your own process of reading, I have attempted to mimic the experience of getting acquainted. What do you think?

✍ Complete This Experiment on Self-Disclosure (Part 2) ✍

Note. You will get the most out of this if you have read through the entire chapter and if you have completed Part I of this experiment (on p. 36) before doing so.

Consider that you now know a little bit more about me than you did when you started reading this chapter. As in Part I of this experiment, look over the following list. Rank order the top three topics that you are willing to tell me about right now. That is, put a "1" next to the topic you might feel most willing to discuss, a "2" next to the topic you are a little bit less willing to discuss and so on. (After you do, which would you feel comfortable discussing with a stranger? Do these differ from those you would discuss with me? Would your choice be different before or after reading this chapter?) To rate your disclosure, see the endnotes of the chapter (p. 72).

1. _____ Hobbies that I have or would like to take up.
2. _____ How much I care about what others think of me.
3. _____ What it takes to hurt my feelings deeply.
4. _____ Things I had trouble with in school.
5. _____ What annoys me most about members of the opposite sex.
6. _____ How important money is to happiness.
7. _____ My feelings about a life hereafter.

BOX 2.2. THE MIMETICS OF PHILEMICS (TEXT MIMICS INTIMACY)

Some qualities highlighted in this chapter—a willingness to interrupt, a process of connecting, and a capacity to change—suggests a mutual, collaborative, real-time interface is necessary for intimacy. If this is so, then how could a relationship between author and reader ever be intimate? But there may be important similarities between the virtual relationship of reader and author and the real-time relationship of two actors. Clearly, you and I are not sharing living quarters, daily routines, or rituals (e.g., anniversaries) (Werner, Altman, & Brown, 1992), and in intimate communication, the differences between correspondence and actual dialogue likely outweigh the similarities. But I believe that we can use text to help understand how intimacy cannot occur between us, and to explore how it possibly could.

In this vein, it may help to highlight the difference between rhetoric, or the study of effective speech, and philemic, which is Davis' (1973) coinage for the study of behaviors through which two interacting individuals construct and communicate an intimate relation. We can examine discourse not just in terms of its effects, but specifically in terms of its potential to draw people together, to shape community, and to foster intimacy (cf. Hauerwas & Burrell, 1989; *affirmative rhetoric*, Fisher, 1992; *ethical-poetical imagination*, Kearney, 1988). This study of the parallel between (temporally fixed) text and (real-time) dialogue may be a discipline in its own right. We should study text for how it fosters intimacy, rather than how it incites a crowd, reasons with logic, or wins a legal argument. If we know how a "text suffers intimacy," we might learn how to correct for its shortcomings. I am suggesting that the science of personal relationships can help to construct a new philemic, a new meaning of the self as a story that is revised with others. This is the narrative self that Kearney (1988) wrote about:

> The ethical imagination bids man to tell and retell the story of himself. And it does so not to shore up the illusion of self-sufficiency, but of fidelity to the other. It is above all the *other* who demands that I remain responsible. . . . Such a model constitutes the self as the reader and the writer of his own life. But it also casts each one of us as a narrator who never ceases to revise, reinterpret and clarify his own story. . . . The notion of personal identity is thus opened up by the narrative imagination to include that of a *communal* identity. . . . In telling its story to the other the imaginative self comes to recognize more clearly its *unlimited* responsibility to others. This responsibility extends beyond my personal history (and also beyond the secluded intimacy of an I-Thou dialogue) to include a collective history. (pp. 395–396)

For Kearney, anyone who tells his story necessarily includes—or must take or embed oneself in—the perspective of the other. Text often serves as the medium through which this inclusion occurs. Is it possible, then, that text contains conditions for some form of intimacy between "storyteller as writer" and "community as reader"? Put another way, can I write with a certain fidelity to the reader so as to mimic some type of intimacy with him or her? I believe answers to this question are available through exploring what we know about intimacy in ongoing relationships. The following list of hypotheses serves two purposes (a) to suggest why it is difficult to mimic

Continued

BOX 2.2 Continued

intimacy in (fixed) text, and (b) to suggest how research could explore parallels for such a mimesis. For example, various researchers have examined how we construct mental representations while we read (cf. discourse processing; Oostendorp & Goldman, 1999). This includes such phenomena as interpretation of context, the creation of emotion and meaning, and temporal continuity-discontinuity. Much can be gained through an interdisciplinary venture that combines the efforts of these discourse analysts and scientists of intimacy. The following hypotheses are a place to begin.

(1) Ongoing revisions of meaning in reading and writing mimic how goals change in ongoing interaction. An author's and reader's goals are revised as they work on a text (e.g., Nystrand, 1982). Neither you or I may know my meaning until the paragraph is complete, just as the goals of talkers change throughout a conversation. However, revisions in the social meanings of speech utterances cannot be studied outside of the "ongoing context" of an interaction. Diez (1984) pointed out that "whatever is ultimately used to examine natural interaction . . . the notion of ongoingness of context and goal definition needs to be included . . . Goals change in an ongoing way throughout an interaction, sometimes in subtle ways, sometimes more drastically. These changes are communicated through individual utterances interpreted in the ongoing flow of discourse" (p. 73). Research on time in reading (e.g., Gross, 1992) or writing (e.g., Matsuhashi, 1982) could show parallels with the time to speak and to receive intimate disclosure.

(2) The timing devices of textual changes mimic the timing of actions. Ricouer (1985) claimed that only fiction (i.e., epics, novels) can explore the varieties of temporal experience that mimic the richness of life. He discussed the narrator's use of a "temporal armature" (the interplay between the time taken to narrate and narrated time; Müller, 1968); e.g., tempo, pauses, insertions, derivations, playing with tenses, and flashbacks. These devices convey a sense of time to the reader about the story but also about the narrator-hero's own time: Some writers effectively help us to anticipate, reminisce, and experience with them. Empathically, we move in time with the narrator just as we might were we to meet in person. Still, you and I are presently interacting in a time of words (*Textzeit*), rather than a time of actions (*Aktzeit;* Weinrich, 1964, in Ricouer, 1985). For us, intimacy can only be vicarious, virtual, or imagined, because we do not touch, sense, or act together. Moreover, the immediacy of strong emotions that intimates have for each other and that enrich their shared actions are impossible here.

(3) Cognitions that emerge from living in relationship mimic those that emerge from a vicarious relationship to the narrator. The reading-writing experience is primarily semantic or anchored in meanings, rather than episodic, or anchored in shared experience. These meanings afford powerful vicarious experiences of authors (cf. Ricouer, 1985, chap. 4), but we will never experience actions together with them. Because of this, the process of

Continue

BOX 2.2 Continued

knowing an author lacks cooperative factors that might otherwise emerge through action. For example, we do not know about the author's knowing of us (*social metacognition*; Hewes & Planalp, 1987; *metaperspective*; Laing, Phillipson, & Lee, 1966). We cannot negotiate what the relationship actually means to us (Acitelli & Duck, 1987), nor do we share a common memory of events witnessed together (Wegner, Giuliano, & Hertel, 1985). Still, our feelings of love may be strongly influenced more by semantics—the language we use and share—than by our experience (see Kövecses, 1991). Vicarious intimacy may impute a sense of sharing with an author. Some people read novels to give themselves a sense of intimacy that they do not have in their relationships. Text becomes more important than face-to-face interaction (see Laing, 1967, 1969). We may even change (revise) our memory of what has happened in our relationship depending on how we create a story about it.

In fact, research on relationships suggests that memory about the story of the relationship may be more "constructed" than real. For example, Orbuch, Veroff, and Holmberg (1991) compared thematic changes that occurred in stories retold by couples in their third year of marriage: "There are clear tendencies for couples to see their courtship as being mutually initiated or initiated by the man in the third year of their marriage more often than they did in their first year. These shifts are interpreted as reflecting a memory change that helps couples see their marriage as fitting normative expectations" (Veroff, Sutherland, Chadiha, & Ortega, 1993, p. 452).

(4) The philemic acts of writer's self-disclosure and reader's feeling understood mimic intimate interactions. Autobiographers make risky decisions about when and how to disclose personal information that may parallel intimates' decisions about self-disclosure (cf. Fisher, 1978). However, an author's disclosure—in bibliotherapy or self-help books as well as autobiography—can have a profound effect on readers, who feel understood and claim: "This person was writing about my life" (see Cornett & Cornett, 1980; Hynes & Wedl, 1990). This happened recently to some who read *The Christmas Box* (Evans, 1995), a story about a woman who visits a stone angel monument to mourn the loss of her child. Readers—many grieving parents with similar experiences—contacted the author. In response he commissioned a new stone angel sculpture, which has become a place of healing for many (Dimmitt, 2000).

Reading is prescribed as therapy precisely because it can spark inner intimacy. Shrodes and Russell (1950) claimed that for bibliotherapy to be effective the reader must experience a three stage process when reading: (a) empathic identification with the character or narrator, (b) a safe catharsis of emotions where the reader has the illusion of both standing apart and of being involved, as both spectator and participant, and (c) an insight or integration of mind and emotions. Thus, bibliotherapy shares a central component of intimate relations: empathic identification or the feeling of being understood (Cahn, 1990).

Continued

BOX 2.2 Continued

Whereas some argue that the claims of self-help books are exaggerated (Rosen, 1987), many family therapists in one study indicated their clients found reading assignments very helpful (Giblin, 1989). Most importantly, some of the most frequently cited works were on divorce and love.

(5) Textual correspondence (love letters, computer dialogue) mimics intimate conversation. Two individuals who send messages back and forth to each other reveal much about time and intimacy. For example, the love letters of Robert Browning and Elizabeth Barrett (Kintner, 1969) contain numerous references to time (e.g., scheduling rendezvous, remembering) and intimate revelations (see epigram to this chapter). These letters are unique for their writer's poetic ability. However, written transactions are unlike ongoing conversations in that the latter are filled with ongoing subtle nonverbal cues such as those involved in lying (e.g., Knapp, Cody, & Reardon, 1987) as well as in intimacy (e.g., Foot, Smith, & Chapman, 1979; Patterson, 1976). These simply do not occur in written language. Nonverbal computer displays might not substitute social presence, but innovative graphics of facial expression through computer conferencing make this an interesting parallel to explore (Acker, 1989).

(6) The balance of predictability and uncertainty in effective speech writing parallels the same balance in relationships. As a writer, I need to anticipate your misunderstandings without becoming too predictable, pedantic, and boring. The following concerns the psychology of composition but it could also reflect on relationships as well: "A highly predictable text is efficient for processing but not effective, because it stimulates little interest. Conversely, a highly unpredictable text may impose unreasonable processing demands and thereby engender confusion or resentment. Text producers must find a workable balance for each situation and audience" (de Beaugrande, 1982, p. 239).

Compare this with the following discussion on uncertainty and intimacy. The real-time continual negotiation of relationship is intersubjective, whereas the writer's and reader's negotiations of meaning is individual and independently subjective:

> Certainty/comfort facilitates continued social interaction, uncertainty/discomfort threatens its survival. We argue that neither state in isolation facilitates social interaction. Without "uncertainty" many of the vitalizing forces in relationships—surprise, novelty, excitement, change—are crippled. By the same token, without a certain degree of predictability (however short-lived), relationships become unduly effortful. The question is again one of *continually negotiated balance.* (Brown & Rogers, 1991, p. 162)

These six sketches of mimesis are purely hypothetical. The ongoingness of context, the presence of nonverbal behaviors, the unpredictability of self-disclosures, the shared past of intimates, all may far exceed even the lover's

Continued

BOX 2.2 Continued

ability to articulate intimacy in writing. Barthes (1984) offered: "To try to write love is to confront the *muck* of language; that region of hysteria where language is both *too much* and *too little*, excessive (by the limitless expansion of the *ego*, by emotive submersion) and impoverished (by the codes on which love diminishes and levels it)" (p. 99). In spite of such limits, I am suggesting there may be ways to construct a philemic—a form of narrative that fosters intimacy and community—by examining (a) the real-time processes of intimate relationships, and (b) the ways in which prose fosters a sense of connection to the author, a sense of "aliveness" (Lanham, 1992).

The study of philemics would also include investigation of what Buck (1989) describes as the "rhetoric of love":

Thus, although the biological foundations of love are common to all human beings, each culture and society may develop definitions of what love is and rules about the circumstance under which love occurs and is expressed. This understanding is often communicated to the member of a culture in songs and stories that instruct them when to love and whom to love and not to love. This is the rhetoric of love, which reflects linguistic cultural definition. (p. 152)

Thus, through story, language and text play an important role in teaching us about intimacy. However, this chapter argues that language and text also have limits on what can be taught. Whereas Buck suggested that cultural text shapes our experience of love, the quote from Barthes suggests that love can never be reliably captured by text. The purpose of philemics is to explore intimacy through text (and story) but also beyond it.

End Notes—Chapter 2

1. The collaborative construction of emotion. Staske (1999) included transcripts of eight interactions between partners about jealousy that provided concrete examples of the transactive and transformational model described here. For example, one couple talks about jealousy in the past and how—in their telling about it—the emotion served to shape (transform) the current relationship. Staske wrote: "These interactant's co-construction of relational jealousy serves in the fashioning of their previous *and* current relational identities. This young woman was once the target of her boyfriend's jealousy, which negatively affected each of them and their relationship . . . however, as a result of both thought and prayer, both he and the relationship have changed for the better" (p. 217). In another transcript, the partners share different views about the amount and quality of time spent together. The female finds herself pursuing more time with her boyfriend, while he juggles other commitments in efforts to make time with her. As the conversation continues, with much interruption and competitive overlaps, it is clear that the couple is working on their shared identity (i.e., moving through transcription to transformation).

2. Viewing one's relationship as a book. In fact, Baxter's (1990) study of relationship development asks participants to view their relationship like a book: "Participants were asked to imagine that their relationship was a book and that they were constructing a 'table of contents' of the book's chapters; a chapter was defined as 'a stage or period in the relationship's history different from other stages or period.' Participants were asked to create a title for each chapter which captured the essence of the relationship during that chapter. Participants were told that they could have as many chapters as they found necessary in describing the 'book' of their relationship" (p. 75).

3. Alternatives to the metaphor of relationship as text. Gergen (1988) critiqued hermeneutic emphasis on the text as a metaphor for human relationship: "the ghost in the text." Brown and Rogers (1991), critiquing a reductionist, linear epistemology, also offered the metaphor of the dance: "When relationships are codefined, ecological structurings, emphasis is placed on the interactive cycles produced and reproduced as relational members move toward, around, against, and away from one another via their distance regulating, communicative behaviors" (p. 163). They also used the metaphor of a jigsaw puzzle that is constantly changing shape as each partner fits in a piece of their own experience. Lerner (1989) implied this metaphor to capture the distancing and pursuit cycles individuals learn from their families. Gergen also mentioned the metaphor of the game. Whereas some relationships may follow game-like patterns, intimacy requires game-free interaction. Oden (1974) explained how intimacy transcends games in relationships.

Finally, Baxter (1992) found that young couples in developing romantic relationships employ different metaphors when asked to describe their relationship as a book with different chapters representing different periods in the courtship. In order of frequency, the root metaphors alluded to were: relationship development as work (e.g., "work through problems," "pass the test": 60% of respondents), a journey of discovery (e.g., "keep finding the new," "going in circles": 57%), an uncontrollable force (e.g., "it engulfed us": 54%), danger (34%), economic exchange (30%), a living organism (30%), and as a game (27%).

4. Self-help books and the honest limitations of words. The Prather's (1988) book is a guide for couples who want to do the hard work of living in the present by not projecting their past images onto their partner. Other contemporary self-help texts follow the same tack (e.g., Hendricks & Hendricks, 1990; Hendrix, 1992; Welwood, 1990). I. Sarnoff and S. Sarnoff (1989, p. 92) developed the idea of complicities or interpersonal defenses—by mutual deception—through which partners cooperate in keeping common fears (about boundaries, love-making, increasing interdependence) from overwhelming them. Their work is important because they show how participation can go awry and keep partners from being present to each other and to the process of their relating. In and of itself, participation does not guarantee intimacy; another crucial ingredient is honesty.

To be effective, self-help books all require a modicum of honesty from the reader. Writers of such books make the implicit assumption that a reader's honesty about whether a book applies to his or her life can help the reader to be honest within their relationship. Of course, readers could collude with authors as well and undermine the intent of the text. This might happen for lonely hearts or those recovering from divorce who experience some vicarious intimacy with the author and use the text to self-justify their own ego or intimacy schema.

✍ HOW TO RATE AND USE THIS EXPERIMENT ON SELF-DISCLOSURE ✍

Psychologists have developed questionnaires that tap individual differences in the tendency to self-disclose at different levels of depth and across a variety of topics (Taylor & Altman, 1966). When just getting acquainted, some individuals may share on fewer topics but very deeply, whereas others may disclose their views and feelings about a broad array of topics but avoid deeper issues. Taylor and Altman asked subjects to rate 671 items on an 11-point scale regarding the degree of intimacy or personal character of the information in each statement. Judges also categorized topics into different areas (e.g., religion, marriage and family, interests, hobbies, habits). The raters were sailors and male college freshman and the ratings were completed in the mid-1960s. Thus, the ratings may or may not apply to individuals today. I chose topics for the two parts of the experiment that were roughly equivalent in intimacy value. (Both lists have equivalent items and they both total to 53.)

The following list gives estimates of the intimacy value (higher scores indicate greater intimacy) in front of each of the statements used in Part I and II of the experiment in this chapter. Compare your ratings from Part I and Part II. Was your top choice lower or higher? Also, add the values of the two topics you chose in Part I. Next, add the value of the two topics you chose in Part II. Did your overall choice of topics become more or less intimate over time?

This experiment may be used to illustrate some of the ideas presented in the chapter. For example, can there be intimacy between an author and a reader? How does this happen? How and why does virtual intimacy change over time? Do the ratings made in 1965 have any meaning today? Is it valid to assign a universal value to a topic?

PART I—SCORING	PART II—SCORING
1. (5.5) How I feel about mercy killings.	1. (2.0) Hobbies that I have/or would like to take up.
2. (8.0) Times I have felt lonely.	2. (8.5) How much I care about what others think of me.
3. (9.0) Lies that I have told my parents.	3. (9.0) What it takes to hurt my feelings deeply.
4. (4.5) My feelings about whether there is a conflict between religious and scientific beliefs.	4. (5.5) Things I had trouble with in school.
5. (6.0) Whom I most admire.	5. (5.0) What annoys me most about members of the opposite sex.
6. (7.0) How I really feel about the people I work for or work with.	6. (6.0) How important money is to happiness.
7. (2.5) As a child, what I wanted to be when I grew up.	7. (6.5) My feelings about a life hereafter.

When we love and value another human being, when we look calmly and attentively at each other, we know, we see that there is something in a man or woman that is not of time. We know it!

—Jacob Needleman (professor of philosopher, author of *Time and the Soul*)

If... we honored the tendency of the soul to move in mysterious ways, we might see that the unpredicted developments that come from the soul can have a positive effect on a relationship.

—Thomas Moore (theologian and former Catholic monk, author of *Soul Mates*)

THOUGHTS ON A NEW SCIENCE

- That we recognize and give equal value to the inner and outer forms of seeing and meeting.

- We provide education and nourishment for each of these forms: solitude, togetherness with one other, community, and spiritual meeting.

- That science helps us to see the value in each, and the best methods for obtaining such value.

3

Unfolding in Time:
Intimacy Across Situations

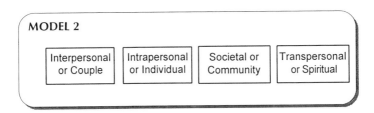

MODEL 2

| Interpersonal or Couple | Intrapersonal or Individual | Societal or Community | Transpersonal or Spiritual |

Do fish complain of the sea for being wet? Or if they did, would that fact itself not strongly suggest that they had not always been, or would not always be, purely aquatic creatures? Then, if we complain of time and take such joy in the seemingly timeless moment, what does that suggest?

It suggests that we have not always been or will not always be purely temporal creatures. It suggests that we were created for eternity.

—from *The Severe Mercy* by Sheldon Vanauken, describing his correspondence with C. S. Lewis (Vanauken, 1980, p. 203)

THIS CHAPTER explores different types of intimacy and argues that—because intimate experience and meaning can manifest in different situations—it is much more prevalent or accessible than we typically think. I aim to speak more directly about the ways in which we experience intimacy in all its possible, especially poetic and spiritual, dimensions. To this end, I borrow readings and mix quotes from different spiritual and mystical traditions as well as from modern psychology. My selections are not meant to convey that one spiritual orientation is better than another. I hope you will add meanings (and references) from your own spiritual orientation that relate to the ideas conveyed.

Intimacy has many interfaces, many "being withs." We experience an ongoing sense of participating or sharing with: of having deeply met, of knowing and connecting, and of allowing and embracing. This sense does not arise in a vacuum, but rather in an encounter, a time of meeting, of being present. We think intimacy occurs mostly with a special person, a life partner, and perhaps with a few other close friends and confidants (Situation 1). But sometimes the sense appears in solitude with ourselves—when contemplating life's mystery or the wonders of this earth (Situation 2). For many, intimacy also occurs in contact with a spiritual source that many choose to call God (Situation

3). And some only experience intimacy in the context of their group, community, or church (Situation 4).

Intimacy is mostly familiar as we experience life with others and, together in time, share life's ups and downs: its confidences and silences, the tragedies and triumphs, plans, mishaps, and memories. Both vivid and memorable is the singular divulgence of a friend's lifelong secret or the extended and deep conversation we have with the stranger just met on a long distance trip. But more often, and with greater nuance and subtlety, we glimpse intimacy within the mundane routines and schedules of our daily, weekly, and ordinary lives. Such intimacy unfolds in time through a process that we participate in shaping and allow ourselves to be shaped by.

But intimacy is not limited to the meetings we have with others. It includes more than the idle conversation that evolves into a forum for two searchers, more than nights of passion, and more than the many types of social situations (with a therapist or pastor, in an emergency room, or at a funeral) in which we typically reveal ourselves, our beliefs, our feelings. In fact, intimacy may not depend on revelation to others (on "self-disclosure") at all, but on just being with others in the ordinary moment. Moreover, we each harbor an inner world, separate from, although influenced by others; a world that summons our attention every day through dreams, strong emotions, memories both painful and joyous, and future hopes and fears. This private, or *intrapersonal*, world is also a place of encounter, of being with, and of knowing. We can feel estranged from ourselves just as much as we can feel distant from others. Alternatively, we can feel a sense of knowing ourselves—knowing what is right for us, likes and dislikes—just as we sense intimacy with others. Thus, intimacy unfolds in both the intrapersonal world (when we gain insight with ourselves) and the *interpersonal* world (when we are revealing with others).

RESEARCH **REFLECTION** 4

TIME AND SELF-CONCEPT: INTIMACY WITH ONESELF AS REFLECTED IN SOME PSYCHOLOGICAL MEASURES

Psychologists have developed questionnaires that tap personality differences in self-alienation, depression, or self-estrangement. Consider how these examples relate to time and how self-concept is tied into time.

1. Time sometimes drags on by without meaning for me.
2. I do not feel like I am getting ahead in life.
3. I am often bored with others and myself.
4. I often don't look forward to the day.

Familiar examples highlight these inner and outer aspects of intimacy. Friendship, romantic love, counseling, or psychotherapy characterize the interpersonal realm, whereas intrapersonal discoveries occur through daily self-reflection, dreaming, meditation, recollection, and through the inspiration to just know more about life. These aspects are woven together; others listen, care, and so help us to love and know ourselves. At the same time, our inner gleanings shape how we share with these listeners. This weaving of inner and outer intimacy is thus a co-creation. It takes one to know and to be vulnerable, but it takes two to listen and share.

The previous examples reveal two basic truths: Intimacy takes time and life changes. As much as a lover's passion may evoke him or her to reveal, as much as a therapist's urgings may coax or warrant, we cannot reveal all of ourselves in one day or one setting. Moreover, experience, the aging process, and capricious laws of chance team up to make each day of our lives different—if only slightly—from the previous ones. Characterized by events beyond our control, by the interplay of inward knowing and outward loving, as well as the unexpected turns of life, intimacy is essentially an ongoing process.

THE JOURNEY TO THE PRESENT

To be enlightened is to be intimate with all things

— *Zen master,* Dogen

Research demonstrates that humans need to feel that they belong and are loved in order to mature and sometimes even survive through infancy (Bowlby, 1969; Werner & Smith, 1982). Other studies indicate that into adulthood, this need for others or for intimacy varies between individuals and from time to time in a single life, as well as to different degrees across the lifespan for all of us (Ainsworth, Blehar, Waters, & Wall, 1978; Hazan & Shaver, 1987). And ultimately, we come face to face with our biology, if not through the chances of illness and disease then through the certitude of death and our mortality. Our need for intimacy may wax and wane throughout life's series of encounters, but it is in that last encounter that many examine how much they have deeply met, known, and loved themselves and others. The balance between separating from and joining with others—in infancy and in death—may be described as perhaps the core task of life and spiritual growth (cf. Mahler, 1968; May, 1969).

It sometimes happens—especially for those who never question life and never search beyond the moment to understand their purpose here—that the deathbed offers the first place of intimate encounter. Stuck between recalling one's past and having to face one's "maker," the dying may go through a process of resolution. Such individuals arrive in the moment where they can *be present with*. They forgive themselves and others, expressing gratitude for the gifts life bestowed, and come to a sense of balance (i.e., of equanimity, weighing life's gains and losses, pains and pleasures). Having spent their time avoiding pain, worrying, chasing after pleasures, or compulsively saving for their retirement, they may feel they have not trusted enough to allow and embrace the full flow of life.

It more often happens that the challenges, troubles, and dissatisfactions of ordinary living cause encounters long before the final hours. Such challenges come in both the interpersonal and intrapersonal realms. A failed relationship, divorce, deep conflict, a problem in one's family, or more generally, not getting what one had hoped and prayed for, all easily disrupt the flow of living. When they do, they may renew the need for the connection and acceptance that interpersonal intimacy provides. And faced with more personal or private difficulty—addiction, indecisiveness about career or marriage, failures, sudden losses, accidents, or psychological problems—we may cry out for that sense of private knowing and security within intrapersonal intimacy.

Our limitations and weaknesses, the reality of our own and other's humanness, may also cause us to look for intimacy in the uncommon (i.e., the road less traveled). What we originally—and perhaps unconsciously—believed would meet our intimacy needs (e.g., the perfect Other or relationship) usually comes up short or deficient. Paradoxically, if we make the commitment to search for a deeper connection and do not run away, then we may find that the troubles or deficiencies that motivated the search actually become our teachers. This deep intimacy, where we appreciate limitation and accept life's imperfections, helps broaden the landscape for encounter. We might stumble into intimacy in those places we never expected to find it.

This relaxing of expectations, journeying into the unknown, represents the basic willingness to be present with whatever arises in the field of experience, however difficult the feeling or emotion. Intimacy goes beyond presence with others or with oneself to a presence with the flow of events in the broader context of living. When we tap into being present for the sake of and in the service of life, we can transcend, support, and bridge the intrapersonal and interpersonal aspects of intimacy. This type of encounter is often difficult to put in words. When people experience it in a sexual encounter, they may say; "You had to be there at the time!" (Schnarch, 1991). The experience has exclusivity, something special about it can only be experienced through direct sharing. And yet, the experience is not limited to the sexual encounter. Paradoxically, there is an inclusiveness to the exclusivity of the experience:

> When we become intimate with all things, we discover rest, well-being, and wholeness in this very body. We recognize that we, and all life around us, are supposed to be here, that we belong here as much as the trees and the sun and the turning earth. There comes a healing, an opening, and a grace. The harmony of all things arises for us like the wisdom of Dame Julian of Norwich, who so beautifully declared, "All shall be well and all manner of

things shall be well." In intimacy we discover a profound sense of belonging and wholeness that allows us to touch all that we encounter. (Kornfield, 1993, p. 336)

To be sure, *transpersonal* intimacy has been discussed mostly within spiritual and religious teachings and texts (e.g., Almaas, 1987; Kornfeld, 1993; Tart, 1983; Wilber, 1979). However, there has been some research on religious beliefs and loneliness. For example, one study found evidence for less loneliness among individuals (females) who reported a stronger relationship with God (Kirpatrick, Shillito, & Kellas, 1999). The transpersonal encounter can be with a lover and with oneself, but usually we identify the transpersonal in encounters with God, beauty, nature, spiritual forces, the universe, or with love itself. Many religions are based on an understanding and respect for transpersonal relationship. Christians seek to emulate Christ in their relationship to God, and so practice love. In Taoism (pronounced dou′iz'm), one seeks to live in accord with the flow of the universe, and so act in harmony and with virtue in interpersonal affairs. Jewish men and women "keep the commandments" as part of their covenant with Jehovah, and so respect others. In the Islamic faith, especially among the Gnostic or mystical Sufis, the divine is viewed as the Beloved—God is Lover—and our loved ones are but manifestations of this divinity.

The eloquence of Jelaluddin Rumi (Persian mystic and poet, 1207-1273), describes this transpersonal intimacy in the poem *Those You Are With,*

> *What is a real connection between people? When the same knowledge*
> *opens a door between them. When the same inner sight exists*
> *in you as in another, you are drawn to be companions . . .*
>
> *Always search for your innermost nature in those you are with.*
> *As rose-oil imbibes from roses.*
> *Even on the grave of a holy man, a holy man lays his face*
> *and hands and takes in light.*

Such intimacy may emerge suddenly and spontaneously as "peak experiences" within a single situation or they may be "plateaus," taking time to develop and to sustain across a variety of situations with others and when alone (Maslow, 1976).

Whether intimacy is private, shared, or transcendent, it always brings one to a deeper time than the busy work schedule or a daily routine can grant. Such routines or social habits are essential for maintaining relationships (Young, 1988). Yet true intimacy can break through or transcend these habits of scheduling. As Young put it, "The most signal characteristic of family, and of friendship which goes beyond exchange of convenience, is that the time which it makes available is in principle unlimited, provided according to need and not according to the expectation of a like return" (p. 245).

Too much controlling and measuring of time in relationships prevents intimacy from arising or deepening. Spontaneity, serendipity, and synchronicity—meaningful coincidence—each characterize the deeper time of intimacy. Of course, setting aside specific times for lovemaking or for meditation or prayer, surely fosters intimacy but such time slots do not guarantee depth. Still, we glimpse something of the eternal within these scheduled resorts. The sense of flow, of timelessness—of not even realizing that time is passing—may transport deeply attuned lovers as well as those in deep meditation.

And so intimacy has many interfaces: in the ordinary conversation of our friendships as well as the transforming dance of sexuality, in the pause for self-reflection and the time given by listening to others, and through facing life's interruptions and challenges as well as appreciating the gifts in each day's uniqueness. Intimacy awakens our sense of being connected, of witnessing and participating in the unfolding. When we learn to be present with, to free ourselves from having to plan everything, to relax our expectations, we may find that—whether we are alone or with others—time "takes care" of itself, of us, and of everything else.

"IN TIME I SEE"—IN · TIM · A · CY

Consciousness of the now is essential to the intimate experience; intimacy is timeless.

—T. P. Malone & P. T. Malone

Two themes help simplify and summarize the previous discussion. First, intimacy can be solitary. Second, real intimacy emerges over time. Intimacy is not merely a sense experience or a state of consciousness only available when with another, as might be suggested by the more common usage of the expression "sexual intimacy." It also may be described by the terms "personal intimacy" or "spiritual intimacy." Moreover, time, change, and the deeper and varied rhythms of life are all reflected in the process of intimacy; it has continuity, an ongoing quality that resides outside but infuses the many separate, single encounters we have. We can become intimate with life itself.

To further elucidate these two central themes, I have played on the word "intimacy" to come up with four different enunciations, that is, different ways of saying in · ti · ma · cy that convey different meanings: Into me; see?, In time I see, In time mates see, Into my sea. These enunciations are called autonyms, because their definition can be found within the parsing and phrasing of the word itself; they are self-defining. The four different meanings of intimacy overlap, each one as important as the next. I think of them as a four-part harmony with distinctive sequences of notes that cyclically weave together and separate out over time. As you read through these, you may identify with one more than another; but I believe they all make up—to varying degrees—most experiences of intimacy. Thus, these autonyms do not represent different types but rather different tones or contours of the intimate process.

Figure 3.1 describes different features of these meanings of intimate process. The five different levels of intimate experience described in the previous chapter (i.e., transcription, translation, etc.) are also shown. The figure conveys the idea that whether by ourselves, with one other, in community, or on the journey of faith, we may experience the different levels of textual transcendence and the qualities of intimacy described earlier. Also, in order to convey the ways in which individuals vary in their tendencies to experience these meanings, I have constructed the following self-assessment tool.

✍ SELF-ASSESSMENT OF FAVORED TYPE OF INTIMACY ✍

For each of the following six pairs of statements circle the one statement with which you are typically or most likely to agree. For example, in the first pair, circle I or F. In the second pair, circle C or R. When you finish, use the scoring below to help assess your preference for type of intimacy. (*Note.* This experiment can only suggest—not determine—preferences.)

1. **I** I enjoy times when I can be alone with nature.

   F I enjoy having a meaningful relationship with God or a spiritual source.

2. **C** I like being part of a close-knit group or community.

   R I like being close with one special person.

3. **F** God cares about me and is concerned about problems I may have.

   R There is a special someone (a spouse or boyfriend/girlfriend) who cares about me and is concerned about problems I may have.

4. **I** I like taking walks or exploring places on my own.

   R I like taking walks or exploring places with a special person.

5. **C** I look forward to relaxing with friends and family on weekends and holidays.

   I I look forward to having more private time on weekends and holidays.

6. **F** I get much from prayer and meditation in solitude.

   C I get much from prayer and meditation within a group (such as church).

To score, count the number of statements preferred in each category:

I = Individual   **F** = Faith   **C** = Community   **R** = Relationship

There are three statements in each category so the highest score you could get is "3." This little scale gives a snapshot of your preference for one type of intimacy over another. A "3" score may indicate a preference for one over another.

Situation of Intimacy

Situation of Intimacy	Autonym	Movement	Qualities	Time	Disharmony
Individuation	into me, see?	self to other to self	boundaries, reaching out	personal story	narcissism, loneliness
Faith	in time I see	self to transcendent	waiting, meet, live, witness	deep touching, eternal sense	noncommital, emptiness
Co-journeying	in time mates see	interpersonal to transcendent	mutual respect	move through time together	codependence, unhealthy symbiosis
Community	into my sea	transcendent to self & others	network of intimates	social cycles	busyness, media dependent

Different levels of textual transcendence (see chap. 2) may be experienced in each of the different situations of intimacy.

FIG. 3.1 Four situations or types of intimacy.

"Into me; see?"—Individuation/Differentiation

It seems likely that the more relational intimacy, individuation, separateness, and privacy promote each other, the more rewarding, harmonious, and enduring an intimate relationship is likely to be. (Prager, 1995, p. 276)

"Into me; see?" reflects a movement from intrapersonal to interpersonal intimacy and back again. One establishes an identity, a boundary for the self—a place where one can retreat, self-reflect, pause, relax, and settle into the sanctuary of one's rhythms and privacy. We say "into me," but it is not a possessed or narcissistic self-absorption in which we withdraw, cut others off, or exploit them. It is not, as described in the previous chapter, mere transcription. The self-reflective "me" communicates that we want to be receptive—to perhaps relax our expectations—in our privacy or distance for now, but we follow "into me" with the invitation of "see?" We are saying "I still want the connection and continuity of relating, but I also need time to just be with or know myself; can you understand that? Can you see into me, too?" Thus, there is openness to the transaction.

This part of the harmony, this looking-in-reaching-out, is often viewed as the key to psychological well-being or self-esteem, as these are discussed in self-help literature or in texts on counseling, psychotherapy, and codependence (cf. "individuation," Jung, 1963; "self-differentiation," Kerr & Bowen, 1988). By saying "into me," we acknowledge our own needs, create boundaries, and embrace the possibility that we can be our own best friend and that we can tolerate aloneness. We can engage in a self-soothing in the face of our partner's anxieties, rejections, uncertainties. By asking "see?" we show a simultaneous willingness to reach out and be vulnerable to the other's response. Their answer may or may not affirm us, but in engaging the whole process of setting boundaries—self-reflecting and outward giving—we experience a readiness to be open. This is individuation or self-differentiation (i.e., a sense of individuality, of wholeness) that balances our separateness with our connection. We stand up for ourselves and we reach out to others. Hillel, the great Jewish sage and scholar (30 B.C.–A.D. 10) implored us to this pulsing in and pulsing out, this inward-outward dance:

> If I am not for myself, who is for me?
> And if I am only for myself, what am I?
> And if not now, when?

It is important to point out that this inward-outward dance or this emphasis on relationship between self and other is found more in Western than Eastern thought. Campbell (1972), in discussing spirituality from the Eastern and Western views, claimed that the Western view places more emphasis on the interpersonal relationship with God, which contrasts with an intrapersonal

RESEARCH   **REFLECTION**   5

THE CAPACITY FOR INTIMACY: BEING IN THE MOMENT

Psychologists (e.g., Shostrom, 1966) have developed questionnaires to try and tap individual capacity for intimacy. The following items represent one such measure that purports to assess individual capacity to develop meaningful relationships, unencumbered by expectations and obligations.

1. I feel free to not do what others expect of me.
2. I like to participate actively in intense discussions.
3. When I really love myself, there will still be those who will not love me.

---

experience of pervasive connectedness and no self-other distinction. The intrapersonal form of intimacy is the ultimate ground of all spiritual or transpersonal experience. Campbell explained, "The ultimate divine mystery is there found immanent within each. It is not 'out there' somewhere. It is within you. And no one has ever been cut off. The only difficulty is, however, that some folk simply don't know how to look within. The fault is no one's, if not one's own. Nor is the problem one of the original Fall of the 'first man,' thousands of years ago, and of exile and atonement. The problem is psychological. And it can be solved" (p. 93).

Thus, the way to enlightenment is wholly within each individual being. In this way, the intrapersonal experience of intimacy is deeply connected with the next part of the melody.

"IN TIME I SEE"—SELF-REMEMBERING, PRESENCE, AND FAITH

My times are in your hands.
— Psalm 31

God can be viewed as another member of a social network who, like other network members, can at times offer help in the coping process. (Pargament et al., 1990, p. 815)

The intimacy reflected in "In time I see" reflects a movement from the self-reflective "me" to the more active "I" (Malone & Malone, 1987). We enter into, embrace, and journey with continuity, change, and varied processes of time. Here, we move from fear, to patience, to faith. We remember that we may be more than any particular "self" or ego-state we happen to be identifying with or defending at any particular moment (Tart, 1987; on Gurdjieff's "self-remembering"). We enter life. We open to the transpersonal intimacy that, over time, infuses our inner reflections and outer connections. Willing to wait for life's answers, we confide or trust in a power or source higher than ourselves. Intimacy embraces this waiting in all its forms (inter-, intra-, and transpersonal), but it is here that waiting is the most powerful. For many, this form of intimacy manifests as a relationship with God.

"Should I marry or should I stay single?" "Will I be happier if I divorce?" Answers to these questions are not entirely available through logic and reason; some part of us recognizes that the answers come from discovery, by living life as fully as we can. In terms of the previous chapter, we immerse ourselves in the transaction without knowing what the outcome will be. Only "in time"—in the moment that spans every opportunity for presence—do the answers come. So this is not a passive "wait-and-see" or "whatever" attitude, but rather an active effort—a decision to concentrate, to be mindful, to "see." Julia Child, the famous gourmet chef, once said, "Life itself is the proper binge."

Time is not simply linear when we let go and live fully; people do not progress from one situation of intimacy to another in some metered series. Coincidence, synchronicity, happenstance, friendships that require the time of nourishment, plateaus and peaks, contractions and expansions, missed opportunities, delays, interruptions, postponements, and being both in and out of synch with one's partner or one's self—all of these become the rich details of a life full of meaning, wholeness and even transcendence. Life becomes the classroom with intimacy—connection, love, knowledge—being the essential curriculum, and time itself is the teacher.

This is the transcendent aspect of "In time I see"; fully living and appreciating life requires a certain—if not complete—degree of letting go, and of listening or tuning in to a deeper rhythm. An appreciation for the passing of time and life's challenges provides a sense of the bigger picture (eternity), and allows us to let go and enjoy.

Time never challenged the Indian or worked against him. Time was for silently marking the passing of the seasons. It was a thing to be enjoyed.

—Tim Giago (on the Native American view of time)

The transpersonal intimacy of an individual's relationship with God is the subject of both personal relationship research and religious studies. In research, Kirkpatrick and Shaver (1992) developed a measure that conceives of one's relationship to God as similar to an attachment to other people.

RESEARCH	REFLECTION	6

MEASURING PERSONAL RELATIONSHIP WITH GOD (FROM KIRKPATRICK & SHAVER, 1992)

1) Would you say you have a personal relationship with God? (yes, no)
2) If yes, which of the following best describes your relationship?

    A)   God is warm, responsive, and supportive.
    A)   God is impersonal, distant, and disinterested.
    B)   God is inconsistent in providing support and response to me.

In Christian religion, this attachment is probably best conveyed in the book of Psalms from the Old Testament. Heald (1987) has designed a devotional study guide to the Psalms entitled *Intimacy with God* that outlines four parts or stages in the journey. First, we long for intimacy with God and come to recognize God's longing for intimacy with us (i.e., "You know me in all things," Psalm 139). Then, we come to know the characteristics of the true friend we have in God: His being righteous, trustworthy, a refuge, and responsive. As we trust that God is a willing confidant, we realize that a worthy response is required. This is a response of reverence, truthfulness, and love for God's word. For example, "I wait for the Lord, my soul does wait, And in His word do I hope" (Psalm 130). This waiting—a sign of devotion and commitment in any outward or worldly relationship—is directed to the inner realm, the inner hearing of intimacy. Finally, Heald's guide shows the fruits of the journey with God: growth in intimacy, praise, and deepening of intimacy. That is, the more we deepen in intimacy with God, the more we want. The Psalms themselves reflect this never-ending desire to keep deepening: "Let us shout joyfully to Him with psalms" (Psalm 95). Seen from this perspective, the transpersonal intimacy of faith is really a continual journey with God.

"IN TIME MATES SEE"—CO-JOURNEYING

"In time mates see" alludes to a two-part melody. The first involves a couple's relation to time. Just as we take our solitary journey with time and life and God, so we may embark on it with a companion. Whether through the convention or sacrament of marriage, a sustained friendship, or perhaps through a series of circumstances in which we find ourselves sharing time with another, we can come to experience unity with our beloved co-journeyer, our "ship mate" so to speak. Here time not only teaches the two so joined; it also records and tells stories. It weaves a history of arrivals and departures, separations and joining. Through the coordinated, and miscoordinated, juggling of schedules, the "time for embracing and for refraining from embracing," two persons allocate their time for being together in a manner that signifies a unity, interdependence, and mutual agreement. Such unity takes, uses, and transforms time. In a sense, time is the unseen resource that partners give to each other freely, not for purposes of exchange (transaction) but from a deep and abiding willingness to love (transform). So in this part of the harmony, "in time" actually means through time; the capacity and the decision to continue cultivating intimacy through the flux. The term *mate* alludes to the impermanence of the commitment; mates really come together for the time being, even when that is a lifetime.

Interestingly, the etymological root of the word "mate" (*gematta*) refers to "being a guest at one's table." Intimacy cultivated over time requires a basic respect, an honoring of the other's personhood. Our treatment of the other as an honored guest (while simultaneously honoring ourself) in the first part of the melody, may provide the strongest foundation for commitment. As they toast to life at their shared table of time, "mates see" the interweaving that a continuing, ongoing relationship provides. They see the routines and the chaos, the plans and the missed opportunities, the separate rhythms that sometimes synchronize, the pacing out of events, the packing them together, and the repertoire of holiday and birthday rituals and anniversaries. Eventually, these fold into a tableau of reminiscence. Time is a shared memory.

"INTO MY SEA"—SPIRITUAL COMMUNITY

> There is the energetic search for a community, as people try one church after another, hoping to have their unnamable hunger for community satisfied. They bemoan the breakdown of family and neighborhoods, longing for a past golden age when intimacy could be found at home or on the city block. (Moore, 1992, p. 92)

So we journey through the uneven process of individuation (into me; see?), the active embracing of life as a teacher (in time I see), and attempts at co-journeying (in time mates see). As we journey, we recognize how intimacy reaches beyond a singular relationship. In fact, it must move beyond the private world of the couple. As stated by one philosopher: "If two people who are involved in a close relationship are not engaged with the larger nature of life, they may only be encased in a symbiotic cocoon that will prevent them from acknowledging each other's reality as well" (Wilner, 1982, p. 32).

A distinction develops between the romantic yearning for and exclusive bonding with "the perfect mate" (cf. "the special relationship," Foundation for Inner Peace, 1975; Williamson, 1994) and the more realistic enjoyment of time with life's many guests. The key to this part of the melody, "my sea," alludes to life as a whole, to our extended network, our community of actual and potential intimates, and to the flow of time that incessantly brings us together and apart in cycles as unpredictable as the weather.

We no longer wait to "live happily ever after" because the whole process of relating—with ourselves and with others—is transpersonal. Every encounter holds the seed of mystery in the other, the Thou, the beloved in all people. "All real living is meeting," wrote Buber (1970). Within such a meeting, we may find a sacredness that supersedes the specialness of a singular commitment. This resembles the transcendence of "in time I see" except with two important differences. First, the "I" relaxes or even vanishes; a selflessness emerges with the lack of any need to assert oneself—almost the polar opposite of "into me; see?" Second, "my sea" reflects a movement out of time, beyond the cause and effect sequences of relating, to a place where many relationships flow together and apart. Intimacy seeks community and we, in our selflessness, in our inclusiveness—not compelled to have a single, special relationship—facilitate such community.

The Vanauken quote at the start of this chapter inspired the following allegory. It helps to elucidate the transcendental aspect of "into my sea":

> This is the story about a fish. All its life, the fish swam around just like it had seen other fish. It never had any question about swimming or about the substance it was swimming around in. This substance was all it knew; it provided food, companionship with other fish, and it helped the fish do its favorite thing, swim. There was never a need to wonder about this happy existence.
>
> One day, as the fish was feeding at the surface of this substance, it darted upward for food and came out of the substance for a little bit longer time than ever before. So much so that it could feel the substance begin to slide or pour off its body. In that moment the fish could see the distinct world of the substance, stretching out in an endless vastness all around it. Then the fish felt it could not breathe and knew that something special was happening.
>
> This event, which went by so quickly, and where the fish saw that it could not live outside of this substance—changed the fish's life. The fish saw, came face to face with that very substance, which sustained its life without ever asking anything from the fish.

This allegory may be interpreted in many ways. The water may be translated as a transcendent principle or source, such as a higher power or God, and the revelation as one in which the transcendent is seen as ordinary—not really so mysterious, other worldly, or supernatural. The very substrate of life itself, water, is found everywhere and in everything. We can always—at every moment—sense the sustaining, omnipresent, and unlimited quality of this transcendent principle.

We can also view the water as time itself or a specific cultural time. It is everywhere, we rarely question it, and it helps us go about our activities. We see that others, mostly, follow and use it much as we do. The revelation consists in discerning the relativity of time, of our culture's arbitrary definition of time. We see how busy everyone is "swimming around," hustling back and forth from one activity to another in their daily routines. They rarely question the pace of life, and rarely pause to see that time is subject to various definitions and uses. The cartoon in Fig. 3.2 may help to show this predicament.

Some understanding of cross-cultural differences in social time helps to explain this analogy between water and time. Some cultures (e.g., Trinidad) are more present-oriented compared to the United States, which is more future-oriented (Jones, 1988). In other cultures (e.g., Brazil), people have more flexible views of time and are not as concerned about punctuality as in the U.S. In a comparative study of six countries, Japan appeared to have the fastest pace of living as measured by the walking speed of randomly chosen pedestrians and the speed of postal clerks to fulfill an order. Indonesia and Taiwan were slower,

"Water?!... What water?"   "Time?!... What time?"

FIG. 3.2. Time as the unseen element or unquestioned medium of social life.

with the United States being more moderate (Levine, 1988). As we look at cultures that follow a more sacred than an industrial time, we see less compulsion for deadlines or for completing projects (see Hall, 1983; Levine, 1998). Importance is placed on what is happening, for example, within a thousand-year period, rather than what happens today. One's actions reflect the cumulative effects of many life times (karma), not the conditioning of our childhood and society.

Perhaps the most vivid distinctions in cultural definitions of time, and also a key to the connection between the transcendent principle and such definitions, can be seen in the calendar time of religious ritual and holidays. Judaism, Christianity, and Islam treat holy days in very different ways, for different times, and different durations. Jews view dawn and dusk as particularly sacred times, giving emphasis to dusk on the eve of sabbath. The Christian celebration of Christmas falls at a time when pagan religions previously worshipped the midwinter sun. And in Islam, worshippers take pre-planned time out of their daily schedule, every day, for prayer. Yet, in all of these observances the practitioners, pious or otherwise, relinquish the "routines" of daily life. In the original meaning of holiday (holy day), time is no longer ordinary; it becomes sacred (Zerubavel, 1981).

The intimacy of "into my sea" represents a move toward sacred time, whether or not initiated by religious ritual. For example, we may be more likely to relax with friends and family on holidays (holy days) and weekends (originally sacred days). We might glimpse that such sacred time need not require religious prescription. Bathing in our friendly sea need not be entirely predicated on ceremony. Further, coming together on holidays does not guarantee intimacy, much like a marriage certificate does not guarantee commitment. But holidays do provide a *cyclic* opportunity to immerse oneself with others. From the point of view of sacred time, it is no coincidence that many long-term breaches in intimacy may heal at special occasions. This may occur at the happy holiday, birth, or wedding as well as at the funeral or hospital after an accident.

HARMONY AND DISHARMONY

The fullness of intimacy comes from all four parts: individuation, faith, co-journeying, and spiritual community. The intimate life weaves these together, sometimes a loose knit, other times tight. When the four threads do not flow together, when we get stuck in one part and neglect others, when we stay too long in one point of the melody, the knit frays and the tangle and snarl of disharmony sets in.

For example, too much "in to me; see?" leads to a lack of sensitivity or caring for others; a self-centered focus on personal needs or solitary journey. Too much "in time I see" leads to procrastination and a lack of active participation within a relationship. We miss the real sense of joining with a partner and with community, of playing, working interdependently, and, especially, seeing things through with others. Too much "in time mates see" leads to absorption and exclusivity within one "special" relationship: "All of one's eggs in one basket," so to speak. Authors give various terms to these extreme forms of imbalance: romantic delusion, codependence, or relationship addiction. Finally, too much "into my sea" leads to a focus on quantity of friendships rather than on quality. We become distracted with too much getting together (a busy social calendar); there is no healthy solitude, burn out may creep in, and even—paradoxically—we feel empty and lonely. Alternatively, we may become spiritually addicted (extreme fundamentalism, zealousness) and fail to face the responsibilities of household and routine.

So we need the solitude and the reaching out of individuation as well as the time alone with just one's beloved for intimacy to deepen. And we need the support of and service to a community that knows us, combined with some relationship to a higher power, for intimacy to become rich, expansive, and timeless. Intimacy has many interfaces, and if we give them each our time, we may find that time gives us all the intimacy we need.

If we had a keen vision of all that is ordinary in human life, it would be like hearing the grass grow or the squirrel's heart beat, and we should die of that roar which is the other side of silence.

—George Eliot (19th century English novelist,
author of *Silas Marner*, and *Middlemarch*)

Science has given us the ultimate of temporal perspectives: the birth and death of the entire universe.

—Michael C. Kearl (Professor of Sociology/Anthropology, author
of the "Sociological Tour Through Cyberspace" website)

If we insist on seeing life in a one-dimensional, linear, and causal way, we will be out of touch with our experiences. We will miss those expansions and compressions of time, those alternations of space that mark the intimate experience. . . . There will be no dance, none of the rhythmic random movements on which all of nature is based.

(Malone & Malone, 1987, p. 107)

THOUGHTS ON A NEW SCIENCE

To some important extent, the same laws that shape physical forces (inside molecular and cosmological events), also shape intimate relations:

- That we can see and learn from these laws by observing nature's images of growth and decay and humanity's images of behavior and society.

- That this will reveal—even in our most mundane interactions— deep truths about our relatedness.

- That, ultimately, science will help us to know our selves and our relations as a function of these laws.

4

The Forces of Time:
The Process of Intimacy

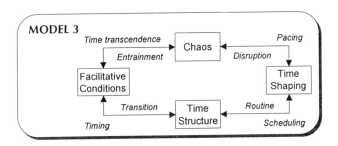

THE PREVIOUS chapter described different forms of intimacy—intrapersonal, interpersonal, and transpersonal—and how time plays a role in each. The current chapter focuses on temporality in relationships, how couples relate to time, and how time impinges on couples. This chapter attempts to build a systematic description of the big picture, which is often lost to couples in the midst of their daily routine, of how relationships proceed in time, and of how partners coordinate their lives together. From this big picture, I hope readers will derive a sense of the wholeness of transpersonal intimacy (see Quality 3, chap. 2). The enlightened activity of continuing to relate with another person through time (In time mates see)—and the coordination this entails—can be seen as a spiritual discipline. On the one hand, this requires extraordinary effort; a certain degree of faith, self-transcendence, mindfulness, concentration, compassion, patience, and an ability to flow is required. On the other hand, it requires a simple understanding of "all that is ordinary in human life," that is, appreciating the warm security of the routines and the little things (timing, pacing) that are shared together.

This chapter outlines a model or tool for representing reality so that many processes that could not be simultaneously perceived are described in a single formulation. Eight functions facilitate the use and influence of time within intimate relationships: scheduling (planning), routine (ritual), timing, transition, rhythm entrainment (coordination), time transcendence, perturbation (disruption), and pacing. The functions represent the ordinary and mundane aspects of our life with another. These functions are derived from four forces that influence and control couples unless or until they learn to harness them: chaos, time shaping, structure, and nurturing conditions (context). Relationships have phases that, like "rhythmic, random movements," change according to the prevalence of these forces. Couples have periods of ups and downs, chaos and routine, as well as periods where they plan their time and periods where they relax and let things happen. A healthy intimate relationship shifts with fluidity from phase to phase without fixating or spending too much time in one phase.

For example, the function of *scheduling* allows partners to shape their time together and provide a structure to the relationship. But unforeseeable circumstances *perturb or disrupt* these schedules and the overscheduled relationship lacks spontaneity and vigor. The function of *transition* allows partners to negotiate their evolving structure and to accept that change is inevitable. If transition is not acknowledged and worked with, then partners feel stuck in old structure and become weary of each other.

I have suggested in previous chapters that individuals, in their innate desire for intimacy, are also driven to experience awakening and transcendence. I believe that couples can harness the four forces through an awareness of the functions that bring them together and take them apart and also through a humble willingness to see the whole process of their shared lives. In fact, couples may experience greater love through an appreciation of the complexity in their relationship. The model described here may be seen as a meditation on such complexity. It is a tool or guide for increasing a couple's awareness and their intimacy. Three core capacities facilitate these aspects of awareness: an ability to flow with events as they unfold in time, being present to the other in the moment without expectations or projections, and a sensitivity to coincidence or synchronicity. These qualities help couples to infuse spirituality into their ordinary lives, bringing the eternal into the temporal, and helping them to listen to that other side of silence. Most importantly, each of these three qualities can be mastered with various practices and patience (e.g., Belitz & Lundstrom, 1997; Csikszentmihalyi, 1990).

FLOW, PRESENCE, AND SYNCHRONICITY

Flow. When things flow, partners experience their relationship as a continuing, uninterrupted phenomenon where they participate with their full being. The expression "things just flowed between us" reveals an emotional sense of continuity and connectedness, a sense of wholeness through time. This flow can occur in any situation or for any duration. Lovemaking, conversations, special occasions with relatives, planning and executing a dinner party, and perhaps an entire period such as a vacation or raising children can reveal flow.

Csikszentmihalyi described four rules for being able to sustain flow, which allow individuals to enjoy life more and help them to deal with the challenges of chaos and disintegration. These rules are setting goals, becoming immersed in the activity, paying attention to what is happening, and learning to enjoy the immediate experience. After the excitement wanes from the beginning of a relationship, efforts must be made to restore flow:

> At this point, the relationship is in danger of becoming a boring routine that might be kept alive by mutual convenience, but is unlikely to provide further enjoyment, or spark a new growth in complexity. The only way to restore flow to the relationship is by finding new challenges in it. These might involve steps as simple as varying the routines of eating, sleeping, or shopping. They might involve making an effort to talk together about new topics of conversation, visiting new places, making new friends. More than anything else they involve paying attention to the partner's own complexity, getting to know her at deeper levels than were necessary in the earlier days of the relationship, supporting him with sympathy and compassion during the inevitable changes that the years bring. (Csikszentmihalyi, 1990, p. 182)

We can also lose a sense of flow by becoming overly controlling of the relationship (e.g., possessiveness, scheduling everything, becoming too goal oriented and busy), or by taking the opposite approach of passivity, avoidance and withdrawal. Too often, relationships deteriorate not because they become boring, but because partners take things for granted, become passive, and take a wait-and-see attitude. Flow requires engaging the other and immersing oneself in the relationship. A sense of purpose or vision, shared goals, or a common dream provides a context and direction for flow.

Presence. Presence provides the key to flow and binds time and intimacy together. Almaas (1986) explained that, for most people, presence is felt in the aesthetic experience of beauty, awe, grandeur or in the "admiration when one witnesses heroism in an individual or group, or the courage and boldness of an explorer" (p. 2). It can also be felt in times of deep and intense emotion. Almaas gave the example of a woman giving birth who "seems to have a fullness. She seems to have a glow, a radiance. The presence is unmistakable, beautiful, and powerful" (p. 4). Intimacy taps into this quality of presence.

Distraction and mindlessness inhibit and destroy presence. We distract ourselves in two ways: through self-absorption (preoccupation and obsessiveness) or, alternatively, we fail to utilize our mental powers to concentrate and attend to the flow of relating. We can be so busy transcribing that we lose sight of the transaction. Self-absorption occurs in one of two ways—projection or scripting. In *projection* we place our own memories, images, and "pictures" of how our partner should be onto the actual being of our partner. We may also project those parts of ourselves that we do not like onto them. Projection includes saying "you hate me" when we hate our partners or seeing one's partner as like our own rejecting or overprotective parent. *Scripting* consists of a series of expectations, usually learned through parental and cultural conditioning, about how events (i.e., interpersonal sequences) proceed. With scripting, we go on automatic and ignore the nuance, spontaneity, and moment-to-moment complexity that arises in relating. Examples of scripting include "No one cares about me" or "I'll show you how to treat me nicely!" Because scripts and projections are central to the way we construe and also enact *sequences* of social behavior, the next chapter describes them in more depth.

Mindlessness comes from failure to pay attention. We may live "in the moment" too literally and become hedonistic, fickle, or capricious. Like flow, mindfulness requires creating new challenges or new categories for seeing the world, being open to the unexpected. Langer (1989) described how our labeling of others, as in blaming or prejudice, destroys our ability to pay attention to their uniqueness and complexity. We see events and others only in the context of the label. So it is with relationships. For example, the hedonistic philosophy of "love the one you're with" can turn into a neglect of the intimacy within a relationship. Being present thus means being present over time as well as in the moment. We need not have our partner directly in front of us in order to be present to them. This ongoing presence transforms marital contracts of commitment into living testimonials. Commitment, like intimacy, must be an ongoing willfulness to presence. Mindful relating requires that we adapt different routines and skills at different times (see Duck, 1988b). It requires the ability to suspend one's use of scripts or projections while listening to another (e.g., Hendrix, 1992); and it also requires the ability to stay in touch with our feelings and emotions throughout relationship change (Amodeo & Amodeo, 1986).

Synchronicity. But flow and presence are not sufficient for seeing the whole process of intimacy through time with another. There must also be meaning. Intimacy is not entirely under our control; time and circumstance conspire to furnish or dismantle our encounters. All relationships—for however long they last—are co-incidental (Peat, 1987). The incidents that are our separate lives coincide. This coincidence is most apparent when we turn a corner onto a rarely traveled street and discover our partner who also never goes that way. Examples include picking up the phone to dial a friend and discovering that person is already on the line, letters passing in the mail, or flying on the same plane. These occasions are relatively short term but they can feel meaningful to us. Everything falls into place and we sense that timing is perfect. They are not merely coincidental, but rather synchronistic; a spiritual aspect is involved. Meaning, in this sense, does not require an overarching context that we refer to. Meaning is inherent in the mystery of the joining.

The ongoing relationship—one that navigates schedules and perturbation, routines and transitions—also embraces and reveals a longer term synchronicity. The concept of synchronicity portrays coincidence as not merely causal or conducted by chance. The magic of intimacy lies in discerning the greater synchronicity or "marvelous correspondence" (see Jung, 1972) of shared lives.

The deep sense of continuity through flow, the fullness and vulnerability of presence, and the mystery and wonder of synchronicity bring intimates to the deeper time or deeper process of their relationship. They are enrolled in a school, are together on a journey, or an exploration; rather than placed within a series of

---

SYNCHRONICITY: The Couple Therapist's View
[From Ritterman, 1995]

Acquiring and maintaining synchronicity may be among the most important bonding skills couples need for forming a good, lasting relationship. Helping couples improve their skills at conflict resolution, communication patterns and sexual functioning, without addressing their time rhythms—if they each live in different biological and psychological time zones—is like trying to dance a waltz to a hard-rock beat.

This attention to time in couples' relationships has traditionally entailed a mechanical arrangement of living patterns so that each can literally take more time for the other. Couples are encouraged to rearrange work schedules, turn down promotions that would make them busier, renegotiate childcare responsibilities, get up an hour earlier, schedule "dates" far away for weekends alone without the kids—a hundred-and-one standard therapeutic prescriptions for shoehorning a little more "quality" time into a time frame already bursting at the seams.

But if the inner experience of that "quality" time is as mechanical as the prescription itself, not much value has been gained. If there is no change in the *inner* sense of the time taken for the kiss, for cleaning up the clothes, the kiss will be perfunctory, duty-bound, without any vital current of compassion or empathy. The therapist's job is not simply to crank out these behavioral assignments, but to try the much more difficult and delicate work of creating a felt pause deep within the bodies and minds of the couple while they are engaging in the task itself—so that it is a living, timeless moment of human synchronicity. (pp. 48-49)

---

meetings, exchanges, or transitions. Flow, presence, and synchronicity signal the deeper process of partner's intimacy and demonstrate that time is more than the measure, increment, or accumulation of their days.

INTIMACY AND THE FOUR FORCES OF TIME

Four forces[1] constitute the deeper, phasic time "on which all of nature is based," including the intimate bond. These are nurturing conditions, chaos, time shaping, and structure or form. All personal relations are, at any one point in time, in some phase that emerges through the activity of these forces. To help understand them, I depict these forces as one of two poles on one of six continuums. These are (a) nurturing conditions—time shaping, (b) chaos—structure, (c) nurturing conditions—chaos, (d) nurturing conditions—structure, (e) chaos—time shaping, (f) structure—time shaping. Each pole is the result of activity occurring at another pole. Tension between these poles can result in psychological tension. However, the cyclic joining of two can result in a shift to a new level of consciousness (increased presence, flow, and meaning).

For example, one pair—nurturing conditions (context) and time shaping (action)—describes how couples shape their life together so as to be responsive to conditions that facilitate or hurt intimacy. This pair also shows how conditions facilitate the couple through transitions and allow them to synchronize their different rhythms. Intimacy occurs when couples are neither stuck in time shaping (constantly doing), nor simply waiting for the right time (only passive). Instead, it occurs when partners are in synch with each other, and balancing action and sensitivity to timing. Another pair—chaos and structure—describes forces of disintegration and reintegration that couples constantly navigate through agreements, the timing of shared events, and their capacity to handle conflict. Intimacy does not occur when couples are in the extreme phase of reeling from chaos or conflict, or the opposite phase of plodding routine and boredom. Instead, intimacy involves the capacity to respond to chaos with accountability to the agreed routine, the right amount of structure or, conversely, the capacity to embrace chaos through novelty and play.

The eight functions also help join the forces. For example, scheduling functions as an action that gives rise to increased structure or form in a relationship. To maintain stability in a relationship, some degree of scheduling is required and scheduling can help when relationships lack predictability and form. Once relationships have structure, however, routines develop. These routines are structural features of the relationship, which facilitate or constrain the need for time shaping. Too much or too little routine will require some shifts or counterbalances in time shaping to maintain a certain level of relational form. Figure 4.1 and Table 4.1 provide illustration and definition of the forces and functions. The remainder of the chapter describes this model in more depth.

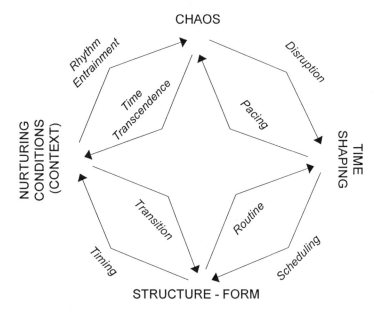

FIG. 4.1. Four forces and eight functions of temporal processes in relationships.

Note. Arrows suggest emergent functions rather than causal relationships. For example, entrainment does not cause chaos; rather, whether partners join rhythms depends on how nurturing conditions interface with chaos. Table 4.1 suggests or hypothesizes how these emergent functions might occur.

TABLE 4.1

DEFINITIONS OF FORCES AND FUNCTIONS

Temporal facet	Description
	FOUR FORCES
1. Nurturing Conditions (Context)	Sensitivity to those conditions and contexts that foster or block intimacy. Experienced as sensitivity.
2. Time Shaping	Actions that influence the couple's future. Experienced as doing.
3. Chaos	Activity of disorganization, disequilibria, dissipation, entropy. Experienced in play, ecstasy, conflict.
4. Structure—Form	The current form or phase that sustains the relationship over time. Experienced as current relationship phase, commitment.
	EIGHT FUNCTIONS
1. Disruption (Perturbation) (Chaos *perturbs* Time Shaping)	When a routine or schedule becomes disjointed or discontinuous or when circumstances prevent or immediately require order. Examples include cancellations, interruptions, kinks in well-laid plans, feeling out of kilter.
2. Scheduling (Time Shaping creates Structure by *scheduling*)	Individual and joint decisions to budget or allocate time to specific tasks, activities, or recreations. These actions influence the form of the relationship. Actions can be effortful, intentional, and mindful, or unintended and mindless.
3. Timing (Structure informs Nurturing Conditions in *timing*)	The capacity of the relationship to accommodate changing conditions that facilitate intimacy; includes sense of right timing, sensitivity to synchronicity, serendipity.
4. Rhythm Entrainment (Nurturing Conditions informs Chaos with *rhythm*)	The ways in which partners' various rhythms—biological, hormonal, sleep-wake cycles, social—follow each other and alternatively diverge over time; represents how one's personal nature interfaces with the more complex and chaotic aspects of the interpersonal system.
5. Pacing (Time Shaping regulates Chaos through *pacing*)	The degree to which partners consider and regulate the length of time, interval, series, or sequence of actions when involved in, approaching, or avoiding some transaction.
6. Routines (Structure moderates Time Shaping with *routine*)	The ways in which relationship structure dictates social habits that the couples engage in together. This includes routines where partners feel stuck, as well as routines that give continuity and spiritual sustenance to the relationship. Neurotic "routines" are scripts that constrain spontaneity.

Continued

TABLE 4.1. (*continued*)

7. Transition (Nurturing Conditions modify Structure through *transition*)	Ways in which conditions change the structure or form of the relationship. This includes changes in roles, degree of cooperation, and in the stage of the relationship. Transitions occur as a linear development in commitment (e.g., meeting > courtship > marriage), a linear disengagement, and they can be cyclical (stability followed by uncertainty).
8. Time Transcendence (Chaos informs Nurturing Conditions through *time transcendence*)	The ways in which both nurturing conditions and chaos allow us to transcend our individuality or limited viewpoints about linear time. This refers to the deeper process of events that have brought partners together for some higher good; provides feelings of joy, ecstasy, wonder, mystery, a sense of timelessness or of losing track of time due to absorption or immersion in the relationship.

NURTURING CONDITIONS (CONTEXT)

Renewing and continuing intimacy requires a clear awareness of ones' inner vulnerabilities and a comfortable perceptiveness about any qualities of uneasy responsiveness in the other. Private urgencies produce magical phantasies of immediate and absolute fittingness, without sufficient playfulness between the two. More leisurely exploring could help discover ways to significant pleasure and connectedness. The wider concept of "foreplay" suggests the usefulness of an awareness of ones' hidden pains and anxieties as a preparation for pacing oneself, from an urgent phantasy of relief to a playful illusion of fulfillment. Instant intimacies can only serve, at best, as exploratory ventures, for which one needs to estimate ones' ability to afford the risk one anticipates. Loving may not yet be earned. (Shor & Sanville, 1978, p. 27)

Put simply, loving relationships take time. This force can be summarized with the following statement: Everything that happens between two people happens because the surrounding conditions allow it; they allow things to happen rather than force them to. There are immediate, or proximal, causes for interpersonal events and there are conditions (often external to and of longer duration than the current situation) that enhance or disturb intimacy. A few analogies may help clarify this idea.

Planting a seed in the garden, releasing a baited hook into the lake, or aiming and shooting a rifle exemplify actions that may or may not lead to certain outcomes. These actions have an associated probability of outcome that depend on secondary or contextual factors. The health of the seed, depth and orientation of planting, soil and weather conditions, and the care given all subsequently influence the maturation of that seed into a colorful flower. Similarly, the type of bait, the depth of one's line, the time of day or season, the hunger of the fish, and the skill of the angler will determine if and when dinner will be caught. And even polished sharpshooters must contend with weather, the quality of the rifle, and their own wavering concentration in order to make a bull's-eye.

Several differences can be noted between these analogies that apply to relationships. First, the duration between action and outcome varies: with planting to maturation being the longest and firing to hitting target the shortest. For example, recall the fictional couple—Jay and Donna—from chapter 1; it was only a few months between the time when they first talked about moving in together and the actual move-in date. Conditions may not have been right for them to move when they did. Second, the degree of perceived control varies; we believe that hitting target is more predictable than catching fish. For example, Donna felt moving in would foster intimacy, but later comes to realize that she may have been a bit pushy. Third, and most importantly, the nature of relationship differs in each analogy. We care for or neglect the seed, pursue and are evaded by the fish, and calibrate or miscalculate the rifle's fire. Similarly, Jay and Donna care or neglect each other, pursue and evade each other, and calibrate or miscalculate those activities that bring them together.

All of these factors—duration from act to outcome, perceived control, and nature of relationship—represent aspects of the facilitative conditions that enter into intimate relationships. Of course, intimacy is not the same as cultivating a plant, pursuing fish, or practicing riflery, but—like these activities and as much as we might deny them—events conspire that are largely beyond our control to either facilitate or inhibit outcomes.

For example, there are those who would like to terminate a relationship but cannot due to factors (e.g., legal or economic barriers, children, other commitments) that were either unforeseeable or actually conditioned by the relationship. When asked to explain why their long-term marriage or engagement fizzled, individuals may simply and honestly respond "things were just not right between us." There is also the common wisdom that "you'll know it when the time is right" for moving in together or marriage. Moreover, the expression "you'll know it when the right one comes along" may be as much a matter of timing or being in the right place at the right time, as it is a matter of compatibility.

> *Knowing when "the time is right" can reflect more than social learning but also a transpersonal consciousness of nurturing conditions.*

Other conventional truisms, such as "some things take time" and "sometimes you just have to let go," reveal the importance of nurturing conditions. In many respects, these secondary conditions, rather than single or immediate causes, facilitate the longer transitions of relationships. What is it that helps relationships move from strangers to acquaintances, from newlyweds to parents, or from long-married partners to divorcees? Over time, partners may learn a sensitivity to the inevitability of transition, that no matter what they do, life has its own turbulence and eddies that move the couple along. Alternatively, partners may learn to recognize such changes and forge a commitment that accommodates them. Here, "timing is everything" as couples learn to dance with each other in short-term interactions as well as long-term phases. Right timing provides a capacity of the evolving relational structure to accommodate those conditions that facilitate intimacy.

Context. Context, or more specifically temporal context, is another term for viewing these unfolding conditions that give relationships meaning and depth. Relationships unfold in many contexts of time. Interactions that may take seconds or minutes occur within situations (e.g., conflict at home, leisure vacations, dining together) that may take hours or days, and many of these situations constitute the longer phases of a relationship. Chapter 6 describes these different temporal contexts and how they are interrelated. Suffice it to say for now that flow, presence, and meaning are all enhanced when we can see the multiple contexts that layer our ongoing relationship. A relationship has meaning when seen and lived in a broader temporal context (cf. Duck, 1994); the colloquial phrase "a meaningful relationship" was coined partly to distinguish ongoing intimacy from a sexual fling or a one-night stand. Also, when we recognize the single interaction (e.g., whether the harsh exchange of words, or the gracious giving of a special gift) as part of a bigger picture, we become more flexible and tolerant. We see that events are transpiring within contexts of time that we cannot fully comprehend or measure. We trust that conditions beyond our control are facilitating our relationship.

| **RESEARCH** | **REFLECTION** | 7 |

TIME COMPETENCY AND NURTURING CONDITIONS

Shostrom (1966) developed a measure that purports to assess "time competency," or the ability to both live in the here and now, as well as tie the past to present, and view the future in a hopeful light. In some ways, this competency is like a capacity to understand nurturing conditions. Here are some example items.

1. My past is a stepping-stone for the future.
2. I do not feel bound by the motto, "Don't waste your time."
3. For me, past, present, and future is a meaningful continuity.

RESEARCH NOTES ON NURTURING CONDITIONS: THE CONCEPT OF YÜAN

The chance to have a relationship is so precious that it must be cherished and not strategically manipulated. (from Chang & Holt, 1991)

The conditions that nurture intimacy (i.e., that allow it to take root, to grow, and to flourish) are numerous, complex, interdependent, and subtle. Much of the research on personal relationships, rooted as it is within the Western empirical tradition, assumes a unidirectional view of causality. This view holds that certain preceding variables (e.g., partner personality, background, style of communication) combine to affect certain antecedent conditions (e.g., marital satisfaction, adjustment, or relationship length). The transpersonal approach to intimacy questions this assumption and begins by assuming a multidirectional view of causality, a view that is more consistent within Eastern philosophical traditions.

In the Buddhist view of causality, the concept of *yüan* (in Chinese, *pratitya* in Sanskrit) is defined as the supporting or secondary condition that brings about events. Yüan is distinguished from the direct or primary cause of the event. Synonyms that are used for yüan are indirect cause, cooperating cause, concurrent occasions, circumstantial conditions, contextual factors, facilitative conditions, and nutritive cause (see Chang & Holt, 1991; Kalupahama, 1975). I have chosen to interpret yüan as nurturing conditions.

Yüan as a Metaphor in Chinese Personal Relationships. Chang and Holt (1991) provided a key introduction to the analysis of the concept of yüan as a metaphor for personal relationships among Chinese. They argued that the Western belief that relationships can be "worked" on through training in communication problems—that is, through self affirmation and interpersonal competence—does not apply to patterns of communication among Eastern populations (Kincaid, 1987; Yum, 1988). They focused on the concept of yüan to explain why: "Yüan is thought to be the chief force that allows contextual factors to play a role in determining whether people will or will not be associated with each other. Chinese will often say, 'I have yüan with another person,' meaning conditions are right for them to be together. This concept plays a significant role in influencing present-day Chinese relationships" (Chang & Holt, 1991; p. 30).

To fully understand the use of yüan within the context of intimate relationships, Chang and Holt also discussed related Buddhist concepts of karma and dependent origination. These ideas are relevant for our general discussion of time, but are too complex to discuss in detail here. Briefly, *karma* refers to the principle of moral law stating that all present actions, good or bad, produce their effects at some unknown point in the future. The doctrine of *reincarnation* is relevant in that events that unfold in one's current life may be due to one's actions within past lives. "Causation . . . is a result of one's acts through various lifetimes and does not stem from some supernatural agency" (p. 33). *Dependent origination* refers to the fact that all phenomena arise or emerge due to various interdependent factors. There is no seeing without vision and an object to be seen, no hearing without the ear and an object to be heard. All events have their context.

A Living Context. Westerners and scientists of personal relationships might argue that these ideas might be relevant for Chinese and other Buddhist cultures but not for Westerners. However, the concept of yüan is relevant for a transpersonal view of intimacy and for later discussion of temporal context. Even if one does not accept the notion of past lives or reincarnation, the concept of yüan, or of nurturing conditions, plays an important counterpoint to the unicausal, action-based idea of time shaping Chang and Holt pointed out that the conditions that nurture relationships have three qualities: They are not completely knowable, they cannot be forced or used to strategize, and they are spontaneous, experienced as a "feeling of fit."

Thus, context may be more than some abstract framework that scholars use to understand and interpret text. Rather, it is a complex set of interdependent conditions that give rise to events. Buddhist views of enlightenment involve gaining insight into this context, to have a deep appreciation for the interconnectedness of events. Context, as discussed here and in later chapters, becomes a way of intimacy rather than a tool for analyzing. If we believe that intimacy can be forced, that we can completely know when such intimacy will happen, or that it can be ultimately analyzed, then we have an unbalanced or distorted view of it. This egoistic view seeks to capture some relational form and to shape it according to our desires. As context, yüan represents that aspect of intimacy that *is ripening* or *is coming to fruition.* No matter how we shape our time with others, the lack of yüan will lead to no intimacy. Conversely, no matter how much yüan we have, unless we "cherish and not just follow it," we may not adequately nourish the time we have with others. Thus, intimacy is an art that combines action and context. Further readings on time and causality in Buddhist thought may be found in Kalupahama (1975), Sinha (1983), and Hayward (1987).

TIME SHAPING (ACTION)

> Marriage too is an attempt to rhyme, to bring two different lives—within the one life of their troth and household—periodically into agreement or consent. The two lives stray apart necessarily, and by desire come together again. . . . But it is the possibility of failure, together with the formal bounds, that turns us back from fantasy, wishful thinking, and self-pity into the real terms and occasions of our lives.
>
> It may be, then, that form serves us best when it works as an obstruction to baffle us and deflect our intended course. It may be that when we no longer know what to do, we have come to our real work, and that when we no longer know which way to go, we have begun our real journey. The mind that is not baffled is not employed. The impeded stream is the one that sings. (Berry, 1985, pp. 171–172)

Relationships do not just float along and deepen in intimacy without both individual and joint efforts to find or create time together. In fact, whereas sensitivity to context allows us to find time, time shaping is a way to create—or control—time. Although conditions we cannot control facilitate intimacy, we do exert some influence. All context requires action, just as all action gains meaning only within a context. The hook requires baiting and lowering, a seed requires soil and watering, and the rifle must be aimed and fired. Similarly, we act in our relationships—deliberately, unconsciously, intentionally, incidentally—in ways that shape time, that make it more or less likely for intimacy to occur. Generally, we plan, schedule, follow, or diverge from routines, and we allocate time to different activities, hopefully balancing personal privacy with periods of closeness. When our actions—time shaping—create intimacy they are likely to involve some artful and skillful balance between control (structure) and vulnerability (chaos).

Interestingly, researchers have found that some people perceive their use of time as more structured and purposive than others; they plan their days more, are less bored with daily routines, and make good use of their time. In one study using the Time Structure Questionnaire (Bond & Feather, 1988), which measures this felt use of time, students who were "married or in a de facto relationship, or divorced, separated, or widowed" had clearly higher scores than singles. Compared to singleness, relationships involve greater time shaping, and just having been in a relationship at some time, may lead to more structured use of time.

RESEARCH **REFLECTION**   8

THE TIME STRUCTURE QUESTIONNAIRE

Bond and Feather (1988) developed the "Time Structure Questionnaire" to assess the degree to which individual structure their time. Consider these example items.

1. Do you plan your activities so that they fall into a particular pattern during the day?
2. Do you think you do enough with your time?
3. Do your main activities during the day fit together in a structured way?

Dimensions of Time Shaping. Time shaping refers to the ways individuals, through management of their time, influence the course of the relationship. Three major dimensions of time shaping behaviors can be distinguished (see Fig. 4.2). The first pertains to how time shaping interfaces with structure and with chaos. Time shaping, through styles or habits of *scheduling,* enables some relational structure to emerge (whether an intermittent friendship, casual dating, or a committed partnership). Also, time shaping—or the lack thereof—contends with unforeseen obstacles or events that disorganize the current structure. For example, partners fall in love at different rates, work through disagreements about a shared future, and manage a household in the face of difficulties such as heavy workloads, accidents, and recovery from disease. Other disorganizing processes include impropriety, dishonesty, and malevolence. Through *pacing,* couples may be better able to embrace this chaos by spacing out activities, not

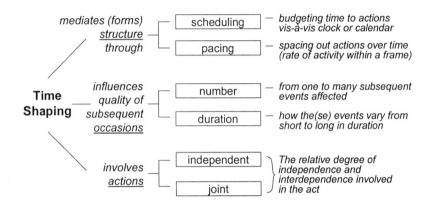

FIG. 4.2. Dimensions of time shaping: structure, occasions, actions.

rushing things, and staying mindful of getting too busy. We are most familiar with pacing through our ability to be vulnerable and patient—to wait with an expectant calmness or to suffer through difficulties without attachment to a particular outcome.

A second dimension pertains to the *duration* and *number* of social occasions subsequently influenced by the time management decision. For example, the decision to have a child entrains a couple's schedule around menstrual cycles for sometimes months or years. In contrast, decisions about when to pick up the children, how much time to spend on a particular outing, or which week to take the summer vacation generally influences fewer intervening events and for shorter periods of time.

A third dimension pertains to the *individual* versus *joint* or negotiated act of budgeting or allotting time. Most Western (cf. American-European, Hall, 1983) cultures treat time as some quantity or commodity; when parceled or budgeted (i.e., "Time is Money"), it is something we can own, share, or give away (cf. the "commodification of time," Daly, 1996). Given our fast cultural pace of work schedules and social calendars, individuals must prioritize these "time packets" alone and together. In order to find intimacy, partners must strike some balance between their individual and joint schedules, as well as between spontaneity and control. A modern paradox emerges: Obsessing about planning and scheduling detracts from the unstructured time for playful intimacy, while conversely a laxity about time shaping can leave couples subject to the rushed, busy, and cluttered schedule typical of our culture. When we obsess about time, we may lose sensitivity to our partners' sharing some feeling or important detail of their inner self. Work addicts, or Type A persons who are so caught up in controlling their own personal schedule, have difficulty with negotiated time budgeting and, subsequently, little time for intimacy.

Trust and Flexibility. As pointed out by several researchers, industrialization and the modern work pace have caused marriages and families to have less control over their private and intimate time (Daly, 1996; Hochschild, 1997). As a result, they need more trust and flexibility. Through trust and interdependence, time shaping becomes more than just the sum of two individual's separate acts of time budgeting. How couples negotiate their joint time depends on interpersonal habits, communication routines, and power balances that partially develop only within the history, the course, or the context of relating. Over time, each partner also discovers their inner priorities for solitude, for friends, and for their mate. If they wish to enjoy each other, they must also consider the priorities of the other and trust that their partner will reciprocate (Scanzoni, 1987). How couples negotiate their joint schedules both depends on and indicates the well-being of the relationship. Power imbalances, conflict, rigidity, boredom, and disunity are directly reflected in one partner recurrently accommodating the other's work schedule or in a long-term routine from which partners never deviate for fear of change.

Flexibility in scheduling occurs so that couples can recognize when "the time is right" and embody the maxim "timing makes all the difference." Healthy couples sense those nurturing or facilitative conditions that afford deeper connections; they are willing to shift schedules when that is appropriate and set aside time for themselves when that is

> *Perhaps the act of scheduling time together is not as mundane as it seems. We may be weaving a context to best embrace life's trials & tribulations.*

appropriate. In this manner, time shaping plays the responsive counterpoint to nurturing conditions. Moreover, it can also cultivate those conditions in which intimacy is most likely to develop.

Of course, conditions do not always facilitate intimacy regardless of how we shape our time. It is at these moments, according to Berry (1985), "when we no longer know what to do, we have come to our real work" (p. 172). For some couples, only reconciliation after an eruption of conflict (or even after an estrangement) may enrich or renew an intimacy in ways that previous compromises could not. Moreover, the inevitability of change in each partner tests the couple's ability to bear witness to impermanence. Couples modify previous schedules according to new circumstances, but these provide little guarantee that events will go smoothly. Try as they might to calibrate time together and balance personal needs, the laws of chaos ultimately challenge intimate time shapers.

Time Shaping interfaces With Chaos and Structure. It is through time shaping that we actively respond to the forces of chaos and structure. Nurturing conditions and time shaping dictate how couples respond in time and to time. By responding to time, partners bring collaboration and continuity to their shared life. In contrast, chaos and structure shape relationships over time and through time. These forces reveal discontinuities and dynamics inherent within intimacy. Chaos and structure tend to operate within a longer time frame than the other forces. There may be long periods of stability before we feel or admit to the chaotic elements. Predictability competes with turbulence, free will meets chance and fortune; and, as they seek to understand what is happening to their relationship, partners' feelings alternate: contentment with surprise, boredom with fascination, courage with fear, serenity with anger, or hopefulness and dismay. One theory even holds that most emotion in a relationship is due to chaos or interrupted patterns of relating (Berscheid, 1983).

But from the transpersonal perspective, this dance of order and chaos has been embraced by such ideas as divine order or God's time. Time is an operator, an incessant force that shapes all the circumstances of our relating. Most importantly, time shaping can harness this force. Through our actions we use relational structures (e.g., dating exclusively, marital commitment) to help us frame difficult circumstances. Otherwise, we fear chaos will take over and we will be left with little time for intimacy. Alternatively, too much structuring (relating purely out of obligation or duty) suffocates us and leaves little space for intimacy. Time shaping, then, is a learned art that works in tandem with chaos and structure.

RESEARCH NOTES ON TIME SHAPING (ACTION): TURNER'S MICROSOCIOLOGY OF INTERACTION

Time shaping refers to actions that arise when two people interact, which then have subsequent effects on their time together. In contrast to nurturing conditions, which refer to the multicausal context of intimacy, time shaping refers to social interaction as the primary cause of actions within that context. Individuals who desire intimacy often time shape (e.g., schedule, establish routines) in order to make intimacy more likely. Conversely, individuals who wish to avoid or modulate intimacy also time shape in ways that make intimacy less likely.

The following discussion borrows from Turner's (1988) thorough review and integration of various theories of social interaction. The central action of intimacy is self-disclosure and, as Turner pointed out, several theories of social interaction regard the self as a pivotal concept. In fact, of the four temporal forces (chaos, time shaping, nurturing conditions, relational structure), time shaping appears most related to the self and the differentiation of the self from the other.

Turner's Model of Social Interaction. Turner (1988) reviewed many classical theories of social interaction within the field of microsociology. He included models of social exchange (e.g., Homans, 1961), ethnomethodology (e.g., Garfinkel, 1967), symbolic interaction (Blumer, 1969), and interaction rituals (e.g., Goffman, 1959), and synthesized these models into a multicausal view of interaction dynamics. Dynamic structuring, Turner suggested, refers to the ways in which social interaction creates a structure within a relationship:

> Structuring is a process in which individuals produce and reproduce patterned sequences of interactive responses. And once created, these established sequences become, in a sense, a "mental template" or "schema" for how those individuals will interact when they resume contact. When such cognitive schemes can be learned by others then successive sets of actors can enter situations and repeat the lines of behavior created by others, often in the distant past. Thus, the process of structuring is, on the one hand, an overt patterning of behaviors in time and space and, on the other hand, a mental modeling of information about what interactive sequences apply to varying types of situations. (p. 149)

I am taking "the process of structuring" to be synonymous with the concept of time shaping. In synthesizing his model of structuring, Turner used both classical theories—for example, Weber's action theory (1978), Durkheim's views of interpersonal structuring (e.g., Durkheim & Mauss, 1963), Spencer's model of interpersonal structuring (1874/1976), Simmel's model of exchange structures (1907/1978), and Mead's model of interactions in society (1934). Turner also integrates more contemporary models, such as Parson's implicit exchange theory (e.g., Parsons, Bales, & Shills, 1953), Goffman's analysis of social framing and interpersonal structuring (e.g., Goffman, 1974), and Giddens' structuration model (1984). I list all these here to portray the extensive amount of investigation into social interaction.

Structuration as Validating the Self. Turner outlined six general rubrics in his synthesis: categorization, regionalization, normatization, ritualization, routinization, and stabilization of resources (see Fig. 4.3, adapted from Turner's Fig. 11.3). Each of these six structuring processes are often used to reaffirm and validate the self. Turner explained:

> To the extent that an interaction endures and is repeated, people's anxiety over self will be reduced, as they use staging cues to organize props and space (regionalize), while at the same time employing rituals to *standardize and sequence time* with clear openings, closings, repairs, and totems (ritualize). Such regionalization and ritualization will also facilitate the stabilization of the resource transfers that are used to confirm self. Thus, I believe that needs to sustain consistent definitions and feelings about self, especially core feelings about one's worth and esteem, are one of the primary motivating forces behind the regionalization, ritualization, and stabilization of the interaction. Social structure must, at the micro level, be able to confirm self; and if such is not the case, then individuals *will seek to change* or leave a structured interaction. (p. 203, italics added)

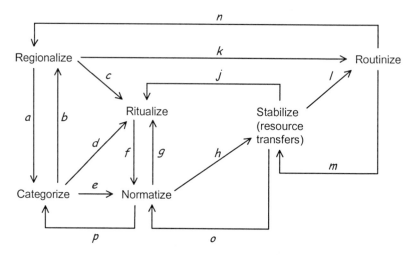

FIG. 4.3. A composite model of structuring dynamics. Adapted with permission from Fig. 11.3 in Turner (1988). See Turner for details on links (*a, b, c,* etc.).

Thus, the maintenance of the self is tied directly into this causal view of how individuals structure their time with others. Turner's synthesis, and most of the authors he reviewed, rests on the presumption that the self can shape time (and intimacy), and that we can control our destiny (with others). Again, this stands in contrast to the concept of nurturing conditions (yüan), where destiny plays a more significant role than the self.

The elements in Turner's model are briefly summarized here. They are the particular processes that individuals navigate with others in order to structure the interaction. Thus, they are not the structure itself but the ways in which structure comes about through joint action. Refer to Fig. 4.3 for his scheme of the following features.

1. Categorization. We often seek to view situations and each other in terms of mutually agreed upon categories. These categories can be classified at three levels of intimacy (as representatives of a category, as persons, as intimates) and three types of situations (work/practical, ceremonial, social). This produces a three-by-three schematic grid. With such a schema, we quickly contextualize situations so that interactions and activities "can be emitted without great deliberate effort." Our close friends are relevant to our self-concept in three types of actions: for achieving a task or goal or owing an emotional response (work/practical), for joining in a collective enterprise with owed personalized responses and a sense of mutual understanding (ceremonial), and for owing informal and emotionally responsive gestures (social).

2. Regionalization. This refers to variables that circumscribe the range of what is possible in an interaction. Spatial regionalization refers to where objects are located in space (e.g., desks, rows), the division of space into regions (offices, corridors), and the number, distribution, and movement of people in that space

(e.g., crowd). For example, we seek out places (e.g., restaurants, bedrooms) that afford more or less intimacy.

3. <u>Normatization</u>. Certain kinds of responses are owed to others—obligations, rights, and duties. These arise from social norms that guide how we act with others and how we make agreements. Normative behavior is creative because as actors, we continually negotiate and renegotiate what our obligations to others are and should be.

4. <u>Ritualization</u>. Rituals are "stereotyped sequences of behavior that symbolically denote and emotionally infuse the ongoing flow of interaction" (p. 161). We use four types of rituals in structuring flow. These are opening and closing rituals (to signal the beginning and ending of an interaction), forming rituals (to create a sense of where the interaction is headed), totemizing rituals (the use of symbols to reaffirm the relationship), and repair rituals (e.g., saying "I am sorry").

5. <u>Routinization</u>. Turner wrote that "routines involve repetitive sequences of mutual signaling and interpreting that are customary and habitual for the parties involved" (p. 162). Whereas interaction requires rituals, it also requires less emotionally infused behavioral sequences that "fill in" time and give predictability to the relationship.

6. <u>Stabilization of Resource Transfers</u>. Our exchanges with others revolve around securing material and symbolic resources that help us to feel included, affirm our self-concept, and promote a sense of *facticity* (i.e., feeling part of a larger solidarity, a sense of participating in a shared reality with others; Garfinkel, 1967). These exchanges also provide a sense of security and create a sense of trust.

Although Turner talked about social interaction in general, his model mentions intimacy at several points. Intimacy is a distinct part of categorization—before we shape time with another, we may decide how intimate the relationship is. Moreover, many of the resources Turner described (self-affirmation, a sense of belonging, a feeling of contribution, security, trust) are essential aspects of interpersonal intimacy. It is important to point out that not all individuals seek an intimate relationship or intimate encounter in order to fulfill security or ego needs and reduce anxiety. Schnarch's (1991) theory of sexual intimacy distinguished between two levels of intimacy that are helpful here. In Level I, or "other-validated," intimacy, interaction is governed more by expectations of reciprocity in self-disclosure and a dependence on the partner's response. In contrast, Level II, or "self-validated," intimacy requires more tolerance of anxiety and separateness (cf. "individuation" in chap. 3) and the ability to persevere when validation is not forthcoming.

Thus, time shaping is a critical aspect of intimacy. It may be that for less mature individuals, there is more urgency around scheduling and a greater need for certainty. The time shaping or structuring of such individuals might be characterized by more rigidity in categorizations and ritualizations. Research that combines the microsociological approach of Turner and theories of self-development in intimacy (see Kerr & Bowen, 1988) should yield more insight into the nature of time shaping between intimate partners.

CHAOS

The following two quotes show different sides to chaos in intimate relations:

> The romantic are the daring: not that you have to go skydiving and tongue kiss your partner at twenty thousand feet while you wonder if your parachute is going to open. But you can, and at least once you should, go skinny-dipping together, scream your heads off on a roller coaster, go horseback riding on the beach, or sing songs even though they're out of key. . . . The purpose of seeking such novelty is to wake ourselves up so we can shake off habit and see our partners, too, with fresh eyes. (Betcher, 1987, p. 45)

> Arguments flare when rhythms don't mesh. When we get angry, we tend to go up-tempo to get our point across, almost always making things worse instead of better. We shout, scream, slam doors, stomp away, even hurl things. . . . When this happens, there is no presence. (Rechtschaffen, 1996, p. 115)

Chaos can be understood in one statement: Everything that happens between two people happens because of entropy, disequilibrium, and the general tendency for things to destabilize (i.e., "things fall apart"). Chaos manifests in intimacy in many ways, including lack of control, play, novelty, argument, vulnerability, conflict, and disintegration. And chaos, like the other forces, is a necessary ingredient in the development of transpersonal intimacy. This is most clearly seen in the sense or feeling of vulnerability. In fact, vulnerability—such a key quality of intimate experience (e.g., Register & Henley, 1992)—reflects a deeper understanding that relationships are impermanent.

As we embrace the vulnerability of intimacy we also learn when and with whom to disclose. Amodeo and Amodeo (1986) explained how to cultivate a quality of flexibility when facing the fear of losing control. Opening up is "not all or nothing—absolute control or no control." They added, "Rather than deciding to shield our vulnerability from everyone, and thus close off any possibility of creating a genuine intimate relationship, we may choose to understand the conditions under which we feel safe to begin trusting another. . . . Intimacy may then gradually grow as we monitor the degree to which we feel safe revealing our real selves to another individual" (p. 39).

Thus, we can use form to break with form and enter into chaos. As they immerse themselves in a co-creative or playful activity, such as dancing, partners synchronize and complement each other. In the flow, "right timing" takes over and gives couples a new freedom. But the co-created form may reside in the whole arrangement of the relationship and not only in the dancing.

By the term *chaos*, I also refer to contemporary theory in mathematics and modern physics. This broad view of chaos as a basic quality of natural systems (explored later; see Research Notes on Chaos) contrasts with our limited perceptions or judgments of chaotic events. Out of fear or jealousy, individuals may imagine or catastrophize all sorts of events as reflecting chaos (e.g., betrayal, abandonment, infidelity). Unfortunately, sometimes these delusions act like self-fulfilling prophecies to eventually bring about the imagined turbulence. So whereas misperceptions about perturbation and jealous delusions may actually facilitate chaos, I mean to distinguish between such perceptions and the more ubiquitous and natural forces of chaos that impinge on relationships over time.[2]

Briefly, chaos theory describes how systems necessarily undergo conditions of turbulence and are continually transformed into new orderings or structures. Human relationships are complex systems that are influenced by chaotic laws. A whole book could be devoted to an application of related concepts (e.g., attraction, iteration, trajectories, bifurcation, periodicity; see Briggs & Peat, 1989). I mainly wish to introduce the idea that those forces operating to destabilize relationships, to diminish and to also reestablish intimacy can be understood with the help of chaos and complexity theory.

RESEARCH   REFLECTION   9

NOVELTY & CHAOS

Relationship researchers (Baxter & Simon, 1993) have developed questionnaires that tap relationship differences in the feeling of what they called "novelty." An examination of these items suggests that too much novelty comes close to chaos in meaning. Is there a distinction between novelty that enhances and diminishes intimacy?

1. Our relationship has too many surprises in it.
2. Our relationship isn't predictable enough for our needs right now.

Chaos also brings in the nonlinear dimension of time. Coincidence, disease, accidents, interruptions, postponements, lateness, miscommunication, forgetfulness and mindlessness can steer relationships off of an otherwise linear trajectory. Chaos can also bring novelty, excitement, and even ecstasy into relationships through such phenomena as surprise, unexpected changes in character, or differences and variations in the timing of sexual arousal. Couples harness these positive aspects of chaos through play, creativity, and artistic endeavor (e.g., music, dance). But we more often think of chaos in negative terms: stress, calamity, breakdowns in communication, violence, abuse, and immorality. These positive and negative perturbations make relationships more than just a series of events that unfold in a straight line or development sequence.

It should come as no surprise that research on courtship and early marriage, as well as on relationship dissolution, demonstrates that both the course of true love—or at least a love that results in marriage—and the course of separation do not always run so smoothly. Huston (1994), asking newlyweds to reflect back on their courtship, found that some couples recalled uneven paths toward marriage and others stalled for long periods before resuming. As might be expected, greater disagreement and expressions of anger were associated with more downturns or interruptions in the courtship period.

Another study (Kurdek, 1991) found that newlyweds are often inadequately prepared for the demands of married life. This is so especially when there is premarital pregnancy or when partners have dysfunctional beliefs about marriage that do not embrace chaos (e.g., believing that disagreement is destructive to relationships, partners cannot change). Finally, even breakups evidence signs of chaos. Finding support for the idea that disengagement may be "messy, uncontrolled, and uncertain" (Duck & Miell, 1986), Lee (1984) showed that many, although not all, individuals are confused and ambivalent about termination. Providing retrospective reports of their breakups, individuals do not always follow through on the terms of their separation and so feel hurt, lonely, angry, and confused.

Grasping features of chaos enhance understanding of transpersonal intimacy.[3] In contrast to the social contracts, steady-state routines, and the coordination of relationship structure, chaos accounts for more of the magic and mystery of intimacy. For example, individuals might feel a perfect match occurs when they follow the same eating habits, explore the same interests, or have the same sleep-wake rhythms as their partners. However, such an ideal unison through time is often absent and a perfect *entrainment* of partners' rhythms fails to emerge or gets easily disrupted by outside forces. Entrainment refers to the coordination of two

RESEARCH   REFLECTION   10

RHYTHM ENTRAINMENT: MORNINGNESS & EVENINGNESS

Various researchers have developed questionnaires to assess individual differences in biological rhythms, specifically the degree to which one is more oriented toward morning or evening (e.g., Horne & Ostberg, 1976; Neubauer, 1992). The following example items have been used to distinguish between morning and evening types. Consider whether you and your partner are similar, whether one of you has entrained their schedule to the other, or whether you have converged over time.

- If you had to do two hours of hard physical work—considering your own "feeling best" rhythm, which would you choose: (a) 8:00 AM–10:00 AM, (b) 11:00 AM–1:00 PM, (c) 3:00 PM–5:00 PM, (d) 7:00 PM–9:00 PM
- During the first half-hour after waking in the morning, how tired do you feel? (a) Very tired, (b) Fairly tired, (c) Fairly refreshed, (d) Very refreshed

different rhythms, timetables, schedules, or clocks. When partners are not entrained, which may be for long periods of time during certain phases of a relationship, they are "out of synch" with each other. At this point, partners must be able to suspend their expectations, cut their partner some slack, and realize that conditions are not right for unity. In short, couples may learn to transcend time through adversity.

However, when circumstances flow and intimacy deepens in the process, couples touch the positive aspects of chaos. This may be experienced as some shade or form of ecstasy. They have a sense of joy or gratitude in being able to share life with this guest. That is, out of the stability offered by relational structure over time, partners may experience new levels of joining and unity. Oden (1974) explained:

> An intimate relationship is ordinarily sustained over a period of time with a shared interpersonal memory, yet it may intensify in ecstatic moments of experiencing that render the other times relatively less vivid. The ecstatic moments, nonetheless, depend on the sustained history of personal covenant for their meaning. Thus there is a dialectical relation between duration and intimacy. (p. 11)

Partners feel a timeless quality to their love, an eternity in their joining. When lovers say "forever" or when the bride and groom say "till death do us part," they *transcend time* through unity. In an important sense, newlyweds forge a pact to face, and hopefully thrive on, chaos together. Alternatively, they may be viewing the present form of the relationship in terms of expectation; the present is defined in terms of the future—and not necessarily "timelessness"—because it is in the future that "obligations," "duties," and "commitments" become viable. [4]

RESEARCH NOTES ON CHAOS: DYNAMIC RELATIONAL SYSTEMS AND THE MANDALA PRINCIPLE

Two views of chaos can be integrated in our understanding of time and intimacy. These are the mathematical theory of chaos (e.g., Prigogine & Stengers, 1984), which views dynamic systems as having as much irregularity, discontinuity, and randomness as pattern, structure, or homogeneity; and ideas in Buddhist philosophy that portray the universe as inherently empty, groundless, and impermanent (e.g., Trungpa, 1991). The mathematical theory describes various features and processes of chaos that the scientist of personal relationships may also discern through research. In fact, recent research (reviewed by Ward, 1995) suggests that chaos theory may improve our understanding of how family systems operate. In contrast, Buddhism provides a phenomenological map and meditation instruction for individuals who seek to witness and embrace the chaos of life through spiritual practice.

From the viewpoint of chaos theory, relationships are dynamic systems that exhibit an inherent, organic instability. Relationships are not entities, nor do they have a structure or form per se. Rather, there are only states of relative stability that may be described within certain probabilistic limits. Thus, relationships do not form, are not maintained, and do not break down. Such terms assume there is an enduring structure, that things happen to that structure, or that the structure goes through a transformation. Through the lens of chaos, these terms tend to reify a nonentity. In fact, relationships are unstable, or "dissipative," systems that "iterate" or "bifurcate." We may observe how systems proceed through certain irreversible trajectories or perturbations. Due to their complexity, they are in continuous interaction with the environment. They exhibit self-generated fluctuations. We can never specify that a relationship is in a given state at a given point in time without also acknowledging our uncertainty (this is similar to the "uncertainty principle" in quantum theory). This continuous flux of dynamic systems echoes the idea of "ongoingness" discussed in the first chapter.

Temporality has a different meaning in chaos than in structure. From structure, time is incidental and socially prescribed; it is given to us in the various social forms and rituals that provide a sense of protection, duration, and the illusion of stability. Relationships manifest and unfold across occasions, situations, or incidents. In contrast, chaos views time as integral or built into the system; time is a fundamental operator that creates the age and the continuity of the system. As they age, relationships are attracted to various states and continuously transition in and out of them. Such an attraction is actually driven by time. These two distinct views of time, as integral and as incidental, also differ from the classic scientific or Newtonian view, where time was viewed as an external parameter or metric used to observe and measure a system.

> *When relationships get chaotic or "messy" it may be time to transcend our limited ego viewpoint and gain insight into the whole system.*

From the view of chaos, relationship structuring (the social rules, guidelines, mores, roles, ceremonies, rituals) is functional only up to a point. Couples use such social functions to navigate through their life cycle and their own aging, but these very functions may show chaotic tendencies. Eventually, each unit system (i.e., a couple), as well as the entire social system (i.e., tradition or institution), is vulnerable to the laws of dissipation, entropy, and randomness (see Adams, 1975). Put another way, human social systems may be inherently nomadic and driven by turbulence. It is through consciousness, effort, cooperation, and forethought (i.e., time shaping) that chaos does not lead to violence, malignant aggression and domination-subordination relationships (see Eisler, 1987; Fromm, 1976).

Relationship Development May Be Characterized by Chaos Theory. Three important concepts from chaos theory—"attractors," "bifurcations," and "iterations"—may be applied to relationships. Attractors are mathematical functions used to describe how systems are drawn to certain states rather than others. "Point," or "static," attractors govern systems in relative equilibrium. Relationships may get off balance for periods of time, but they tend to return to some balance or equilibrium. Theories that describe relationships as sequential exchanges or as a series of interactions (e.g., Berscheid, 1983, 1985; Scanzoni, 1979) tend to assume the existence of "static" attractors.

Periodic attractors govern systems that go through periods of stability and instability, or that oscillate back and forth between various states. Relationship theories that describe dialectical cycles of relationship development (e.g., Altman, Vinsel, & Brown, 1981; Baxter, 1988)—where couples experience periods of openness and closedness, periods of routine, and periods of novelty—assume "periodic" attractors as fundamental.

Finally, many systems are characterized by disequilibrium (i.e., systems that change suddenly and transform into a new system). These are governed by "chaotic" or "strange" attractors. There is no explicit theory of relationship change that assumes the existence of such attractors (although see McCall, 1988; Vallacher & Nowak, 1994). The model developed in the previous chapters of this book attempts to show how relationships evolve in multiple temporal contexts and that disequilibrium as well as stasis and oscillation can all emerge in the relational system.

As a system changes over time, we can observe critical transition points in its history; the rapid fluctuations taking place may amplify in number to a point where the whole system has to adapt a new mode of functioning. These points of transition are called "bifurcations," as the system takes a path or branch that cannot be predicted. As a system "bifurcates," it becomes increasingly complex and difficult to measure in a single situation. Moreover, small or subtle changes that exist at an earlier point in the history of a system may become more significant and lead to an unpredictable bifurcation later on. In fact, research shows that when couples get locked into a certain cycle of miscommunication, there comes a "point of no return." The system has, so to speak, "bifurcated" to the point where marital therapy is of little help to such couples (Gottman, 1994a, 1994b).

Mathematically, iteration is "a computational procedure in which replication of a cycle of operations produces results which approximate the desired result more and more closely" (*Webster's Ninth New Collegiate Dictionary*). Such cycling is a central quality of dynamic living systems. Because living systems are very sensitive to initial and external conditions, certain states become more pronounced with each cycle and eventually produce a sudden or unpredictable shift. Different systems display different sensitivities to the effects of iterations. Vulnerability is not something that resides within the relationship structure, per se, but in how the state of the system is sensitive to changing external conditions.

Other authors have suggested that chaos theory may apply to the study of social systems (see Eisler, 1987; Ward, 1995). Relationships may be viewed as systems that sometimes are governed by "static" attractors, and sometimes by "periodic" and "chaotic" attractors. They are always in some cycle of iteration and are attracted to some bifurcation point. Viewed in this way, relationships are not strictly reified along some path of development or progress; they are not merely the sum total of interaction sequences. They are whole, dynamic systems exhibiting an ongoing tendency toward self-transformation.

The Mandala Principle: Orderly Chaos. The mathematical view of chaos differs from the view held by Trungpa (1991), who described the Mandala principle in Buddhist philosophy. This principle should be distinguished from discussions of the figural mandala as presented in religious iconography or Jungian psychology. As an icon or symbol, the mandala is a schematized representation of the cosmos, usually represented as a "concentric configuration of geometric shapes each of which contains an image or attribute of a deity" (*Random House Webster's College Dictionary*, 1992). For Carl Jung, the mandala was a symbol representing the effort toward individuation and self-transcendence, as discussed in the previous chapter. Figure 4.1 is a sort of mandala.

As a principle in Buddhist cosmology, the mandala represents orderly chaos and the ability to work with the confusion, ignorance, and suffering we experience in our lives. Because of our ignorance—our lack of intimacy with ourselves—we create a self-existing circle of pain and suffering. The mandala gives us a perspective on this circle and teaches us that all states of confusion are "eminently workable." For in Buddhism, enlightenment is actually born out of confusion. Trungpa (1991) explained:

> The word *mandala* literally means "association," "society." The Tibetan word for mandala is *kyilkhor, kyil* means "center," *khor* means "fringe," "gestalt," "area around." It is a way of looking at situations in terms of relativity: if that exists, this exists; if this exists, that exists. Things exist interdependently, and that interdependent existence of things happens in the fashion of orderly chaos. (p. 15)

Trungpa said that you cannot go through life or through relationships without getting hurt. You cannot have a plan or manual that describes how to respond in every possible situation that might come up in an evolving and dynamic relationship. In fact, chaos may come from an egoistic having to have, or to maintain, a specific viewpoint or position. Relationships are organic; chaos reminds us about this organic nature of intimacy.

In Buddhism, the capacity to embrace the chaos and the structure, the ability to take the mandala perspective, is one way of describing a transcendent or transpersonal experience. One possesses an ability to be present to many events happening at once and a capacity to embrace multiple temporal contexts. According to Trungpa (1991):

> The point is that one sees the totality, the whole area. One begins to have an extraordinary panoramic vision with no boundaries. . . . It is an entirely new approach to time and space. You can approach time because it is timeless; you can approach space because it is spaceless. There is a direction because there are no directions at the same time. This opens up tremendous possibilities of another way of looking at the whole thing. At the same time of course, there's no reference point, therefore you can't keep track of it. Wanting to keep track of it would be comparable to wanting to attend one's own funeral. (p. 71)

STRUCTURE (FORM)

> Form is not seen as the result of some central plan or program. . . . Rather, form is constructed in the process of acting under specific task demands. The many contributing elements of a system exert constraints upon one another under these circumstances, markedly reducing the degrees of freedom for these elements and resulting in the system self-organizing into one or a few recognizable behavioral forms. (Eckerman, 1993, p. 343)

> Families live on the cusp between the internal time needs associated with intimacy and rejuvenation and the unrelenting external forces of a sociotemporal order that demands compliance and diligent attentiveness. . . . In light of the dramatic increases in the number of women and teenage children in the paid workforce, there appears to be an increasing imbalance between the family's ability to control time and the imposed schedules of a variety of institutions. (Daly, 1996, p. 142).

Taken together, the above two quotes point to the fact that relational forms are not self-generated as much as they emerge from an interaction between couples' own actions, from society, and from the past. Over time, as they make agreements, address problems, coordinate schedules, and settle into routines, couples inject some security and organization into their relationship. Their time shaping, whether in spite of or because of chaos, gives rise to some relationship form. Actually, their relationship structure is not entirely under their direct control. Societal (work/organizational, sex-role, religious or legal) conventions (specific task demands) dictate or restrict when and how they become intimate. As the quote by Daly above suggests, these dictates have increased to the point of diminished time for intimacy. In addition to their actions and societal convention, couples inherit patterns of relating from previous generations, and genetic or sociobiological factors influence mate selection and commitment. Structure also refers to the whole range of intimate behavior, from the structure analyzable in communication sequences (e.g., postural changes, topic shifting, nonverbal cueing; see Scheflen, 1973) to the structure provided by kinship systems in different cultures (see Adams, 1975).

There are prescriptive tendencies (rituals) in society for certain relationship structures and sequences to be more common than others. Conjugal forms develop (as institutions) to provide some supportive vehicle through which partners can sustain intimacy, raise children, and presumably live more comfortable lives. Until recently, heterosexual monogamy with an associated marriage contract served as the primary norm of commitment in Western culture (Murray, 1994). With increased numbers of stepfamilies, premarital pregnancies, cohabitation without marriage, and greater acceptance of alternative relationship or family structures (e.g., homosexuality, single parents by choice), this marital norm is changing. Regardless of their conformity to or deviation from the marital norm, their decision to continue through time indicates that couples have assumed some generic form of closeness (in scientific language, "a close relationship situation," Scanzoni, 1987).

Thus, structure plays the counterpoint to chaos and refers to those tendencies—contractual, conventional or otherwise—toward continuity (and ultimately toward permanence) that couples either inherit or innovate. The inheritance comes from many places and occasions. Examples include traditions (e.g., marrying only by class or race, religious rituals in the marriage ceremony), annual or calendrical rituals (e.g., getting engaged on Valentine's Day), the historical epoch (e.g., less restraint due to sexual liberation the 1960s), the cultural milieu (e.g., greater caution due to "sexual harassment" in the 1990s), and socialization and sex role learning (e.g., man as bread winner). And as they grow through adolescence, potential partners face a barrage of information about how to conduct their commitments: from romantic imagery in popular songs, movies, and literature, to religious dictates and sex education in the public schools.

> *The form that any relationship takes keeps changing shape; yet, over time each relation has a signature—recognizable & distinct from others.*

The innovation of structure may occur in several ways: through the force of time shaping and the associated acts of *scheduling* and *routines* (e.g., prenuptial agreements, engagement dates, and marriage arrangements) or through nurturing conditions and the associated sensitivity to *transition* and *timing*. These innovations may be discerned in two disparate phenomena in the research literature: the Romeo and Juliet effect and the transition to parenthood.

Research on the *Romeo and Juliet effect* (Driscoll, Davis, & Lipetz, 1972) describes those couples who reported increases in romantic love when their parents interfered with their dating. However, after marriage, parental interference had no influence on romantic love. For those who remained unmarried, decreases in parental interference were actually associated with declines in romantic love. Thus, for some young couples, attraction may be primarily due to their being threatened by parents. Importantly, there may be a specific window of time where this rebellion or reactance effect may hold. Unless they *schedule* to marry within this window, young lovers may miss their *timing* for staying in love until marriage. This phenomenon is but one example of what may be a "sensitive period," or critical transition point in the development of a relational system (cf. Bornstein, 1989).

Another such phenomenon is the transition to parenthood. Most research on families suggests that the arrival of the first child is the single greatest disrupter and, as such, has the most enduring effect on relationship structure. For example, research shows that some of the "inevitable" perturbations in a new parent's schedule may be mitigated if partners can reschedule time to accommodate intimacy in new ways (e.g., Worthington, Buston, & Hammonds, 1989). Other research shows that couples may schedule their pregnancy such that the child provides a barrier to marital perturbation (e.g., Morgan & Rindfuss, 1985). Clearly, there are ways of adapting new *routines* so that couples can be more sensitive to this first-child *transition*.

These examples highlight the inherent instability and developmental quality of structure, and that relational form must always be viewed in context of other forces. This instability is an intrinsic feature of the ongoingness of intimacy, which can be discerned (in time I see) through an understanding of the forces outlined here. Hopefully, couples' sensitivity to these forces (nurturing conditions), their ability to thrive on chaos, their skills at time management, and an appreciation for continuity (structure) will make them happy witnesses to what life, with all its changes, has to offer (in time mates see).

RESEARCH NOTES ON RELATIONSHIP FORMS AND STRUCTURES: DISCERNING PATTERNS

There are many ways of studying and approaching relationship structure. We know more about the various forms and structures that relationships take than about any of the other temporal forces described here. Social scientists have studied the norms and rules individuals use to construct and maintain a relationship (e.g., Bilmes, 1986) and have theorized about the nature of social structure (Blau, 1975). The structure of families has been analyzed in detail and from various perspectives. To name a few, there are historical studies (e.g., Demos & Boocock, 1978), analyses of role differentiation (e.g., Nye, 1976), and sex role patterns (e.g., Stoll, 1974). The study of structuralism—analysis of an underlying order to society—claims that these social structures operate independently of our consciousness of them (Lévi-Strauss, 1963; Saussure, 1959). Others claim that we create structure through our discourse, the mutual interpretation of social rules and sanctions (e.g., Bilmes, 1986). Thus, social structure has been studied in sociological theory, in research on the family, and as a way in which humans create order in their world.

Social scientists have used a variety of terms to describe and explain the forms that relationships and specific interactions may take. These include social rules, norms, roles, institutions, and rituals. Research has examined everything from topic control in conversation (Lennard & Bernstein, 1969), to body movements in interaction (Birdwhistell, 1970), to genetic factors that constrain kinship selection in certain cultures (Ballonoff, 1974). Thus, there is a structure or pattern that can be discerned in moment-to-moment interaction, as there is a pattern of mate selection dictated by kinship ties in many cultures. These may seem like disparate areas of study, but they each deal with the ways in which relationships possess or come to possess form.

Structure as Highly Patterned Sequences of Interaction. Implicit in all these approaches is the idea that most relationships either have or develop certain patterns of regular interaction. Throughout any given period of history and in any given culture, a society will have numerous forms of relationships in which intimacy may develop: marriage (husband-wife), friends, siblings, relatives, master-slave, kinsman-kinswoman, worker-employer, student-teacher, the prostitute and the partner. Relationship structure refers to highly patterned sequences of behavior that have any of several functions. These sequences serve as a norm or guideline due to regularity or frequency of occurrence within a population, subpopulation, group, clique, or a set of roles. Such sequences are intelligible and provide a frame or meaning with which to engage in social discourse (see Bilmes, 1986).

Structure as Dependent on Rules. One main way in which we create, recognize, and change structure is through convention or rules of conduct (e.g., contracts, agreements; cf. "normatization," Turner, 1988). Rules imply a moral code of behavior, but they are known (and followed) as rules because of how they are *interpreted* in light of the presence or absence of the subsequent sanctions. Bilmes (1986) argued that rules are rules because they have an intrinsic meaning that does not change from one context to another. Of course, new rules may develop or proliferate in a culture (e.g., increased cohabitation in contemporary society). Individuals may prefer lifestyles that are seen as deviant from tradition or certain norms (e.g., homosexuality). Also, rules may also be fuzzy or not clearly understood and they may be broken from time to time. These variations, however, are mutations in form; they can be studied and understood in and of themselves and are not merely the results of chaos and randomness. The breakdown or fuzziness of rules does not necessarily imply the operation of chaos. All societies are characterized by relational forms that may be labeled deviant when seen from the perspective of another culture.

Historical/Cultural Variations in Sexual Relationships. For example, Bullough (1976; also see Kohler, 1975) reviews anthropological and historical data to show how the availability and societal regulation (e.g., through religion) of sexual partners has led to widely distinctive types of mating routines and rituals (homosexuality, prostitution, polygamy, monogamy) throughout history and in different cultures. His work is interesting for the magnitude of diversity in sexual relations described. These range from moral codes regarding adultery in the Inca empire to the informal sexual relations developing between hoboes and young boys in the United States in the 1890s, to the more contemporary development of nudism in the Western World (also see "Love Lines" pp. 194-202 in chap. 6). When considering the rich diversity of form throughout history and culture, it is difficult to prescribe any particular one as ideal, although many argue that marriage is essentially the most functional for the species.

Is Marriage the Most Viable Form? Whereas it remains an empirical question whether intimacy can be experienced to the same extent in all of these forms, anthropological evidence suggests that marriage supporting children throughout the life cycle is essential for providing the basis in which secure social attachments can flourish. Reviewing cross-cultural evidence, anthropologist Murray (1994) believed that all cultures that survive are built on marriage; he viewed the increasing rates of illegitimacy (children born out of wedlock) in the United States as jeopardizing its future.

Because marriage has been the most common or conventional form of intimate relationship, many authors have projected their own interpretation of its purpose as a structure in society. It is interesting to contrast views from different authors to show how such views may be influenced by the era in which they write. At the turn of this century, one author (who purports to give a scientific view of "A History of Matrimonial Institutions") revealed his own subjective valuation of eugenics, or the improvement of human qualities through control of breeding: "Everywhere men and women are marrying in utter contempt of the way of science. Domestic animals are literally better bred than human beings. . . . Under the plea of "romantic love" we blindly yield to sexual attraction in choosing our mates, selfishly ignoring the welfare of the race" (Howard, 1904/1964, p. 258).

Contrast this with those writing during the period of sexual liberation in the 1960s and 1970s. Describing the "new intimacy" of "open-ended marriage," Mazur (1973) encouraged the reader to march to the tune of a different drummer, proclaiming "relational innovators are constantly accosted with negative terms such as promiscuity, adultery, and infidelity" (p. 13). He regarded "traditional monogamy, with its rigid requirement for exclusive devotion and affection . . . to be a culturally approved mass neurosis" (p. 12). By contrasting these two views of marriage, we can see how strong individual values about relationship form can depend on the ethos of the contemporary culture. The science of eugenics was apparently popular to some at the turn of the century as free sex was popular to some in the 1960s. It remains to be seen whether the anthropological viewpoint of "illegitimacy" taken by Murray will be seen as reflecting the current ethos of our apparently fragmenting culture.

Recent Investigations. Most recently, the scientific investigation of relationship forms has been in areas relevant to more current changes in our society. This includes cohabitation (e.g., Bumpass & Sweet, 1991; Teachman & Polonko, 1990; Thomson & Colella, 1992), gay and lesbian relationships (Kurdek, 1993), changes in sex-role behaviors, and the increased formation of step-families (e.g., Thomson, McLanahan, & Curtin, 1992). This research helps to show how different forms of relationship are worthy of study in their own right and that rules that apply to marriage relationships may or may not apply to these different forms. Scanzoni (1987) argued for researchers to adapt a more tolerant view of families that does not adhere to the traditional marital form.

Relationship Stage as Structure. Structure is particularly relevant to our investigation of time because we mostly experience structure through the different stages of a relationship. That is, relationships apparently transform in a qualitative manner such that partners experience a new sense of commitment at each stage. Partners often know—or at least it matters to them and they take the time to negotiate—whether they have moved from casual to serious dating, to engagement to marriage. Importantly, relationship stage may be more relevant for a couple than the mere duration.

For example, Stanley and Markman (1992) distinguished between different types of commitment in their research with couples. Personal dedication (e.g., a willingness to sacrifice, desire for permanence, viewing the relationship as a team) differs from constraint commitment (e.g., investment of possessions/money, pressure from family/friends, difficulty of termination), with the latter relating more to structural aspects of the relationship. The researchers found that the stage of the relationship (e.g., dating, engaged, married with children) was a better predictor of constraint commitment than was the time the couple was together.

CONCLUSION

As a process, intimacy is hard to analyze into separate bits. This chapter has attempted to describe those basic temporal forces that intimate couples inevitably experience and sometimes harness (e.g., chaos). I have tried to delineate relationships (links in Fig. 4.1) between these forces, and to show how partner interaction mediates these relationships. I am suggesting that these fundamental forces can be touched through intimate relationships, and that—in some existential sense—this is the purpose of intimacy.

Thus, the deepest aspects of the intimate experience are infused with forces from nature. These forces are glimpsed in the natural phases that shape the intimate relationship. For example, through vulnerability we embrace chaos, through acceptance and the sense of preciousness we embrace nurturing conditions, through ordinary routines we embrace structure, and through our responsiveness to disruption we act. The next chapter revisits these forces as they operate in the stories or scripts we create about our relationships.

1. **Temporal forces: Finding the right name.** I hesitate to use the word "forces" for several reasons. The term *force* often implies an external dynamic or potential that exerts strength and can possibly overwhelm us. Of course, this may be true with each of the four points discussed here (the auspiciousness of "just the right conditions," the looming presence of deadlines or the points of major decision—"no turning back," the overwhelming periods of chaos, and feeling stifled and stuck by too much structure). But these forces do not have to manifest in such a dramatic fashion. They are more like ways of experiencing time—phenomenological quadrants—than physical operations.

Alternatively, these points may be seen as temporal tendencies that may or may not be external to the relationship. Time—whether it manifests in nurturance, action, chaos, or structure—is neither external or internal; couples manifest these qualities through their intimacy and their intimacy deepens by how they meet these points as forces. I like the phrase "temporal radiants" to capture the illuminating and circular–concentric quality of time. That is, each of the four points can illuminate intimacy and help couples to center their attention on what is happening at any give point in time. The four points have effects that ripple out, like pebbles in a pool, and interlace with each other. I decide to use force because it is the more dramatic metaphor that (I am guessing) is more understandable.

2. **Perspectives on perturbation and disruption.** The term *perturbation* has a specific meaning in chaos theory. In physical systems it refers to a change that takes place when the system is destabilized by some nonsystem disturbance in the environment (e.g., Vallacher & Nowak, 1994). Whether this destabilization is real versus imagined or projected is a significant fact in the growth and dissolution of a relationship. I think that what we often believe to be a "disruption" (i.e., from a planned action, an interruption, or expected sequence or script) is, from a larger perspective, a perturbation in an otherwise relatively stable system. Similarly, the concept of "dissipation" in chaos theory may be interpreted, at one point in time, as "dissolution" or a breakup in a relationship. But, as the course of relationships can be chaotic, breakups may or may not last. What we thought was an ending may have just been a dissipative flourish in the system. Thus, as with other terms used for the eight functions described in this chapter (e.g., rhythm entrainment), I intend to point readers in the direction of thinking about the big picture rather than formulating a precise operation. From the egoistic point of view of any one individual (time shaper) a chaotic event (perturbation) is seen as a disruption. From the point of view of yüan, the same chaotic event may reveal the opportunity to transcend.

3. **Chaos and conflict: A Research example.** Couples may be happier when they believe that conflict or disagreements are part and parcel of their time together. Crohan (1992), in a longitudinal study of newlyweds, asked 282 couples if they agreed with the following statements: (a) disagreements can always be settled if you just talk about them, (b) couples should try to avoid disagreements, and (c) disagreements in a marriage are healthy. Those couples who had a healthy attitude toward conflict (e.g., did not avoid it) were happier when assessed both within their first and later in their third year of marriage.

Crohan commented that "research shows that conflicts in marriage can serve potentially valuable functions, such as promoting relationship satisfaction and stability, increasing partners' understanding of each other and building up the couple's feelings of intimacy and trust in being able to handle the problems that arise in their relationship (Braiker & Kelley, 1979)" (Crohan, 1992, pp. 99-100). In line with the view of chaos presented here, conflict and perturbation is an integral part of the temporal portrait that partners paint together. Apparently, those who can accept this can shape their time together in ways that benefit their well-being.

4. **Types of timelessness.** Fraser (1975) described two types of timelessness that are "normally mixed, even in the most commonly available ecstasy, that of sexual union" (p. 308). These first he labeled the "ecstasy of the dance," in which individuals lose

themselves through continuous, rhythmic change; where there is an emphasis on continual becoming and a de-emphasis on permanence. The second, the "ecstasy of the forest," gives individuals a sense of awe or beauty, with an emphasis on permanence and perpetual Being (see chap. 6 on "process and sequence").

Fraser postulated an instinctual drive to seek both forms of timelessness. The drive to identify with permanence—"We instinctively seek permanent relationships and we are fulfilled when we believe we have identified them"—and the drive to seek the unpredictable, the discontinuous, the unexpected. Perhaps the act of marriage, as a social ritual practiced for many centuries, implicitly recognizes this double desire. Newlyweds embrace the dance knowing that, if they are also going to make it through the forest, they had better square up their obligations.

Explanatory processes are triggered when a schema that has worked well in the past to understand events in a relationship no longer works easily. Then *a much wider range of knowledge* must be scanned to come up with a more adequate explanation. That explanation, then, can be used to update, modify or sometimes replace the original schema. . . . We have learned from our data that relational schemas are far from static. (Planalp & Rivers, 1996, pp. 318–319; italics added)

As appealing as it might seem to an insecurely attached person to have a relationship with an unconditionally loving God, it might be difficult for someone holding negative mental models of attachment figures to believe that such a relationship is possible. Instead, one is most likely to have a profound, powerful religious experience if one holds a combination of negative self-model and positive model of others—namely, those with a preoccupied (anxious/ambivalent) attachment style. (Kirkpatrick, 1997, p. 961)

I haven't got time for the pain, not since I've known you.
—Carly Simon & Jacob Brackman (lyrics from the song "Haven't Got Time for the Pain")

THOUGHTS ON A NEW SCIENCE

- That we understand the purpose and meaning of our feelings of separateness, pain, and longing.

- That we have a clear perception of our own schemas and learn that these are reflections of a deeper path to wisdom.

- That all the stories we have ever known—of god, of love and of longing—are reflections of this deeper path.

- That science—as a study of these reflections—reveals the codes and the sequences for unraveling the mystery of our emotional pain and liberation.

5

Time, Addiction, and Intimacy:

Scripts, Archescripts, & Holoscripts[*]

MODEL 4

| Scripts | | Archescripts | Holoscript |

Many who suffer the pitfalls of addictive lifestyles have fallen into dysfunctional patterns while seeking a higher, more creative and meaningful way to relate in this mundane world. They often tell me that they were born feeling like strangers in a strange land, and have lived with a deep sense of isolation. . . These people are more interested in seeking a way out or back to that "other place" where they truly feel at home than bothering to try to make it here in this world. And they may choose addictive relationships, sex, chemical highs, overeating, causes, or gurus to fill the empty spaces within their hearts, the gaps of unfulfillment. They will give their power away to almost anyone or anything; so desperate are they to find that something or someone to guide them home. (Small, 1991, p. 37)

UP UNTIL now, I have described a somewhat ideal state of affairs. Many people do not experience all, if any, of the forms of intimacy described earlier. Few spend the time to develop qualities of presence and flow. Life seems to run smoothly without any special awareness of temporal qualities (e.g., routine, pacing) and the deep experience of intimacy may be rare. Indeed, in their review of research on intimacy, Berscheid and Reis (1998) concluded: ". . .most relationships never become highly intimate, even when the participants are initially attracted to each other and are not particularly averse to intimacy" (p. 225). Relationships have their "dark sides" of jealousy, envy, sexual coercion, violence, and obsessive love (see Cupach & Spitzberg, 1994, for research on these phenomena). So, the current view of intimacy and wholeness may be just

---

* An earlier version of this chapter was presented at the 1993 International Association of Transactional Analysis (Minneapolis, MN).

too idealistic. I have presented abstract theory rather than concrete reality. Relationships more often stumble along than flow, and individuals keep lowering their expectations about what their marriage or relationships should be. They may crave too much closeness (insecurity, dependency, loneliness, depression) or not crave it enough (avoidance, spiritual emptiness, alienation, social anxiety, narcissism).

This chapter addresses some of these blocks to intimacy, or at least places them in the context of transpersonal intimacy. Drawing from a broad range of ideas, I hope to show that many have touched on the relations between time, intimacy, and spirituality. In particular, this chapter attempts to integrate different theories of personality and personal growth; for example, transactional analysis (e.g., Berne, 1964, 1976) and Jungian archetypal theory (e.g., Jung, 1972; and more recent adaptations in Estés, 1992; Moore, 1994). These theories indicate that deeper psychic and metaphysical scripts inform our ways—and our difficulties—of loving. Paradoxically, blocks to intimacy actually contain ingredients for discovering intimacy. In the realm of intrapersonal intimacy, loneliness can be a gateway into the solitude necessary for a deeper intrapersonal intimacy (Malone & Malone, 1987), and depression can bring one to search and care for their soul (Moore, 1991).

Blocks to Interpersonal Intimacy:
Relationship Addiction and Insecure Attachment

One roadblock to interpersonal intimacy (like loneliness or depression) is addiction; namely, the addictions alternatively described as relationship, romance, sex addiction, codependence, or love addiction (cf. "merger" or "fusion," Prager, 1991). The following discussion uses the term addiction to refer to a broad set of internal psychological barriers to interpersonal intimacy. Importantly, there are strong parallels between interpersonal addiction and the well-researched construct of insecure attachment styles (Hazan & Shaver, 1987; and review by Berscheid & Reis, 1998; pp. 218–220).[1] The latter refers to dispositional tendencies to avoid or experience anxiety and ambivalence in close relationships.

Although relationship addiction has received attention in the popular literature for the past decade, social scientists have only recently examined the phenomena more closely (e.g., Fuller & Warner, 2000; Le Poire, Hallett, & Giles, 1998). Thus, like the term *intimacy*, these addictions have not always been clearly or, at least operationally, defined. Lyon and Greenberg (1991) list symptoms from their review of the literature on co-dependence:

"(a) intense and unstable interpersonal relationships, (b) inability to tolerate being alone, accompanied by frantic efforts to avoid being alone, (c) chronic feelings of boredom and emptiness, (d) subordinating one's own needs to those of the person with whom one is involved, (e) overwhelming desire for acceptance and affection, (f) external referencing, (g) dishonesty and denial, and (h) low self-worth"

There is much controversy over whether the concept of co-dependence is useful (Kaminer, 1992; Katz & Liu, 1991). For example, Schaef (1989) argues for clearer distinctions between sexual, romance, and relationship addictions and the recovery literature actually uses different tools for sexual (see *Hope and Recovery*, 1987), and relationship addiction (Augustine Fellowship, 1986). Schaef neatly summarized the differences between the three types of "love" addictions: "Sexual addicts 'come on,' romance addicts 'move on,' and relationship addicts 'hang on' " (p. 101). Others claim "love is an ideal vehicle for addiction because it can so exclusively claim a person's consciousness" (Peele & Brodsky, 1975, p. 25). Whether one agrees with these ideas, it is difficult to be intimate with oneself, with another person or with some transcendent power if an individual experiences but a few of the eight symptoms listed by Lyon and Greenberg (1991). My point here is that, together, the symptoms represent a syndrome of nonintimacy.

From a transpersonal perspective, addictions represent spiritual longings. Relationship addicts feel an emptiness that they hope others will fill. Small (1991) related that many of her clients with addiction issues have had mystical experiences since childhood. She viewed addiction as a thwarted attempt to regain those spiritual highs by looking to outside sources rather than into oneself (also see discussion of attachment in Almaas, 1987).[2] In fact, research by Kirkpatrick (1997, 1998) suggests that God can become a substitute attachment figure for individuals who have insecure (anxious and avoidant) attachment styles. Kirkpatrick and Shaver (1990) found that individuals who reported anxious attachment patterns with their mothers (in childhood) also reported higher rates of religious conversion in adulthood than others. These findings suggest that we are deeply motivated to feel connected and whole in our relation to the world and others. When our internal schemas and scripts tell us that we are not whole, we find haven in the image of a loving God.

RESEARCH	REFLECTION	11

ATTACHMENT TO GOD

Kirkpatrick (1997, 1998) has studied the relationship between attachment styles (Hazan & Shaver, 1987; Bartholomew & Horowitz, 1991) and images of God (Benson & Spilka, 1973) (see RESEARCH REFLECTION 6, p. 85). The following items are adaptations of some of these measures.

Attachment Style	*Image of God*
1. I am comfortable getting close to others and don't worry about being alone. (Secure)	1. God (or a higher power) is forgiving, loving, and accepting. (Loving God)
2. I am uncomfortable getting close to others and worry about being rejected or abandoned. (Insecure)	2. God (or my higher power) is distant and unavailable. (Distant God)

Chapter Premises. Three major premises of this chapter are:

1. Relationship addiction entails the compulsive use of certain scripts about how to behave with others and how others should behave.
2. Transpersonal insights or openness to transpersonal intimacy increases the capacity to revise or rewrite these habitual scripts.
3. Addictive tendencies center on attachment to certain scripts, whereas transpersonal (healthy, spiritual) tendencies center on a willingness to participate in a larger story (transcend scripts).

Recall from chapter 2 that interpersonal intimacy requires more than mere tran*script*ion in text. If we just act from our own subjective scripts, where we project our own images (transcribe) without the dialogue of translation or transaction, than we do not enter the real-time, face-to-face, give and take necessary for an intimate meeting. Relationship addicts have difficulty in moving beyond transcription. They seek out others so they can obtain or secure some resource from them (e.g., sex, romance, affection, love, praise, power, time) as a way to fill up some felt emptiness. They seek to enforce routines that their partner will follow and "procure" these resources. Addicts collude; they do not want and cannot accept changes in the relationship because these threaten their "supply or stash." They cannot distinguish between love and need (see Merton, 1985). Again, research supports these ideas. A recent study shows that reports of more openness to experience correlates positively with secure attachment and negatively with anxious or avoidant attachment (Mickelson, Kessler, & Shaver, 1997).

ADDICTIVE SCRIPTS, TIME, AND INNER WORK

By definition, scripts entail some potential sequence of actions that unfold when activated by interpersonal circumstances or conditions. Scripts have a special relationship to time in that they provide a method for introducing order into the flow of social occasions. They also are based in the past. In addiction, the order provided by scripts and the attachment to the past itself becomes more important than the flow and spontaneity of meeting another—that is, relationship addicts or insecurely attached individuals try to control intimacy. Insecurely attached persons are less open to changing their views of their partner than are securely attached persons (Mikulincer & Arad, 1999). Recovery from addiction (or becoming more secure) is a process in which addicts restructure (re-script) a relatively fixed (compulsive, habitual) and linear repertoire of scripts so as to become more flexible (improvisational, spontaneous) and intimate in their close relationships.

This chapter presents a model of intimacy as it relates to scripted time and hopes to show that individuals can become more intimate as they "work on" and become aware of their internal scripts. In some ways, this chapter is a response to the recent overemphasis on cognitive and perceptual processes in close relationship research (see Fletcher & Fitness, 1996). It attempts to integrate the academic construct of cognitive scripts (e.g., M. W. Baldwin, 1995) with the transpersonal theme outlined in earlier chapters and the popular literature on relationship improvement (e.g., Gray, 1992; Hendrix, 1992).

The model proposed here suggests that, as a process, intimacy occurs when two or more individuals: (a) recognize, communicate, and change their own addictive scripts—in short, they are willing to reveal character flaws or darker, more hidden aspects of their selves; or (b) embrace how they unconsciously and mindlessly project latent scripts onto each other (archescript)—in short, they learn more about these hidden parts of their being and find a deep commonality (similarity or complementarity) to these parts. Whereas scripts leave us stuck in the past, archescripts are a resource of past wisdom. The process of revealing wisdom to oneself and another leads partners to (c) recognize and feel that, in time, they are part of a shared holistic reality—via the self, relationship, family, community, and the universe—often only dimly perceived (holoscript).

RELATIONSHIPS IN TIME:
DEFINING SCRIPTS, ARCHESCRIPTS, HOLOSCRIPTS

> People often feel reluctant to get quiet and move into the present moment for fear that unexpressed emotions, old and new, may arise. At some level, they recognize that there is an emotional price to be paid for slowing down long enough to experience the feelings they have been trying to outrace. (Erkel, 1995, p. 36)

In relationships, we follow certain courses of action according to: (a) the scripts we learn from society, our parents and our personal history, (b) the archescripts, inherited from the common history of male-female relationships, that shape personal scripts, and (c) the holoscript, or most universal script, that guides the interrelationship of all things. Table 5.1 briefly sketches some distinctions between scripts, archescripts, and holoscript.

TABLE 5.1

SOME DISTINCTIONS BETWEEN SCRIPTS, ARCHESCRIPT, AND HOLOSCRIPT

Script	Concrete	Learned	Individual	Linear	Stuck in past
Archescript	↑ ↓	Innate	Individual is Universal	Multilinear	Wisdom from past
Holoscript	Abstract	Meta-physical	Universal in Everything	Omnilinear	Past woven with present and future

Definitions. Of the three, *script* is the most consciously accessible; it is widely used in common vernacular even outside the field of psychology. Some individuals in recovery and psychotherapy talk about changing "the tapes in my head" and use affirmations (e.g., "I am loved and I am lovable"), or positive self-talk to override scripts they feel they learned from their parents. The term *archescript* is a variation on Jung's archetype (1972), which he defined as the latent images or templates that reside in the collective unconscious of humanity. These archetypes serve to organize and shape our personal experience of the world and our own unconscious. In contrast to archetype, with its emphasis on category or structure, I use arche*script* to emphasize the flux, process, and more changeable aspects of unconscious relationship. This archescript serves as a deep grammar for our more conscious scripts and, as such, we project onto our actual relationships.

Finally, holoscript is an adaptation of Bohm's (1980) metaphysical term *holomovement,* which he defined as the undivided wholeness or totality of the universe through which all specific manifestations are "enfolded" and "unfolded" (see Quality 3, in chap. 2). For Bohm, every particular aspect of the universe contains within it some representation of the whole universe; that is, the whole universe is collapsed or enfolded within that piece. Conversely, when we become aware of the wholeness represented in a fragment of the universe, the universe then unfolds before us. That is, like a hologram, "the form and structure of the entire object may be said to be *enfolded* within each region of the photographic record. When one shines light on any region, this form and structure are then *unfolded* to give a recognizable image of the whole object once again" (Bohm, 1980, p. 177). Bohm used holo*movement* to emphasize the dynamic and continuous quality of interactions between regions that only appear autonomous. This concept explains that—at both the macro or universal and the micro or particulate level—everything is dynamically related to everything else. I use the term holo*script* to refer to stories about universal intimacy or a living cosmology that connects all living and inanimate aspects of existence. As such, the universe is a feeling universe (cf. "the Gaia hypothesis," Barlow, 1997).[3]

Such cosmologies are reflected in the wisdom of ancient or native cultures (Amerindian, Aboriginal, Egyptian) that reveal a strong and sustaining connection to the earth. In modern times, the ideas are reflected in the process philosophy of Whitehead (1929), the process psychology of Schaef (1992), a holonomic model of history/ecology (Argüelles, 1988), and Maturana and Varela's (1980) biological theory of autopoiesis. These ideas or stories describe time in more natural and cyclical terms than as some abstract progression. In the realm of human relationships, the concept of wholeness has been portrayed as androgyny or a transpersonal embracing of both "masculine" and "feminine" qualities within oneself and in an intimate relationship (e.g., Colegrave, 1979; Singer, 1977).

Comparing Script Levels: The Case of "The Child." The distinction between script, archescript, and holoscript can be elucidated through a comparative analysis of any one human role image: for example, mother, father, child, martyr, hero, or warrior. The example of a child is used here. In Berne's (1964) transactional psychology, the *child ego state* consists of feelings, impulses, and spontaneous actions that are often recorded in early experiences with one's parents. One's life script derives, in part, from the Adapted Child, which is that version of the Natural Child that has been socialized to accommodate to others' expectations and to often deny feelings, impulses, and spontaneous actions. In Jung's archetypal psychology, the archetype of the eternal child or *puer aeternus* (see Hillman,1979; von Franz, 1981) reflects a direct connection with spirituality, with searching and idealistic questing, with staying forever young and—in neurotic form—avoiding responsibility, denying reality, becoming self-absorbed and narcissistic.

Following a Jungian analysis of literature, authors have identified the *puer* in various mythic and popular characters: Icarus, the Little Prince, Hippolytus, Billy Budd, Peter Pan. In cosmology (and the estimation of a holoscript), we find that the image of the child is prevalent in nearly all creation myths (see Neumann, 1954). The process of Becoming that proceeds from Being is symbolized in the image of a growing child, or the two basic forces of the universe—the Creative and the Receptive, Yin and Yang, Masculine and Feminine—continually interact to *give birth to* the material or phenomenal world. From the perspective of Bohm's holomovement, reality itself is the child of continuous implication and explication. From the perspective of androgyny, the child is inherently bisexual—immanently whole—only society teaches it opposing scripts about sexuality that distort this wholeness.

As we proceed from script to holoscript, experience becomes less immediate, more abstract, more universal, less cognitive, and more spiritual. With some training or therapy we can immediately observe a thought and recognize it as a Child ego state ("I am no good, I should be ashamed of myself"). We can read a book or see a movie about a character, such as *Peter Pan* or *Cinderella*, identify with the character's trials, and so come to an understanding of our archescripts. But this process is more elaborate—often involving active imagination, journaling, guided imagery, dream work (Baldwin, 1991; Singer, 1972) and is so less immediate. We can also meditate, pray, and act in ways that are "in accord with the nature of things" (as prescribed by Taoism) or "God's Will" (as Christianity suggests) and hope to follow the holoscript (see Moore, 1992, or Cooper, 1992, for help along these lines).

RECURRING PROBLEMS

We cannot notice our scripts, work with archescripts, or follow the holoscript when we are addicted; yet, it is the very recurrence of pain and the repetitive discomfort of not getting what we want that leads us on a spiritual journey or into recovery. In a sense, it is time's recurrent or cyclical aspect that challenges the linear and unidirectional assumption that underlies scripts. Forrester (1992) alluded to this in an essay on repetition in psychoanalysis: "Repetition is inherent in the very idea of a symptom . . . [as in] Freud's conception of the symptom as the *return* of the repressed" (p. 289). Any relationship that contains intimacy also contains recurring conflicts and complexities, born of two changing individuals with different scripts. When met with presence, this conflict becomes "grist for the mill" and leads individuals to do the deeply personal work of recovery, of spiritual journey, and of intimacy. Jung called this self-examination a "confrontation with the complex" (complex is Jung's term for "hang-up" or some personal issue, Matoon, 1985). In fact, the notion that "our treasure lies where we stumble" reflects the complex in the interpersonal work of intimacy. Thus, whenever a couple faces the same issues over and over, they have a shared opportunity to revise unconscious scripts.

As individuals, we can loosen the hold of a lifescript on our limited sense of self and glimpse greater (and perhaps ancient) meanings of life. At center stage in this individuation (cf. enantiodromia, Jung, 1921; redecisional, R. Goulding & M. Goulding, 1987) process is the recurrent meeting with others or with a specific other—an intimate. And he or she may become more than just another person, but a beloved other, as together, we open to time's greater rhythms and rewrite scripts from childhood.

A REVIEW: FROM SCRIPTS TO HOLOSCRIPT

The next sections provide an interdisciplinary review of previous writing and attempt to establish some links between the constructs of script, archescript, and holoscript. I bring together somewhat disparate fields of study to show that we already know much about how to recognize and work with relationship problems. However, there has been little dialogue across these fields of study.

SCRIPTS

The following discussion seeks to clarify the usage of script, which has at least four different shades of meaning. These are *social psychological*, or how we deliberate on which roles to take in social interaction; *conversational* or the manner, often learned from stereotypes about gender, of social discourse; strictly *cognitive*, or the ways in which we organize information about social action sequences; and *psychodynamic*, or unconscious action patterns (routines) we follow based on either childhood experiences or archetypes. Regarding intimacy, we inherit scripts about our sexuality (e.g., sex role scripts), or about how we "should" interact with others. The different uses that follow all apply to the intimate situation.

Social Psychology and Personality. Scripts serve to structure, navigate, and ritualize our social discourse and interaction. Goffman (1967) recognized the prevalence of ritual in every human interaction. Commenting on Goffman, Turner (1988) wrote: "Indeed, every interaction is punctuated with opening and closing rituals; and it is such routine rituals that signal actor's involvement in a context, smooth the sequencing of interaction in this context, and reinforce the larger cultural and structural context.... In this process, actors affirm their mutual involvement in, as well as dictate the sequencing of, the interaction" (p. 92). Rituals, routines, and roles are the social arenas in which we both learn and enact scripts. Social psychologists view scripts as attempts to regulate, maintain, or enhance one's own self-image in the face of social situations. Miell and Duck (1986) discovered that during the development of friendship, individuals distinguish between a new partner "script" from a close friend "script," where the former keeps the level of discussion general and limited.

Murray's (1938) theory of personality or personology shows how one's own life story or life theme shapes interpersonal sequences. Personology views the individual's life as a story with recurrent themes organized around unfulfilled or thwarted childhood needs. Whereas Murray did not use the term "script," he distinguished between "proceedings," "serial programs," and "schedules." He showed how individuals organize their time to satisfy major (often childhood) needs. A proceeding is an interaction between a person and one or more others that completes a pattern of behavior. Serial programs organize proceedings toward subgoals and major goals, and schedules are ways in which individuals organize the timing of these programs. These motives are often unconscious and often involve others. From the personological viewpoint, love relationships are stories in which each partner tries to fulfill both their own and the other's needs according to idiosyncratic programs and schedules. Love relationships are schedules of complementary need fulfillment.

Conversational. Research on gender differences in self-disclosure (e.g., Gottman, 1979; Tannen, 1990) suggests that males and females follow different conversational scripts associated with learned sex roles. These scripts underlie communication differences that can hinder or even prohibit intimacy.

For example, Tannen (1990) described the myriad ways in which gender-based styles of communication (she uses the term "genderlects") lead to misunderstandings and inevitable conflict between the sexes. Tannen characterized scripts men tend to follow, such as "Trust me," "I'll fix it for you," "I'll explain it to you," "Who do you think you're talking to?" and "Don't tell me what to do" in which conversation centers around competition, ego protection, problem solving, and getting things done. These differ from women's conversational trends, such as "Be nice," "Talk to me!," "Let's you and I. . . . ," "Don't you agree?," where the emphasis is on intimacy, inclusion, and cooperation. Tannen pointed out how partners, because of their different ways of framing conversation, often talk at cross purposes that can lead to incremental misunderstandings and communication breakdown (cf. "complementary schismogenesis"; Bateson, 1972). Thus, it is possible to habitually use scripts in conversation that lock partners into a sequence of communication where intimacy becomes less and less probable. In fact, research suggests that the conversation of healthy couples is less rigidly patterned and less predictable (Gottman, Markman, & Notarius, 1977; Gottman, Notarius, Gonso, & Markman, 1976).

Cognitive. The field of social cognition often defines a script as an event schema or a "preconception about a sequence of events likely to occur in a particular kind of situation" (Brehm & Kassin, 1990). Individuals have scripts for first dates (Pryor & Merluzzi, 1985), relationship breakups (Battaglia, Richard, Datteri, & Lord, 1998), the expression of anger in close relationships (Fehr & Baldwin, 1996), persuasion (Rule, Bisanz, & Kohn, 1985) and nuclear war (Fiske, Pratto, & Pavelchak, 1983), and they will readily complete an unfinished sequence when given incomplete scripts (Bower, Black, & Turner, 1979). This research suggests that individuals often encode and recall information according to their preconceptions about how things "should" proceed, rather than how events actually do or did proceed. Moreover, strong expectations about a given sequence of events may lead to expectancy confirming behaviors or self-fulfilling prophecies, where we bias an interaction in our favor.

> *Scripts—a useful metaphor for computers and understanding cognition—may have a lot more to tell us about the soul then we realize.*

Psychodynamic. Besides Jung's archetypal analysis of the unconscious (see below), authors have developed ideas about how unconscious scripts play a role in intimate relationships. Such scripts may originate in the drama of one's family of origin (Berne's Life Script theory), from fixation at a particular stage of development (Hendrix's Imago theory, 1992), or as self-crafted life stories (McAdams' Thematic Lines theory, 1985).

Eric Berne, the personality theorist who developed transactional analysis (TA), carried out the most extensive analysis of psychodynamic scripts. In Berne's theory, a script is a "preconscious life plan" that originates from early parental influence about how to carry out certain behaviors, and an ultimate compliance with those parental injunctions. In TA theory, games are segments of these larger scripts. TA therapists use scripts to help clients observe limiting scripts and choose new, healthier ways of behaving. Berne (1964) described the most common game played between spouses as "If It Weren't For You" but there are others: "Kick Me," "Now I've Got You, You Son of a Bitch," "See What You Made Me Do," and "I'm Only Trying to Help You." He also described the games of addicts, called "Alcoholic," which involves several roles: Persecutor, which is "typically played by a member of the opposite sex, usually the spouse;" Rescuer; and others. Berne also described sexual games, such as "Let's You and Him Fight" where two men fight for a woman.

Berne and his followers (see Kahler, 1978; Steiner, 1974) are important reading for a full analysis of temporality in intimacy. For example, Kahler elaborated on "time structure scripts" or "process scripts" that help to understand how we "script ourselves in" to a locked view of time:

1. <u>The Never Script</u>: "I never make it. As a child I was forbidden by my parents to do the things that I most wanted to do."
2. <u>The After Script</u>: "Things may be OK now but something bad will happen."
3. <u>The Always Script</u>: "If that's what you want to do, you can just spend the rest of your life doing it. You've made your bed now lie in it."
4. <u>The Until Script</u>: "You can't have fun until. . . ."
5. <u>The Almost Script</u>: "I almost make it. If only, if only. . . ."
6. <u>The Dead End Script</u>: "I've made no plans after 'retirement': the kids grow up; menopause, etc."

Berne also viewed intimacy as one of six primary ways that individuals structure their time. In comparison to the other ways (withdrawal, rituals, activities, pastimes, and games), intimacy is the ultimate "I'm OK, You're OK Experience." This reinforces the basic premise that intimacy and time are closely aligned. Intimacy requires an acceptance of oneself and the other "as is"—not how we have been (past) or hope that we will be (future). Partners must relinquish the linear time, goals, and games when either afraid or blaming or trying to change each other.

Oden (1974) devoted his book *Game Free* to an application of Berne's ideas about script to the topics of intimacy, time, and theology. Oden agreed that scripts such as "Nobody loves me" or "No matter how hard I try. . . ." prevent intimacy. Yet he critiqued TA, asking "After Intimacy, What?" Emphasizing that intimacy is only one way to get love and affirmation from others, Oden urged us to a broader view of time in relationships:

> The exceptionally high value placed upon intimacy and the corresponding rejection of other modes of structuring time is a peculiarly class-oriented value assumption. The urgent, almost frenetic, quest for intimacy is endemic to upper-middle-class, white-collar, competitive, upwardly socially mobile Americans who are in fact the principal clientele of psychotherapy. . . . Psychotherapy and group processes in general have been notoriously irrelevant to the values of class strata other than the one from which their basic clientele is drawn. . . . After intimacy we must still learn to be accountable to our neighbors within the structure of human community. . . . A more circumspect understanding of reality will see the interpersonal within the context of the social, and social in the context of the historical, and the historical as inclusive not only of its past and present, but of its future and finally its end. So when you and I meet, we meet in the midst of a history that reaches far beyond our interpersonal meeting (p. 90).

Oden simultaneously helped us to see that transpersonal intimacy is as important as interpersonal intimacy and that we must see the larger script, or the bigger story (holoscript) in which our personal scripts are embedded. More recent critiques follow a similar tack to that of Oden's (e.g., Hillman & Ventura, 1992; Schaef, 1987) and show how cultural dynamics influence how we structure our time.

Hendrix's Imago theory (Hendrix, 1992) combines Erickson's model of life span development (e.g., Erikson, 1964) with attachment theory (e.g., Mahler, 1968). This model of therapy provides tools to help individuals examine how they project images (imago) of their parents onto their romantic partners. Hendrix's model has significance for the discussion of addiction, time, and intimacy in that—like Freud's psychosexual stage theory—individuals can become fixated (wounded in childhood) around one style of attachment and subsequently, and addictively, seek out relationships in attempt to heal this wound. Hendrix believed that—using questionnaires and self-analysis—we can break the pattern of dysfunctional relationships. His term *imago* is like a lifescript about loving and attachment (also see Horney, 1942).

McAdams (1985, 1989) follows in the tradition of Murray in analyzing the stories people share about their lives, and, further, in describing the unconscious themes (thematic lines), archetypal motifs (imagoes), critical events (nuclear episodes), and story structure (narrative complexity) of those stories. In essence, McAdams provided analytical tools for studying the scripts of individuals. Importantly, he viewed life stories as having two essential themes: power (agency) and intimacy (communion). He also developed the idea of a generativity script (following Erickson), or a script about what one is going to do in the future (later stages) of one's life. McAdams also discussed other author's work on a "script theory" of personality (e.g., Tomkins, 1979).

Summary and Discussion. The analysis of scripts across independent fields of study suggests that it has broad appeal and utility. This is in basic research (social cognition), communication studies (Tannen), as well as in applications to individual (Berne) and couple's therapy (Hendrix). This prevalence suggests that scripts serve a critical function in helping to organize the sequence of meaningful interpersonal events. In previous approaches, scripts have their origin in social conditioning, either through parental or cultural (e.g., sex role) influences. That is, scripts have been seen as helping the individual self to organize the world and navigate through relationships. They function to represent, control, or maintain the current reality, even if that is a broad, historical reality (Oden). In contrast to these approaches, the current model hypothesizes that scripts have their origin in transpersonal or psychospiritual processes. Scripts can function to not only represent but also change reality and create a deeper intimacy, or sense of connection. In fact, scripts may be seen to have their origin in deeper, more soulful aspects of the personality, sometimes called "archetypes."

ARCHESCRIPTS

> Our ancestors had to learn how to utter words; words made stories possible and stories demanded and generated temporal frameworks. The expanding capacity for storytelling brought with it story thinking, which helped push the horizons of time further into the future and the past. (Fraser, 1975, p. 175)

A different understanding of intimacy comes from either a spiritual or Jungian analysis of stories and myths about men and women. Theme, plot and character structure provide helpful clues about how individuals project certain desires and outcomes in intimate relationships. Jung (1972) and his followers claimed that each person possesses unconscious images of particular characters that potentiate and reflect universal principles. Key archetypes in intimate relationships are the *anima*, which is Jung's term for the soul of a man from which he derives feelings, emotions, nurturing, and vulnerability; and the *animus,* which is the soul of a woman from which she derives opinions, certainty, and active creativity. There is also the *shadow* or the darker, impulsive, passionate, irrational side of both men and women, in which denied feelings and hurts are repressed and in which spiritual ideals lie dormant. These archetypes are part of many stories of romance, marriage, and the conquests and defeats of lovers.

> *Stories of love and of the spiritual journey have been humanity's most powerful ways of dealing with mortality— connecting the eternal with an ancient aloneness.*

A wealth of literature applies these archetypes to interpersonal relationships (Bolen, 1984; Colegrave, 1979; Hillman, 1985; Johnson, 1983; Kast, 1986; Leonard, 1986; Pearson, 1989; Sanford, 1980; Singer, 1977; Small, 1991; Young-Eisendrath, 1984; Zweig & Abrams, 1991). I focus on the *process of interaction* (cf. *integration of imagoes,* McAdams, 1985) that takes place between the archetypes—thus, the term *archescript.* In Jungian theory, individuals seek to integrate their contrasexual nature (i.e., anima for man and animus for woman). Several authors use the term *androgyny* to label this integration and believe that with such integration (i.e., individuation) the individual touches broader transpersonal and metaphysical forces (Colegrave, 1979; Singer, 1977). For example:

> We need to think of ourselves no longer as exclusively 'masculine' or exclusively 'feminine' but rather as whole beings in whom the opposite qualities are ever-present. . . . The androgyne is a symbol of the Self par excellence. But more than that the androgyne is a *representation in human form* of the principle of wholeness. (Singer, 1977, pp. 271– 272)

Others claim that the failure to integrate the shadow leads to codependence and projecting our "dark side" or personal "monsters" onto our partners (Small, 1991; Welwood, 1990). The shadow embodies the unclaimed "transpersonal wholeness" that we fear because we believe powerful spiritual forces might overwhelm us. Small (1991) describes some symptoms of the failure to integrate the shadow:

> I will fall madly in love with someone who is not available or appropriate for me (a married man, a priest, a well-known womanizer). My deep ability to relate and care is wasted on irrelevant "romantic" pursuits that keep me excited and preoccupied with the thrill of drama and newness. I am therefore spared from having to make myself truly vulnerable in relationships that are ongoing and real. My passionate nature is being misdirected. (p. 50)

Because they are primarily unconscious, archetypes can mostly be known through personal dream work, creative work and play such as art and poetry, journaling, and by exploring feeling reactions to stories (e.g., Hannah, 1981; Kaplan-Williams, 1991).[4] Jungian analyses of stories provide keys to understanding the intimate process underlying the notion of archescript. That is, a story describes a progression or series of events that transpire between characters over time. Partners, without them even knowing about it, act out such ancient stories—often in diluted, or compressed, forms (interacting scripts). But these stories reflect a deeper, evolutionary tendency for story telling in the human species, a tendency acknowledged by Jung in his discussion of the "collective unconscious" or reservoir for all events and images that have occurred to humans throughout time. Thus, archescripts denote an ancient substrate of humanity that helps us to understand, organize, and experience relationships over time. Margulis and Sagan (1991) wrote: "Our species *homo sapiens* would be better named *homo seriatim*, claims neurobiologist William Calvin, because our distinguishing feature is that we narrate in series, we tell stories, we write in linear prose, and plan ahead. . . .The story of how animals learned to perceive time is no ordinary story: it is the story *of* stories, the story that tells us where the sense of story-telling comes from, how it arose" (pp. 143–145). Through insight into these origins, individuals can recognize how current self-limiting scripts are essentially universal and impersonal; they do not have to identify with them or compulsively follow them. In fact, the sense of connection that the relationship addict was looking for on the outside, with another, may now be found on the inside, through a deeper connection to the self.

Stories may give the listener some preverbal or sensual access to a primitive and distinguishing characteristic of humanity: consciousness of time. We are a species that—through our perception of series and linearity—has consciousness of our own mortality and some understanding of how sexuality, or procreation, can mitigate the death of our species (cf. "the romantic solution," Becker, 1973). In this way, stories about love and relationships—particularly those that have withstood the test of history and different cultures—can give insight into archescripts. For this reason, a Jungian analysis of stories is important. More important is our own personal reactions to such stories, and how we use them to do inner work on our scripts.

Stories that have been subject to such an analysis include ancient myths of Greece and Rome (e.g., Zeus-Hera or Aphrodite-Ares; see Bolen, 1984), Tristan and

Iseult (Johnson, 1983), *Beauty and the Beast* (Leonard, 1986), Sir Gawain and Lady Ragnell (Young-Eisendrath, 1984), and *Pygmalion* (Kast, 1986). Jungian analysts suggest that each individual discovers which stories (in fiction, cinema, art, myth, fantasy) seem to resonate with their own way of living in an intimate relationship.

Bible study offers another rich place to examine archescripts. The ways in which Elijah, the Prodigal son, and Jesus communicated with God reveal different pathways between archescript and holoscript. For example, Agudo (1978) pointed out that Elijah found God in "the tiny whispering sound" rather than the terrible forces of nature (1 Kings 20:11-13). Bush (1978) showed that although the prodigal son projected shame and guilt onto his father, his father embraced him with forgiveness and joy. Hagberg and Guelich (1989) also related different Bible stories to different stages on one's spiritual journey. For

---

RESEARCH **REFLECTION**

LOVE IS A STORY: A MODEL OF RELATIONSHIPS THROUGH TIME

Sternberg (1998) developed a view of relationships that fits with the script-archescript model. In essence, the stories we tell about our relationships have patterns and themes similar to the kinds of stories we learn through our culture. Sternberg has classified over 25 different stories into six different types. Consider some of the examples of items Sternberg uses for some of these types and the story lines they represent. You may notice some archetypal themes in these stories. Also note Sternberg includes *The Addiction Story*.

ASSYMETRICAL STORIES (e.g., *Teacher–Student, Police, Pornography, Horror*)
For example, *The Sacrifice Story*
Example item: I believe sacrifice is a key part of true love.

OBJECT STORIES (PERSON AS OBJECT) (e.g., *Science Fiction, Collection, Art*)
For example, *The Art Story*
Example: It is very important to me that my partner always looks good.

OBJECT STORIES (RELATIONSHIP AS OBJECT) (e.g., *House and Home, Game*)
For example, *The Religion Story*
Example: I believe that in the best relationships, people help each other draw closer to God.

COORDINATION STORIES (e.g., *Sewing and Knitting, Garden, Business, Travel*)
For example, *The Addiction Story*
Example: I am almost totally dependent on my partner for my happiness.

NARRATIVE STORIES (*Theatre, Humor, Mystery*)
For example, *The Science Story*
Example: I like to sit back and objectively analyze and discuss different aspects of my relationship with my partner.

GENRE STORIES
For example, *The War Story*
Example item: I actually like to fight with my partner.

example, the story of Job's search for meaning in his suffering (Job 26-28) reflects a crisis point in one's journey inward. Alternatively, Joseph's forgiving his brothers after selling him into slavery (Genesis 45:1-15) may help one to understand their own deeper calling or vision in life.

It is important to stress that, however it's done, the exploration of archescripts is a private and creative act. Again, it is the sequence of events, the unfolding of the story, that is important, and not the analysis of character (archetype). It is in the narrative rhythm—the reciprocal interchange, development, and denouement—where we experience the intimate connection. It is in the coming together of lovers or of individuals with God through periods of chaos that we experience a move toward integration, toward androgyny, toward wholeness. Unlike the psychodynamic approach to scripts (e.g., Imagoes), an understanding of one's archescripts comes from the collective wisdom found in stories and one's personal reflections and absorption in these stories.

Summary and Discussion. Human beings have the distinguishing capacity to intentionally look far into the past and far ahead into the future. This process shows us—as humanity—to ourselves. We have the opportunity to see beyond our current, idiosyncratic, and often limiting ways (scripts) of organizing time. Throughout history, stories from myth and religion guide us to different parts of our inner world (child, hero, shadow), which can interact in harmful as well as harmonious and healthful ways. When we turn to this inner world, and learn from it, we gain insight into working with the recurrent problems in our relationships. We realize we are not alone and that we do not have to depend on our own particular way of organizing interpersonal sequences. This is a step to greater intimacy. Just as these archescripts inform scripts, the holoscript—or unifying story—informs archescripts.

HOLOSCRIPT

> The interweaving of aboriginal continuity and civilizational advance...
>
> —J. Arguëlles (from *Earth Ascending*)

> We have come a long, long way from those ancestors of ours whose ideas of Time cannot have been very different from those of the Australian aborigines. Passing time, once almost meaningless, is now the inescapable beat, like that of the engine of some space ship, of the whole vast universe; we seem to be utterly at its mercy; while any idea, once so all-important, of the Great Time, the eternal dream time, the other time of gods and heroes and mythology, seems to have vanished.
>
> —J. B. Priestly, 1964, p. 123.

The concept of holoscript—as a metaphysical idea—is difficult to convey in words, but the sense of unity or wholeness is key. We have this sense of wholeness when the multiple situations (characters, plots) of good story/narrative

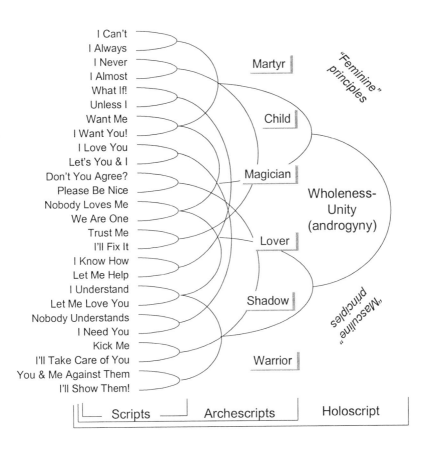

FIG. 5.1. Relations between scripts, archescripts, and holoscript.

This rough illustration of examples of scripts and archescripts is not meant to convey a specific ordering or taxonomy. The unity of the holoscript (at right), bifurcates into "masculine" and "feminine" principles, which manifest in different archescript combinations. For example, the Warrior embodies certain stereotypical masculine principles of strength, alertness, and perseverance. The Child represents a merging of the two principles. Habitual scripts (shown at left) that flow from archescripts are most accessible to consciousness.

reveal coherence. Modern physics has given us a similar view of unity in the idea of time-space continuum. Time is somewhat metaphorical and similar to Eastern Mysticism (cf. Capra, 1975; Prigogine & Stengers 1984). As such, human beings are part of a dynamic whole, represented in each human interaction at all points in time. According to this view, time is indivisible and eternal; we have all been here before and known each other at a very intimate level for countless life times. We are born into this world knowing this at some level but, through social conditioning, this ancient memory of eternal connection is erased.

The holoscript subsumes both collective archescripts and the individual scripts (Berne's games) that are enacted within relationships (see Fig. 5.1). At any given point in time, one partner acts out a script (e.g., "Don't tell me what to do!") and the other responds with his or her own script (e.g., "But I need you!") (left side of Fig. 5.1). This action-reaction indicates an archescript embodied within the relationship—especially if the couple keep acting it out in an obsessive manner. For example, "Don't tell me what to do!" may reflect masculine independence of the woman's animus, and "But I need you!" may reflect the male becoming more vulnerable to his own anima. The archescript subsumes and shapes the script. At the next, holoscript, level, these scenarios of conflict really portray an unconscious seeking of unity or wholeness. Images of wholeness have been described in three perspectives: the marriage of opposites (masculine and feminine aspects), the new physics view, and the holographic model.

Holoscript as Unifying "Masculine" and "Feminine" Aspects. To elucidate this wholeness of the holoscript we can return to the previous chapter. There I suggested that the dynamic whole of intimate process consists of various temporal forces: nurturing conditions (context and allowing things to unfold), time shaping (action and planning or controlling time), relational structure (cultural conventions and forms for negotiating intimacy), and chaos (tendencies toward instability). These forces can be seen as reflecting both "masculine" and "feminine" principles. Nurturing conditions and chaos reflect the receptive, formless, and changeable aspects of the "feminine" and structure and time shaping reflect the more active, forming, and steady aspects of the "masculine." Wholeness comes from embracing both of these principles. Writing about feminine consciousness, Colegrave related the ancient Chinese Story of 'The Rainmaker'—which is clearly about being receptive to nurturing conditions. This can also be viewed as a story about the wise man or magician archetype:

> It concerns a remote Chinese village stricken with drought. The harvest is in danger and the people face starvation. The villagers pray and sacrifice, but no rain falls. Eventually, in desperation, they send far afield for a rainmaker. When the little old man arrives they ask him what he needs to perform his magic. "Nothing" he replies "except a quite room where I may be alone." He lives quietly there for two days and on the third day it rains.
> The magic of the rainmaker is his capacity to allow things to happen rather than to cause them. The villagers had been frantically trying to make the rain come; the Rainmaker simply created space for the rain to fall. Because he willed nothing and asked nothing, he exerted a very different influence from the deliberate, organizing impulse of the masculine, and revealed by his example that not everything can be forced, some things have just to be allowed to happen. (Colegrave, 1979, pp. 102–103).

Hillman (1985), in his analysis of the anima archetype as a "mediatrix" or guide to the unknown or unconscious, describes her more chaotic or crazy qualities. He writes, intermittently quoting from Jung: "She would also 'unleash forces' of the collective unconscious, for across her bridge roll fantasies, projections, emotions that make a person's consciousness unconscious and collective. . . . A mediatrix to the eternally unknowable, she is the bridge *both* over the river into the trees *and* into the sludge and quicksand" (pp. 132–133).

Both Colegrave and Hillman demonstrated that the anima and more feminine aspects of the unconscious embody the universal forces of chaos and nurturing conditions within the psyche of each individual. Conversely, the animus and more masculine aspects embody the forces of relational structure and time shaping. Colegrave (1979) described masculine consciousness as "structuring human life" instead of "participating instinctively in the rhythms of nature." Much feminist analysis has deplored this dialectical separation—for example, aligning the female with nature and the male with culture (Dinnerstein, 1976)—and seeks to transcend the "gender polarity" (Benjamin, 1988). However, the pop-psychology book *Men are From Mars, Women are From Venus* (Gray, 1992) only reifies this dialectic. This has been the number one selling book in the United States, based on book sales from 1994 to 1998 (*USA Today*, February 11, 1999). Its popularity appears due to the author's ability to accurately convey the important differences between men and women that keep them from experiencing intimacy together.

Gray provides numerous examples that, seen from the current perspective, support the view that masculine consciousness is attracted to time shaping and structure and female consciousness is attracted to chaos and nurturing conditions. For example, Gray showed sex differences in the cycle of intimacy, using the metaphors "men are like rubber bands" and "women are like waves." For women, mood, emotion, and self-esteem all naturally cycle from a period of "cresting," feeling an abundance of love, fulfillment, and nurturing qualities, to a period of "crashing," of dark, vague, and diffuse feeling. According to Gray, women rise and fall in their ability to love themselves. When the wave crashes, their mood suddenly changes without any external or apparent reason and they need to talk to deepen into the "well" and clarify feelings. Crashing occurs when their need for intimacy seems the most salient or heightened. It is through this cycle that women embody the temporal forces of chaos (vague, diffuse, dark feeling) and nurturing conditions (abundance of love, fulfillment).

In contrast, according to Gray, men continually pull away for independence and get close again for intimacy. When the rubber band is "limp," men need their opportunities to feel potent and to take action that shapes a world independent of their female partner. When they experience too much independence, aloneness (i.e., the rubber band is too tight) then men desire contact and closeness again. Either too much dependence (feeling limp and without independent potency) or too much independence (feeling too isolated) triggers the man to take action by moving close or away. This intimacy cycle, I believe, shows how men embody the temporal forces of time shaping (by taking action) and temporal form (by setting up routines of closeness-distance). While Gray does not talk about transpersonal intimacy, his work can be seen as helping couples to see the "big story" that has characterized male-female relationships for centuries. Gray's work is one example of self-help books designed to teach "personal relationship skills." By helping couples understand their natural differences, Gray is teaching them how to be present, flowing, and patient.

Gray also did not advocate androgyny, but instead the honoring and respecting of sex differences in intimacy. Transpersonal psychology also tends to view transcendence in the androgynous image of the marriage of opposites. In fact, research suggests couples are happier when both partners possess both stereotypical masculine and feminine personality traits rather than only the "sex-typed" personality of their sex (i.e., only the man as active and independent and only the woman as nurturing and caring) (Antill, 1983; Ickes, 1985).[5] Welwood (1990), a transpersonal psychologist, believes that marriage can facilitate such integration and put the couple in touch with the universal principles of a bigger story:

> *The study of what human intimacy can become likely entails the future study of the story of humanity; and that big, sacred, story may actually takes us there.*

> Whenever two halves of life come together—consciousness and form, passion and discipline, male and female, heaven and earth—a new world of possibilities comes into being. In this sense, two people joining their lives in marriage are engaging in a sacred activity because they are creating a cosmos in miniature—where all the different sides of themselves, personal and transpersonal, can be included. . . . If two people are to make good use of the chaos arising between them, and not become overwhelmed by it, they must accord wisdom and truth a central place in their relationship. Then the natural order of things can unfold, for a sacred order has been established. (pp. 186, 188)

Whether we ascribe to a feminist, androgynous, or "Mars–Venus" view of intimacy, there are many ways in which universal principles are represented in intimate relationships. Couples experience periods of expansion and contraction: times when the relationship suffers from withdrawal, separation, and alienation and periods of unification, growth, and companionship. These temporal patterns reveal a deeper process of universal principles (see Holoscript Diagram; Fig. 5.1)

Holoscript and the New Physics. Modern physics has derived several principles about the nature of time and the universe (see Briggs & Peat, 1989; Hines, 1996; Wolff, 1999): universal laws of order and of chaos constantly interact with each other; time is a function of the expansion and contraction of the universe; and every part of a complex system contains the whole of that system. The course of a human relationship follows these universal principles, but also—according to the logic of the new physics—implicates, enfolds, or contains them. Modern physics, particularly chaos and complexity theory, indicates that phenomena do not change or evolve in a strictly linear process of development and decay. There are inherent instabilities, periods of nonequilibrium and turbulence that can erupt into consciousness at any time. Wolff (1999) explains that these precarious and uncertain qualities reflect the archetype of the trickster (shadow, clown, juggler, coyote, Hermes) who lurks at the border between chaos and structure to bring our consciousness into the moment: "Bringing order out of chaos and chaos from order requires the trickster's prestidigitation, for the trickster is always upsetting the established order of things in surprising ways" (p. 184). Wolff (1999) draws a clear parallel between the trickster and the chaotic qualities of nature:

> Mathematics and the laws of physics are marvelous inventions in bringing order out of chaos. They seem to be "out there," as real as Mars's elliptical orbit and Earth's spherical shape. They are as true as a pendulum's steady time-keeping period and as unwavering as the frequency of a laser's directed light.
>
> But not quite. The laser's frequency has some fluctuations in it, unpredictable and unwanted. The Earth's spherical shape is not quite real either. She seems to bulge more at the equator and has a distinctive pear shape perturbation to her roundness. Mar's orbit is continually being perturbed as well by the other planets and the asteroid belt, and even the pendulum's steady to-and-fro movement eventually slows to a nervous twitching. (p. 189)

Every human relationship is a complex system and the dance of intimacy— of uniting and separating, pursuing and being pursued, of disclosing and withholding—is continually marked by periods of instability and stability. At some basic level, what we experience in our attachments, surrendering, in our loving, are reflections of the order and chaos of the universe. That is, in the dance of intimacy, the periods of separation (whether through conflict, misunderstanding, addiction, withdrawal, abuse, or even planned partings) with all the attendant feelings we experience, are actually manifestations of the holoscript in a period of contraction, stabilization, ordering. When we come together, meet, unite, experience closeness, tenderness, and understanding; this too is a reflection of the holoscript. Intimacy, like time, is the process of expressing this holistic interaction. Intimacy is not just about being close or about separation, but rather about the entire—*whole*—process that our relationships continually reflect. This process is reflected in the creation myths seen across many world religions (Campbell, 1972). The Hindu myths of Shiva (destroyer, chaotic, passive energy) and Shakti (creator, active energy) (Kast, 1986), and the Egyptian myth of Nut (heaven) being lifted above Geb (earth) by Shu (self) (Neumann, 1954), are examples of archescripts reflecting the structuring and chaotic forces of the universe.

The Holographic Model. In his discussion of holonomy (i.e., the law or principle governing whole systems) Argüelles (1988) theorizes that an *aboriginal synaesthetic* condition once existed in which science (knowledge), art (expression), and the sacred order were married together. His allusion to aboriginal referred to the Australian aboriginal culture that conceives of "dream time" as a seamless sacred whole where, through ritual and totems, aborigines could draw strength and courage. In the modern age, planetary consciousness has reached an opposite condition, *mechanistic psychosensory alienation.* There is a "loss of a sacred view, a splintering of knowledge, the divorce of art and science, and the general collective confusion caused by an explosion of information without a coherent knowledge structure to contain it" (p. 60). Argüelles explained that we are moving out of the modern age into the posthistoric, holonomic age, where "art, science, and sacred order are unified into a single image, a primary configuration that nonetheless contains the whole story" (p. 132). By whole story, Argüelles referred to the history of the earth, our relationship to it, and to the future where we resonate in a relationship to the universe. Thus, in discussing holonomy, Argüelles is really describing a form of intimacy at the level of planetary consciousness.

Other authors have used the concept of the hologram in a more experiential, or immediate, psychological context. Schaef (1992) described the possibility of coming to a sense of the holomovement through living in process and deep process work. Deep processes have to do with processes, often emotional, that bypass logical, rational understanding and that often have to do with being socialized into an addictive society:

> Because we do not live in a culture that respects and facilitates our processes as children, because few (if any) of us have been process-parented, because as children we don't have the internal or external tools to process what happens to us, because we have been raised to believe in controlling or denying our internal processes (through addictions and other methods of control), and because we have tried to fit in, most of us carry many unfinished, aborted, pushed-down process inside of us that are rumbling around, waiting to be healed and integrated. (p. 146)

Schaef suggested that as we pay attention to our internal processes (become intimate with ourselves), we also take part in a "participatory universe" or holomovement.

The holoscript, or the Great Story in which we all participate, is a new paradigm of wholeness informed by different sources: physicist's discussions of holomovement and chaos theory, Argüelles' exploration of holonomy, and individuals exploring their own spirituality through the living process of recovering through addiction. As we transcend rigid social structures and scripts that dictate interpersonal relationships, as we grow in consciousness of scripts and archescripts, we will begin to see how relationships can also inform us about the holoscript.

SUMMARY

Figure 5.1 sketches some purely speculative relations between script, archescript, and holoscript. The figure implies that the scripts we use to negotiate our close relationships are shaped by deeper soulful longings toward unity, as reflected in the archetypes. These archetypes—or images about our humanity—are shaped by a larger universal tendency toward wholeness. Most of the world's religions are based on this tendency and the belief in a universal entity or process that embodies wholeness (e.g., God). These religions portray how a single human being (e.g., Buddha, Christ, Mohammed) struggled to know, and be known by this wholeness. Their stories of transpersonal intimacy continue to provide (every day to millions) a model or schema for understanding the relationship between this (time-limited) life and something eternal and divine. In a parallel but limited way, the relationship between scripts, archescripts, and holoscript provides a model for understanding the relation between our interpersonal styles and universal processes. I end this chapter with the following quote, which expresses this relation in yet another way.

> There is an important correlation between the personal experience of an intimate relationship and our relationship with God. Intimacy is being known and knowing. In the experience of being known by another and being accepted for who we are, we grow in the consciousness that it is wonderful that we exist. We come slowly to believe that the parts of ourselves that we find unacceptable, that we hate or are ashamed of or embarrassed by, can in fact be accepted by someone else. We then learn to own and love every aspect of ourselves, our history, the gamut of our feelings, even our sinfulness. When we have been deeply affirmed by someone who really knows us, who has gotten behind all our facades and false fronts, we know that God loves us also, precisely because of the fact that he knows us and causes us to exist. (Bush, 1978, p. 48)

End Notes—Chapter 5

1. Parallels between addiction and insecure attachment. There appears to be strong overlap between descriptions of addiction and insecure attachment, but both concepts are fuzzy. As Berscheid and Reis (1998) pointed out, there is "surprisingly little consensus about the precise nature and operation of attachment schemata" (p. 219). I think there is much room for cross talk between those writing about relationship addiction/ codependency and researchers who study attachment working models or schemata. Readers who are familiar with the attachment paradigm may wish to view the current chapter as an attempt to enrich the attachment (internal working model) paradigm.

2. Relationship addiction as a cultural story or by-product. It is important to note that the current discussion of addiction would not have been possible 100 years ago, and may simply be a by-product of the growing self-consciousness of this millenium. Reports of recovery from sexual or romance addiction, as argued by Jamieson (1998) offer a "story" of "dawning self-knowledge" that fits with a culture that overwhelms us with choice and that barrages us with stories about how we should be as "healthy," and "real" men and women. The theme of understanding intimacy in an historical context is discussed throughout this book in several places (e.g., see previous references to Ricouer, Oden in this chapter, and Luhmann in next chapter). Together, these authors' writings imply that all meanings of reflective consciousness (of intrapersonal intimacy) require consciousness of history. Perhaps the problem of relationship addiction entails the perception that the desired "other" may not be part of one's own projected history and, accordingly, one's self-concept is threatened.

3. Holoscript is not a new idea. Like the thing it refers to, the concept of holomovement is complex. In trying to explain it briefly, we diminish our understanding of it. However, Bohm's metaphysical and cosmological concepts are not new and may be elaborated on from other perspectives. Process metaphysics (e.g., Whitehead, 1968) and Hua-Yen Buddhism (e.g., Chang, 1974) both present views of reality as holistic, interdependent, intercausal, or interpenetrating (see Odin, 1982). For example, according to Whitehead (1968): "In a certain sense, everything is everywhere at all times." Odin (1982) compared these two views and cites the work of Fa-tsang (643-712 A.D.), who was the Third Patriarch of Zen Buddhism and grand systematizer of the Hua-yen sect, to demonstrate the Hua-yen vision of "simultaneous inter-reflection and infinite realms-embracing-realms. In Fa-tsang's words: "In each of the lion's eyes, in its ears, limbs, and so forth, down to each and every single hair, there is a golden lion. All the lions embraced by each and every hair simultaneously and instantaneously enter into one single hair. Thus, in each and every hair there are an infinite number of lions" (cited in Chang, 1974; p. 229).

4. Archetypes and the conscious personality. Feinstein and Krippner (1988) and Pearson (1989, 1991) suggest more direct and conscious access to archetypes is possible, and have developed methods (e.g., personality questionnaires) for this purpose. For example, Pearson distinguishes between the archetypes of innocent, orphan, wanderer, warrior, martyr, and magician. An individual identified with the orphan will be more apt to agree with the statement "I want someone to take care of me," whereas an individual identified with the warrior will more likely say "Winning isn't the best thing in life, it is the only thing!" Research is needed to explore parallels between Pearson's view of conscious archetypes and scripts (see Fig. 5.1). For more updated information about Pearson's work visit www.herowithin.com.

5. Psychological research on gender-stereotyped traits and Jungian psychology. As mentioned in the preface, the audience interested in personal relationships appears to be split between scientific or academic and popular or lay readers. This split occurs between those interested in Mars-Venus or Jungian views of masculinity, femininity, and androgyny and personality psychologists who study gender–stereotyped traits. Several personality measures exist that assess the degree to which an individual identifies with stereotypically masculine (instrumental) or feminine (expressive) personality traits and a great deal of research has examined how this gender orientation correlates with other factors. Interested readers should consult this research and also the theoretical work of Janet T. Spence, who highlights the many nuances and complexities involved in individual's identification with gender-stereotyped traits (see Swann, Langlois, & Gilbert, 1999). For example, a recent study suggests that intimate love correlates with expressive and androgynous traits for men but not for women (Varga, 1998). This and other studies suggest that broad (Mars-Venus or Jungian) notions of feminine–masculine traits may not always be useful and can sometimes contribute to sexist views of men and women.

The answer to the problem and the sorrow of time is one thing and one thing only: the experience of meaning.

—Jacob Needleman (professor of philosophy, author of *Time and the Soul*)

No communication is totally independent of context, and all meaning has an important contextual component . . . A man and a woman on good terms, who have lived together for fifteen or more years, do not always have to spell things out. When he comes through the door after a day at the office, she may not have to utter a word. He knows from the way she moves what kind of day she had . . . In contrast, when one moves from personal relationships to courts of law or to computers or mathematics, nothing can be taken for granted, because these activities are low context and must be spelled out. (Hall, 1983, p. 56)

THOUGHTS ON A NEW SCIENCE

- That we develop a new consciousness of multiple contexts, where we see how relationships (intimacy) shape and are shaped by meanings across these contexts.

- That all roots of misunderstanding are dissolved and each perspective—each claim to scientific knowledge—is welcomed and embraced as part of the whole.

- That we see how we weave our knowledge together and, in so doing, are able to give it, make it useful, and benefit others.

- That this transdisciplinary meeting serves the development of the consciousness of humanity.

6

Temporal Context in Love and Science: The Weave of Temporal Sensitivity

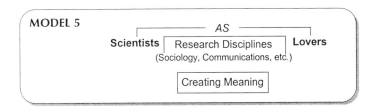

Nature has linked her kinds into a net, not into a chain; men are incapable of following anything but a chain, since they cannot express in words more than one thing at a time.

—Haller (cited in Margulis & Sagan, 1991, p. 146)

THIS CHAPTER attempts to bridge the gap between two widely disparate perspectives. The first perspective deals with our common, personal views of time as we experience it and also how spirituality (our notions of paradise, timelessness, or eternity) plays a role within these personal views. The second perspective deals with the scientific view of time as researchers, who study personal relationships, continually construct it and as they develop ideas and methods for studying time's role within personal relationships. I seek to formulate a language that will convey meanings for both those who seek a personal understanding of time and intimacy and students of personal relationships who seek a scientific understanding of temporality. This bridge or language rests on the relatively complex concept of temporal context. Although this concept has been described previously, this chapter builds a more complete definition. In its essence, the concept attempts to "express in words more than one thing at a time."

This chapter also follows through with the transpersonal theme outlined earlier. Previous chapters described transpersonal intimacy almost as a possibility or contingency. It is a type of intimacy (into my sea), a feature of time in relationships (time transcendence), the latent structure of our relationship stories (holoscript), and the outcome of partners transacting meanings that move them beyond their projective texts (textual transcendence). This chapter assumes

155

the transpersonal experience of intimacy to be more imminent and near than transcendent, or more actual and immediate than potential. That is, transpersonal processes are not ephemeral, epiphenomenal, or without substance; they are directly accessible, knowable, and meaningful. The metaphor of couples weaving meaning together appeals to this imminent aspect of transpersonal intimacy. We are always weaving context together; the activity is open and perpetually unfinished. Social scientists can also stand to gain from seeing their own work as a weaving (a temporal articulation from the wholeness of time) rather than a particular recording of phenomena (an atemporal objectification of events) (Faulconer & Williams, 1987).

Overall, then, this chapter forms a bridge between two different ways of knowing time. There is experience: For example, Donna and Jay learn to get along with each other as they adapt to each other's rhythms and schedules and, as a result, Jay's ability to be intimate shifts. Then there is research: For example, partners who show patterns of accommodating each other are compared with those who do not in order to determine whether intimacy precedes or follows this accommodation. Figure 6.1 summarizes some distinctions made in this chapter.

This chapter begins by articulating two ways to bridge the gap between the two perspectives. First, it explores the different meanings of two words, *time* and *temporality*, and argues that psychology and personal relationship research could focus more on temporality. It then develops the meaning of the term *temporal context*, hoping to show how it can help merge the personal and scientific way of knowing. Second, it elaborates on the commonalties of personal and scientific knowledge by drawing parallels between the ways lovers and scientists know. In addition, it describes the importance of appreciating *process* as distinct from mere *sequence*.

The remainder of the chapter examines context and temporal context within the social sciences. For the different areas of social science, entire books can be devoted to temporal context and intimate relations. Thus, only two fields are

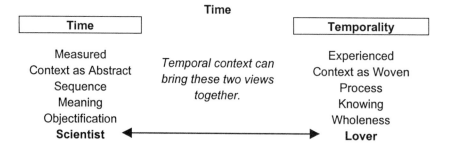

FIG. 6.1. Distinctions between the "Scientist" and "Lover" approach to time.

focused on, communication and sociology. Within these fields, I highlight research studies that are temporally sensitive (see "Research Notes" sections). I also provide overviews from evolutionary behavior, chronobiology (biological clocks), and social psychology. The role of our culture's influence on context is a recurring theme in this chapter. Unless we are international travelers, we often take culture for granted. To bring some perspective here, I also introduce some feminist commentary on the role of time in communication and sociology.

TIME AND TEMPORALITY

The meaning of temporal context requires an understanding of the two terms, *temporal* and *context*. This section defines temporal, distinguishing it from time, and the next section defines context. Following the writings of others (Fraser, 1987; Sinha; 1983; Slife, 1993), I draw a distinction between time and temporality. As we typically use it, time refers to a succession of moments as independent, objective, measured, and usable. This meaning presumes that the world can be divided into subjective reality and objective fact. In contrast, temporality refers to actual change and ongoingness, to the world that we create as we participate in it, where there is no subject/object distinction. Time is a framework we impose that captures succession, change, or evolution. Temporality is the actual activity or process of succession and change. Time implies a distinctive change in something so that it is now other than what it was in the past. Temporality is itself the phenomenological quality of changefulness. This changefulness is complete and directly knowable within itself; conception or thought does not mediate it.

One way to understand this distinction is by trying a two-part experiment. In the first part, look at a digital clock that has digits for the 60 seconds of a minute. Watch the clock for at least two minutes so that you can see the minutes change. It is important to pay close and continuous attention and to be free from distractions. As you see the numbers change—01 02 03 . . . 59 60 01—you may have the sensation that time is incremental (one second builds or follows upon the next). You can try this with the second hand of an analog clock too. If you only focus on the second hand and not the surrounding 12 numbers, the sensation of change will be less incremental. Now imagine that you are looking at a digital clock and, instead of numbers, you are watching a series of images or symbols that have no particular meaning to you: 〈 ⊃ ⌋ ∩ ⌋ ⌉ 〉. Or, instead, you are watching a random series of numbers: 32 07 11 61 44. You are still likely to have a sensation of change but not, necessarily, of time. From this illustration, you may get a sense of how time is something that we have constructed from our use of numbers and counting.

For the second part of the experiment, watch something other than a clock that has change woven into it. This can be passing clouds, the surface of a lake or pond, or the wind in the trees. You can also let the water run from a faucet or place an ice cube on a plate. You can place your hand on your heart and follow the rise and fall of your abdomen as you breathe. Again, pay close and continuous attention for at least a few minutes, but do not keep track of the time. Ignore time and focus on change. As you pay close attention, you will notice different feelings than those you experienced when watching the clock. These may have a more organic and connected feel to them.

The experiences of watching the time of a clock and directly experiencing the temporality of change parallel the perspectives already described. Our personal experiences, strongly influenced by the fast-paced, time-starved culture, are focused on time (Gleick, 1999), even though moments of change and temporality are accessible to us. Similarly, the scientific study of intimacy uses time as a metric even though intimacy is more about temporality.

FROM CONTEXT TO TEMPORAL CONTEXT

Before examining temporal context, it helps to see how context can be atemporal; in fact, we usually think of it in this way. The most literal definition of context reads: "the parts of a written or spoken statement that precede or follow a specific word or passage, usually influencing its meaning or effect" (from the *Random House Dictionary of English Language*, 1969). Thus, context often implies the cognition or awareness of a sequence. But the meaning of the term is not restricted to sequence. Alternative definitions indicate "to weave together, to form, construct, or compose as by interweaving of parts." The *Oxford English Dictionary* provides an early example: *"the skynne is composed & context and woven with threds and vaynes"* (1541). Thus, context can mean togetherness and creativity as well as the more literal reading of how events fit in a sequence. In either case, context does not necessarily imply a temporal or dynamic property. It may simply refer to the static, unchangeable reading of signs and symbols, words and phrases.

The following example, sometimes used to illustrate a Gestalt principle of perception called "reference frames" demonstrates the effect of spatial, but not temporal, context. This figure, without any reference frame, may seem ambiguous to you. Unless you project or tacitly assume some reference frame or sequential context, the meaning (as a singularity) will remain ambiguous. Suppose you read it as falling in the following sequence:

You will be satisfied in concluding that the figure is not a pair of meaningless lines and recognize the pattern as the number 13 on subsequent presentations.

But now suppose that an alternative sequence were displayed:

Clearly, the meaning of a singularity depends on how it fits together with its surroundings. Although you are just looking at unchanging figures, the example also demonstrates the active and creative feature of context; we create meaning by interpreting a singularity when we may not even have enough information, when we lack sufficient context. So, even in this simple example, we can see that context involves the dependence, togetherness, and creativity of weaving in addition to the implication of sequence.

As noted in chapter 4, temporal context refers to a "living" medium through which intimacy is created and develops (cf. yüan). Chapter 1 described how three main contexts—interactions, situations, and phases—weave together to continually shape, and be shaped by, couple's experience of intimacy. It is difficult to furnish one single referent of temporal context and so I use it in different ways throughout the chapter. Table 6.1 lists different meanings of temporal context. Sometimes it refers to the actual cultural or historical situation of a couple, sometimes to the ways couples frame their communication to each other, and sometimes to the retrospective or prospective accounts couples give of their time together. It also combines how couples use private time and how society shapes the way intimacy proceeds through public and sacred time. This chameleon-like definition of temporal context appeals to the main thrust of the chapter; namely, that meaning is created through a variety of dynamic sources.

In fact, various authors use context in different ways because they *contextualize* relationships in different ways. Context can be viewed as the scenic backdrop against which individuals carry on their relationships. When seen in this way, context is abstract and objective. In fact, researchers have recently begun to operationalize temporal context in their study of marriage.[1] Alternatively, context may be understood as inseparable from the conduct of relationships and intertwined with it so completely that it cannot be viewed merely as a "scene" or framework. Recall the allegory from chapter 3 about the fish that emerges from the water and experiences that which sustained her all her life. Here, context provides sustenance and transcendence; it creates the very fabric of life and our awareness of it is a form of intimacy. This idea was echoed in the discussion of yüan in chapter 4, where context was seen as a living phenomenon (a complex set of interdependent conditions that give rise to events), a way of intimacy rather than a tool for analyzing. Thus, there is at least two different uses of context: one as abstract and static and one as real and dynamic. The main thesis of this chapter is that both the experience and the study of intimacy require embracing a *real* and *dynamic* context.

TABLE 6.1

DIFFERENT USES OF THE TERM TEMPORAL CONTEXT

Meaning	Reference	Example
Communication Scenarios	The placement of a phrase within a sequence of interchanges that gives the phrase meaning. The phrase changes meaning by when it occurs in a scenario.	The husband uses one word "Ready?" when asking his wife if she is ready to order food and later if she is ready to leave the restaurant.
Hierarchy of communication contexts	Refers to the idea that communications are nested in this order of contexts: domains > situations > events > acts (see Hymes, 1972; Leeds-Hurwitz, 1989).	At the restaurant (domain), he saw that it was time to order (situation); when she looked up from the menu (situation), he asked "Ready?" (act).
Account-making (perspectives on relationship history)	In talking about their relationship (past or future), partners narrate events with different interpretations, twists, or spins (see Harvey, Weber, & Orbuch, 1990).	Jay and Donna have different stories about how they first met and how it affected them.
Private versus public time	Events that occur between two intimates have their own context that may be separate from or overlap with events that occur when in their public roles.	On their way up the hill Jack told Jill a secret. This private act did not stop them from fetching water. Clandestine affairs have a history that runs concurrent to public life.
Sacred versus mundane time	Events during a spiritual or religious occasion have their own context that may overlap or be separate from experiences of mundane events.	As with most mornings, Donna liked looking at Jay as he slept. The fact that this was their first Christmas morning made him even more angelic to her.
Marriage (Commitment)	Refers to having made a commitment to stay with someone across time; thereby creating a prospective context (e.g., fidelity; shared investments) and a history unique to that marriage.	"My husband has been there for me and he continues to be there for me and we have been able to overcome difficulties because of our commitment to each other."
Transpersonal	Refers to experiencing the "big picture" of many overlapping contexts within a relationship and of being able to transcend differences and changes that keep occurring.	"God saved our marriage. When we rededicated our lives to the Lord, we had divorce papers ready to be signed . . ." (from Warren, 1995, p. 150).

TABLE 6.1 (*Continued*)

Methodological vs. Real time	Researchers use time-limited methods (experiments, surveys) that only partly capture the ongoing events of the real relationship (Kelly & McGrath, 1988).	The experiment asked partners to talk about 3 topics of importance; but when the couple left they spontaneously talked about what really bothered them.
Cultural meaning	Refers to a specific period within a culture that—because of important news stories, life styles, and fashions—phrases and behaviors have special meaning (Gollub, 1991).	In the 1960s, you might have been able to form a "meaningful" relationship if you gave the right person the "peace sign."
High versus Low context Cultures (Hall, 1983)	Refers to the fact that low context cultures require explicit, concrete, and literal communications, whereas high context cultures entail more allusive, relational meanings in communication.	In the United States asking for directions means getting concrete instructions. In Latin America, asking means knowing the person whether he or she wants to come, who is along the way, etc.
Scientific (empirical) versus Personal (experiential)	Although researchers *examine* sequences and orders of events that are independent of them, lovers *create* sequences of togetherness and mutual dependence.	Buck's (1989) theory views emotion within an evolutionary context. Through marriage, Jay and Donna have created a context of mutual respect.
Disciplinary context (academic)	Implicit temporal contexts of research disciplines; some take cultural history as their guide, while others use evolution, biological cycles, family generations, etc.	Anthropologists view mating rituals as driven by the cultural era. Biologists view such rituals as evolving certain complexities that enhanced survival.
Historical Reference (Luhmann, 1976)	Refers to how one refers to the history of one's own culture in the context of the past; a culture that is divorced from its past is "context-free."	For their careers, families move from city to city and gradually lose touch with relatives, friends, and a sense of tradition that kept them tied to the past.
Paradigm or "Taking for Granted" (Baert, 1992)	Scientists and lovers take methods for granted as the way to do things. They evoke a temporal context when they say "It has always been done that way." They may not actively reflect about what they do to perpetuate their own version of reality.	Taking-for-granted happens in relationships. Borys (1991) said: "Love can be as simple as giving Susan more attention than I give the T.V. Yet if I fail to make these simple gestures, ... my relationship with Susan will not be one of love, but one of neglect" (p. 46).

LOVERS AND SCIENTISTS: KNOWLEDGE FOR THEM BOTH

Time is context-bound. Anomalous themes have developed around the supposed objectivity of linear time. Rather than time being an objective entity that has certain "effects" on the mind and behavior, time is considered to be shared (intersubjective) organization of reality. The scientist is not seen as an objective observer, but a participant/observer in which his or her own culture is paramount. (Slife, 1993, p. 220)

At first glance, lovers and scientists seem to move in different worlds, find meaning in different ways, and struggle with different problems. Lovers find meaning in relationship to their partner or beloved; scientists find meaning in the search for truth. Lovers seek involvement, togetherness, and joy, and thereby learn to dialogue, care, trust, and surrender. Scientists use method, precision, and factual analysis, and thereby discern some regularity, pattern, or quirk of nature. To navigate the river of belonging, lovers bring their full attention, their souls. To observe and to understand, scientists bring their measures, their technology. The knowledge of science is external, precise, and impersonal. The knowledge of love is involving, sensual, and existential (cf. Reid, 1962). Certainly, these two groups contextualize the world in a distinct and separate manner.

However, when we pay close attention to how they know, the differences between lovers and scientists seem more apparent than real. Bronowski long argued against the common view of science as the mere accumulation of facts: Science is "a way of giving order, and therefore of giving unity and intelligibility, to the facts of nature" (Bronowski, 1962). True, they may seek unity in a different way (e.g., through organizing data, rather than in making time for togetherness), but it is still some form of unity they seek. Lovers, too, may know in different ways (e.g., through sensuality rather than analysis), but it is still some form of knowledge they seek. In certain senses, both scientists and lovers seek unity and knowledge; they also seek identity or certainty throughout the changes that they separately face. And because they both know that their purpose lies not simply in their daily routine, or in the methodological details, they also aspire toward fresher understandings: a love now revitalized or a paradigm now shifted. To create a transpersonal science of intimacy, I believe it is helpful to clarify these similarities (the processes of knowing, of identifying, and of transcending) and to synthesize them.

First, both groups seek knowledge. True lovers want to "know" their partner, if only in the biblical sense. They also—at least Don Juans or purveyors of sexual manuals—have their "methods" and "observations." Conversely, in its methods as well as its aims, the whole project of science may be interpreted as some Freudian sublimation of the sexual instinct. But whether or not all knowledge is sexual, both scientists and lovers enjoy discovery at some point. They derive satisfaction from exploring and from the metamorphosis, if not the fruition, of their search. Nature can disclose itself in ways that surprise researchers, just as lovers can chance on secrets that their beloved has kept hidden. The persistence of anomalies in science can lead to shifts in theory and method just as two lovers' differences can lead to a restructuring of the relationship. And knowledge is a collaboration too. Scientists must contend with their society. Peer reviews, research symposia, and conferences signal that scientific knowledge is somewhat consensual (Roth, 1987). When a research paper is accepted in a professional journal it indicates some consensual validation; that is, the contribution was deemed worthy as an advancement of knowledge. Similarly, lovers define the status of their love by how they accept and reject each other, how they agree and disagree, in their own private research community of two.

Second, as they come to know, both groups ultimately face the intermin ble dance of change. Lovers seek a permanence or continuity to their love and attempt to fix their relationship in time, to achieve some sense of security, or some protection against infidelity, abandonment, or betrayal. Scientists also hone the reliability of their measures in hopes that their discoveries are more valid than erroneous, that they hold up under further scrutiny. Within the jargon of modern psychotherapy, intimates sometimes borrow a scientific metaphor when they feel known or seen and say "I feel *validated* by you" or "I appreciate your *feedback*" (Sarnoff & Sarnoff, 1989). By wanting to know, both scientists and lovers assume some stability, some underlying pattern or identity that can be

> *The thirst for knowing hints at a meta-motive in humanity—lovers and scientists take different "objects" to know but the process they engage in fulfills a similar need.*

carved out of the flux. They both seek to reify and affirm this identity in their own way—through showing love or through validation, by demonstrating trustworthiness or by discerning regularity against the random background.

Finally, and most importantly, both groups come to believe or sense that their knowledge has limits and imperfections. Patterns identified today are only a piece of the whole; they can fray or change with time and unpredictable forces. Intimates do not live in laboratories where all variables can be monitored; and as faithful as they may be in representing nature, telescopes and microscopes are just that, *re*-presenters or tools. Bronowski (1978) reminded us that "there is no permanence to scientific concepts because they are only our interpretations of natural phenomena. . . . We merely make a temporary invention which covers that part of the world accessible to us at that moment" (p. 96).

Biases must be accounted for, factored in, and ultimately transcended in order to create a clearer and bigger picture. Such transcendence takes time and patience (cf. in time I see). Knowledge is more often cumulative than sudden and it accrues through the life mindfully led or the details carefully organized. The discipline of a science does not grow without a paradigm shift. The love of a relationship stagnates when partners behave within stereotypical routines— however comfortable or secure—that do not admit change. Both lovers and scientists must be willing to abandon their steadfast and seemingly "objective" viewpoints, and to some extent, their identities. Transcendence happens in two ways in this path of knowledge: The ability to transcend the details, the "small stuff," and the ability to move ahead, to surrender one's identity in the commonplace or the status quo, and face the unknown future.

Keller (1983), in her biography of Barbara McClintock, described how this pioneer geneticist held views that went against the prevailing paradigm of her peers. Her vision took years of painstaking, detailed documentation and it led to a major shift in our knowledge of genetics. Keller wrote:

> A deep reverence for nature, a capacity for union with that which is to be known—these reflect a different image of science from that of a purely rational enterprise. Yet the two images have coexisted throughout history. We are familiar with the idea that forms of mysticism—a commitment to the unity of experience, the oneness of nature, the fundamental mystery underlying the laws of nature—plays an essential role in the process of scientific discovery. Einstein called it "cosmic religiosity." In turn, the experience of creative insight reinforces these commitments, fostering a sense of the limitations of the scientific method, and an appreciation of other ways of knowing. (p. 201)

Mystery inspires the attuned lover as well as the attentive scientist, and requires a transformation of their approach. The world is filled with subtle changes that escape the casual observer or partner. In a manner that defines a lover's sensitivity as well as a scientist's precision, mindfulness of this world requires examining assumptions, recategorizing our past, and contextualizing experience (or data) in new and creative ways (see Langer, 1989). Keller described how McClintock had access to "another way of knowing" because she was emotionally invested in her attention to complexity and irregularity: "Her answer is simple. Over and over again, she tells us one must have time to look, the patience to "hear what the material has to say to you," the openness to "let it come to you." Above all, one must have "a feeling for the organism" (p. 198).

Thus, the impersonal methods of science may differ from the involving passions of lovers, and their objectives also vary, but certain processes are common to both. For in order to know, we must have the patience to explore and to listen; and as we discover, we appreciate change and complexity until we gradually surrender particular views in light of the bigger picture. Nature gradually reveals its intimations just as love reveals its gifts. This is both the hard work and the joy on the path of knowledge.

THE APPRECIATION OF PROCESS AND SEQUENCE

Do not be bewildered by the surfaces; in the depths all becomes law.
—Rainer Maria Rilke

It is a fact of nature that intimacy rarely occurs as a singular event. Patterns emerge in time, not in one secret shared or one statistical test. Beneath the conversations of lovers, beneath the series of research findings, lies a deeper process. Lovers who arrive "face-to-face without intermediary" (Levinas, 1987) and scientists who come to a "feeling for the organism" begin their journeys on the surface but gradually articulate a deeper meaning. We often vacillate between these two levels of time: between understanding what is happening (the sequence of *time*, of actions and events) and involving ourselves within it (embracing the *temporal* process). Intimacy, by its very nature, centers and vitalizes this vacillation. Intimacy brings together and contextualizes our mundane and our divine longings. That is, intimacy takes us from time to temporality and back again as we seek to know (without objectifying).

Whereas science is often equated with the empirical analysis of causal change, transpersonal science looks for the wholeness or the interconnectedness of actions and events. Much has been written about different types of knowing that pertain to a process–wholeness versus a causal–sequence distinction. Authors distinguish intuitive from intellective knowing (e.g., Hayward, 1987; also see Gardner, 1984), "intimate" knowing from "separate" knowing in women's studies (Belenky et al., 1986), and contextual from componential intelligence (Sternberg, 1988). In a parallel fashion, philosophers make the distinction between flow and sequential time (e.g., Neville, 1993) and between a "temporal articulation" of wholeness and an "atemporal objectification" of causality (Faulconer & Williams, 1985). Intuitive-connected knowing is often associated with understanding of process, whereas intellective-componential reasoning is often associated with analysis of sequence.

In bridging these distinctions, we can learn about intimacy in a new way. As defined here, a transpersonal analysis seeks to understand sequence and embrace process, to honor both the intellectual and the intuitive. Strict rational empiricism—gathering evidence, the distillation of fact—tends to emphasize causal sequence over inter-connectedness. In contrast, a transpersonal approach seeks unity from evidence and increased consciousness from studying both the causal sequence and the deeper process. Transpersonal science appreciates transformation within the mundane, the extraordinary within the ordinary, the universal within the personal.

Philosophy offers many ideas that aid this articulation. Buber (1970), contrasted the "It-world" and the "You-world." The It-world emerges from experience, and is mediated by the past, conditional, causal, and measurable; it is populated by separate identities or egos. The You-world emerges through living participation, of joining with others in full consciousness; it is a world populated by persons, rather than egos, entering into relationship with other persons. For Buber, the I that says "I–It" resembles the empiricist who isolates particulars and, through logic and theory, attempts to join them together, to understand them but without the participation of relationship. The You of the I–You world is more than an aggregation of qualities. Through presence and participation, "You" always emerges whole in the consciousness of "I" or self. The You also appears as a deeper continuity and so cannot be known from an analysis of some sequence or series of encounters. According to Buber (1970):

> The man who has acquired an I and says I-It assumes a position before
> things but does not confront them in the current of reciprocity. He bends
> down to examine particulars under the objectifying magnifying glass of
> close scrutiny, or he uses the objectifying telescope of distant vision to
> arrange them as mere scenery. In his contemplation he isolates them
> without any feeling for the exclusive. . . . Only now he experiences things
> as aggregates of qualities. . . . Only now does he place things in a spatio-
> temporal-causal context; only now does each receive its place, its course,
> its measurability, its conditionality. (pp. 80–81)

Feminist philosophers (e.g., Benjamin, 1988; Keller, 1986) echo Buber in their attempts to address a central problem for love: how to know and love the other (i.e., You) without completely objectifying them and their particular attributes. The title of one book sums up their argument: *From a Broken Web: Separation, Sexism, and Self* (Keller, 1986). In the I–It world, a world inhabited by both lovers and scientists, time's course and sequence requires us to construct the other from memory, from past recollections of their qualities. In the I–You world, in the time of relationship, "the current of reciprocity" obviates the need for such construction or assembly. "The You appears in time, but in that of a process that is fulfilled in itself—a process lived through not as a piece that is part of a constant and organized sequence but in a 'duration' whose purely intensive dimension can be determined only by starting from You. It appears simultaneously as acting on and as acted upon, but not as if it had been fitted into a causal chain; rather as, in its reciprocity with the I, the beginning and end of the event" (Keller, p. 81).

Other philosophers (Bergson, 1911; Levinas, 1987), claim that time is not intellectual abstraction or sensation of order but a process that permeates our consciousness of the other. Levinas equated time with the "always of relationship, an aspiration and an awaiting." Time and intimacy are woven together in our consciousness at a deep, existential level. Time has the wholeness and enduring quality (Bergson's *durée*, Levinas' *eternal alterity*) that we weave into our consciousness of relationships with others.

Consciousness of such weaving entails the capacity to perceive and live in multiple temporal contexts. At one level, these are the temporal contexts of the self, the other person, and the creative iterations that arise from joining together. At a more spiritual level, philosophers describe a transcendence of context. Buber talked about the "eternal you" of God and the "thirst for something spread out in time, for duration" (p. 162; also see Hassel, 1985, on "the secular transcendent"). Levinas (1987) writes: "to care for one's neighbor more than oneself, to take on responsibility for the Other, . . . is to enter into a *sacred* rather than an ontological or epistemological history" (p. 24). Thus, the You-world is ultimately timeless and also a place where—through salvation, enlightenment, or divine grace—we can become conscious of an ultimate or sacred context, namely, eternity (Neville, 1993).

Fraser (1975) hypothesized an instinctual drive for two experiences of this timelessness: the desire for continuity (permanent relationship) and the desire for the unexpected. We resolve this existential tension toward Being (the search for continuity) and Becoming (the enjoyment of uncertainty) in the context of social institutions (in civilization's hope for the true, the good and the beautiful). We try to balance continuity and uncertainty in our mutual participation through religion, science, the arts, politics, and the moral life. A deep temporal structure, one that combines the two instincts, underlies all our institutions, including courtship and marriage. Such institutions provide signposts that allow us to encounter the deeper process of timelessness and return to the surface sequence of timeliness, the duties and responsibilities of one's social roles (cf. Berger, 1980, on how the secularization of modernity may obscure these signposts).

Because they persist, social institutions endow us with a sense of certainty, a sense born from the socialized expectation of sequence in routines, timetables, and anniversaries. We feel secure and happy when we follow role obligations as parents, spouses, and workers. But institutions also provide a context for the unknown, the mystery that lies in waiting for and enjoying the true, the good, and the beautiful. However, in and of themselves, institutions cannot center and animate the soul as can intimacy. They can and do rob us of a self, take away our time, and leave us feeling empty (cf. "caught by the system;" Malone & Malone, 1987). Intimacy is thus challenged by and challenges institution. On the one hand, we need the certainty of knowing that our partner will fulfill duties. On the other hand, we want to change and become.

These tensions exist for scientists as well. As in choosing marriage with a particular person, to invest time in a particular line of research, involves choosing a particular from the general (from "the *unchosen* absolute"; see Hassel, 1985). Such choice brings risk, uncertainty, and obligation. The lover who gives in marriage, who embraces the other exclusively, in "the current of reciprocity," must also learn to be responsible and responsive in the I–It world. The empiricist who desires to really know (have a feeling for) their subject must also learn how not to objectify and fragment it. Lovers face the dialectical problem of either overanalyzing their relationships on one hand or by failing to be mindful and thoughtful of their partner on the other. By focusing on prediction and particulars, scientists of personal relationships can get caught up in trivial commonsense aspects of relationships and fail to appreciate the more complex and ongoing revelation of lover to lover, the "duration" of a fulfilling intimacy.

The ability to do meaningful research on intimacy depends upon how researchers address these tensions in themselves and in their ability to develop the "big picture" (i.e., increasingly accurate models of relationship complexity). Dialectical theories of relationship change (e.g., separateness–closeness; instability–predictability; openness–closedness) represent one step in this direction (Altman et al., 1981; Baxter, 1988, 1990; Bochner, 1976; Conville, 1991; Montgomery, 1993; Wilmot, 1987). A transpersonal approach could also help to create a new sense of meaning. We lose perspective by focusing on the empirical march of the It-world and neglect the true, the good, and the beautiful of the You-world. We gain perspective by enriching the context of study to include both worlds, one unfolding in time, and one that—through the spiritual aspects of intimacy and the deeper, scientific commitment to mystery—transcends time.

TEMPORAL CONTEXT IN THE SOCIAL SCIENCES

Much has been written about the role of context in the creation of meaning in social relations (see Tracy, 1998). Bateson (1979) acknowledged that nothing has meaning except it be contextualized. Examples are given of how a single utterance, behavior, or sign takes on different meaning depending upon preceding or subsequent conditions or upon the way the perceiver frames, and "situates" (Leeds-Hurwitz, 1989) these surrounding features, or "punctuates" a communication sequence (Watzlawick, 1976). Watzlawick gave the example of U.S. soldiers who experienced confusion when courting English women during and after World War II. Kissing in the English cultural pattern came considerably later than in the American, and so was interpreted as a radical escalation in sexual intimacy by the women who then either ran away (to the soldier's chagrin) or offered themselves sexually (to the soldier's amazement).

Gergen (1988) explained how his good friends approach each other at a social gathering where he then observed Ross reaching out and momentarily touch Laura's hair. Gergen used context in two ways to help him understand this action. If Ross had told him a week ago that he was madly in love with Laura, Gergen would use a *retrospective context*, where events occurring prior to the action help to define it (as a sign of affection). If Laura smiles and takes Ross's hand, Gergen would use an *emergent context*, where events that follow the act help to define it (as perhaps a request to show their status as a hand-holding couple). Here context is defined by reference to past and present, in horizontal time. Analyses of context are not limited to such anecdotal accounts. Researchers have examined the role of context using quantitative (e.g., McGill, 1989) as well as qualitative methodologies (e.g., Belenky et al., 1986).

Two fields in particular, communication studies and sociology, offer important theoretical insight into temporal context. Communication scientists examine context to show how communication works in interpersonal interaction (conversation, dialogue; see Tracy, 1998). Sociologists view context in terms of self and society, how social selves are defined in terms of the wider social and cultural context, and how these selves change this context. Three other approaches toward understanding temporal context are discussed in this chapter: evolutionary, chronobiological, and social psychological. Figure 6.2 provides an outline of the remaining sections of this chapter. As you read through this cross-disciplinary approach, keep in mind the central focus (as depicted in Fig. 6.2): Intimate relations both use, and are shaped by, various temporal contexts to create meaning (deeper intimacy).

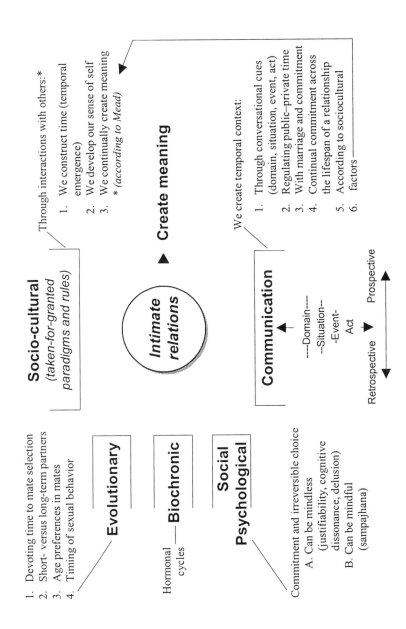

FIG. 6.2. Temporal contexts in the social sciences (outline of text in chapter)

COMMUNICATION AND TEMPORAL CONTEXT

> Meaning-making, many (but not all) discourse scholars argue, requires study
> of naturally occurring discourse. Not only is it essential to study talk in its
> everyday contexts, but to aggregate instances, as is necessary in quantitative
> analyses that seek to assess causal relationships, is to ignore what is key:
> meaning-making as a highly local process, dependent on the situation and
> the particular moves and countermoves of its people. (Tracy, 1998, p. 7)

Much of our communication with others depends on context. Context helps
reduce uncertainty in social situations. Social competence, or the ability to
communicate well and to be understood, requires the capacity to monitor social
contexts, and to be in tune or "in synch" with the social occasion. This section
describes five processes of or related to context use in communication. These
are: (a) the ways we use context in conversation and communication to cue,
imply special meaning, and ultimately shape intimacy; (b) the importance of
temporal context for maintaining a couple's "private" world of intimacy; (c) the
shared perception of temporal context as the subjective substrate for commitment
and marriage; (d) the ways couples use their time (i.e., weave temporal context)
to create meaning throughout marriage; and (e) the role of culture as it impacts
how we communicate about and share time in personal relationships. Following
this analysis of communication process, I introduce the reader to some of the
research in behavioral communication sequences within couples. Here I hope to
show that research examining even brief, time-limited interaction sequences can
benefit from adapting a framework of multiple temporal contexts.

Contextual Cues in Conversation Shape Intimacy

Through socialization, individuals learn how to recognize and to give
"contextualization cues" (Gumperz, 1982), information supplied *during* an
interaction that helps participants understand unspoken assumptions and
appropriately interpret verbal and nonverbal acts. Attempts at deepening and
maintaining (and even preventing or destroying) intimacy require a variety of
acts in which intimates monitor each other for the "right time" to say something
and for evidence that the communication act involves seeking affinity (Daly &
Kresier, 1994). Whole books and popular magazine articles are devoted to this
topic (e.g., Sills, 1987). Davis (1973) described how in the "getting to know
you" phase of intimacy, contextualization cues are crucial:

> Each intimate can enhance the probability that the other will respond in
> the hoped-for way to his own questions concerning the other's crucial
> secrets if he asks them directly, that is, at those times and places when
> and where the other is unusually disposed to disclose. The "right time"
> for inquiry and revelation is when each feels especially close to the
> other—as, for instance, when they have both just finished listening to a

favorite concerto together. The "wrong time" is when each feels especially distant from the other—as, for instance, when one is preoccupied with a toothache or headache, when one has been offended by the other, or when one has observed the other engaging in behavior unbecoming his image of an intimate. (p. 113)

When communicators share a joint history, a common culture, or a mutual familiarity with situations, they tacitly locate themselves and their communication within different temporal contexts; meaning becomes clear and the conversation flows. Chapple (1970) identified the smooth coordination of communication "turn-taking" as "mutual entrainment." Hall (1983) described the general flow between people as "interpersonal synchrony." This smoothness is characteristic of intimate dialogue. Intimates who know each other for some time do not often require contextualization cues to understand each other; meaning is a given (intentional) rather than something to be searched for (referential).

Leeds-Hurwitz (1989) reviewed the literature on context in everyday communication. She described levels within a hierarchy of contexts that communicators use (cf. Hymes, 1972). In this model, the highest level of meaning is derived from the physical setting, or domain (e.g., school, church, bedroom), in which the behavior occurs. This is followed, in turn, by the narrower contexts of situation, events, and acts. A situation has a single purpose, topic, or group of participants, and lasts for a specific amount of time (e.g., show-and-tell at school, community announcements at church). Within situations are events or sets of interactions (e.g., Johnny's turtle is part of show-and-tell). Lastly, events are comprised of acts, or gestures, actions, or utterances (e.g., Johnny holding up the turtle, the pastor forgetting to mention someone's name). In this nested model, a set of acts constitutes longer events that constitute usually longer situations that constitute domains. Awareness or the ability to monitor, clarify, or signal these nested relationships allows for clearer meanings and security against breakdowns in communication. Thus, Johnny holding up his turtle during church would have entirely different meaning (mischief á la Tom Sawyer) than in school during show-and-tell.

RESEARCH	REFLECTION	13

CONTEXT & WORKING THROUGH: MEANING IN CONFLICT

A breakdown in context can lead to conflict. Researchers have developed a questionnaire that taps how partners process through difficulties with communication skills (Burleson, Kunkel, Samter, & Werking, 1996). The *conflict management* scale assesses whether one's partner can reach mutually satisfying solutions. Consider these items (adapted from Burleson et al., 1996) and the meaning of "working through" as synonymous with repairing context.

1. My partner helps me see that even the best of relationships has its conflicts or disagreements that need to be worked through.
2. My partner makes me believe it's possible to resolve our conflict or disagreements that need to be worked through.

These ideas are directly relevant for intimacy. In a sense, intimacy is always "nested" (vertically or upward) in time, so much as to minimize the effort of communication. But intimacy—as presence for—also situates horizontally as the present connecting the past and future. In the earlier example provided by Gergen, Laura may "just know" what Ross means by touching her hair; the somatic immediacy and sensuality of lovers is itself a context. Laura need not refer backward to a retrospective context or forward to some emergent context to understand. Nor need she refer upward to the situation or domain; Ross's act is a simple reflection of his abiding love for her. Intimacy weaves from and within both vertical and horizontal time (see epigram quote by Hall at beginning of chapter).

Leeds-Hurwitz (1989) pointed out that "no one context by itself creates anything: it is the combination of holding a set of possible contexts in common that has the potential for creating a sense of group" (p. 74). This sense of group hearkens to the quality of wholeness, togetherness, or belonging within the definition of context as weaving. Individuals gain a sense of belonging with others, of participating in some common purpose or future, because they reside in multiple temporal contexts.

In fact, intimates may be endeared to each other's idiosyncrasies or particular habits because such habits are familiar; they are nested within temporal contexts the couple has created together. Knapp (1984) describes how intimates have unique speech patterns or personal idioms that signal their special, intimate status to each other: "As a result of their relationship history, intimates often develop an interpersonal jargon with private symbols and private meanings, known only to the intimate pair. In addition, they develop words and phrases commonly used by others that have *special meaning* for them" (p. 25, italics added). The special meaning lies in the fact that partner nicknames, expressions of affection, or sexual euphemisms refer to the joint history (temporal context) that is privately theirs. Interestingly, research shows that idiom use may be more frequent in young couples, during their identity formation stage, but more important for enduring satisfaction among midlife couples (Bruess & Pearson, 1993).

Temporal Context and the Developing, Private World of Couples

Although intimate communication touches our depths, and leads to changes in these depths, it also has a practical function for scheduling of privacy. First, intimate communication touches upon those aspects of our selves that are deep and private. Different types psychotherapy indicate that for a relationship to mature there must be greater vulnerability in communication, a willingness to disclose one's private self (Fisher & Stricker, 1982; Sarnoff & Sarnoff, 1989). Second, just as the self has these deeper aspects, so does time. Society, through its calendars and institutions, provides guidelines for segregating time domains: private from public, sacred and profane (Fraser, 1987). Intimate partners have needs either for private time or for spiritual time and these may or may not overlap. Third, intimate communication, through the course of a relationship, usually leads to changes in the self of both partners. Theory and research suggests that couple's communication changes who they are (Levinger, 1983; Stephen, 1985). Finally, how a couple regulates their private and public time, alone and together, may be critical to the development of the relationship (cf. Altman et al., 1981; on privacy regulation).

Different authors have distinguished between private and public time (Zerubavel, 1981) and between sacred and profane time (Hall, 1983; Zerubavel, 1981). We get personal or private time by controlling our social accessibility, by how we schedule our time to create social distance, a sort of temporal boundary. Conversely, public time includes shared schedules and the commitments, social routines and obligations that sustain public life. The distinction between sacred and profane time is defined by how one engages their imagination, spends time in contemplation, or cultivates spirituality (through creativity, religion, ritual, ceremony, or spiritual practice) as a counterpoint to the explicit, formulated, talked about, or ordinary clock time of society.

One's ability to regulate or control their time for privacy or spirituality, as well as friends or work, also provides identity and freedom. "Uninterrupted availability can be a sign of either great devotion if done freely or of slavery if done involuntarily" (Fraser, 1987, p. 193). So it is for intimates who devote themselves to a joint identity as a couple and yet desire their autonomy within the relationship. The weaving of temporal context arises from how intimates balance their private-public time and the sacred-profane time both alone and together as a couple. Society makes these contexts easier to navigate by segregating time for couples (e.g., weekends for private time, holidays for sacred time, see Zerubavel, 1981).

> *Both the self and time have private and public dimensions. Intimacy moves between these dimensions and enriches our experience of both.*

Intimate partners exercise their freedom to move back and forth across private-public boundaries through signals (Knapp, 1984), which reify their status as an intimate pair (Duck, 1994). Again, Knapp provided examples from his research: "Sometimes it was necessary for the couple to communicate something in front of others without actually saying it. Thus, 'What's new?' was interpreted by one couple as 'I'm bored and ready to leave'; for another couple, 'Let's go for a bike ride' meant 'Let's go outside and smoke some dope'" (p. 226). The nonverbal cues that intimates give each other can be so subtle as to leave even their friends spellbound in believing that any communication occurred at all.

But how do couples get to this state of "private unity," or do people select others with whom this intimacy is more likely to begin with? Some research models of communication, including "fixed-sequence" models, suggest that individuals use information from their interactions with their partner at successive stages of commitment to determine future suitability. Alternatively, "circular–

causal" models indicate that commitment may depend on how partners become more interdependent through communication over time (Levinger, 1983). In the fixed-sequence view, time progresses independently of the couple; in the circular–causal view, intimates contextualize time as ongoing and cyclical. Stephen (1985), whose research supports the latter view, suggested:

> Both partner's views of the world are subtly eroded, altered, and recast through conversation, leading eventually to the construction of a "couple reality" or "homodynamic code" (Kreckel, 1982), a private system of meaning that is fully accessible only to couple members themselves . . . Beliefs, attitudes, values, and individual frameworks for interpreting reality are reworked to accommodate divergent views. This process gradually generates a "micro-culture" (Berger & Kellner, 1964; Fine, 1979), which serves to orient couple members with regard to each other and aspects of the world beyond their relationship. (p. 957).

The "micro-culture" of privacy only gradually develops and emerges over time rather than as the result of some sequence. Partners join together in developing this culture through the mutual regulation of private time as a couple. But their micro-culture is also subject to change, and as the relationship develops, partners face difficulties in learning how to get along. Ideally, the nature of communication changes to enrich the couple as they face changes in their public lives and private selves.

Private Selves Through Public Time: Marriage as Creation of Temporal Context

But how do couples stay together through these changes? Love and marriage is the typical response to this question. Marital engagement and the wedding ceremony are themselves forms of communication, from the (private) couple to their (public) society. In a sense, marriage is a temporal context in public time: It communicates an agreement about the future exclusivity or privacy of the couple. This agreement may or may not be imbued with private or sacred time. Do they see their wedding as a spiritual event? Is their marriage a way of getting more private time or of bringing their families together for more shared, public time? Answers to these questions depend as much on cultural and marriage rituals as on the families' and the partners' own wishes. The meaning of marriage depends on how both the couple and society contextualize it. Such meanings also change over the duration of a marriage.

For example, from a completely impersonal angle, the ritual of marriage (e.g., a shower, the wedding) may merely be a "transition event" (Surra & Huston, 1987) and have little spiritual meaning. In the minds of newlyweds, the decision to marry may occur as a result of an impersonal, causal sequence rather than some transcendent principle: "Respondents tend to explain why the probability of marriage changed in terms of causal chains and that these causal chains are sometimes long, complex, and consequential for respondents. One man said, for instance, "A conflict she had with her family was a big influence in that it led to our decision to live together, which, in turn, led to our finding out we had similar routines and ways of doing things" (Surra & Huston, 1987, p. 114). For those considering commitment or for the newly committed, marriage may just be the appropriate or convenient next step in a sequence and not, necessarily, an appeal to unity. Similarly, marriage can be reduced to a formal contract rather than held as a covenant or sacred agreement (cf. "sacramental couple," Gallagher, Maloney, Rousseau, & Wilczak, 1989).

Alternatively, the sacred time of marriage ceremony can sustain a couple for some time afterward (beyond the honeymoon phase). Here, the wedding represents an announcement of unity as well as a commitment to transcend differences and hardships that arise. In contrast to Surra and Huston's research on newlyweds, another study asked long-term marriage partners to retrospect on their reasons for marrying. In these couples, getting married for love—as opposed to external, impersonal circumstances—was associated with a more enduring commitment with less marital problems (Swensen, Eskew, & Kohlhepp, 1981; Swensen & Trahaug, 1985). Brothers (1994) summarized this research:

> What makes some marriages endure while others fail? . . . [Psychologists] got the answer when they asked this key question: "Why did you marry your spouse when you did, instead of marrying somebody else, or staying single?" Some said they married "because it was time" or "it was expected," or "my parents wanted grandchildren." And the researchers found that these marriages were less likely to last than those who married "because I love her," or "I wanted to spend the rest of my life with this person," or in other ways showed that, from the beginning, they were committed to the chosen spouse. This commitment indicated lasting love. (p. 56)

Partners also negotiate meanings as they construe their reasons for marriage. These may be complicit or collusive meanings, pacts to keep each other from growing. They may also be mutual validations (cf. "mutual identity confirmation," Knudson, 1985), ways of reaffirming self through threats to one's self-concept (Reis & Shaver, 1988), or threats to loving itself (Sarnoff & Sarnoff, 1989). In cocreating the future, a healthy marriage becomes more of a process of communication rather than a single event or episode, a way of reducing uncertainty rather than some absolute reduction in certainty (C. R. Berger, 1988). Actually, in another study (see Levinger, Faunce, & Rands, 1976, in Levinger & Rands, 1985), where long married couples were asked what contributed most to their high marital satisfaction, two conclusions emerged. First, marriage was seen as a process (e.g., one wife said: "Marriage is not a constant; it's an ever-changing, growing, moving-ahead kind of process"). Second, marital compatibility required effort in mutual problem solving (e.g., "working together and sharing"). Thus, whether a relationship remains healthy may depend on an understanding of intimacy as a process and the shared collaboration of meaning in that process.

The aforementioned studies suggest that for some younger couples and for longer term married partners who are less satisfied with their relationship, marriage may be seen in terms of causality, in sequential "causal chains." For more happily married couples and for older couples who reflect on the success of their marriage, commitment is seen as an enduring love and an ongoing process. This hearkens to the transpersonal theme discussed in previous chapters and to the fact that a successful marriage may depend on building a transpersonal context. Warren (1995) surveyed 100 of the most happily married couples he could find. Calling these "triumphant marriages," Warren (1995) discovered that spirituality (i.e., *inside, quest, eternal, and enduring*) was one secret of success:

> The 100 couples in our sample consistently cited some form of spirituality as crucial to the development of their extremely healthy marriages. . . . Spirituality involves what is *inside*. It is built around a *quest* for deeper *meaning*, for a clearer sense about profound and *eternal* matters. Marriages that involve two people who share experiences, thoughts, concerns, and involvement in these areas of life tend to hold together and become richer *over time*. These marriages usually are extremely close and ultimately healthy. (pp. 151-161 italics added)

Marriage Across the Life Span: The Continual Creation of Meaning

The formal contract of marriage often increases a couple's sense of certainty. But the certainty of that contract must be continually negotiated across the life span (cf. "affinity maintenance," Daly & Kreiser, 1994). If the relationship is based solely on contractual rules and stereotypical routines—if they are too rule conscious (Raush, 1981)—the couple has entered into the I–It world and may be captured by it. In order to sustain intimacy over time, intimates must continually "re-synthesize" the meaning of their relationship by confirming each other's views of it. Gottman and Silver (1999), based on years of research, viewed the continual creation of meaning as one of the fundamental principles for making marriages work. Marital quality appears to depend on strategic communications that indicate a desire for affinity between partners, including sensitivity, spirituality, and honesty (see Daly & Kreiser, 1994). But maintaining these communications is a precious weave; at various points in its history, a relationship goes through some disintegration unless or until there is re-synthesis:

> Members have entered Disintegration when they begin noticing their relationship, noticing it instead of being in it. Something is askew, out of kilter. What they notice is Difference; Difference is becoming problematic. The problematic differences they encounter include the dialectical oppositions of time, affect, and intimacy. Encountering such difference shoves a relational partner out of ordinary routines so that the

relationship is observed as if from the outside. . . . The routine becomes momentarily strange, and they see what they had looked through before. (Conville, 1991, p. 93)

Conville suggested that ongoing awareness of differences requires communication work. Such work resolves the "Difference" and, once again, the couple resynthesizes a new sense of unity. The ability to shift from disruption to new routines depends on how partners confirm each other amidst the inconstant process of defining and redefining their relationship (see *calibration*, p. 289).

Conville also argued, echoing Raush (1981), that the lack of supporting community and kinship networks of postindustrial society leaves couples without a context to negotiate through periods of disintegration. The burden to develop rules continually rests on the shoulders of the couple. He cited research by Parks and Adelman (1983), where the best predictor of certainty in a relationship is one partner's communication with the other's social network of friends and family. More recent research indicates that marital satisfaction is higher for those who have a shared family network as well as separate friends in comparison to those who have little or no shared family (Stein, Bush, Ross, & Ward, 1992). Thus, when the relationship is secure and governed by routine, couples weave context by communicating by themselves, in private time. When relationships experience undue pressure and routines are broken, the couple may weave a wider net in public time. These breaks in routine, the perception that "something is askew, out of kilter" indicates a fraying within the couple's temporal context. It then makes sense to seek for connectedness that links them to the broader temporal context of society. From the transpersonal perspective, a deeper weaving emerges where the couple blends their private and public time of their support network.

> *Healthy marriages appear to require the partners continued ability to "construct" the marriage by balancing their public identity with their private intimacy.*

Research suggests that time relates to marital well-being when time spent together is not empty activity or even pleasant; but rather, when it enriches the self of married partners (Reissman, Aron, & Bergen, 1993). Other research has shown that just staying together over time is no guarantee of satisfaction. In fact, love may decrease over the later years of marriage after the children have gone and after retirement (Swensen et al., 1981). In this study, retired partners who had developed a self beyond their stereotypical roles and had greater self-awareness (i.e., greater ego development), expressed more affection, worked through unexpressed feelings, and generally disclosed more to each other.

Still, other research shows that "among heterosexual couples, young men have less desire for their partner's companionship than do young women, but the tables turn as the couple ages" (Blumstein & Schwartz, 1983). Apparently, stereotypical routines tend to give men more time away from home in the earlier stages of marriage. As they get older, their desire for private time with their partner increases—often to the chagrin of some of their wives. Blumstein and Schwartz provided the following example from one 66-year-old wife telling about her husband of 44 years:

> I have to say that I would like more time by myself. . . . His needs are different from mine, and sometimes I would like him around and sometimes I just don't. . . . He can just feel alone even when I'm in the room, whereas I really need to be alone. He would prefer to do everything with me in the room. He doesn't even need to read alone, whereas I like to go off and really have some private time. . . . This has been much more intense ever since he retired because he wants to fill up all that time with me and I want to go over and see the children and do things for them. . . . I have been hoping that he will get active in one of those organizations or something because I am not going to be with him all the time. (p. 177)

This account reveals much about the relation of time to intimacy that may not emerge until stereotypical routines subside in retirement (see Dressler, 1973). The wife's claim that "he wants to fill up all that time with me" reflects different needs for private time but also different meanings of intimacy. Perhaps the husband cannot tolerate aloneness or perhaps, in coming closer to death, he longs for connection. Either way, how couples decide to spend their time requires communication and resynthesis after transitions, even after retirement. According to Conville: "the routine becomes momentarily strange, and they see what they had looked through before." When the wife indicates "I am not going to be with him all the time," her wish for separateness may be that she cares about him or that—in an awareness of death—she recognizes the need in herself to work through the ultimate separation from her husband. Either way, and as the previous research suggests (Swensen et al., 1981), the ability to love later on and throughout life may be depend on maturity in self-intimacy (ego development) and the willingness to keep resynthesizing, and reweaving, the temporal context of that love.

Time's Cultural Context: The Polychronic Weave and Feminism

Thus far, communication has been linked to temporal context in several ways. Couples require context for communication to occur at "the right time." Through loving communication, commitment, and social support, couples learn to use time for weaving a deeper and wider context that contributes to marital satisfaction over the life span. Speaking to this wider view, Hall (1983) made a distinction between high context or polychronic, cultures and low context, or monochronic, cultures. In low context cultures, communication depends upon explicit, overt, and literal explanations. With emphasis on tasks, schedules, and procedures, time tends to be more monochronic or linear. High context cultures are defined by communication, where meaning is more often assumed; personal relationships are not given intrinsic value because of the roles, jobs, or situations involved. In such cultures, polychronic time "brings people together and accentuates highly personalized relationships." Hall argued that "if you value people, you must hear them out and cannot cut them off simply because of a schedule" (p. 50). Polychronic time (P-time) emphasizes communion, whereas monochronic time (M-time) emphasizes communication.

There are parallels between polychronic time or high context cultures and intimacy. In such cultures, there is less concern about time management and scheduling and more emphasis on social networks, the family, the community, and close friends. High context means that individuals require less effort when communicating; the context is a given just as it is for the sensuality or conversational flow of intimacy. Hall argued that the networking aspect of intimacy seems to be more comfortable for women than men and that "at the preconscious level, M-time is male time and P-time is female time." He gave the example of how women "can raise several children at once, run a household, hold a job, be a wife, mother, nurse, tutor, chauffeur, and general fixer upper" (p. 49). They are less oriented to the compartmentalized, segmented world and can juggle many times at once.

As suggested in chap. 2 (p. 53), the capacity for intimacy requires sensitivity to multiple temporal contexts. Research has, in fact, shown that women tend to be more comfortable with intimate self-disclosure than men (e.g., Cline, 1989; Dindia & Allen, 1992; Hacker, 1981). Also, separate studies have found that wives' perceptions of a marriage (e.g., understanding of their husbands) predict marital well-being to a greater degree than husbands' perception (e.g., Acitelli, Douvan, & Veroff, 1993; Barry, 1970; Sillars, 1985). These findings suggest that the smooth functioning of the relationship depends on women's communication skills. In another vein, feminists have argued that women's or matriarchal time is categorically different from the "his-story" of patriarchy. They speak of time in organic metaphors—as generative, labyrinthine, spiral, web-like—and found in the cycles and rhythms of nature and women's bodies (Forman & Sowton, 1989; Keller, 1986; Kristeva, 1981; Johnson, 1991; Starhawk, 1979). When viewed from this critical feminist perspective, time—as how society contextualizes it—is something that we may need to be more conscious of. Sociology views time from this viewpoint; one broader than that of communication science, yet no less important to the study of intimacy.

RESEARCH NOTES: BEHAVIORAL AND SEQUENTIAL ANALYSIS OF INTIMATE COMMUNICATION

A host of studies examines sequences of behavior communication between married partners. These studies explore how these sequences relate to marital satisfaction and adjustment. For example, Gottman (1982) examined conversational sequences that discriminate satisfied from dissatisfied couples along three dimensions: perception and the exchange of negative emotion, lack of emotional responsiveness on the husband's part to adequately receive the emotional intent of his wife's message, and the linkage of arousal during negative emotional exchanges. In dissatisfied marriages, partners more often receive messages as having a negative impact and respond, in kind, with a negative message. In satisfied marriages, wives tend to be more agreeable and responsive to their husband's complaints and displays of negativity and so can de-escalate a conflict situation. Finally, as degree of conflict increases in a conversation, couples exhibit a coupling of their physiological responses; that is, skin conductance (a measure of nonspecific sympathetic arousal), gross motor activity, and various heart rate indices showed that as arousal increased in one partner, it also increased in the other. Gottman's research suggests that communication between dissatisfied partners is relatively inflexible or "locked-in" in comparison to satisfied partners, who are more positive and can independently de-escalate in conflict situations.

A key methodology in Gottman's and other communication research is to videotape or audiotape partner conversations and examine the probability that certain forms of communication in one partner follow similar or different forms in their wife or husband. These probabilities are studied using sophisticated statistical techniques—Time Series, Markov chain, and Lag sequential methods—that allow researchers to track particular verbal sequential patterns and conduct statistical tests for the reliability of their appearance within particular couple types. For example, Ting-Toomey (1983) developed the Intimate Negotiation Coding System (INCS) to examine the highly affectional style of interaction between intimate partners; that is, emotionally toned messages that reveal the emotional state of the speaker while appealing to or rejecting the emotional experience of the listener. The coding system consists of 3 types of verbal behaviors that subsume 12 different coding categories. These are (a) *integrative behavior*, which reveals one's affective state while simultaneously affirming the other (confirming, coaxing, compromising, or agreement messages); (b) *disintegrative behavior*, which reveals one's affective state while rejecting the ideas or feelings of the other (confronting, complaining,

---

RESEARCH **REFLECTION** $\boxed{14}$

COMMUNICATION APPREHENSION IN MARRIAGE

Powers and Hutchinson (1979) developed a measure to assess communication apprehension that applies to both marriage and dating partners. This approach implies that the capacity for intimacy requires relatively less apprehension to disclose oneself. Interestingly, apprehension is itself a way that the self relates to time with one's partner, in terms of looking forward to or being hesitant. Consider these items.

1. I look forward to evening talks with my partner.
2. I never hesitate to tell my partner my needs.
3. I am hesitant to develop a "deep" conversation with my partner.

defending, and disagreement messages); and (c) *descriptive behavior*, which facilitates information flow through either socioemotional or task-oriented statements or questions.

Ting-Toomey (1983) discriminated between different levels of marital adjustment in a nonclinical sample of couples who were videotaped while discussing a marital conflict situation. Among highly adjusted couples, she found the following reciprocal chains of interaction to be the most likely: confirming messages followed by (→) a socioemotional descriptive statement; socioemotional description → socioemotional question; and task-oriented question → task-oriented description. Thus, in these couples, partners either confirm or match each other's statements that "level" the interaction and get to the feelings or the task at hand. Within the low adjustment marital group a different chain emerged indicating long strings of reciprocal interactions with confront → confront, confront → defend, complain → defend, defend → complain as key sequences. As in the results of Gottman's research, less satisfied and less affectionate couples tend to reciprocate negative affect in spiraling cycles of disintegrative behavior. These surface sequences of interaction reveal a problematic system of communication: Couples are more likely to blame each other, and defend or justify in response, rather than focus on the task or feelings at hand. In a sense, such couples are operating more in the I-It world described by Buber than in an I-You one. Instead of affirming the other, they defend themselves and get locked into a sequence of reaction rather than a process of intimacy.

The methods of conversational analysis used by Ting-Toomey and Gottman are not the only ones (cf. Raush, 1965, 1972; Krueger & Smith, 1982). The pragmatic perspective of human communication (Fisher, 1978; Watzlawick, Beavin, & Jackson, 1967) has spawned research into relational control, or negotiation issues regarding dominance and submission, leadership and deference, and who has the right to define the relationship (Millar & Rogers, 1976; Rogers, 1972). Within this perspective, one study in particular exemplifies sensitivity to more than one temporal context.

Zeitlow and VanLear (1991) examined differences in control acts in the conversations of couples of various duration (Marriage groups averaging 6, 29, and 46 years). The categories of behavioral control (based on the coding system of Ellis, Fisher, Drecksel, Hoch, & Werbel, 1979) were acts of domineering (e.g., demands, challenges), structuring (e.g., disagreement), equivalence (neutral, noncommittal), deference (agreement), and submissiveness. The researchers found that control sequences depended on marital duration and marital satisfaction. For example, elderly couples showed the most predictable patterns, using more equivalence-equivalence than other couples, whereas short-term couples were the least patterned in their talk. The authors also found that the relation between marital satisfaction and control sequences varied between the three marriage groups. The authors reached several conclusions about marital duration, satisfaction, and communication sequences.

For short-term couples: "Overall, the key to high satisfaction for short-term couples seems to be refraining from too much deference. Deference may be somewhat dysfunctional as a control mode for short-term couples, and may reflect an inability of the couple to resolve the issue of dominance. Or, it may reflect a tendency for one partner to withdraw from involvement or to retreat from the discussion of sensitive problem topics" (p. 781).

For mid-life couples: "The number and intensity of problems seem to peak during intermediate marital stages (Stinnet et al., 1972). Structuring functions to introduce new ideas and refine old ones (Ellis, 1979), and its use is necessary when couples are required to address salient problems. Thus, the ability to negotiate control in ways that result in open communication about problems (without escalating conflict) may be an essential characteristic of mid-life couple" (p. 781).

For elderly couples: "Unlike problems that face pre-retired couples, the problems that confront long-term couples (e.g., retirement, disability, memory loss, a lower energy level, the death of friends, etc.), are less resolvable in nature (Dresler, 1973). Since no amount of talk can resolve or forestall these crises, structuring may not play a central role in the adaptation process for elderly couples. In brief, deference may be both appropriate and functional for these couples, while higher rates of structuring among dissatisfied older couples may be symptomatic of frustration amid unresolved (and unresolvable) conflict" (p. 782)

These results imply that—in order to be satisfied—couples who have been together for varying lengths of time require the use of very different communication strategies, especially when it comes to resolving conflict. The research does not indicate whether couples—who have a particular communication style—must wait until they get to a certain point when that style will prove more effective. Some couples may fare better in mid-life, while some fare better in retirement. The authors suggest that happy couples must keep changing how they communicate across time (see preceding section on "Marriage across the life span").

The previous studies show how communication researchers analyze the detailed patterns of marital interaction. Although this research examines marital satisfaction and adjustment, it does not explore intimacy per se. Prager (1991; following Rausch et al., 1974) developed a coding system for assessing conflict management style among couples of different intimacy statures (following Orlofsky, Marcia, & Lesser, 1973, and Whitbourne & Weinstock, 1979). Using a semistructured interview (Tesch & Whitbourne, 1982), Prager asked members of each couple about their relationship. She classified individuals into four categories. These were: (a) *Intimate* individuals, who characterized their relationships as enduring, open, highly involved, caring, respectful with sharing of leisure and responsibility; (b) *Merger* individuals, who characterized their relationships as enduring, involved and open, but with an unequal balance of power and a lack of autonomy on the part of at least one partner; (c) *Pseudointimates*, who viewed their long-term relationships as lacking open communication and high involvement; and

(d) *Preintimates*, who related to their partners on a deep emotional level but had made no long term commitment to the relationship.

Prager (1991) discovered sex differences between the relationship of intimacy status and conflict management sequences; but such differences held for individuals and not for couples. For example, Pseudointimate women replied to coercive acts (e.g., commanding, rejecting, attacking) almost exclusively with cognitive acts (e.g., seeking information, suggesting, reasoning), and Merger women were more likely to reciprocate coercion with coercion. There was a marginal finding that Merger males were more likely to follow affective strategies of negotiation (e.g., humor, accepting, appealing) with coercive acts. Whereas intimacy status had no relationship to sequential analyses, Merger women used more overall affective and less cognitive strategies than Pseudointimate women and Merger couples (Merger men who were paired with Merger women) were the most coercive group in the sample. These results—on intimacy status—accord with the above research by Gottman (1982) and by Ting-Toomey (1983) on marital adjustment and point to the problem of fusion (cf. codependency and relationship addiction, chap. 5) among Merger couples. Prager (1991) explained:

> The concept of Merger closely resembles the notion of fusion in object relations theory (e.g., Karpel, 1976). Fusion refers to the process by which two minimally individuated persons form a close relationship: the two identities become blurred and individual differences are suppressed to "keep peace" in the relationship. The unique aspects of each partner come to embody threats to the relationship, to their "closeness," and to each partner's sense of self (Rausch et al., 1974). When differences do arise, this is tremendously anxiety provoking for one or both partners, and "everything we have dreamed or feared becomes the enemy, embodied now in the antagonist before us" (Henry, 1971; quoted by Rausch et al., 1974, p. 41). (p. 522)

Thus, merger couples are more likely to resort to, and reciprocate coercive strategies to minimize (apparent) differences between them; they show "lack of focus upon the problem at hand, and (put) greater focus upon emotional manipulation of the partner" (Prager, 1991, p. 522). Apparently, this manipulation preserves the sense of fusion and closeness that is threatened by independence. Prager's work ties in to the discussion of relationship addiction described in the previous chapter. As described there, relationship addiction is associated with loss of clear ego boundaries and poor maintenance of self-esteem. The addictive desire for "keeping the relationship at any cost" and the associated fear of loss overshadows the reasoning skills, empathy, and assertiveness sometimes necessary to manage and resolve conflicts that arise. Put another way, the relationship form is more important than relational meaning.

SOCIOLOGY AND TEMPORAL CONTEXT

> Intimacy is not only a personal choice governed by individual desires and
> capabilities. It is also a culturally patterned arrangement, infused with values
> and beliefs legitimized by the surrounding society. (Wood, 1993, p. 54)

Sociologists have studied the topic of time for nearly a century. This section
reviews some of these notions and some recent demographic research on
relationship transition across the life span. Bergmann (1992) reviewed the work
of classical writers on time in sociology (e.g., Durkheim, Schütz, Sorokin and
Merton, and Mead) integrating this work within six themes. These are: time
perspective and time orientation; temporal ordering and social structure: the
social construction of time schedules; the time structure of specific social
systems and professions: the economy, the legal system, the family, and formal
organizations; the evolution of social consciousness of time; social change and
time; and the concern of time in social theory and methodology. Bergmann's
valuable and extensive review touches on the idea of temporal context in several
places. For example, writing about time perspective, he reviewed Luhmann's
(e.g., 1976) work on how history, through social evolution, has become
"context-free." Through increased social differentiation (i.e. class systems) and
less stratification of society, time becomes more reflexive within one's own
social system, rather than simply determined by the past (e.g., tradition,
ancestry). Unlike the past, in modern society "the future became a socially
dependent quantity. Today it is understood as feasible, capable of being planned,
and dependent on present decisions" (W. Bergmann, 1992, p. 90).

I first focus on Bergmann's sixth topic category: time in the social theory of
Mead. From the sociological viewpoint, intimacy is influenced by longer
societal or historical patterns or prescriptions. Thus, this section also considers
how time and intimacy is a social construction. I also review research related to
Bergmann's third topic area, time within the family or marital system, focusing
on the demographic study of life span transitions.

Mead's Sociology of Time

Of the various theories of time in sociology, the work of George Herbert Mead
has perhaps the greatest relevance to the study of personal relationships. There
are three ideas from Mead that show an important connection between time and
interpersonal relationships. First, time is "emergent" or constructed; that is,
individuals actually create new futures and symbolically reconstruct the past
(see Baert, 1992). Second, individuals develop a self-concept, or gain identity,
primarily through their interaction with others—a process labeled "symbolic
interactionism" (Blumer, 1969). The third idea combines the previous two. Any
meaning we create in a situation or about our self-concept is "historically open"
or continually subject to revision depending upon the feedback we give to and
receive from others.

McHugh (1968) elaborated on Mead's concept of temporal emergence to show how we define social situations. "The past influences the symbolic definition of the present, the definition of the present is influenced by inferences about the future, and the events of the future will reconstruct our definition of the past" (p. 24). McHugh gave two examples. First, cultural heroes may write their memoirs by coloring the past to give any current success more meaning. Second, when we miss an airplane because of a lack of seating, we may be angry until we later feel otherwise on discovering it has crashed. Thus, meaning is never self-evident, it depends on authorship and feedback from the social world. As such, temporal context is self-evolving. Even not acting has consequences for meaning. The following example shows how these ideas have relevance in intimate relations. McHugh explained:

> The sociological emphasis on feedback results from the realization that the social meaning of an object may have to be revised, that a definition at one point in time may undergo considerable revision at another. ("I thought it was love, but was it lust?"). . . . After all, although the actor observes, he is not solely an observer. He is searching out a definition. Let us assume that a lover is uncertain as to whether the state of his affair is love or lust. Imagine how active would be the procedure of uncertainty: probably stalled behavior, which would be such as to firmly commit oneself to neither love or lust, and yet so formulated as behavior to be seen by the other as either. (pp. 39–40)

The second idea—symbolic interactionism—indicates that the self first evolves only gradually through interaction with others during childhood. Because we create a self by taking the attitudes and perspectives of others ("altercasting"), the self-concept is essentially more public than private. With this process comes a growing awareness and acceptance of a "generalized other" that helps individuals to differentiate their unique identity. Davis (1973), using Mead's ideas of the generalized other and self-definition, described how intimacy allows for an intensification of individuality.

> An individual's mental image of his intimate, which he internalizes to play the accompaniment for his own responses to the situations he encounters, may strike dissonant as well as sympathetic chords. Consequently, he is constantly presented with occasions when he can contrast his personal responses with those he takes to be his intimate's. He often has the opportunity, in other words, to hone his singularity against the grinding wheel of his internalized companion. It is important to notice further that when he sharpens his self against a single intimate or *specified other*, the edge produced is much finer (presuming the other has a coherent self) than that effected by his coarser (less defined) reference group or *generalized other*, whose place his intimate has taken. (p. 190)

As in the previous section of communication, meaning is dynamic, but it does not emerge through the words exchanged between partners. Rather, meaning evolves within the self and through the self's definition of situations, specifically when with an intimate other. Recent research on the "Michelangelo Phenomenon" in close relationships confirms these ideas (Drigotas, Rusbult, Wieselquist, & Whitton, 1999). Essentially, through a series of studies with couples, the authors discovered "a congenial pattern of interdependence in which close partners sculpt one another in such a manner as to bring each person closer to his or her ideal self" (p. 320). In other words, one's self concept emerges and is continually molded through interactions with the specified other. Most importantly, the researchers found that the process of behaviorally affirming one's ideal self through couple interaction plays a powerful role in shaping both personal and couple well-being.

The third idea emphasizes the fact that meaning is a continuous process of adjustment and revision; that is, time keeps "emerging" as we symbolically interact with others. Duck (1994) explained:

> For Mead, the constant passage of time gives rise to events for which a person requires adaptive preparations but, more than this, the relationship between individual and society as a whole (or between individual and specific others) is a ceaseless process of adjustment. The adjustment involves the interaction between individuals and a community of other minds acting as a framework for the interpretation of personal meaning. Our ability to continually reflect on or adjust to the other person in an interaction (e.g., by seeing self as an object for that other person or by taking account of that other person's response as we communicate) is also a perpetually unfinished task. (p. 70)

This "perpetually unfinished task" points to the historically open aspect of Mead's views on time and the quality of "ongoingness" described in previous chapters. Duck used the phrase "temporal context" to indicate that self and society create meaning together and in time. Through the openness of time, claimed Duck, individuals relate "not only *in* contexts but *on* contexts." He used the following example of a kiss to demonstrate that a kiss is not just a kiss:

> Why should not the value of a kiss also take on different value according to the time and personal context of meaning in which the kiss occurs? Well, of course it does, depending on whether the kiss is from a lover, a relative at a wedding, or Judas Iscariot. However, let us go further. A kiss from the same lover can vary in value, on a first meeting, after six months of separation, after a fight, and as a ritual on waking in the morning. In each case, the value depends on the meaning attached to the kiss *at the time* and *in context*. (p. 72; italics added)

These ideas from Mead lead us back to the time-intimacy equation. That is, one's behavior in a relationship may or may not symbolize intimacy; it depends on the timing of the action and its meaning within a temporal context. Moreover, the symbolic weight of intimacy we ascribe to a particular action may actually determine our understanding of time (e.g., "You really did love me after all we had been through!").

Toward a Temporalised Sociology: Personal
Relationships as Structured by Time

Baert (1992) maintained that Mead overlooked the unacknowledged, latent structural conditions of human action and their interrelationship with longer time spans, with what the structuralists called *longue durée* (Braudel, 1969; Foucault, 1972). Simply put, there are forms of routine or habitual interaction patterns that are passed down from one generation to another until they become less accessible to conscious self-reflection (cf. Luhmann, 1976). Such patterns may have consequences that were unintended by their social creators. In this way, aspects of the self that were acquired through "symbolic interaction" may have a cultural rigidity—a set way of seeing the social world. However, it is possible, argued Baert, to "self-monitor" or self-reflect on one's own personal and social conditions in order to control one's individual destiny. With self-monitoring, individuals and collectives become conscious and change those latent structural conditions that exist across a longer time span, and that were hitherto unacknowledged and imprisoning (see Braudel, 1969).

> *To some extent, the intimate other helps us to author our own identity, which—as a function of time—we can take for granted or create anew.*

We can realize that certain social conditions (e.g., rituals, norms, and rules for relationships) may be unintended or taken for granted and that we can act to alter them. Baert's reassessment of Mead suggests that temporal context can be fixed in our unconscious or taken for granted; it comes as the result of some tacit agreement about how to know, live with, and influence others. Thus, partners not only have a hand in authoring their own relationship history ("self-monitoring of the first order"), but in revising deeply held assumptions about personal relationships in general ("self-monitoring of the second order").

This deeper context is similar to the idea of a scientific paradigm, and Baert applied his view to a reassessment of Kuhn's work, the *Structure of Scientific Revolutions*. Scientists often take the predominant paradigm for granted in a manner similar to how partners may take each other for granted, or how society may take its institutions (such as marriage and the family) for granted. We can now return to the similarities of lovers and scientists discussed at the beginning of this chapter, but with more sensitivity to the wider temporal context. Baert's analysis persuades sociologists to pay more attention to the wider temporal context (the *longue durée)* in which this "taken-for-granted" quality arises. Baert is quoted at length because of the interesting parallels with the earlier distinction between surface sequence and deeper process, and the importance of sensitivity to temporal context for nurturing intimacy:

> What I described as "self-monitoring of the first order" comes into play whenever the scientists are involved in what Kuhn called "puzzle-solving activities." . . . Scientists take for granted certain rules, assumptions and

procedures, which are typical of the dominant paradigm. In most cases, it was established long before they entered the scientific community or even long before they were born. . . .The cognitive acquisition of the paradigm is such that most of its assumptions and rules are what I have called "taken for granted." . . . Scientists are aware of the assumptions and rules they are following, but they regard them as beyond question or often even as obvious. . . . In periods of crisis, there is an erosion of the taken-for-granted character of many rules and assumptions of the dominant paradigm. . . . The concept of paradigm implies that beneath the puzzle-solving activities of scientists lies the rhythm of the *longue durée*; that is, the mental frameworks which have survived for a long time and in which the scientists have been enclaved. Behind that self-reflective monitoring of the first order, which is embedded in the daily routine of normal scientists, lies a deeper, less conscious and less accessible level (Baert, 1992, pp. 129–133)."

The two features involved in paradigm shifts, the taken-for-granted character of rules and the unintended consequences of following those rules, can be compared to the work couples do in marital and family therapy. To see this parallel, substitute the term *partners* for *scientists* in the previous quote, *conflict* for *puzzle-solving activity*, and *routine* ("the same old, same old") for *paradigm*. That is, as partners work through and solve the problems that underlie their conflicts, they may actually revise and deepen the meaning of their marriage. Most importantly, they may learn to abandon old habits (rules, see chap. 4) or pre-conceptions (Imagos, scripts; see chap. 5). In so doing, their experience of intimacy may deepen and their relationships become more stable.

Some forms of marriage and family therapy focus on the inheritance of rules and the unintended consequences of following those rules. For example, family

RESEARCH   REFLECTION   15

FAMILY SECRETS: INHERITING PARADIGMS ACROSS GENERATIONS

Communication scientists have studied the types as well as the functions of family secrets that individuals are reluctant to reveal to others (Vangelisti & Caughlin, 1997). This research suggests that family secrets are an important part of intimacy. Researchers describe a range of taboo topics (e.g., marital problems, financial information, substance use, premarital pregnancy) that are revealed more often than conventional information (e.g., physical health, religion, personality conflicts), suggesting that ethical considerations are relevant. The following lists some of the functions of secrets (and representative items).

1. **Fear of Evaluation** (The secret would shatter my partner's beliefs about me and my family).
2. **Maintenance** (I keep the secret to prevent stress for my family).
3. **Defense** (My partner might use this information against me).
4. **Privacy** (Our family greatly values privacy).
5. **Bonding** (Having this secret makes my family more cohesive).

and sex therapists (Kerr & Bowen, 1988; Schnarch, 1991) encourage clients to examine the intergenerational transmission of rules and ideas about intimacy and eroticism, of how one's family of origin shapes ideas about sexuality and distance-pursuer dynamics. This transgenerational perspective of marital therapy suggests a certain loyalty to the paradigm of one's family, or to keeping family secrets (Boszormenyi-Nagy, 1974; Boszormenyi-Nagy & Spark, 1973; Knudson, 1985). There is a family system of accountability, a "trans-generational ledger of entitlements," that married partners combine from their respective family's pasts (see related research on divorce below). The couple develops a network of multilateral obligations or a "deep ethical context" (Boszormenyi-Nagy, 1974) in which they develop rules and procedures for finding ethically valid solutions to the inequities and imbalances of living together in time.

Therapy consists in realizing the importance of the loyalty and secrecy implications: both for staying married (they provide a deep temporal context for commitment) and for reappraising assumptions for how loyalties may be stifling the marriage. The transgenerational paradigm informs the "puzzle-solving activities" or conflicts couples face. However, as their awareness of the unintended consequences of their loyalties increase, couples can shift away from these inherited and less conscious ways of marriage. We can pay attention to the deeper structural conditions (longue duree, paradigm, transgenerational ledger). In so doing, we see that intimacy develops through a deeper, perhaps ethical, weaving of time.

A Feminist Perspective

There is another point to be made about the deeper, structural aspects of time and paradigm shifts that brings in a feminist perspective. Kristeva (1981) argued that there are two types of temporality, cyclical or repetitive and monumental or eternal, that are linked to female subjectivity and intuition. She associated cycle with gestation, biological rhythm, and with a regularity and unison that brings pleasure (*jouissance*). Monumental or eternal time (cf. "Great Time," Priestley, 1964) is associated with an all-encompassing feeling and with "various myths of resurrection which, in all religious beliefs, perpetuate the vestige of an anterior or concomitant maternal cult, right up to its most recent elaboration, Christianity, in which the body of the Virgin Mother does not die" (p. 17). Kristeva argued that most of modern history (as recorded), with its emphasis on progress and linear development, has overshadowed this deeper matriarchal time (also see Eisler, 1987).

What does all this have to do with intimacy? Johnson (1991), in her own personal account of intimate sexual relationships, showed that self reflection and a willingness to act differently from her established patterns of love-making led to some deeper awakening of intimacy in her life. She described how her feelings of guilt around sexual pleasure, and her ideas about the work ethic and Puritanism were derived from patriarchal and repressive views of sexuality. These views often lead her to define intimacy as "the feeling of being most possessed" and to try to control her partner's time to keep this feeling going. But in her sexual awakening, Johnson realized that there is an abundance of time, always available and continually renewable. Her revelation seems like a direct experience of the eternal, monumental time described by Kristeva:

> Though we live in present time and enjoy every moment of this thoroughly for itself alone, we also know that in some other present moment, we will all be on the creative plateau from which an infinite number of paths lead to an infinity of possibilities. . . . Because we also have the advantage of living in spiral—not linear—time, we have no concern about the time it takes. There is an abundance of time. . . . I experience this intimacy with every woman I see and meet and talk with every day. Every bite of food I eat has been grown and prepared by the hands of women whose hearts beat in my breast; every article of clothing I wear, every tool I use—everything is created out of this love. My life is deep and rich and satisfying beyond telling. . . . I thought as I observed this union of freedom, integrity, power, and creativity in my mind's eye, "This is intimacy!" (pp. 253–254)

Johnson's personal reflections may be difficult for traditionalists who view marriage as a sacred covenant with a paternal God. The view of time within Christianity is clearly more historical/sequential than the one Johnson or Kristeva appeals to. The point here is not that revisionist feminism is right, but that the desire for and experience of intimacy may be as spiritual in homosexual relationships (see Barret & Barzan, 1996) as, for example, in Catholic marriages.

RESEARCH NOTES: DEMOGRAPHICS ON RELATIONSHIP TRANSITIONS

In recent years, a host of studies have explored demographic trends in the age and timing of transitions from various relationship stages or states to subsequent stages or states. These studies suggest that societal norms influence how relationships develop and also how we attach meaning to certain phases of a relationship. Much of this research examines temporal factors surrounding adulthood and marriage. For example, Marini (1978) has examined the transition to adulthood in several ways. These include the commitment to wed, the order of events in making that transition (e.g., marrying and having a child before or after leaving education) (Marini, 1984a), the relationship between women's educational attainment and the timing of their entry into parenthood (Marini, 1984b), and social conformity to certain sequencing norms that mark the transition to adulthood (Marini, 1984c). Longitudinal studies examine how parental resources and other factors influence the age when young adults leave home and go to a semi-independent residence versus a premarital or married residence (Goldscheider & DaVanzo, 1989). Moreover, scholars of family history have taken a broad historical view in examining the timing of transition to adulthood, paying particular attention to demographics that compare age of marriage, household establishment, headship of a household, and workforce participation across two different centuries (Modell, Furstenberg, & Hershberg, 1976). The following synopses provide some examples of this type of research.

The Transition to Parenting

The timing of the transition to marriage is one sociodemographic marker in the study of families. Another critical transition is the beginning of parenting, that is, first time motherhood and fatherhood. One study of first birth during adolescence found that the sequencing of childbirth (premarital birth vs. premarital conception, postmarital birth vs. postmarital conception) was related to later marital stability as a function of the age of the woman at marriage (McLaughlin, Grady, Billy, Landale, & Winges; 1986). The authors claimed "young women who marry prior to childbirth—whether the conception is premarital or postmarital—experience greater stability in later years than those who delay marriage, implying that the trend of rising nonmarital birthrates may result in reduced marital stability in the future. However, we also discovered evidence indicating that this effect has attenuated in recent years" (McLaughlin et al. 1986, p. 18). In a more fine-tuned study, women were questioned at six different intervals before, during, and after their pregnancy (prepregnant, 1st, 2nd, and 3rd trimester, 1 month and 3 months postpartum). Ruble, Hackel, Fleming, and Stangor (1988) found that women report decreasing satisfaction with their husbands and their relationship postpartum as compared to during pregnancy. This dissatisfaction was due to violations of expectations the woman had about how much their partner would participate in housework and child care.

An even more complex picture emerges in a recent study of predictors of negative marital interactions (conflict, withdrawal) throughout the transition to parenthood—prenatally and at 3, 12, and 24 months postpartum (Cox, Paley, Burchinal, & Payne, 1999). In general, the authors found that negative interactions increase after birth until the end of the child's first year. However, the rate of change in these interactions depended on a host of factors, such as whether the pregnancy was planned, the child's gender, problem-solving communication ability, and depressive symptoms in the parents. The authors concluded that there is great variability in couples' responses to the birth of their first child.

Serial Marriage

The phenomena of serial marriages is also gaining increased research interest is. Brody, Neubaum, and Forehand (1988) cited census data suggesting increases in serial marriages within the general population. They estimated that around one third of all young adults today are projected to remarry following divorce (Cherlin, 1981). Other studies suggest that remarriage is becoming less frequent (Norton & Moorman, 1987) and depends on a host of factors (e.g., gender, age of marital disruption, religion; see Wu, 1994). The phenomena of serial marriage is also a lodestone for the study of temporal context. Although data are lacking on the timing of the transition from one marriage to another, the authors argue that the security of remarriage may depend on the timing of courtship and marriage postdivorce (see Rodgers & Conrad, 1986). The lack of security is particularly seen on the effects it has on the adjustment and behavior of young children as well as adolescents.

Divorce

Divorce or some other form of marital dissolution is another key transition in marriage relationships. Thornton and Rodgers (1987) conducted a demographic study that discriminated between the influence of individual and historical time on marital dissolution. They wished to answer the following questions: "Which specific aspect of historical time—birth cohort, marital cohort, or period—can best explain trends in marital dissolution? How do the dimensions of individual time—age, age at marriage, and marital duration—interact and combine to influence marital stability? And how have the historical trends modified the basic effects of personal time?" (p. 19). For example, the authors found that from 1922 to 1929 divorce rates increased slowly, declined sharply after the depression, than rebounded to predepression levels—trends that were consistent regardless of length of marriage. Whereas these effects point to the influence of historical time, other data demonstrate that divorce rates decline sharply with age and marital duration, reflecting the influence of personal time. Overall, the authors conclude that young age at marriage increases the likelihood of marital dissolution relatively independent of historical or period influences. Trends and fluctuations of the last half-century influenced levels of separation and divorce but have not changed the patterns of dissolution across individual time.

This complex study compares well with data from Morgan and Rindfuss (1985), who examined the effect of several sequencing variables on marital disruption in a large population survey. For example, they compared the timing and sequencing of first birth at different time intervals post marriage and with those couples who had children before marriage. Similar to results found by others (McLaughlin et al., 1986), delaying births within a marriage does not increase the stabilizing effect of parenthood on a marriage. However, age at marriage does have a negative effect, with earlier marriages leading to divorce regardless of marriage duration and ages.

Still other studies have examined determinants of divorce over the life course (Feng, Giarrusso, Bengtson, & Frye, 1999; Frisbie, Opitz, & Kelly, 1985; Norton & Moorman, 1987; South & Spitze, 1986). These studies support the idea that certain predisposing factors—such as wife's participation in the work force or history of divorce in the family—influence divorce. Other variables (e.g., number of children at home) have little or inconsistent effects. South and Spitze (1986) found that wife's education decreases the probability of divorce at early marital durations but increases it at later durations. The authors argued "that a more highly educated woman may be more likely to find an alternative partner in later years, once children are grown and no longer present a barrier to dissolution" (p. 589). Many of these demographic studies find the tendency for marital disruption to be linked to early age at marriage (Carlson & Stinson, 1982). Interestingly, researchers have studied the effects of inter-generational processes on marital stability, finding that parental divorce increases the likelihood of children's divorce (Amato & Booth, 1997), especially from parents to daughters (Feng et al., 1999).

Distal and Proximal Causes of Divorce

A recent longitudinal study combines both predisposing (distal) factors, such as age at marriage, and more immediate marital problems (proximal) as predictors of divorce (Amato & Rogers, 1997). This is an important study as it combines different temporal contexts within a longitudinal framework and so is sensitive to process. As such, it has more temporal sensitivity than previously mentioned studies in this section. That is, the previous studies show which factors predict divorce, but they do not show how they do it. The researchers collected data from over 1,000 respondents for three periods from 1980 to 1992. The authors distinguished a variety of different distal predictors, including age at marriage, prior cohabitation, race, marital duration, income, church attendance, and parental divorce, among others. Proximal predictors were both husband's and wife's 1980 ratings of marital problems due to anger, jealousy, infidelity, moodiness, drug use, spending money, among others. The study contained a number of interesting features. Most importantly, the authors wished to show that the influence of distal factors on divorce was mediated by, or depended on, proximal factors.

Findings showed that among the proximal predictors, extramarital sex was one of the strongest predictors of divorce. Others included drug use, not home enough, and irritating habits. Best distal predictors were parental divorce, lack of church attendance, remarriage, and younger age at marriage. The researchers also found that the proximal predictors mediated the effects of parental divorce, church attendance, and other distal predictors. In other words, it seems that variables at the time of marriage (e.g., age, parental divorce) contribute to a constellation of marital problems, which, in turn, predict divorce. Thus, it may not be that lack of church attendance or parental divorce is predictive of divorce, per se. Rather, these variables predispose couples to having more problems with difficulties such as jealousy, moodiness, or irritating habits.

Decade Effects

It is difficult to summarize the myriad of multivariate findings that relate to historical, period, cohort, and age effects on the timing of transitions in relationships. I provide this overview to give the reader a sense of the dynamic aspects of the sociological context. Research shows that different decades and ages imply different norms about when it is appropriate (for maximizing marital success) to make certain relationship transitions (e.g., Mare, 1991). Gollub (1991) developed a framework for analyzing the social tone of different decades. He called it "Time Signatures" (i.e., comprised of economic outlook, technological conditions, social and political environment, and cultural climate). He explained that all individuals within a generation have a "Birthmark" that distinguishes them from their cohorts. Gollub argued that "our Time Signatures and Birthmarks combine to give each of us a special, *time-based* personality" (p. 7). I would argue that each couple has its own time-based personality as well.

Suffice it to say that many apparent "background" factors are woven into the fabric of each relationship; the individual and joint authorship of each relationship may either enhance or diminish the impact of these demographic threads.

OTHER TEMPORAL CONTEXTS OF INTIMACY

As we have seen, couples both create temporal context through communication as well as use communication to understand context. Context both shapes and is shaped by the unique mutual history of the couple, as well as by the more enduring historical contexts of their family and their culture. So created, temporal context is colored by changes across the life span of the couple and by how the couple uses time along the private-public and sacred–profane dimensions. When combined, these various aspects of temporality (e.g., in communication, from society) manifest as an ongoing weaving of intimacy.

Other temporal contexts play a significant, although less apparent, role in the weaving of intimacy. Even the historical epoch we live in (perhaps however broadly defined) plays a role (see *Love Line*, bottom of page through p. 202). Although communication and social behavior may be more accessible (and modifiable), these other temporal contexts reveal aspects of time and intimacy that require more effort to be mindful of and to change. The first temporal context pertains to the span of human evolution and the work by evolutionary psychologists that suggest how sex differences prevent intimacy from enduring (e.g., Wright, 1994). The second deals with biological cycles, such hormonal rhythms that influence sexual behavior across weekly and monthly time schedules (Cutler, 1991). The third relates to the automatic effects of social influence and the gradual, cumulative effects of escalating commitment in social situations. These effects often lead to decreases in awareness or increases in social delusion (variably referred to as "the foot-in-the-door technique," e.g., Cialdini, 1985; "habituation to violence," Geen, 1981; or "media cultivation of public attitudes" (Gerbner, Gross, Morgan, & Signorelli, 1986). I refer to each of these contexts as *evolutionary*, *chronobiological* and *social psychological*.

Evolutionary Time: Genetic Substrates of Intimacy

This section reviews both empirical and speculative views on the influence of evolution on time in sexual and nonsexual intimacy. For example, evolution may

LOVE LINE: A RANDOM WALK THROUGH THE HISTORICAL CONTEXT OF INTIMACY & MARRIAGE (from Stephens, 1996)	PREHISTORY *The wedding ring as we know it stems from the ancient German practice of offering a ring to a bride on the tip of a sword—a pledge of union.*	323 BC *The Egyptian wife has plenty of power over her husband: He must pay a fine to his first wife, for example, if he wishes to marry a second one.*

dictate how much time we devote to mate selection, decisions about choosing short-
versus long-term partners, age preferences in our mates, and even the timing of
behavior during intercourse. Nonsexual intimacy may be the most recent advancement
in evolution and may represent a shift in the evolution of human consciousness
(Adamopoulos, 1991).

Research on evolutionary psychology assumes that our feelings toward
romantic partners are genetic in origin (Kenrick & Simpson, 1996; Shackelford
& Buss, 1997). The cover article of a recent issue of *Time* magazine ("Our
Cheating Hearts"; Wright, 1994), sums up this basic argument: "Our everyday,
ever shifting attitudes toward a mate or prospective mate—trust, suspicion,
rhapsody, revulsion, warmth, iciness—are the handiwork of natural selection that
remain with us today because in the past they led to behaviors that helped spread
genes" (p. 46). For women, gene preservation depended on securing "high male-
parental investment," or a mate who could provide good genes, a sense of security
for the duration of child bearing and child rearing, and fatherly love. For men, gene
preservation depended on his social dominance, sexual fertility, and fidelity in as
many mates as possible. The sex difference is captured by the idea that, genetically
speaking, women are monogamous and men are polygamous.

Buss (1989a, 1989b) collected data to substantiate evolutionary claims about
sex differences in human mate preferences. Using data from 33 countries, females
were found to value cues to *resource acquisition* in potential mates more highly
than males, whereas males valued *reproductive capacity* in prospective partners
more than did females (Buss, 1989a). Buss' research is a test of parental
investment theory (Trivers, 1972). This theory claims that, among *Homo Sapiens*,
females should be more selective in seeking a mate because they are typically the
sex who has to invest more in their offspring (i.e., a 9-month gestation that requires
time, energy, resources, and foreclosed alternatives). For Buss, this translates to
females seeking partners with attributes such as ambition, industriousness, and
earning capacity. For men, female fertility and reproductive value are strongly age-
dependent and Buss argued that males will show a preference for "relative *youth*
and *physical attractiveness*" in potential mates because of their links with fertility
and reproductive value" (p. 3). Buss also argued that paternity confidence is a
strong factor in mate selection for men; men want a chaste partner because it
reassures that their offspring will be identifiably theirs. Thus, Buss (1989a)
hypothesized that in addition to youth and physical attractiveness, males would

1ST CENTURY AD

*With the emergence of Christianity, Roman marriage changes from a
procreative duty into a choice. Marriage requires female consent, and the
role of "wife" takes on as much dignity as that of "friend." But "love" isn't
necessary for marriage. In Greece, Plutarch calls love a "frenzy" and says
that "those who are in love must be forgiven as though ill." Meanwhile,
virginity is glorified, sexual connection is deemed foul, and homosexuality is
punishable by death.*

value chastity more than females: "Assuming some temporal stability to behavioral proclivities, chastity would also provide a cue to the *future* fidelity of a selected mate. A male failing to express such a preference would risk wasting the time and effort involved in courtship and would risk investing in offspring that were not his (Daly & Wilson, 1983; Dickemann, 1981)" (p. 3).

This quote, and much of the logic of evolutionary theory, contextualizes time as a resource to be invested in the making of successful offspring. This logic views time as linear, progressive, and subject to waste if genetic security is not attained. Buss' results showed that sex differences in the preferences for the characteristics of "good financial prospect" and "ambition and industriousness" were in the predicted direction; females valued these qualities significantly more than males. Alternatively, the findings showed that males prefer youthful and good-looking mates and females prefer mates older than themselves. Preferences for chastity (no previous experience in sexual intercourse) showed marked variation among countries and so did not corroborate the hypothesis that males preferred chastity more than females.

Buss concluded that there is cross-cultural stability in sex differences in mate preference that confirm an evolutionary viewpoint. However, it should be pointed out that he ignored differences in preferences for casual sexual partners versus long-term (or marriage) partners (see Kenrick & Keefe, 1989; Kenrick & Trost, 1989). He downplayed the finding in his data that "*both* sexes ranked characteristics "kind-understanding" and "intelligent" higher than earning power and attractiveness in all samples, suggesting that species-typical mate preferences may be more potent than sex-linked preferences" (p. 12). Although genetically based sex differences in mate selection exist, such differences may be outweighed by partner similarities due to culture and education.

There is another curious research study that points to sex differences in sexual interest (see Buss & Schmitt, 1993). Subjects were approached by surveyors of the opposite sex and asked either directly for a date that night, to go back to the surveyor's apartment that night, or to have sex with the surveyor that night. Although both sexes responded affirmatively to the first question 50% of the time, more and more males said yes to the second and third requests (69% and 75%), and less and less females agreed to the requests (6% and 0%, respectively). This supports the common sense belief that women are more discriminating and men are more eager.

3RD – 4TH CENTURIES	5TH CENTURY

3RD – 4TH CENTURIES

5TH CENTURY

*In India, Brahmin priest Vatsyayana, believed to be a lifelong celibate and ascetic, writes the erotic classic, the **Kama Sutra**. In Europe, Jovian, a maverick monk, is excommunicated in 385 A.D. on the grounds of heresy and blasphemy for calling marriage superior to celibacy.*

Religion governs marriage. Almost all weddings in the Roman Empire now include an ecclesiastical benediction, and marriage is considered a sacrament. In the centuries to come, Emperor Justinian will make adultery a capital offense and divorce nearly impossible.

In a recent formulation of sexual strategies theory, Buss and Schmitt (1993) gave a central role to the concept of temporal context. They define temporal context in reference to short- or long-term mating and argued that how males and females adapt sexually depends on their different sensitivities to temporal context. For example, females are devoted to identifying a long-term partner who can invest in her and her child over the long term; males are devoted more to short-term, competitive strategies for gaining access to fertile females. Buss and Schmitt wrote: "Sexual strategies theory specifies that evolved psychological mechanisms are exquisitely sensitive to context and, in particular, to the temporal dimension of context" (p. 209).

In their research on gender differences in age preference, Kenrick and Trost (1989) reviewed several studies of "lonely hearts" advertisements as an unobtrusive measure of mating preferences; findings clearly show females tend to seek older males, whereas males seek younger females (Bolig, Stein, & McKenry, 1984; Cameron, Oskamp, & Sparks, 1977; Harrison & Saeed, 1977; Lynn & Bolig, 1985). Kenrick and Trost (1989) reported data, however, that supports a "Time-Qualified Parental Investment Model." They found a significant gender by age interaction for both the minimum and maximum age specified in dating advertisements. Females, at all ages, were interested in males that were a decade older then themselves. In contrast, male preferences changed as they got older; males in their twenties preferred partners ranging from five years older to five years younger and males in their 50s and 60s prefer females much younger than themselves. These data are important because they show how the temporal context of age may qualify generalizations about sex differences in mate selection preference. Thus, the temporal weave becomes evident even within the evolutionary model; changes in the life span may enhance or diminish genetic effects.

Margulis and Sagan (1991) give an interdisciplinary review of the literature on the evolution of human sexuality, focusing on the origins and functions of sexual/hormonal cycling, genitalia, and orgasm. They attempted to explain the evolutionary origins of sexual intercourse and orgasm, questioning the particular benefit to species preservation that complex sexual behavior has over meiosis in asexual organisms. For example, they argued that orgasm gave the female the ability to discern between those male partners who were willing to pleasure them to the point of sexual satisfaction, and thereby, in addition to the suction effect of her

6ᵀᴴ CENTURY

Buddhists and Hindus in India begin to practice Tantrism in an attempt to transform the human body into a mystical one. Through maithuna (ceremonial sex), human union becomes a sacred act.

939

In one of the first known attempts to suppress the ancient Japanese practice of phallic worship, a large phallic image that had been displayed and worshipped in Kyoto is moved to a less prominent place.

orgasm, assure fertilization. Thus, the ability of males to time the genital stimulation and sexual arousal of their partners may be genetically controlled. From this radical viewpoint, Margulis and Sagan (1991) concluded:

> In its early evolution the clitoris had no evolutionary significance; it came into existence because of the advantage its counterpart, the penis, gave sperm competing males. . . . The retention of the clitoris led to clitoral orgasm, which allowed greater female choice in the selection of mates. Infants—always at risk—may also have been better protected by mothers whose men were willing to indulge them in clitoral orgasm. Natural selection retains male penises and ejaculations; males are born of females whose embryology they share. From an evolutionary perspective, it is the presence of the penis that gives the female opportunity to quiver in delight as he releases spermless streams. (p. 86)

For these authors, the pacing of sexual intercourse and stimulation may be under genetic control. As Cutler (1991) suggested, an important key to sexual harmony within a marriage depends upon how well the male reads the desires and arousals of his partner, rather than vice versa. Although there is much variation in this "sexual symphony" across different couples, Margulis and Sagan appeared to suggest that there are certain evolutionary origins of the clitoral orgasm that require males to pay special attention to how they time their behavior during intercourse.

The work of Adamopoulus (1991) on nonsexual intimacy (closeness or mutual self-disclosure) contrasts with these sociobiological, evolutionary views that emphasize the importance of sexuality (e.g., reproductive value in Buss's work, and sexual orgasm in Margulis and Sagan). Focusing more on recorded history and civilization than on our evolutionary apelike ancestors, Adamopoulus (1992) argued that societies are governed by the exchange of resources, and that societal evolution is marked by an increase in symbolic or abstract—over concrete or materialistic—exchanges of goods. According to an analysis of literature from different time periods (e.g., ancient Greece, romantic literature in the 1800s) he argues that in past centuries close relationships were based upon concrete exchanges (e.g., wives seen as property), and they more recently are focused on personality and symbolic displays of affection. He also suggested that intimacy, as a feature of interpersonal behavior, was only distinguished from association (affiliation), formality, and dominance fairly late in cultural evolution. In comparison to social structures of

1477

Margery Brews of England writes the earliest known valentine to her "Right Worshipful and well-beloved Valentine," hoping that he'll make her "the merriest maiden on the ground" despite a meager dowry.

16TH CENTURY

Some 400 years before **The Joy of Sex** *comes India's* **Ananga Ranga,** *which shows husband and wife how to keep a marriage lively with 32 sexual positions.*

1536

John Calvin creates a code of morals that limits engagements to six weeks and prohibits revelry at weddings.

resource exchange (trading, give and take) and dominance (e.g., subordination, slavery), intimacy involves more complex interpersonal structures that may require much longer periods of time to evolve.

Adamopoulos' ideas about cultural evolution are important to view in distinction to sociobiological, genetic views. First, the nonsexual aspects of intimacy may be more a function of culture than of some biological imperative. Freud, in fact, viewed mature love as a result of cultural sublimation of infantile sexual drives (see Bettelheim, 1984). Second, the symbolic exchanges involved in nonsexual intimacy imply that it is both a phylogenetic achievement—the earlier forms of exchange (trading, dominance, formality) are integrated and synthesized through intimate relationships—and a transcendence of those concrete forms of exchange. As Adamopoulos explained it, arranged marriages transform into reciprocal self-disclosure, sexual relations transform into romantic love, and self-sacrificing altruism transforms into commitment and trust.

Clearly, views of love and sexual relations have changed throughout recorded history and across cultures, suggesting that the historical (or epochal-cultural) context is yet another temporal context through which we can understand intimacy. In fact, a mere examination of a historical timetable of forms of rules and social mores about marriage and intimacy (absent any bio-evolutionary or cultural-evolutionary scheme) suggests no specific linear development. Such a timetable is provided by Stephens (1996) and is reproduced in *Love Line* (beginning on p. 194, see below). This table represents a random walk through time rather than an attempt to show a linear development.

To summarize, the evolutionary perspective of intimacy suggests a temporal context serves as a moral guide. Popular articles (like in *Time* magazine) that focus on genetic reasons for the demise of monogamy (infidelity and divorce) implore us to become more self-aware of our genetic heritage. Human beings are not apes. A moral code is a cultural solution to selfish genetic preservation:

> Maybe for starters, men and women will realize that their constantly fluctuating perceptions of a mate are essentially illusions, created for the (rather absurd, really) purpose of genetic proliferation, and that these illusion can do harm. Thus, men might beware the restlessness designed by natural selection to encourage polygyny. We are potentially moral animals—which is more than any other animal can say—but we are not naturally moral animals. The first step to being moral is to realize how thoroughly we aren't. (Wright, 1994, pp. 51–52)

1613	1625
Don Juan comes to life in Tirso de Molina's play the Joker of Seville. ♡	While Puritan author William Gouge is advising wives to address their mates openly as "Husband" and never as "sweet, sweeting, heart, sweetheart, love, joy, dear, duck, chick, or pigsnie," English adventurer Thomas Morton establishes "Merry Mount," a plantation in the Massachusetts Bay Colony where Whites and Native Americans openly engage in sexual relations.

Chroniobiological Time: The Hormonal Symphony

> Recognizing a time to embrace and a time to refrain from embracing can
> promote the health and well being of the reproductive endocrine system
> of individual women. (Cutler, 1999, p. 1)

As noted earlier in this chapter, an entire book could be written on each of the temporal contexts (e.g., evolutionary, chronobiological) overviewed here. This is probably the most true for a discussion of the role of sexual biology and sexual rhythms. Research on human aging (Medina, 1996), the evolution of the human life course (Wachter & Finch, 1997), hormonal changes during marital conflict (Kiecolt-Glaser et al. 1996), and exercise and biological rhythms (Reilly, Atkinson, & Waterhouse, 1997), each suggests that human interpersonal and sexual behavior can be influenced by biological rhythms. Still, we know very little about these influences. Most research in this area has focused on female hormonal cycles, but some findings also suggest cyclic changes in male testosterone levels (Lips, 1997).[2]

Cutler (1991) has conducted several studies on hormonal rhythms in adult women and on human sex pheromones. She claims that you can enhance your health, well-being, and sexual life by taking control of your hormonal rhythms. Reviewing the results of various research studies, Cutler concluded that there are windows of time when sexual activity is most conducive to physical health, particularly for women. She made the following claims:

- Whereas regular (weekly) sexual intercourse is closely linked with regular menstrual cycles of close to 29.5 days, sporadic sex or celibacy appears to be associated with irregular menstruation.
- Males have a critical period for sexual potency (testosterone levels and the volume of ejaculate); when deprived of sex, these factors increase until a certain point when potency declines.
- Weekly sex is associated with fertile-type cycle lengths; the 12-day luteal phase (the span from ovulation to the start of menstruation) is optimized when there is regular sex.
- Women who have a sporadic sex pattern may have an inadequate luteal phase length, frequently rendering them subfertile. These women are likely to be the ones most vulnerable to fibrocystic breast disease, uterine cancer, and other maladies.
- Female masturbation on a regular schedule cannot substitute for sexual intercourse in helping to entrain a fertile menstrual cycle.

c. 1750	1896
As out-of-wedlock pregnancies increase, some New England towns attempt to prohibit "bundling"—a practice wherein courting couples are allowed to sleep together so long as they remain fully dressed or have a "bundling board" between them.	*John Rice gives May Irwin the first movie kiss, which looks more like a peck. But the press harrumphs that the "unbridled kissing, magnified to gargantuan proportions and repeated thrice, is absolutely loathsome."*

- Men's hormonal levels show seasonal variations, with peaks in September–October and troughs in July–August.
- The sex hormones cycle in men on an individual basis (and so appear less locked in to a particular cycle), as compared to the cycle in women, which tends to be more harmonic within their social group.

Because of these findings, Cutler suggested that monogamy is the healthiest lifestyle for the sexual cycle; how partners make use of their time to exploit this cycle can be critical to health, in pre- as well as postmenopausal females. She offered various prescriptions about time management (cf. Knopf & Seiler, 1991):

> Intimacy seems to be dispensable, but as my studies show, it is not. We need intimacy—often and regularly. Regularity in intimate contact, in sex, must be maintained in order for benefits to continue and accrue. . . . I do not believe in the truth of the untested myth that "quality time" in our important relationships can substitute for quantity. . . . Adults should make active choices rather than fall ignorantly into the romantic notion that "we don't need to plan and everything will turn out all right. (Cutler, 1991, pp. 39–40)

Cutler believed that hormonal time is critical; it is so critical that she suggests couples prioritize their schedules around it. This suggestion hearkens back to the discussion in earlier chapters about the importance of listening and tuning into one's own bodily cycles, rather than being merely driven by the "metronomic society." Such listening is a form of personal intimacy (in to me see?) that, according to Cutler, enhances interpersonal intimacy (in time mates see).

Cutler also provided evidence showing how fertile women cycle in phase with the lunar cycle: "The reproductive biology of a fertile woman shows a harmonic relationship between her cycling body and the moon's cycling body" (p. 231). Outside of these monthly cycles are annual changes in fertility and male potency. Orlock's (1993, p. 124) review of research suggests that the best times for conception are the fall and spring equinox.

Other female writers have argued that even raped woman may feign orgasm to prevent fertilization (cf. Margulis & Sagan, 1991), or that the power involved in mothering is only one source of strength and identity (Janeway, 1981); women have choices, and they can be selective. Cutler's conclusions give primary status to the hormonal cycles of women—and the man's ability to synchronize with it—as a key to satisfaction in marriage. The ideas she

1910	1960s
The company that makes **Hallmark Cards** *is established in Kansas City, Missouri.* ♡	*Scenes from a sexual revolution. On May 9, 1960, the FDA approves the first birth control pill. Matchmaking hits prime time with* **The Dating Game** *in 1965. The U.S. Supreme Court voids all laws against miscegenation in 1967. In the fall following the Summer of Love, feminists crash the 1968 Miss America pageant, proclaiming "women's liberation" and urging women to throw fake eyelashes, dishcloths, Playboy, Vogue, and their bras into "freedom trashcans."*

expressed are consistent with our earlier discussion of women being more polychronic in nature (Hall, 1983) and with wife's perceptions being more critical to marital satisfaction than men. Research on hormonal cycles provides insights to how time and intimacy are complexly interrelated, and adds another thread to the precious weave of context. Most important, the biochronic context is extremely dynamic and changeable. Men and women want different things at different times; sometimes their endogenous rhythms are mutually entrained and sometimes they are not. As we discussed earlier, how couples use their time, pace their interactions, and learn to synchronize their rhythms is what intimacy is all about.

Social Psychological Time: Commitment and the Progressive Irreversibility of Choice

Previous sections have alluded to a general understanding of commitment and it's importance for understanding context. As reviewed by Brickman et al. (1987), many of the most dramatic and influential experiments in social psychology demonstrate how justifiable increments in small commitments often lead to unforeseeable and negative consequences. A rapid and polarizing escalation in debilitating conflict that even hurts one's own self-interest may result from an initial use of only one coercive threat (Deutsch & Krauss, 1960). In the famous Milgram (1974) study on obedience, subjects accept money for playing their role (as teacher) in an experiment, and deliver initially mild but incrementally painful shocks to another person before they are confronted with the fact that they are inflicting pain and suffering on this other person. Brickman et al. pointed out that most criminals start with minor offenses, and the major crimes and atrocities of the past century (Watergate, the Jonestown suicides, the My Lai Massacre, the emergence of Nazi concentration camps) did not appear "full-blown" all at once. They were the result of gradual increments in commitment and the *justifiable* belief that the worst will not happen. Even addictive behaviors (e.g., smoking, alcoholism) may start out for extrinsic—and apparently innocent—reasons, such as to gain acceptance or to do something new. Brickman et al. (1987) explain the cumulative nature of behavioral involvements often intensifies the motivation behind the earlier actions in a sequence:

1975	1980-1981	1996
Unable to find any law prohibiting same-sex marriage, Clela Rorex, a county clerk in Boulder, Colorado, marries Dave Zamora and Ave McCord.	*Doctors begin to notice rare forms of pneumonia and cancer killing young gay men. Soon it becomes clear that this infectious disease, AIDS, is not exclusive to homosexual males.*	*The U.S. Congress passes the Defense Marriage Act, defining marriage narrowly as the official link between a man and a woman.*

There is a sense in which each act in the sequence is incomplete in itself, or is complete only momentarily, but soon comes to serve as a kind of lead-in to the acts that follow. These acts tend to finish, justify, and place into perspective the earlier acts and also to extend them in a way that motivates still further developments. We are engaged by our own behavior in somewhat the same way we can be engaged by soap operas or comic strips. In isolation, each episode of a soap opera, a comic strip, or a baseball season is meaningless. After a while, however, each episode serves to answer a question left over from a previous episode and, soon, to pose a question that will need answer in the next episode. The fact that there is a delay between episodes (as there is between most episodes of the same behavior) may raise the tension level involved in this process and enhance its overall effectiveness. (Auble, Franks, Soraci, 1979) (p. 166)

Temporal context is woven into the incremental nature of commitment. Our failure to consider this context results in the lack of insight about the various mechanisms Brickman et al, outlined: the intensification of earlier motivation, failure to see the situation unfold because of a need to complete a meaningless sequence, and tension due to delay between episodes. The forms of social ignorance that led to the atrocities of Jonestown, My Lai, and Nazi Germany can be seen as a problem of context. We commit to a view or way of doing things and then stubbornly cling to that view in the face of hardship, difficulty and even destruction. Different versions of this commitment process have been offered to explain why partners stay in relationships that are dissatisfying, problematic, and even abusive and violent.

Using Rusbult's investment model of commitment (e.g., Rusbult & Buunk, 1993), Rusbult and Martz (1992) surveyed women who sought refuge at a shelter for abused women. Commitment, rather than satisfaction, determined whether or not women returned to their abusive partners. When women have poor alternatives (e.g., lower education level, little money on hand) and have endured the relationship before, they are likely to go back regardless of their dissatisfaction. One version of cognitive dissonance theory (Festinger, 1957) suggests that we commit ourselves to a line of action by justifying our efforts in the face of difficulties and odds; that is, we come to like what we suffer for, or at least what we feel dissonant about (Aronson & Mills, 1959).

Delusion in Buddhist Psychology. This process of maligning commitment is similar to the process of delusion described in Buddhist psychology (Salzberg, 1993). Delusion is based on "unwise attention" where we respond to feelings of uncertainty (worry, confusion, stupor, helplessness, bewilderment) by clinging to some view just to give us a sense of security. By holding on to any view that we settle on, we than conceal the proximate cause (i.e., the uncertainty) of the initial clinging. Instead of paying attention to and relating to the feelings of uncertainty, we react to them with unwise attention.

Sampajhana—awareness of context—is essential to mindfulness and promotes a state of mind where delusion is less apt to arise. For example, in certain social situations, we do not blurt out what is only true without first thinking. We may sensitively combine information in the situation to discern what is useful—what, in the social context, is helpful rather than what gives us immediate pleasure or reduces our uncertainty. In social psychological situations of incremental commitment, we are often driven to confirm our initial commitment and to reduce the uncertainty we feel as the situation proceeds in an unforseeable direction (e.g., increased shocks, increase costs by staying at Jonestown). In short, we justify our initial choice in order to save face, clinging to a view of ourselves as a consistent person.

Sampajhana, an antidote to mindless commitment, is the ability to see this situation with a tenderness, spaciousness, and openness instead of becoming lost in our own story or script about how things should proceed. Interestingly, when we are deluded "we are engaged by our own behavior in somewhat the same way we can be engaged by soap operas or comic strips." We fail to have vision, to appreciate the larger, dynamic temporal context of which we are part. Subjects in the Milgram experiment would never say they would hurt another at the beginning of the experiment, but each small step led to an increased lack of vision. From the Buddhist perspective, the mistakes made at My Lai or in Nazi Germany are not due to some inherent evil but due to "unwise attention."

Intimacy may play a key mediating role in the development of this context awareness. Interestingly, in the Milgram studies, the degree of increased shock varied as a function of the physical distance between the experimenter and the confederate subject. When experimenters were separated in a different room from the subject, they administered highest level intensity shocks (with the confederate displaying an intense and prolonged agonized scream) 65% of the time. When seated in the same room as the subject, full obedience dropped to 40%, and when subjects were required to physically grasp the victim's hand and force it onto a metal shock plate, full obedience dropped to 30%. Thus, physical closeness and visibility led to less incremental commitment. Perhaps the more we can objectify or distance ourselves from another (I-It), the more mindlessly we behave and the less likely we can appreciate the situations we weave with others.

CONCLUSION

There are many different ways of conceptualizing and examining temporal context. Each has relevance for the process of intimacy in personal relationships. In addition to the most accessible temporal context provided by communication and social roles and situations, couples may be influenced by evolutionary-genetic time, biochronic-hormonal time, and the cumulative aspects of social commitment by virtue of their participation in social situations. The lack of awareness of these temporal influences may be seen as a moral issue; it seems that a healthy commitment to monogamy entails an ongoing moral choice that considers these temporal contexts. Regarding evolution, if we were to just follow our genetic impulses and attitudes, monogamy would continue to suffer and the moral fabric of society would fall apart (cf. Murray, 1994). Regarding hormones, monogamy appears to be the best choice for sustaining sexual regularity and the health and pleasure associated with it (Cutler, 1991). But, when entered into mindlessly and when we justify our painful efforts to maintain it, monogamy can also become a context for violence and abuse. These temporal contexts of evolution, hormonal cycles, and social commitments are not background factors that converge like causal sequences on relationship behaviors. Rather, our behavior shapes the effects of these dynamics. Through communication, mindfulness, self-monitoring (Baert), and an openness to new ways of seeing (sampajhana), we may be able to experience intimacy with ongoingness and depth.

End Notes—Chapter 6

1. **Empirical study of context.** Some researchers have operationalized context for empirical analysis. Godwin and Scanzoni (1989) included context as a variable in their statistical analysis of marital joint decision-making. Using self-report data of 188 married couples to measure context and an audiotaped interaction to assess process, these researchers distinguished between context and process variables as determining the outcome of the couple's discussion about their decision making in different areas (e.g., household chores, money, childbearing decisions). The context variables were both partner's perceptions of their love/caring, cooperativeness during past conflicts, commitment to the relationship, the degree of modernity (versus traditionalism) in gender role preferences, and the inequality of economic resources (income). Process variables were amount of measured coerciveness and control during the audiotaped decision-making interaction.

Interestingly, under the specifications of the statistical model they use (structural equations modeling, LISREL), the authors referred to the context variables as "exogenous variables"; that is, they are the background or distal causes of couple consensus in comparison to the immediate or proximal causes of interaction process. Whereas such context variables as wive's level of love and husband's past cooperativeness were significant predictors of consensus, the combination of both husbands' and wives' process data were stronger predictors.

Other authors have referred to context as a background or mediating factor. Bradbury and Fincham (1988, 1989) proposed a contextual model of marital interaction for understanding the relationship between behavior and satisfaction within marriages. Kurdek (1991) used this model to examine marital stability among newlywed couples. The contextual model distinguishes between proximal context (momentary thoughts and feelings) that provides the immediate environment for processing events, and distal context (personality traits, moods, preexisting relationship variables, and variables that emerge over the course of the relationship) or the emergent background of the relationship. Bradbury and Fincham (1989) wrote:

> The importance of the elements in the distal context lies in their potential to influence (a) variables in the proximal context and (b) the processing stage. For example, the wife's proximal context at the outset of an

interaction is likely to be a function not only of her thoughts and feelings about existing circumstances, but also of more stable factors such as her chronic mood state. . . . Moreover, elements in the distal context may be modified gradually as a function of the thoughts and feelings that comprise the proximal context. For example, a husband may become more trusting of his wife on the basis of the thoughts and feelings prompted by the things she says or does in their relationship. (p. 123)

This model, although it gives a central role to context as the mediator in marital interaction, views context "as a framework for organizing and conceptualizing mediating processes in marital interaction." Context becomes yet another variable in a causal scheme that distinguishes between processes and outcomes. Both Godwin and Scanzoni (1989) and Bradbury and Fincham (1989) viewed context and process as separate empirical categories. As we shall see, such an *atemporal* view of context fails to embrace critical aspects of intimacy. I also cite these authors to show that context is referred to as a background ("exogenous" or "framework") factor not only in theory but in research practice. This point anticipates the discussion in the next chapter (chap. 7) in which I argue that temporal context is not only a woven part of intimacy but that it can and should be measured as such.

2. More on biological clocks. Although most of the research has been conducted on women, Sheehy (1998) makes a convincing case for a male sexual life cycle, with some men experiencing a menopausal passage in middle age. She describes "symptoms of irritability, a feeling of sluggishness, and mild to moderate mood swings" (p. 186) as well as "the greatest fear, the phobic event that may become a self-fulfilling prophecy, is intermittent problems in gaining and sustaining an erection" (p. 186). There is also some evidence for increased sexual behavior during the summer months when testosterone reaches a seasonal maximum (Reilly, Atkison, & Waterhouse, 1997; citing Smolensky, 1992). Beyond these findings, there are still many questions that remain unanswered. For example, do partners that exercise together, have sex on a regular basis, follow similar sleep-wake cycles, similar eating cycles, and continue to follow these similar rhythms across different life-stages experience intimacy in qualitative different ways than partners who share only some of these concordant cycles?

Self-disclosure and close relationships do not necessarily develop over time in a parallel, incremental, and continuous fashion. People may wish to believe so and therefore may report a sequential progression on questionnaire surveys when they reconstruct their relationship from memory. However, research done with couples *over time* indicates that temporal patterns are, in fact, flexible and varied. (Derlega, Metts, Petronio, & Margulis, 1993, pp. 26–27, italics added)

We predicted ratings of satisfaction with the relationship from the variables in our study. Two attributes showed an increasing pattern of correlation with success: finding time to be with each other and willingness to change in response to each other. In other words, higher scores on these attributes become more predictive *over time* of satisfaction in relationships (Sternberg, 1998, p. 154, italics added)

THOUGHTS ON A NEW SCIENCE

- That we find a method and grammar that makes for a clearer and useful exploration of time as it is shaped and shaped by intimate relations.

7

In Search of the Temporal in Personal Relationship Research: From Temporal Initiative to Temporal Scale

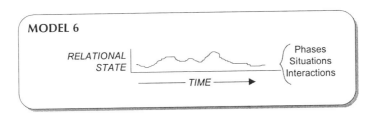

> The universe is not a museum with its specimens in glass cases. Nor is the universe a perfectly drilled regiment with its ranks in step, marching forward with undisturbed poise. Such notions belong to the fable of modern science—a very useful fable when understood for what it is. Science deals with large average effects, important within certain modes of observation. But in the history of human thought no scientific conclusion has ever survived unmodified by radical increase in our subtleties of relevant knowledge. (Whitehead, 1968, p. 90)

THEORETICAL WRITINGS in the social sciences call for a more refined, temporally based, view of social relationships. One representative of this "temporal initiative" is the burgeoning interdisciplinary field of personal relationships (PR). This chapter has four objectives: (a) to review temporal issues across different areas of the social sciences; (b) to identify biases in scientific thinking that predispose us to ignore or minimize the importance of time; (c) to develop a model that views PRs in three temporal contexts: interactional–sequential, exchange–situational, and phasic–transitional; and (d) to use this model to interpret a set of studies in terms of temporal contextualization and temporal extension. In chapter 8, several theories of personal relationships are examined for their temporal features. This next chapter has two main objectives: to use the tripartite contextual model to review existing theories that contribute to our understanding of temporal structure in

PRs; and to sketch a unified grammar of temporality in PRs; that is, to articulate some of the interrelationships across the three temporal contexts.

Background and Overview

Social scientists and analysts of the field of psychology, bearing various models, methods and research concerns, have been decrying the lack of a time-sensitive view within their respective disciplines for some time (e.g., Abbott, 1988; Duck & Sants, 1983; Faulconer & Williams, 1985; Giddens, 1984; Gottman, 1982; Hollis, 1987; Kelly & McGrath, 1988; Rosnow, 1981; Scanzoni, 1987; Sprey, 2000). The common voice across these disciplines suggests a paradigmatic revision of the nature of social phenomena as inherently dynamic and embedded within temporal contexts of various shapes and widths. As a whole, social scientists are becoming increasingly aware that temporal factors may provide alternative explanations for their research findings. Researchers face various problems: an inability to generalize research findings beyond the temporal context within which the data were collected, a failure to consider temporal parameters in research designs, and either statistical or database restrictions that prohibit testing of temporal assumptions about the phenomena under study.

Advances in statistical reasoning and methodology may alleviate some of these problems (Gottman & Rushe, 1993), but without a temporal theory such advances provide insufficient explanations of relationships that exist in time. All current efforts toward the building of such a theory may be called the "temporal initiative," which is only partly underway. The central claim of this chapter is that researchers, as well as the lay public, do not have a language for talking about or investigating time and change in human relationships. A coherent language will make us more aware of the role time plays in human relationships and will give momentum to the temporal initiative. It may be possible to construct such a "temporal grammar"—both with the models presented in previous chapters and now through a review of existing research and theory on personal relationships.

The first part of this chapter presents evidence of the temporal initiative and reviews theoretical and methodological biases that prevent appreciation of temporal context in social psychology (and PR research). Next, the argument is presented that time-sensitive methodologies are necessary (cf. Gottman & Roy; 1987; Kelly & McGrath, 1988; Kenny, 1988;) but insufficient for the understanding of social temporality and that social psychology lacks a coherent theory to compensate for this insufficiency. As a representative of social science, the multidisciplinary field of close relationships (Berscheid & Reis, 1998; Duck, 1988a) contains various models that describe social interaction, relationship development, and relationship dissolution, all of which implicate a temporal dimension.

Within this field, however, there has been no explicit attempt to integrate these models on a single dimension. In response to this lack of integration, this chapter introduces a descriptive model that considers relationships across different temporal contexts. This model also integrates models discussed in previous chapters. Using this contextual model, a temporal scale is developed that classifies research according to degree of temporal contextualization, that is, how much the research presents relationships as dynamic and changing. This chapter concludes with a subjective, but systematic, review of exemplary personal relationship research according to this new scale. Chapter 8 reviews several (although not all) theories within the field of personal relationships and interprets them within the language of the contextual model. On the basis of this review, a temporal grammar for relationships is outlined. Box 7.1 (next page) provides an outline and map to help you through the key aspects of this chapter.

THE TEMPORAL INITIATIVE: A REVIEW OF REVIEWS

Social psychology, and other disciplines that examine human relationships, is searching for a new paradigm. This search is influenced by *contextualists* who feel that in order to be meaningful, the study of human relationships must consider the surrounding context—history, meaning, change (e.g., Rosnow & Georgoudi, 1986). The search has also been influenced by *interactionists* who criticize experimental research—because it ignores the interactions of many variables that occur in real settings—as largely artificial and irrelevant to important human concerns (e.g., Strickland, Aboud, & Gergen, 1976; sections IV and V). The search is being conducted through cross-disciplinary approaches to social relationships (e.g., Cupach & Spitzberg, 1994; Duck, 1988a; Fletcher & Fitness, 1996; Petronio, 2000;), and by others who attempt to articulate a view of human action that is grounded in temporality (Faulconer & Williams, 1985; Slife, 1993; Vallacher & Nowak, 1994). The beginning of

> *The search is on for a language that translates between the real-time process of human relating and the methods used to measure that relating.*

the temporal initiative occurred in the 1960s and 1970s amidst "crisis" claims that social psychological research is trivial, irrelevant (e.g., Ring, 1967), historically bound, and culturally determined (Gergen, 1973). In response to this crisis, many have challenged researchers to develop theory and design research that examines social interaction in a more natural, ongoing, temporal context rather than in a reductionistic, static, experimental context (e.g., Carlson, 1984; Rosnow, 1981; Rosnow & Georgoudi, 1986; Snyder & Ickes, 1985; Sprey, 2000).

We can meet this challenge if we integrate temporality with an interdisciplinary perspective of social behavior. The emerging paradigm should concentrate on social phenomena as processual, as occurring across and within different levels of analysis and disciplines (refer to Table 6.1, pp. 160-161). These levels, or temporal contexts, include but are not limited to: (a) the personal history of individuals within relationships, (b) person-to-person interaction sequences, (c) the variability

BOX 7.1. CHAPTER OVERVIEW AND MAP

This chapter is somewhat more technical than previous ones. The following outline and map (opposite page) may be helpful in getting an overview of the purpose and flow of the chapter.

The Temporal Initiative: Social scientists are trying to formulate a language for translating between the real-time processes that occur in the systems they study (system time) and the methods they use to study those processes (method time).

Biases in Personal Relationship (PR) Research: To formulate that language within the PR field, it helps to identify biases that prevent appreciation of temporal factors.

Temporal Scale: Some research methods are more sensitive to real-time (ongoing) phenomena than others. The development of a temporal scale represents one way to assess this sensitivity and address biases.

The Tripartite Contextual Model: To help develop a temporal scale, I distinguish between three temporal contexts of increasing width: interactional (sequences), cross-situational (exchanges), and developmental (phases).

Dynamic Basis of the Contextual Model: The contextual model is not just a typology. Distinguishing contexts is less important than understanding the *dynamics* within and the *relationships* between the three contexts. These help us to understand the dynamic, ongoing, ever-evolving nature of PRs.

Static and Dynamic Factors: Thus, research should explore *how* relationship states come about, such as attraction, liking, marital satisfaction, and stability. To do so, research should identify the processual nature of context, such as procession in interactions, salience in exchanges, and continuity from phase to phase. (see Fig. 7.1)

Elements of a Temporal Scale: Based on the above, I propose two basic elements of a temporal scale, *extension* and *contextualization*. Extension refers to the number of observations made and the interval between observations. Contextualization refers to the number of temporal contexts observed and any assessment of the relationships between contexts.

Probability and Creating a Temporal Portrait: I propose that through the use of a temporal scale any research study can be assessed in terms of how probable the description it provides is a valid representation of the temporal (ongoing) nature of the system under study. (This probability is also called the external validity of the temporal dimension or temporal validity). (see Fig. 7.2)

Application of the Temporal Scale: To help demonstrate use of the temporal scale I estimate the temporal validity of 9 PR studies (see Table 7.1)

BOX 7.1. (CONTINUED)

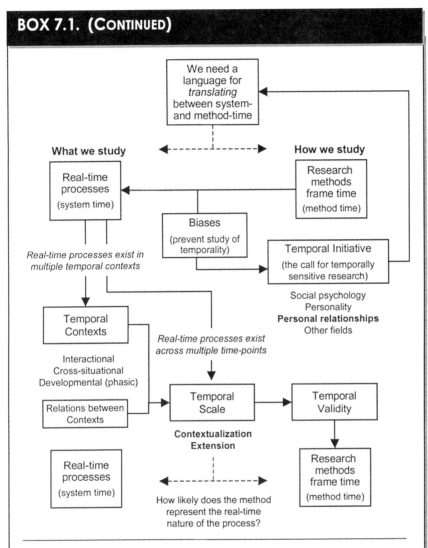

This chapter develops a temporal scale as a way of translating between real-time processes (what we study) and methodological time (how we study). Two basic assumptions are made: (1) real-time processes exist in multiple temporal contexts, and (2) real-time processes exist across multiple time-points. Any given research study cannot assess all the temporal contexts and all the time-points that make up the real-time process. However, across research studies we can estimate how well the methods used represent or approximate that process (temporal validity). This is the purpose of the temporal scale.

of interpersonal behavior across situations, (d) developmental changes in relationships, and (e) the phases of sociocultural and sociobiological history that may effect human relationships at a particular point in societal evolution (refer to *Love Line* in chap. 6, pp. 194-202). Consideration of these different temporal contexts would bring together thinking from the areas of personality theory, communication theory, social psychology, family and marriage studies, human development, sociobiology, anthropology, and ethnology. Without this *intertemporal* paradigm, there is some risk of wasting efforts on research that either distorts or poorly represents the ongoing nature of human social behavior.

Recent writings have, in fact, specifically addressed an interdisciplinary revision of social time (Fraser, 1987; Young, 1988). The current call for a more time-sensitive view of social phenomena is so widespread within the social sciences that it is difficult to focus our vision on a single "disciplinary matrix" (Kuhn, 1970). The current analysis takes the field of close, personal relationships to be such a matrix or paradigm case. The following section highlights the larger cross-disciplinary search for temporality before examining PR research.

Cross-Disciplinary Search for Temporality

Social Psychology. In a historical analysis of the field of social psychology, Pepitone (1981) identifies two broad classifications of dominant theoretical schools—the social psychology of the individual or of the relation—and claimed that theory and research have been pervasively weighted toward the former; a bias he labeled "individuocentric." Pepitone called for "adequate" theories that focus more on interactional, adaptational, and distal (e.g., historical, political) causes rather than intraindividual, cognitive, or proximate (e.g., biological) causes of social behavior. Pepitone accented the dynamic aspects of both individuals and relations as they are influenced by and adapt to the changing biological, ecological, and sociocultural contexts in which they are embedded. Huston and Robins (1982) provided a methodological parallel to Pepitone, calling specifically for research that integrates both proximal and distal causes of social interaction. In the past 20 years, researchers have begun to answer these calls (e.g., quotes that head this chapter by Derlega et al. and Sternberg).

Zajonc (1980) gave an historical review of social cognition and claimed that, unlike perception in ordinary psychophysics (where stimuli remain constant in response to perception), social perception involves an object-observer interaction through which social stimuli (persons) are influenced by how they are perceived. Social perception is an "inconstant" process that necessitates successive measurement strategies. Similarly, Brickman, Dunkel-Schetter, and Abbey (1987) integrate studies in impression formation, compliance, obedience, and persuasion to derive a developmental model of decision-making and commitment. They claimed that "many things that appear to be single decisions turn out, upon closer examination, to represent the cumulative process of a series of steps, choices, or decisions" (p. 153). More recently, Vallacher and Nowak (1994) proposed a "dynamical social psychology" that incorporated ideas from chaos theory into traditional areas of social psychology (e.g., attitude change, conformity).

Personality. Theoretical attempts to integrate personality and social psychology (e.g., Baron & Boudreau, 1987; Buss, 1987; Snyder & Ickes, 1985) suggest a dynamic view of person-situation interaction because such interaction evolves over time (cf. "serials" and "proceedings," Murray, 1938). Snyder and Ickes (1985) reviewed three major perspectives on the role of personality in social behavior: the dispositionalist (traits determine behavior), situationalist (social situations determine behavior), and interactionist (behavior is determined by both personality and situations). Snyder and Ickes seemed to endorse a "dynamic version of the interactional strategy" and emphasize the importance of situations when individuals interact. They argue that individuals select situations that favor the expression of their personality traits and feedback from the situations often lead to a sequence of modifications in the expression of the trait. This dynamism implies a temporal sequence in which individuals "select, evoke, or manipulate" (Buss, 1987) from their environment and where their environment provides "affordances" (Baron & Boudreau, 1987) for the realization or manifestation of one's personality.

Despite our common sense belief that people have an identity, a continuity of personality, or show the same traits across different situations, research has failed to provide strong evidence for cross-situational predictability of behavior (e.g., Mischel, 1968). In an attempt to address this problem, Epstein (1979) demonstrated that measures of behavior are often not reliable, because individuals have not been assessed over multiple time periods. The prototypical experiment isolates persons within single temporal frames. This method introduces a bias that has kept researchers from considering a more dynamic view of personality in and over time. More recently, there has been a move in personality research from "inferred personalities" to "personality in action." Fiske (1988) points out that in most of these programs (e.g., Klinger, 1987; Luborsky, Sackheim, & Christoph, 1979; Paul, 1987) "the investigator is studying relationships between behaviors that are temporally adjacent, as one would expect in studies of personality in action (p. 829)." Thus, in terms of theory, method, and new research programs, the field of personality has also been seeking a more articulate view of temporality (also see Funder, Parke, Tomlinson-Keasey, & Widaman, 1993).

The Study of Personal Relationships. In the *Annual Review of Psychology*, the field of personal relationships was first reviewed by Huston and Levinger (1978) then by Clark and Reis (1988), and more recently by Berscheid (1994). The authors of the first review indicated that more than two thirds of the research at that time focused on impression, attraction, and encounters rather than "ongoing relationships." They asserted that their review is part of a wider attempt (e.g., Altman & Taylor, 1973) to "create languages for describing the development of relationships." Clark and Reis (1988) repeat this assertion in their call for research on relationship history, spontaneous everyday behavior, and "critical time periods" in relationship transitions. Gaining access to these temporal contexts has apparently been a major methodological obstacle: "Relationships are interactive, dyadic, and time-bound, necessitating special methodologies" concluded Clark and Reis (1988, p. 662). Interestingly, Berscheid (1994) noted that relationship scholars must be sensitive to methodological techniques because of the "temporal nature" of relationships.

The call for a focus on relations rather than individuals (Pepitone, 1981), stimulus inconstancy rather than constancy in social perception (Zajonc, 1980), and serial processes rather than a single-decision in commitment (Brickman et al., 1987) implies dissatisfaction with atemporal concepts of social phenomena. Similarly, research trends focusing more on person-situation interaction rather than either person or situation alone (Snyder & Ickes, 1985), and on ongoing relationships rather than encounters and impressions (Clark & Reis, 1988; Huston & Levinger, 1978) points to a boundary condition—a present limit within the scientific paradigm—that confronts other social scientists as well.

Other Fields. In communication science and marital studies, Gottman (1982) argued that a new language of "temporal form" is required to describe relationship pattern (see also Heaton, 1991; Millar & Rogers, 1976). Most recently, Sprey (2000) argued that theory within the field of family studies needs to view marriage as a nonlinear process. Baxter and others (e.g., Baxter, 1988; Conville, 1991) advanced a dialectical perspective on couple communication. In theoretical sociology, Abbott (1988) argued that the sociologists' view of the world is rooted in the General Linear Model, a view that examines "fixed entities" rather than events and calls for a sequential model of reality, "narrative patterns" that evolve through time. Scanzoni (1987) examined the paradigm currently prevailing within family studies and claims that it is "time to refocus our thinking." He suggested that scientists view the family less as a fixed (and idealized) image—the "contemporary traditional family"—and more as a developmental phenomenon (e.g., "conjugal succession") that occurs within an ever-changing sociocultural context. In their methodological monograph on time, Kelly and McGrath (1988) outlined ways in which behavioral scientists can construct time-sensitive research designs that distinguish between the individual, situational, and temporal factors that are present and ongoing within any research setting.

The common voice across each of these reviews speaks to a "temporal initiative." This is a widespread perception that the prevailing epistemology (or way of knowing) that governs the social scientists' perception of social reality is limited. The limitation appears to be rooted in both methodological and theoretical shortcomings that prevent the incorporation of temporality into researcher's construal of reality (Faulconer & Williams, 1985). More importantly, current research is beginning to address a revision of social reality into a temporally based, historically determinate, and processual or sequential context in which persons, situations, relationships, and various social contexts *cohere intertemporally*. This initiative is paradigmatic in the sense that relational phenomena that comes under the purview of separate subdisciplines can be grouped together as presenting a particular and common "puzzle-solution" (Kuhn, 1970). That is, the same problems are facing researchers from closely related areas of the social sciences. Versions of this puzzle differ depending on whether one is concerned with its historical causes (e.g., Pepitone, 1981; Zajonc, 1980), methodological limitations (e.g., Abbott, 1988; Clark & Reis, 1988), logical premises (Hollis, 1987), or sociological constraints (e.g., Giddens, 1984; Scanzoni, 1979). The first step toward a solution will likely require the explicit articulation of some common language of temporal form in human relationships and the trajectories those relationships take.

Previous theoretical work may provide keystone concepts for a common language. Such concepts include Mead's "symbolic interactionism" (1934, see previous chapter), Murray's "proceedings" and "serials" (1938, see chap. 5), Lewin's "contemporaneity" (1951), Gouldner's "reciprocity" (1960), Goffman's "consequentiality" (1967), and Bandura's "reciprocal determinism" (1977). Not only have these terms seen relatively wide usage within their respective disciplines, they each explicitly account for human behavior as it unfolds within time. There are also more recently advanced concepts that could enrich this temporal lexicon within the study of personal relationships. These terms include Gottman's "temporal form" (1982a), Kelley et al.'s "interchain causal connections" (1983) and Werner and Haggard's (1985) "salience," "sequence," "temporal scale," and "pace and rhythm." Moreover, there are other coinages from McGrath and colleagues, such as time allocation, cycle, continuity versus change (McGrath, 1988), temporal order, temporal interval, temporal scale (Kelly & McGrath, 1988), entrainment, mesh, and tempo (McGrath & Kelly, 1986). Future researchers who operationalize these terms would pioneer attempts to flesh out the specifics of a temporal lexicon for interpersonal processes. The problem lies though, not in the development of a lexicon, but in the lack of a grammar that would contextualizes the various terms, showing how they interrelate.

THE FIELD OF PERSONAL RELATIONSHIPS

As already noted, this field is particularly troubled by the lack of a coherent temporal language. Clark and Reis' (1988) review of methodological developments suggested that these new tools will allow researchers to address questions of a more temporal nature: "Because the central phenomena in the new field of interpersonal relations are interactional in their essence, methodological expansion is especially valuable. . . . Paradigms focusing on the behavior of individuals in isolation need to be supplemented by paradigms focusing on interdependence, relationships, and influence" (Kenny, 1988, p. 651).

Duck and colleagues (Acitelli & Duck, 1987; Duck & Pond, 1989; Duck & Sants, 1983), attempted to reframe the field of PRs more in an epistemological sense than from methodological strategy. It is not the tools that will teach us more about relationships as much as a process orientation or way of seeing the world as process (see also Cate & Lloyd, 1988; Reis & Shaver, 1988). This orientation or way of knowing views PRs as (a) inherently negotiated through ongoing communication, (b) variable depending upon who is describing the process, and (c) as understood by their participants in a non-rational, albeit emotional and somewhat unpredictable manner. Duck and Sants (1983) suggested that this new view charts "the geographic course of a relationship" as well as "the characteristic tides, fluctuations, and behavior of the relationship within and beyond those bounds" (p. 39). Again, the problem is not that researchers lack consensus on the need for this process view, but rather that they lack a guiding theory for it. Recent reviews of the field indicates the continued lack of such guidance (Berscheid, 1994; Berscheid & Reis, 1998).

Whether it is through methodological and statistical innovations (Clark & Reis, 1988; Raudenbush, Brennan, & Barnett, 1995), or a renewed process perspective, the interdisciplinary field of personal relationships (as a representative of social science) is seeking an understanding of time that has hitherto been lacking. It is not clear, however, that innovations in methodology or perspective innovation, although necessary, will be sufficient for this understanding. Because of both theoretical and empirical epistemological biases (cf. MacKay, 1988), an alternative view may be required that construes social reality as inherently processual and temporal, not individuocentric, stimulus constant, non-sequential, fixed, or patternless.[1] The dialogue between research and theory plays a pivotal role in scientific progress. Such progress can be facilitated by a coherent grammar for understanding relationships in time, a grammar that avoids reduction to a single level of explanation (e.g., to the individual). Such a grammar should explicate the relation between the particular research context in which social behavior is studied and each of the broader temporal contexts in which the relationship is situated. It should also address biases and assumptions about the nature of time. In this regard, it is instructive to review some biases that keep the aforementioned arguments from actively facilitating research.

Biases Preventing Appreciation of Temporal Context [2]

A number of texts treat the role of time within a social or interpersonal context (Cottle & Klineberg, 1974; Doob, 1971; Fraser, 1987; Gurvitch, 1964; Yaker, Osmond & Cheek, 1971). Since 1972, the *International Society for the Study of Time* (e.g., Fraser, Lawrence & Haber, 1986; see www.studyoftime.org) has included presentations dealing with social time and there is now a new research journal devoted to social time: *Time and Society* (1992, Sage Publications).

Thus, although time may be said to be the primary language of the historian or the physicist, social scientists attempt to also speak that language (also see Kearl, 2000). Kelly and McGrath (1988) claimed that social psychologists and other social scientists interested in social relations have been lacking an adequate empirical appreciation of time in their investigations. Literature from the temporal initiative contains analyses of those biases that may be preventing such appreciation. The following categorization is meant to be a survey of a broad area of research and the listed biases are overlapping and interdependent.

The Individuocentric Bias. Pepitone (1981) claimed that research has focused on the individual rather than the relationship because social psychology has inherited methodological doctrines (norms about "how psychologists should think about and practice psychology") associated with the concept of psychology as a natural empirical science. Pepitone listed the doctrines of empiricism, objectivism, behaviorism, reductionism, materialism, mechanism, universalism, and individualism as each contributing to the historical tendency for social psychologists to reductively explain social behavior to the individual. As long as this reductive tendency exists, psychologists will neglect the more global, distal, and contextual factors (e.g., environment, economy) through which relationships evolve. Reductive explanations of relationships place emphasis on the *intra*psychic (rather than *inter*psychic) events of those relationships' participants; they tend to neglect how those events are successively causal and consequential within the relationship as it evolves.

Methodological Convenience Biases. The prevailing tendency within personal relationship research has been to use participant reports (Ruano, Bruce, & Mcdermott, 1969, cited in Kelley et al., 1983, p. 452) or subjective responses of one partner in a relationship at one point in time (Brehm, 1985). Much data is collected on college students whose viewpoint is subject to a number of idiosyncrasies (e.g., readily compliant, relatively nonintrospective, having stage-specific attitudes; Sears; 1986) that limit generalization to relationships that are more ongoing or at subsequent developmental phases (marriage, divorce).

Methodological reviews (e.g., Gottman, 1982; Harvey, Christensen, & McClintock, 1983; Huston & Levinger, 1978; Huston & Robins, 1982) of close relationship and social interaction research reveal a prevailing focus on individual functioning (e.g., personality) to explain interactional processes. This is due, in part, to the advantages that questionnaires afford in terms of ease of access to private events (Harvey, Christensen, & McClintock, 1983), the relative ease of data collection, and the greater amount of effort required to carry out studies on rate (e.g., duration, latency) measures of social interaction (Hartup, 1979). Huston and Robins (1982, p. 918) claimed that "the resources and care necessary to do causal research on relationships make such work extremely difficult." Whereas researchers have long been able to apply sequential analysis methodologies to behavioral observation data (Gottman, 1982; Lamb, Suomi, & Stephenson, 1979) historical reviews of marriage and family research (e.g., Broderick, 1988; Nye, 1988) indicate that methodologists rely on interviews, global self-reports, or accessible demographic survey databases.

> Analyses employing demographic variables and secondary data have a high likelihood of being published in medium- to high-prestige journals. Since tenure and promotion depend largely on such publications, the temptation to conduct this type of research is considerable. But the correlations found are usually low and those that are found are difficult to interpret, since they are typically atheoretical; thus the contributions to knowledge are not very great. Family research needed to go through this stage in 1937, 1947, and 1957, but most of it in 1987 represents arrested development in the evolution of family research. (Nye, 1988, p. 314)

Methodological inconvenience, whether it is due to publication pressures or to the lack of either theory or time, results in the avoidance of either sequential-interactional research strategies (micro-analytic data collection) or longitudinal-developmental stage studies (macro-analytic). Although there are statistical problems involved in measuring change (Cronbach & Furby, 1970) and in relying on cross-sectional data to infer relational processes (e.g., Spanier, Lewis, & Cole, 1975), the inconveniences caused by these problems should not restrict our view of relationships as "ongoing" as often as they do.

Truncation of Perspective. Truncation of perspective represents the bias (of temporal context) of a disciplinary orientation. For example, patterns of relationship options (e.g., cohabitation versus marriage) over time tend to be analyzed in the sociological domain, changes in feelings of love or satisfaction tend to be the province of psychologists, and probabilities of certain communication sequences are assessed by communication scientists. Working within their respective paradigms, scientists do not analyze the interrelationships between events occurring in one temporal domain with events that occur at another level of analysis (although see Milardo, Johnson, & Huston, 1983; Zeitlow & Van Lear, 1991). Clark and Reis (1988) pointed out that studies have not been conducted that discriminate between method and relationship effects. First, the study of ongoing relationships tends to be relegated to survey and correlational designs whereas the study of stranger interaction tends to be relegated to experimental designs. Second, the study of ongoing relationships tends to be descriptive whereas the studies of cause-and-effect processes are confined to the laboratory. And finally, the study of ongoing relationships in the field tends to use aggregated measurements, whereas fine-grained analyses of process are confined to the laboratory. The Clark and Reis review reads like an apology for those researchers who have been overcommitted to experimental research. Experimentalism brings with it certain assumptions about causality and temporal sequence that are not entirely applicable to the study of ongoing relationships, especially regarding the phenomena of intimacy.

Assumptions From the Natural Sciences. The experimentalist bias, inherited in part from the natural sciences (Kelly & McGrath, 1988), has been observed and critiqued by researchers in personality (Epstein, 1979, p. 1121), social psychology (Snyder & Ickes, 1985, p. 1227), and personal relationships (Clark & Reis, 1988). Social psychologists have argued that the emphasis on prediction, control, and the reductionist logic of experimentalism desensitizes us to the broader historical context in which behavior occurs (Gergen, 1973); the "one-hour" experiment truncates our view of persons (Carlson, 1984). Berscheid (1986), lamenting the "pervasiveness of reductionistic dogma," suggests that the "systems" approach (e.g., Bertalanffy, 1968) will increase the "likelihood that questions of process will receive more attention, and questions of static structure will be regarded as less interesting" (p. 283).

Rosnow (1981), after reviewing the rise of experimentalism in social psychology, showed how it has failed to face the crises of artifacts (e.g., experimenter-expectancy bias), ethics (e.g., the problem of informed consent in volunteer subjects), and relevance (e.g., most research is trivial; Ring, 1967). Rosnow claimed the classical or mechanistic epistemology that gave rise to experimentalism is inappropriate for understanding the biocultural and sociocultural factors that influence interpersonal behavior. The reconstruction of social psychology requires theories of change. Such theories may view change as (a) unilinear progression and adaptation, (b) recursive or cyclic progression and development, or (c) dialectical conflict and resolution. Rosnow argued that the reconstruction of social psychology requires the incorporation of a "diachronic systems" view,

> *If science views relationships in cause–effect sequences ("part" time), how can it understand systems that transcends those sequences ("whole" time)?*

where we view a system in transhistorical context, as opposed to the common, experimentalist "synchronic entity" approach, where the focus is on an individual within a single time frame (cf. "whole time" vs. "part time," Gioscia, 1971, p. 79).

Similarly, Kelly and McGrath (1988) claimed that "the temporal features of the processes underlying human behavior often take place in a different time domain that is far more macro than the critical events in many areas of physical science" (p. 23). They described two pairs of assumptions that behavioral scientists have borrowed from the natural sciences: that processes are inertial and linear, and that change is instantaneous and persistent. They then claimed that much of human behavior is cyclic, rhythmic, or oscillatory and that some changes, for example, in attitude formation, take time to develop and do not always persist.

Taken together, these claims assume that human behavior occurs in a much richer temporal context than physical particles, and that natural science methodology does not adequately capture this richness. All that happens in a relationship cannot be reduced to chains of cause-and-effect sequences; human love is rich precisely because it can transcend such chains. Those theories that consider this richness and provide clear operation-conception linkages will be more likely to examine, convey, and explain the temporal reality of their human subjects. The model proposed here attempts to regard relationships through multiple temporal lenses so that we can explore and understand the relationship *between* processes rather than just focus on simple cause and effects. The model might help in at least four ways, it should: (a) prevent theoretical fixation on singular instances or within a singular temporal context; (b) address the atemporality biases just listed; (c) allow psychologists to assess relationships and research about relationships in temporal terms through use of a temporal scale; and (d) provide a grammar for explaining temporality that articulates relationships within an existing lexicon.

TOWARD AN INTERDISCIPLINARY MODEL OF TEMPORAL SCALE

At least three different uses of the term *temporal scale* can be applied to our study of personal relationships, including: the scale a culture uses in its orientation toward time—some cultures being future-oriented and others being present-oriented (Jones, 1988); the scale scientists use in translating between laboratory time and the natural timing of events in the observed system (Kelly & McGrath, 1988), and the durations and cycles in which relationship processes unfold (Werner & Haggard, 1985). There are also at least three different worlds of time or "temporalities" (Fraser, 1987): biotemporality, or the timing of events in living systems (e.g., entrainment to biological clocks, McGrath & Kelly, 1986), nootemporality, or the subjective, psychological world of time; and sociotemporality, or the effects that society has on the structure and pace of life (cf. "time-geography," Giddens, 1984).

The current model attempts to incorporate and interweave each of these definitions. Unlike the common, "classical Newtonian paradigm", which structures time into linear, divisible, successive units (McGrath & Kelly, 1986), the current model assumes that time exists in different contexts, that it can be scaled in more than one way. This assumption is based on the "Einsteinian" or new physics view, where time is abstract and relational with "the viewpoint of the observer constituting an integral feature of the measurement of time" (McGrath & Kelly, 1986, p. 32). The culture, the experimental situation, the relationship itself, and their biological, psychological, and sociological currents represent different contexts in which scientists can attempt to understand time in personal relationships. As previous models have tried to show, time "unfolds" as a function of intimacy (chap. 3), manifests in various forces and features (chap. 4), and it interpenetrates both our personal problems and cosmic processes (chap. 5).

Kelly and McGrath (1988) distinguished between "the processes of natural systems [that] unfold according to their own timing" and the artificial time constructed by experimenters to examine behavior. They claimed that social science lacks a theory of temporal scale that could "map between experimental time and system time in some systematic fashion" and that one prerequisite for a temporal scale is "a conceptual formulation of the system itself that is virtually fully developed in its dynamics" (p. 94). Whereas Kelly and McGrath focused on the experimental method, any methodological insensitivity to temporality results in some imposition of interval or temporal frame on the naturally endogenous system process (e.g., cycle).[3] For this reason, a dynamic conceptualization of a system may facilitate the rigorous use and interpretation of time-sensitive research designs.

In the field of personal relationships, Werner and Haggard (1985) identifed some features of this dynamic conceptualization. For them, temporal scale means duration, a quality measured both externally (e.g., by clocks) and internally (psychologically), and they distinguish between linear and cyclical temporal scale. These authors used scale to refer to length, stage, and events of a relationship and reviewed the concept of linear scale as it has been used in various studies and theories. For example, there are norms for length of utterance in relationships (e.g., Argyle, 1978), and stages of relationship have been defined by psychological qualities that change over time (e.g., Altman & Taylor, 1973).

Werner and Haggard (1985) also described cyclical scale, the frequency and duration of recurrent relationship events. Anniversaries and the routines of daily living typify these recurrent events. Research examples of cyclical scale include Altman and his colleagues' work on cycles of privacy regulation in which intimacy is sometimes sought and sometimes avoided (Altman et al., 1981). There is also research (e.g., Rowles, 1981) that describes the psychological meaning of interaction routines within social networks, and research (Lee, 1969) showing how women who seek an abortion appear to "cycle" through their social network until they find support. Werner and Haggard demonstrated how conceptions of scale (and of the other temporal qualities of sequence, rhythm, and salience) are already woven into existing research and theories.

Taken together, Werner and Haggard's (1985) conceptions of scale, Fraser's (1987) three temporalities, Kelly and McGrath's distinction (1988) between "system (real) time" and "experimental (methodological) time" serve to illustrate the idea that time is relative. It is constructed and operationalized according to the ways in which theorists frame observed events. By adapting this relative (Einsteinian) view of time, we run the risk of having as many different conceptions or contexts of time as there are observers.

To help avoid this risk, we can classify most current conceptualizations of relationships into a minimum of three overlapping temporal contexts: interactional, cross-situational, and developmental. *Interactional* refers to the sequence of give and take, communication, and basic (verbal and nonverbal) information exchange that occurs within a singular interaction between two people. *Cross-situational* refers to the development and exchange of psychological properties (e.g., affection, intimacy, interdependence) that occurs within but more often across the situations that two people share. *Developmental* refers to the development and transitions of the relationship as it evolves through different phases or stages. The next sections illustrate these different contexts, describe how they are analyzed, discuss their processual nature, and then discuss how they might be integrated within a single temporal scale.

ILLUSTRATION OF THE CONTEXTUAL MODEL

The basic structure of the contextual model can be highlighted with the following illustration. Recall from chapter 2 that even though my communication to you is fixed in writing on this page, it is possible to imagine that you and I are in the process of interaction. There has been sequence and development of an idea. I first introduced the concept of temporal context in personal relationships, described three such contexts, and now intend to illustrate each. At each point, you have presumably responded with some degree of understanding. As we proceeded through this brief paragraph, we have, for the sake of rough illustration, been in a sequence of interaction.

Now suppose that the ideas of this chapter prompted you to correspond with me; you would have propelled our relationship into at least two separate interaction sequences. Your correspondence, in effect, suggests that the

---

RESEARCH **REFLECTION** 16

SITUATIONS DEFINED BY RESOURCE EXCHANGE (TRANSACTIONS)

In defining situations according to the exchange of resources, the model outlined here borrows from resource exchange theories of relationships. These theories assume that relationships are governed by exchange principles similar to those in the marketplace (see "transaction" in chap. 2). Importantly, the resources exchanged involve intangibles such as love, information, and social status, as well as tangibles like services (Foa & Foa, 1974). Haslam (1995) developed a questionnaire to assess these resources in relationships. Following are some factors and example items. Reflect back on chapter 2, and consider what I (as author) might have as a resource to exchange.

- **Communal sharing** (If this person need help, you would cancel plans to give it).
- **Equality matching** (You often take turns doing things).
- **Authority ranking** (One of you calls the shots in the relationship).
- **Market pricing** (How much this person gets from you depends on how much he or she puts in).
- **Love** (This person gives you affection).
- **Information** (This person advises you).

influence (positive or negative) of reading has enough of an effect on you to lead to your action. There is either some reward or anticipated reward from correspondence that outweighs the cost of inaction. But you may not even take immediate action; you may only think or contemplate about what I have written. Whatever your responses, they would now exist in at least two temporal contexts: the two sequences of interaction and the balancing of rewards and costs that led to the development of a new situation (i.e., your written or contemplative response).

In all likelihood, however, you and I have never met; although we may have interacted or exchanged ideas in the previous two paragraphs, we are still strangers or, at best, potential acquaintances. Assume, however, that over the course of a few years we chance to meet and discover some common interests. Our relationship can take several different trajectories at that point (e.g., continued acquaintance, perhaps even friendship). Our relationship would then show signs of change that are not adequately captured by interaction or exchange language alone; there has been some transition, some entry into a new phase. It is possible that we may have a single interaction or a significant exchange that propels us into that new phase. However, were we to describe it only as an interaction, we would not capture or convey our new and different feelings about each other (i.e., the discontinuity in our psychological orientation toward each other). In other relationships, interactions may accumulate into exchanges, and exchanges may accumulate into phases. But phases may be comprised of only one interaction (e.g., love at first sight), and many exchanges may occur in a single phase (e.g., a one-night-stand) (see Fig. 7.1). The previous illustration cleaves a trifold distinction between the otherwise simultaneous, inter-weaved existence of the multiple timelines in intimate relations. Before we can understand this simultaneous, processual, cross-contextual nature of relationships, it first may help to have a concrete unit for analyzing relationships within each context.

UNITS OF ANALYSIS AND CRITERION STATES WITHIN THE THREE CONTEXTS

There are a number of ways to describe how relationships change and continue across time. The proposed (tripartite) model, following ideas discussed in previous chapters, suggests three basic overlapping units of contextual analysis. These are changes in partner's actions and perceptions within the sequential-interactive context, changes in how partners coordinate outcomes (e.g., rewards and costs) within the situational–exchange context, and critical relationship decisions and choices within the phasic–transitional context. The first context entails actions and perceptions of relatively limited duration. A single conversation, with all its nonverbal, paraverbal, and psychophysiological aspects, is the prototype for this context: Husband says a; wife says b in response; husband expresses c, and so on with concurrent changes in affect, arousal, and cognition.

The second context tends to be of intermediate duration and includes a variety of overlapping, sequential-interactions that may be identified and ordered by the emotional, cognitive, or behavioral outcomes they yield.[4] In this context, self-disclosure, feelings of love, and emotive exchanges become regulated through rules, routines, and socially or self-prescribed norms (e.g., habits and their deviations; Young, 1988). Each partner's search for, interpretation of, and response to these outcomes, is influenced by enduring personality traits (e.g., unity-thema; Murray, 1938), as well as the partner's ongoing revision of their mutual definition of the relationship (Morton & Douglas; 1981). For example, under a reciprocity (tit-for-tat) rule, Jay may concede to socialize with Donna's friends this weekend only if she consents to go to the hockey game next Saturday. She is likely to agree only because she knows (from past interactions) that his aloof shyness, which annoys her in the situation with her friends, is outweighed by her enjoyment of their shared passion at the game. Jay's and Donna's communication and behavior together entail a sequence, but this sequence is regulated by rules made salient by the psychological situation and by social motives. Such motives supersede and, in fact, give some narrative structure to this sequential frame. Jay and Donna are seeking some outcome that gives shape to their interaction.

Returning to the language of person–situation interactionism (Snyder & Ickes, 1985), a person selects and manipulates a situation (e.g., "I think I want to have some private time with her tonight so how can I help set the mood for that?"). In turn, the situation evokes behaviors (Buss, 1987) that are oriented toward some outcome. When two individuals schedule their time across situations in a relationship (see Clarke, Allen, & Salinas, 1986), their outcomes become coordinated to varying degrees of interdependence (Kelley & Thibaut, 1978). In the previous example, Donna may vacillate in her decision to accompany Jay to the hockey game, or she may immediately agree to go. Over time, however, their relationship consists of a series of situational outcomes that (either cyclically, again and again, or cumulatively, in an increasing fashion) satisfy or dissatisfy conditions for coordinating future outcomes. This second temporal context is identified by changes that occur across psychological situations, so defined by the cognitive, emotional, and behavioral effects these situations yield.

The third context brackets the previous ones inside decisions or choices that partners are, more or less, normatively (i.e., through conformity) scheduled to make. For example, the early work of Huston, Surra, Fitzgerald, and Cate (1981) delineated events such as "first date," "first kiss," "first sexual intercourse" in courtship. Argyle and Henderson (1985, p. 130) reviewed several critical periods of marriage: married without children → child bearing → preschool children, oldest child 5 → school children, oldest 6—12 → teenagers → first child gone to last leaving home → empty nest to retirement. Braiker and Kelley (1979) classified couples in four stages: the first two distinguished

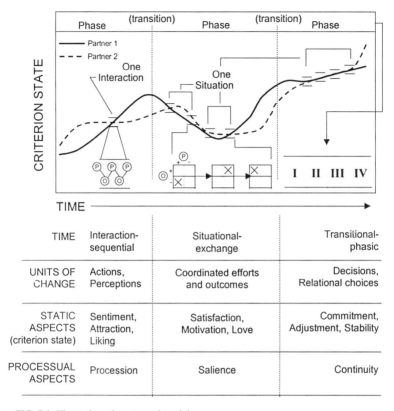

TIME	Interaction-sequential	Situational-exchange	Transitional-phasic
UNITS OF CHANGE	Actions, Perceptions	Coordinated efforts and outcomes	Decisions, Relational choices
STATIC ASPECTS (criterion state)	Sentiment, Attraction, Liking	Satisfaction, Motivation, Love	Commitment, Adjustment, Stability
PROCESSUAL ASPECTS	Procession	Salience	Continuity

FIG. 7.1. Illustration of contextual model.

psychologically and the latter two institutionally: casual dating, serious dating, engaged, married.

Figure 7.1 presents an overview of each of these contexts and the various temporal distinctions under discussion. The top of the figure represents two individuals (solid and broken line) who show continuing relative, although cyclical, increases in some criterion state (vertical axis; e.g., love, interdependence) over time (horizontal axis). The figure depicts different phases, transitions between phases, different situations within these phases, and interactions as well. As suggested by the figure, different temporal contexts can be simultaneously applied to analyze continuous change. For example, interactions can be analyzed within situations as well as within phases and transitions. The figure also represents interactions as a P (partner) > O (other) sequence and it represents exchanges through the relative benefits (+) and costs (-) of acting.

As suggested by the figure, the three basic contexts represent demarcations on a continua rather than discrete nominal categories. The units of analysis within each of these frames are features of relating (what I call *relata*) that are driven by three prototypic or ideal "clocks." At the molecular level, these are the biological rhythms of the two individuals that become entrained (McGrath & Kelly, 1988) or cohere to varying degrees within certain cycles. At the broader level, relata are those social "project clocks" (Helson, Mitchell, & Moane, 1984) and age-related changes that couples adhere to with varying degrees of temporal conformity: some being early (e.g., sex on the first date) and some being late (e.g., having children after age 35) (cf. "hyperchronic" vs. "hypochronic," Gioscia, 1971; see also Kenrick & Trost, 1989). At the intermediate level, relata represent a synthesis of both biological and social mechanisms. These syntheses manifest in the psychological experiences or states of relating, self-disclosure, social exchange, love, and intimacy.

These three clocks are only features of contexts (rather than integral to them) in that each context should not be equated with its corresponding clock. Clearly, biology has an effect on interaction (e.g., Chapple, 1970) and social norms are based, in part, on age-related events (e.g., Young, 1988). Additionally, it is important to recognize that psychological states are not only relevant at the situational or exchange level. Much theory and research in personal relationships has been devoted to understanding and predicting a variety of psychological, relational, and interactional states. The present model attempts to incorporate these static features only as brackets within which relational

> *The use of multiple time-frames may help to increase our understanding of complex relationship systems and provide tools for more accurate study.*

processes unfold. They are not outcomes that are the end result of tightly coupled processes, chained together in a progressive, linear, future-oriented framework. Still, personal relationships and their inhabitants do experience important psychological states as outcomes. A temporal model of relationships should not neglect them.

Static Features in a Dynamic Context. Perhaps the most examined states within the study of personal relationships have, broadly stated, been sentiment (attraction, liking), satisfaction (motivation, love), and commitment (adjustment and stability). Research has been conducted to examine these in relationships of varying types. For example, attraction has been explored among acquaintances (Byrne, Ervin, & Lamberth, 1970, Touhey, 1972), among daters (Rubin, 1970), and in marriage (Levinger, 1976). Satisfaction has been studied among all kinds of close relationship (see Sternberg & Hojjat, 1997)—from students "in love" (Hendrick, 1988) to married couples (Antill, 1983). Commitment has been examined among daters (Hill, Peplau, & Rubin, 1976; Michaels, Acock, & Edwards; 1986), friends (Rusbult, 1983), and married (Masters & Johnson, 1974), as well as divorced, individuals (Hetherington, 1976). However, there has been little systematic investigation of how attraction, satisfaction, and commitment changes across these different relationship phases or how these states mean different things to individuals at different stages in their relationships. Certainly, satisfaction with a dating partner is not the same as satisfaction with a long-term marriage. Also, these three criterion states may or may not be related to each other (a) within a given couple, (b) within a given temporal context across couples, (c) across temporal contexts, and across couples. Partners may be satisfied with each other but they do not necessarily like or are strongly committed to each other (cf. Sternberg's mismatching on love, 1986) and their lack of quarreling (a highly specialized form of interaction) may or may not indicate that they are happy together (Levinger, 1983).

There is also a historical tendency for research to associate these three criterion states with the corresponding three temporal contexts introduced earlier: Attraction is experienced in an interaction context (Byrne et al., 1970), satisfaction in an interdependence context (Thibaut & Kelley, 1959), and commitment in a social choice context (e.g., exit, voice, loyalty, neglect; Rusbult, 1987). Within the first context, researchers refer to sentiments (Heider, 1958): to feelings, attractions, interests, likes, and dislikes. Within the second context, researchers talk about relational and situational rules (Argyle, Furnham, & Graham, 1981): about decision outcomes, relationship rewards, satisfaction levels, investments, trusts, equities, self-disclosures, and the exchange rules that govern these factors (Burgess & Huston, 1979). Within the third context, the focus is on the events or trends that propel the relationships into different phases (Baxter & Bullis, 1986). One purpose of the current model is to uncouple these states from any specific context or any specific clock. The model should allow us to examine how attraction, satisfaction, and commitment develop across interactions, situations, and phases, and, separately, how they are each regulated by biotemporal, nootemporal, and sociotemporal clocks.

By viewing states and clocks together, the current model may also help to determine whether temporal patterns in one context parallel or predict temporal patterns or outcomes in other contexts. These parallels may be explored at two major levels of analysis: both the idiographic (examining individual differences on a couple by couple basis) and the nomothetic (examining statistical patterns across different samples). In the example of a couple, states experienced within one context (e.g., Mary's concern about Jack's shyness with her friends) may reflect a couple's experience in another context (e.g., concern whether they are compatible enough to get married). This, in turn, can constrain or facilitate events within yet another context (e.g., Jack avoids the topic of shyness whenever Mary specifically confronts him about it). In the example of statistical summaries, the temporal profile that eventuates in "hitting-it-off" (Gottman, 1983) may or may not parallel the temporal profile that delineates those behavior-outcome contingencies of social exchange (Kelley, 1979). The latter may in turn parallel the (typically longer) temporal profile that a couple navigates when dissolving their commitment (Lee, 1984). Again, the criterion states in this particular example—"hitting-it-off" or "not-hitting-it-off," cooperative or individualistic decisions, and dissolving versus not dissolving the relationship—are of interest as they serve to demarcate the temporal profiles that precede and succeed them.

I offer another example. Consider research on the transition to marriage, which suggests that communication and self-disclosure may have a critical period for emergence. Lewis (1973), working within his Premarital Dyadic Framework, showed that mutual self-disclosure at an early point in courtship is predictive of continuing versus broken-up couples 2 years later; but self-disclosure at the later time did not discriminate these couples. Using retrospective accounts of recently married couples, Braiker and Kelley (1979) found that close communication was associated with increased interdependence and love in earlier but not later stages of development. Interestingly, Baxter (1988) suggested that early on in relationships, individuals are faced with the dilemma of deciding how vulnerable to make themselves and how fragile such disclosures could make the relationship. Interpreted in this light, the findings by Lewis and Braiker and Kelley suggest that how and when couples are intimate with each other (i.e., how they navigate an openness–closedness dialectic) should occur during a critical initial period of a relationship if the relationship is to continue.

That is, *interactions* may be modulated (e.g., playing "hard to get") because of the desire to coordinate *situational* outcomes (e.g., make him show me that he likes me), which are themselves shaped by unpredictability of commitment at these early *stages*. One purpose of the current model is to specify how states associated with these temporal contexts actually cohere to give rise to this and other critical periods. As a model, however, the focus of explanation should be on the processes that surround, trigger, or predicate these states. Distinctions between state and process is important because of the prevailing tendency for researchers to focus almost entirely on static aspects of personal relationships.

DYNAMIC BASIS OF THE CONTEXTUAL MODEL[5]

The illustration used earlier, of my relationship to you, is clearly not as complex as examples of those personal relationships in which outcomes are continually coordinated and in which each partner's decisions propel the relationship through a weave of states, transitions, and phases. I could have described any one of a number of distinctive scenarios. Consider the following situations: a married couple argue about how they should schedule their private time after the first baby arrives, or new acquaintances open up sensitive topic areas that neither individual feels ready to discuss. In these examples, marriage and new acquaintances are references to phase; coordination of the after-baby schedule, and the salience of the sensitive topic areas refer to the exchange situation. The argument and opening up indicate the interaction sequence. It should be stressed that these single sentence descriptions are aggregates of the proceedings: they combine many events that occur within the three temporal contexts. They are better construed as summary referents rather than indices. They do not distinctively access the processual and ongoing aspects of relationships.

Still, a temporal language of relationships could, in its most rudimentary aspects, take on the following schematic form of single-sentence description:

	a	*b*	*c*	*d*	*e*
Grammatical element:	Reference to a phase or a transition	Reference to relational status (involves noun use)	Reference to interaction sequence (involves verb use)	Relation between preceding (c) and following (d)	References to situational exchange
Possible examples:	Temporal preposition (e.g., before, after, during).	Couple, first dating, friends, newlyweds, etc.	Went, argued, kissed, necked, exchanged gifts, eloped, etc.	About, according to, within, following, at the same time as, etc.	Hug, drive, discuss, dine, schedule, sleep
Illustration 1:	future (with baby)	married couple	argued	about	scheduling private time
Illustration 2:	began	newly acquainted	discuss	(to)	risky topics

Thus, "the *married* couple *argued* about the *scheduling of their future private time*" and "the *newly acquainted* couple began to *discuss risky topics*." This sentence-based language would effectively isolate or frame each temporal context although it would not be processual; it would not describe the dynamic relationship of these occurrences across contexts. To ascertain these cross-temporal relationships, we need research that is sensitive to temporality. For Illustration 1, research suggests that after childbirth (a transitional–phasic referent), partners show less coordination of housework (an exchange referent) and reported decreases in couple closeness (e.g., the amount of time they spend together, an interactional referent) (see chap. 6; Ruble, Hackle, Fleming, & Stangor, 1988). For Illustration 2, research suggests that the satisfaction female undergraduates experience with new acquaintances (a phasic referent) is associated with the degree to which these acquaintances initiate communication in interactions, whereas satisfaction with known friends is associated with emotional support in interactions (Buhrmester, Furman, Wittenberg, & Reis; 1988). The single sentence, whether it describes a couple or the aggregated research findings of many couples, can partially reflect cross-temporal dynamics and influences.

Procession, Salience, and Continuity

Relationships are ever-evolving over time; that is, they occur across measurable units of time. They have continuity across phases. They also evolve in time; that is, they show changes within a particular measurable unit of time. Each interaction has procession; that is, interactions proceed in time. For their participants, relationships also have an "ongoing" quality about them; partners derive and share cognitive and emotional representations of their relationships as existing in time. These representations are temporally salient (Werner & Haggard, 1985). Depending on their exchanges and the situation they find themselves in, partners invariably focus on either the past, present, or future of their relationship. These dynamic properties of relationships—continuity, procession, and salience—also cannot be captured by single sentence descriptors.

The biases (e.g., individuocentric, methodological convenience) addressed in the discussion of the temporal initiative cannot be overcome without a model that somehow considers the procession of interaction sequence, the changing salience of the psychological situation, and the continuity within transition and phase. Fraser's (1987) model may aid our understanding of these dynamics in that the biotemporal world infuses and entrains our interactions (Chapple, 1970; Warner, 1979), the nootemporal world constrains and facilitates situational salience (Argyle, Furnham, & Graham, 1981), and the sociotemporal world shapes our experience of transition and phase (e.g., Young, 1988). But these temporalities and dynamic distinctions should not be merely descriptive, they should provide an understanding of how our conceptions of time can either help or hurt our comprehension of relationship phenomena and how our atemporal conceptions of relationships constrain our appreciation of time.

As explored in the next chapter, other theories have addressed or attempted to incorporate these dynamic elements; that is procession, continuity, or salience. There are models, usually typified as "stage" or "phase" models, that emphasize the *discontinuous* over the *continuous* aspects of relational development (Kerckhoff & Davis, 1962; Lewis, 1972, 1973; Murstein, 1976; Reiss, 1960; Scanzoni, 1979). There are dynamic or interactional models that emphasize the *process* over the *stasis* within relationships (Argyle, 1978; Baxter, 1988; Kelley et al., 1983; Knudson, 1983; Reis & Shaver, 1988). Two relational models that address the psychological salience of time are Altman and Taylor's social penetration theory (1973) and Kelley and Thibaut's interdependence theory (1978; Kelley, 1979). These theories demonstrate that cognitions, memories, and expectations—and individual's communication of these thoughts—help structure interactions and the development of the relationship (see also Duck & Pond, 1989).

Distinguishing processual aspects of the three contexts gives an opportunity to measure them or at least to consider how researchers could measure them. After considering the dynamic factors mentioned above, I believe it is possible to construct a temporal scale, a scale that empirically assesses the processual aspects of relationships.

ELEMENTS OF A TEMPORAL SCALE: PROBABILITY AND THE EXTERNAL VALIDITY OF TEMPORAL FACTORS

Accurate assessment of the "ongoing" qualities of relationships is more likely if the unit of scaling centers on their processual aspects. Similarly, our measures of relationships should be applied in terms of temporal patterns and trends rather than of singularly framed events, subjective summaries, or behavioral aggregates. This unit of scale may be called the relata[6] to help focus empirical attention on the actual relating that occurs, on the active proceedings rather than on the causal agents and outcomes that bracket them.

The temporal scale can be used to evaluate analyses and research investigations of personal relationships. Theoretically, higher values on this scale indicate that a study of personal relationships has a greater probability of representing the processual nature of the phenomena under study. Higher values indicate that the manner in which the analysis was conducted gives it greater external validity with respect to temporal patterns (Kelly & McGrath, 1988). External validity with regard to time means that the temporal context in which social behavior is examined is similar to the temporal context to which researchers wish to generalize their findings (Campbell & Stanley, 1966). Because relationships exist in several temporal contexts (i.e., they are ongoing), a research study should contain explicit references to each context whenever possible. Moreover, those studies that examine the interrelationships (statistical interactions) between human interaction, social situation, and relationship phase would also have a greater external validity. The primary purpose of the temporal scale is to increase sensitivity to temporal issues among those scientists who assess personal relationships and who assume those relationships to be ongoing.

Temporal Extension[7] and Temporal Contextualization

Researchers can identify specific data sources that reflect each of the three contexts to varying degrees. The degree to which a study includes reference to many temporal contexts may be called its degree of *temporal contextualization*. If a relationship process is only assessed at a single point in time, as is the case with most experiments, then the resulting data can, when it contains sensitive references to each temporal context, be used to construct a probabilistic portrait of the process as it exists in time. In other words, if we only assess a couple at one time point we may still capture temporal aspects of the relation if we carefully assess the relationship phase, the current situation, and a current interaction. In addition to temporal contextualization, a research design should have *temporal extension*, that is, researchers should specify the number of observations across time and the interval between these observations (cf. "periodicity," Kelly & McGrath, 1988).

Contextualization and extension are the two dimensions of the temporal scale. Contextualization is the gradation of temporal relata such that higher values refer to descriptions that are sensitive to the effects of each of the three temporal contexts.

Temporal extension refers to the degree to which multiple points in time have been welded into the description of the relata. Thus, higher values on this scale would reflect studies that assess phasic continuity, situational salience, and interactional procession or studies that coordinate different contexts. Such studies would remain sensitive to information about multiple observations (e.g., cycle and rhythm) within the different temporalities. Lower values would be given to descriptions that focus on behavior only within one context and over a limited duration.

Illustrating Extension and Contextualization. These two dimensions may be illustrated through the example of a phenomena that has not been extensively researched: the effects on a couple's relationship during and after they have been visited by one of the partner's parents (cf. Silverstein, 1992). An example of low contextualization would be research that did not consider the length of visitation, the pattern(s) of interaction that occurred, or the phase in which the visitation took place. High contextualization would consider all temporal parameters and relationships (e.g., how often the parents visit; biological cycles of the partners; the satisfaction from previous visits). In the same example, low temporal extension would be characterized by research on the couple's self-report only about one visit. High extension would describe several changes in self-report occurring across successive visits.

Figure 7.2 may help to illustrate both extension and contextualization. Although both dimensions are continuous we measure them according to some standard or interval, such as minutes, hours, or days. Figure 7.2 (under the heading "Interval") shows extension and degree of contextualization across five discrete interval levels. If the description is based on measurements only across minutes, or only across days, or only across months, the degree of contextualization is low. If our description includes references to changes across minutes that occur within a certain day within a certain year of the relationship, then the degree of contextualization is high. Each description would specify current action-perception aspects of the interaction, coordinated-outcome aspects of the situation, and decision-choices of the phase. Most research fails to consider this degree of contextualization due to the biases listed in the first section of this chapter.

Recall that a single sentence-based description of relationships can include and isolate each of the temporal contexts but cannot, as such, convey change within relationship. In contrast, the ideal empirical unit of analysis would describe the relationship across time or between two sentence-based descriptions. It would describe each temporal context with a certain degree of extension. As shown in the left half of Fig. 7.2 (under the heading "Temporal Extension"), the degree to which the description captures process will vary as a function of the interval between the two statements. If the statements refer to a change across seconds or minutes, their differences will probably be seen in interactional terms. For example, Jay said "I love you" and, moments later, Donna began to cry. . . . He then hugged her. The greater the number of these second-to-second or minute-to-minute observations, the more likely we will represent the interactional context. Figure 7.2 represents this by showing that as we proceed from two observations (T_2) to many (T_{2+n}), there is an increased probability of representing the interactional context (depicted by increased shading in the figure).

Alternatively, if the statements refer to change across months or years, their differences will probably be seen in phasic terms. For example, Jay and Donna met in June . . . They were engaged by September. If the two descriptions are separated by days or a week, it is more likely that situational exchanges will be detected; but it is also possible that important transitions or significant

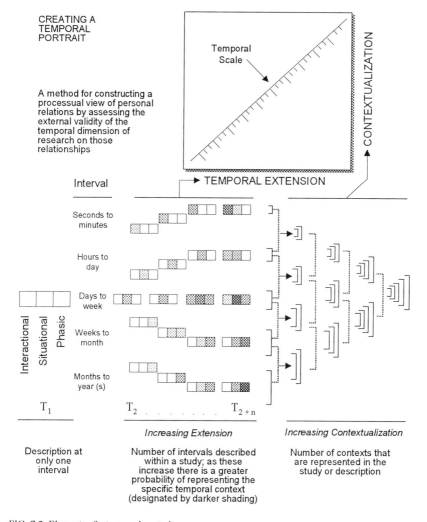

FIG. 7.2. Elements of a temporal portrait.

interactions would be discerned. For example, The first time that Donna picked up the laundry for Jay was the week after he met her parents. . . . The following day Jay surprised her with flowers at work. Either longitudinal or cross-sectional comparisons of relata across minutes, hours, and months will allow researchers to better isolate the effects of these different contexts.

Researchers do not often seek an understanding of phase by examining interactions over minutes or an understanding of self-disclosure by using years as the interval of measurement. However, there are temporally compact, extended, or cyclical relationship phenomena that do not readily conform to the model shown in Fig. 7.2. Acts of engagement, marriage, conceiving a child, or revealing important secrets take seconds or minutes, but these critical events are better described as transitional than interactional; honeymoons or divorce proceedings take days or weeks, but these events are also transitional rather than situational. Overseas long-distance relationships, especially those conducted through mail, may take months to expedite an interaction or social exchange. Traveling salespeople, visits with relatives, and periodic health concerns all entail relatively long-term cycles that constitute interactions and exchanges as well as phases. It is precisely these compacted, extended and cyclical types of relata that cannot be understood just through high extension—through analyses that measure behavior across many points in time. Such relata also cohere across several temporal contexts. Honeymoons contain many interactions and situations and also mark an important phase in the relationship. These many exceptions, the anomalous texture of relationships, require a temporal scale that integrates extension with contextualization (see top portion of Fig. 7.2). As suggested by the interface of the two diagrams in Fig. 7.2, temporal extension gives greater access to the processes of a given context which, in turn, will allow us to better detect the relationship between contexts. By examining and conducting research with an eye on both of these dimensions, we gain a better understanding of process.

To borrow a cinematic metaphor, a sufficiently detailed (i.e., resolved), well-organized (i.e., contextualized) single snapshot from an ongoing movie stream can provide invaluable information about the entire movie.[8] Research that assesses behavior during single interaction sequences can help discern the conditional probabilities of the behavioral trends that occur in all interactions (e.g., Gottman, 1979). Experimental research that analyzes psychological outcomes (e.g., satisfaction) across different interpersonal situations might be used to determine the probability of certain shared outcomes in ongoing relationships (e.g., McClintock & Liebrand, 1988). Analysis of couples' decisions to marry, even if based on their retrospective accounts, can help us determine the factors that led up to this decision. Moreover, such self-reports might be used to determine whether the cumulative shape of shared outcomes will result in marriage (e.g., Huston, Surra, Fitzgerald, & Cate, 1981) or in other critical turning points (Baxter, 1984).

Probability in Constructing a Temporal Portrait. Researchers put together their observations in order to describe some phenomena. A temporal portrait refers to the description of some relationship phenomena that we are interested in understanding. This could be anything such as jealousy, envy, equity, sexual pursuit, breakups, passion, or intimacy. In the current model, probability refers to the probability that this portrait (description, research study) represents the ongoing, temporal qualities of the phenomena as it occurs once we are no longer observing it (Kelly & McGrath, 1988). An observation of a relationship phenomena is time sensitive *to the degree* to which the observation is able to represent that phenomena within the broader temporal contexts of the relationship. With sufficient detail in the research design and a temporal language, the researcher could take a set of observations (data) from a single point in time and construct a probabilistic portrait of the process. This detail, or temporal extension, increases with the number of measurements taken across time and with the sensitivity of the statistical methods used to detect trends across these data points.

To some extent, the validity of a temporal portrait depends on the level of detail or number of intervals in the analysis. Recall (see Fig. 7.1) that relationships change through the actions and perceptions which occur in an interaction, the coordination of efforts and outcomes within a situation, and the decisions made within a phase. If we are interested in a temporal understanding of relationship actions (violence, arguments, lovemaking) than we should assess interaction sequences across multiple intervals that last seconds to minutes. The probability that our description accurately represents the action increases as some function of the number of intervals used in the study of the interaction. Similarly, the probability our description accurately represents a trend in coordinated efforts or outcomes (e.g., satisfaction, love, motivation) depends on intervals (temporal extension) used in the analyses of situations. The probability that a particular decision-choice trend (e.g., have a child, move in together) is validly represented depends on temporal extension in the analyses of phases and transitions. The greater the extension across all trends—that is, the higher the value on the temporal scale—the more temporally valid is our data.

> *The more our measures are temporally refined and historically broad, the more complete and accurate a picture of relationship stories will emerge.*

Probabilities are not linear predictions of events. For example, the goal is not to be able to predict that if Jay and Donna do not kiss by the sixth date they will not get married. (This linear view of probability is supported by the empirical, general linear model that emphasizes causal relationships between instances (Abbott, 1988) and by a formal logic that neglects time (Hayakawa, 1972; Korzybski, 1958).) In the current model, probability is stated in terms of coherence, coordination, or calibration (see chap. 8) across the three temporal frames. Relationships are not comprised of a series of divisible instances wherein the collection of data from one instant yields important information about other instances or even about the relationship (i.e., relationships are not merely a string of relationship states; Duck & Sants, 1983). Rather, relationships are inherently transformational; they are comprised of trends that span and shape interactions, interdependencies, and phases. In short, a relationship is always ongoing within intratemporal frames and embedded within intertemporal context. Researchers who can identify these frames and contexts can begin to construct a temporal portrait of relationship process.

A Note on Longitudinal Designs. The need for longitudinal designs in personal relationship research (e.g., Clark & Reis, 1988) appears to be based on the premise that we can only understand process with the temporal extension this methodology affords. However, experimental, correlational, and survey designs, predominantly taking measurements in order of seconds or minutes, may be used to understand social exchange phenomena (e.g., McClintock & Liebrand, 1988). These types of research designs may be helpful even though their results bear a less probable (external validity) relationship to the processes of exchange that occur in ongoing personal relationships than do the results of cross-situational designs. Longitudinal studies are extremely helpful but not essential for our understanding of process. As already noted, even if we collect data at a single point in time or of a single duration, we can put together a picture of process if we have a temporal scale and a grammar for discussing time. Although I have introduced a scale (see Fig. 7.2), a useful grammar cannot be constructed without first reviewing how other theories of personal relationships have understood time. I take up this task in chapter 8.

In summary, the proposed model assumes that higher values on a temporal scale results in a clearer picture of relationship processes. This is similar to the logic of personological research (McAdams, 1985; H. A. Murray, 1938) where individual life stories are assessed through a multi-form approach including pencil-and-paper tests, situational exercises, interviews, and group decision-making processes. The more the assessment is refined and broad in scope, the more complete a picture of the personal story emerges. Analogously, experimental snap shots may tell a thousand words, but unless they are sufficiently informative about several temporal contexts, those thousand words may not be able to furnish us with a story.

PRELIMINARY APPLICATION OF THE TEMPORAL SCALE: AN ILLUSTRATIVE REVIEW OF RESEARCH

One of the earliest studies done on attraction demonstrates how the lack of temporal data in the face of a certain pattern of results requires inferences to time. In the 1940s, Festinger Schacter, and Back (1988) were puzzled by a particular set of findings in their study on how proximity (living next to someone) influenced friendship in a dormitory complex. They predicted and found that closeness of subject's dormitory neighbor was associated with greater likelihood of friendship. More specifically, there were five apartments on each floor and those who lived nearer the stairwells were expected and found to receive more sociometric (e.g., more popular, more liked) choices than others. The authors reasoned that students were more likely to pass these particular apartments in leaving and coming back to their apartment. However, there was also a high frequency of sociometric choices that individuals in the lower floor middle apartment (i.e., apartment "c" in a row of a—b—c—d—e; with "c" nonadjacent to the stairwell) received from upper floor residents. Given this "only finding inconsistent with (the) hypotheses," the authors then proceeded to construct a post-hoc test and explanation:

> Let us assume that *within any given time interval* the probability of a passive contact occurring between residents of houses which are one unit apart is greater than the probability of a contact between residents of houses 2 units apart and so on. The probability of a passive contact occurring between residents living 4 units apart would be lowest. . . .
>
> The resident of house c will generally have made contact with all others living in the row sooner than any other resident. If *enough time is allowed to elapse* one might be relatively certain that all residents would have had at least one passive contact with all others in the row, but the resident in house c will have had the greatest number of such contacts. (Festinger et al., 1988, pp. 120–121, italics added)

The authors then pointed out that it is impossible to "check these derivations specifically against the data available" but, to support the previous reasoning, they do show a peak of choices in the middle apartments for lower floor residents. This single example is important for three reasons: (a) a temporal feature is inferred to explain anomalous results when no measure across time is taken; (b) the hypothesis about time can still be given some test without this time-sensitive measurement; and (c) studies with minimal extension and contextualization offer glimpses into temporal processes—provided there is some careful inferences to these dimensions.

Many other studies on personal relationships follow the pattern of Festinger et al.'s seminal work. All indicate that temporality is a prevalent, although secondary, source for explanations about anomalous relationship phenomena. To demonstrate application of the temporal scale, I have chosen nine studies from 1970s and 1980s that vary in time sensitivity, (i.e., in contextualization and extension) and that focus on different temporal contexts. It is important to emphasize that the following illustration is only an initial attempt to provide researchers with a heuristic for coding the temporality of personal relationship research. Because it is qualitative and subjective, some will question the representation of studies, and disagree with my coding scheme and/or with value assignment to the studies. Again, this is an initial application to demonstrate that studies do differ on temporality and that these differences can be systematically investigated. I make no claims to reliability or thoroughness; this review attempts to introduce new ways of thinking about the temporal sensitivity of research investigations.

Method

Each of the studies was examined for references in their method and results sections to each of the following parameters. *Context* includes any reference of relationship phase (e.g., acquaintance, married), interaction variables (e.g., reciprocity), or exchange process as either an independent, dependent, predictor, or criterion variable. *Outcome* includes any reference to a relationship state (e.g., liking, breakups) as a criterion or dependent variable.

Extension includes references to the number of times a variable was either manipulated (as in a repeated measure design) or assessed (as in frequency, change, or pre-post test measures). *Time* refers to explicit inclusion of a temporal dimension as a predictor (as in external clock, calendrical, or age-related effects), a criterion (as in use of frequency, duration, or trend data), or in the phenomena under investigation itself (e.g., effect of memory on future relationship events, turning points, critical time periods). Each study may make several and different references to these four parameters. For the sake of brevity, only one set of findings was examined that explicitly or implicitly incorporated time. These findings were then summarized in a brief description of the study (see Table 7.1).

Estimate of Temporal Scale

After identifying the parameters for the description of a particular set of results, I estimated the degree of contextualization and extension of the description. The method for estimation was entirely subjective. I compared studies against each other to arrive at some gradation system. However, numerical differences correspond to temporal differences in the studies that likely represent some non-ordinal, interval scale. No attempt is made to describe the potential range of values that could be ascribed to the two dimensions, the meaning of their zero points, or their non-linear (e.g., logarithmic) aspects. The following coding scheme is derived for the purposes of demonstrating temporal scale solely as a heuristic device.

Contextualization. In some research, the research participants or subjects (Ss) do not interact at all. In such research, minimal reference to any temporal context received a rating of "0." For each reference to a context beyond this lack of exposure, a value of "1" was assigned. Measurement references—whether pertaining to occurrences or self-reports, to predictors or criteria from different contexts—were also assigned a value of "1." These included attraction (e.g., interest, liking) as the outcome or predictor of some interaction, satisfaction (e.g., rewards, alternatives) as the outcome or predictor of an exchange, and commitment (stability, dissolution) as the outcome or predictor of a phase.

Results that investigated statistical interactions across temporal contexts, as well as results that focused on trends across contexts (e.g., using a temporal pattern as a predictor) and between contexts (e.g., turning-points) received higher values than results that treated contexts as separate phenomena. All values within a given study were summed to give a total estimate of contextualization.

Extension. Those descriptions that only assessed relationships (through aggregation or survey methods) at one point in time were given a value of zero unless the assessment included reports on other points in time. Follow-up studies, such as the prediction of break-ups from one set of variables, received a value of "1." Pretest posttest designs that assessed the same set of variables twice received a "2." In multitrial or repeated measure designs, a value of "1" was assigned for each trial. Frequency, duration, or other rate data was given a value of "1" for each point in time if continuous changes were plotted and assessed in this data, or if this data was itself the object of attention in the investigation. In the latter case, any explicit inclusion of time (e.g., season, turning point) as a predictor criterion was also assigned a value of "1." When rate data was not examined continuously but was broken down into separate categories (e.g., couples who date each other once, twice, three times a week versus examination across the dates within each couple), the number of categories was halved to give an estimate of extension. All values within a given study were summed to give a total estimate of extension.

Qualitative Placement of Nine Studies

The studies examined a host of relationship phenomena including attraction as a result of mere exposure to a stranger (Saegert, Zajonc, & Swapp; 1973), reciprocity of intimacy for both spouses and strangers (Morton, 1978), and changes in interaction with subjects' premarital social network as a function of changes in relationship status across a three month period (Milardo, Johnson & Huston, 1983). Table 7.1 lists the descriptions of nine studies in chronological order.

Description of Studies' Content. The summary descriptions show that a full range of contexts and outcomes were included across the nine studies. Mere exposure to another with little interaction (Saegert et al., 1973) represents a minimal degree of context and was evaluated as such (.5). Other researchers focused on two contexts. Byrne et al. (1970) examined the relation between initial acquaintance interaction and subsequent dating interest (phasic transition). Hill et al. (1976) predicted breakups (phasic transition) 2 years after assessment of relative involvement (situational outcome). At the other extreme, research using retrospective accounts of turning-points in relationships assessed multiple contexts. Baxter and Bullis (1986) examined the association turning points had to changes in commitment (a phasic reference), to relationship talk (interaction referent), and to satisfaction (exchange referent) (Baxter & Bullis, 1986).

TABLE 7.1

TEMPORAL DESCRIPTION OF 9 SELECTED STUDIES AND
ESTIMATED PLACEMENT ON TEMPORAL SCALE

(Study #) Author(s)/Date	Description of Study	Contextu-alization[a]	Extension[b]
(1) Byrne et al. (1970)	Behavior, liking,[O] and 3-mo. follow-up[E] of dating interest assessed in 44 male-female pairs returning from ½-hour acquaintance date[C]	Effect of acquaintance (1) on liking (1) (i.e., two contexts represented)	3 months (1) (i.e., 1 point in time)
	Code for Study:	2	1
(2) Lewis (1973)	Dissolution and continuance[O] of 91 dating couples[C] predicted over 2-year period[E] using changes in self-report indices of rapport,[C] self-disclosure, role-fit[C] (and other indices)	Couples (1) + Rapport (1) + Role-fit (1) (i.e., 3 contexts represented)	Pre-post test of indices (2) (i.e., 2 points in time)
	Code for Study:	3	2
(3) Saegert et al. (1973)	Assessed effects of frequency (0, 1, 2, 5, or 10 times)[E] of minimum (40 seconds) contact[C] with different task partners on liking[O] of those different partners (48 female undergraduates)	Minimal interaction (.5)	Categorical frequency (2.5) (5 points in time)
	Code for Study:	.5	2.5
(4) Hill et al. (1976)	2-year follow-up study[E] to predict breakups[O] in 103 dating couples[C] with self-reports (love, involvement);[C] time of school year[T] shown to effect timing of breakups	Breakups (1) determined from relative interest (e.g., love) (1)	2 year (1) + time of year (1) (2 distinct uses of extension)
	Code for Study:	2	2
(5) Morton (1978)	Compared 24 married vs. stranger[C] pairs on reciprocity[C] of intimacy[O] across 3 trials[E] in both intimate and nonintimate[C-T] tasks	Phase (married, stranger); by Interaction (2) by Exchange (2) (i.e., 2 x 2 = 4)	Trials (3) with Topic of discus-sion repeated (2)
	Code for Study:	4	5

Continued

TABLE 7.1 (*continued*)

(6) Archer & Burleson (1980)	<u>Liking for</u>[O] <u>confederate</u>[C(O)] in 66 male students in a <u>sequence of 7</u>[E] <u>topic discussions</u>[C] with personal revelation of other controlled either <u>early or late</u>[T] in an <u>(un)chosen</u>[C] sequence	Discussion (1) Situation (chosen, unchosen) (1)	Sequence repeated (7)
	Code for Study:	2	8
(7) Rusbult (1983)	<u>Once every 12 weeks</u>[E] <u>dating individuals</u>[C] (<u>M</u> length=4 weeks, n=34) rated <u>exchange</u>[C] variables (rewards, costs, alternatives)—used to predict <u>commitment</u>[C] and <u>satisfaction</u>[O]	Dating (1) Exchange (1) to predict leave/staying (1)	Weeks (12)
	Code for Study:	3	12
(8) Milardo et al. (1983)	<u>Duration and frequency</u>[T-O] of <u>interaction</u>[C] with network among Ss (n=89) in <u>regressed, stabilized, or advanced</u>[T-C] relationships <u>(dating, engaged)</u>[C] at <u>2 points (3 months apart)</u>[E]	Phase-change (3) on interaction (2) in different networks (2)	3 months (2) and time (2)
	Code for Study:	7	4
(9) Baxter & Bullis (1986)	Study correlated retrospections on <u>turning points</u>[T-C] of partners (n = 80) in <u>romantic relationships</u>[C] with <u>change</u>[C-E] in <u>commitment</u>[O] and <u>satisfaction</u>[O]; examines turning points that involved <u>talk</u>[C]	Turning points (4), romance (1), talk (1)	Change reported (1) (i.e., change was reported not measured)
	Code for Study:	6	1

Note. Underlined and superscripted terms or phrases are references to the following: **C** = temporal context (number of contexts in study), **O** = outcome assessed (e.g., liking, commitment, satisfaction), **E** = extension (number over time), **T** = temporal methods or variables (e.g., turning points, seasons, advanced relations).

[a] Degree of contextualization is based on the number of contexts used in analysis, any interaction among these contexts, or variables that were contextualized within the research design (e.g., control of timing disclosure in Archer and Burleson, 1980).
[b] Degree of temporal extension is based on number of points in time at which data is assessed (repeated = repeated measures) and/or sensitivity (to temporal shape or event).

The studies also vary in the degree to which they refer to temporal factors. Research by Saegert et al. (1973) is an example of a study that lacked explicit inclusion of a temporal factor. These researchers manipulated the number of times subjects were exposed to others in an ostensible experiment on taste (rating of different flavors). As predicted by the mere exposure theory of liking, greater exposure resulted in greater liking for the other. In this study, however, the data were not analyzed for changes in liking that occur across each encounter. We were not told whether increases in liking occur with each exposure. Rather, subjects were categorized by five separate conditions of increasing frequency of exposure to the other subjects (0, 1, 2, 5, 10 times). Only their overall liking at the end of the study was assessed; the greater number of exposures, the greater the liking. There was no reference to changes in liking that may have occurred across each encounter.

In contrast to this absence of reference to change is research on changes in dating status and changes in social network. Milardo et al. (1983) examined relationship changes within different temporal contexts. These authors categorized relationships into those that had changed status across a 3-month period into one of three groups: "either advanced in stage (e.g., those moving from casually to exclusively dating), remained stable, or deteriorated (e.g., moving from exclusively dating to casually dating or termination)" (p. 969). This categorization is then used to predict changes in subjects' interactions with other people in their social network. Thus, explicit reference is made to temporal changes at both the phasic and interactional levels.

Contextualization. Contextualization ranges from .5 in the mere exposure study to 7 in Milardo et al.'s (1983) study. Greater contextualization is coded when a study examines several contexts together (e.g., as in a statistical interaction) versus separately. A distinction between studies that examine contexts separately versus together can be highlighted through comparison of Lewis (1973) with Morton (1978). Lewis gathered self-report data from couples at instances 2 years apart. These reports assessed couples' perceptions of role fit in the relationship (e.g., the fitting together of the interpersonal roles of two persons, initiating the social system of a comprehensive dyad, p. 23), and their perceptions of rapport or mutual liking. I classified perceptions of role fit as an exchange referent (how well two partners are coordinating their investments; a score of "1") and perceptions of rapport or mutual liking as an interaction referent (also a "1"). Lewis, comparing the reports of couples who had continued or dissolved their relationship (phase referent; a "1"), examined changes and differences in these perceptions. The interaction among these three contexts, however, was not made clear from Lewis' analysis and presentation of the data. Thus, whereas the study referred to three contexts (total score of "3"), it did not co-vary them in such a way as to assess their relationship to one another.

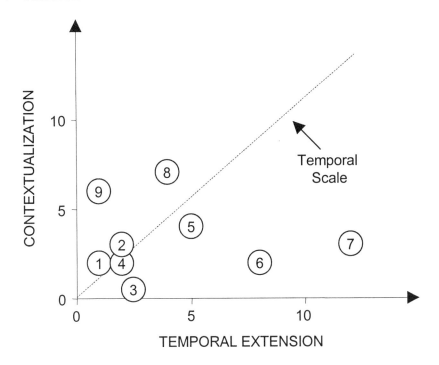

FIG. 7.3. Estimated placement of nine research studies on temporal scale (values from 'Code for Study' in Table 7.1.)

In contrast, Morton (1978) examined the process of self-disclosure in married versus stranger pairs as *a function* of relationship phase, topic type (intimate vs. nonintimate), and three successive trials of discussion. Among the results, two-way interactions indicated that "spouses became less reciprocal over time relative to strangers" (p. 77) and "strangers tend to guard private facts in discussing intimate topics, and spouses tended to introduce private facts into otherwise trivial topics" (p. 78). The first finding documents the effect of phase on the temporal regulation of intimacy and the latter finding highlights the joint effect of phase and situational pressures (i.e., topic) to disclose. Each of these interactions received a score of "2" for a total of 4 points.

Extension. The extension of the nine studies varied from 1 (for follow-up designs) to 12 (Rusbult, 1983); the latter is a serial examination of social exchange variables on a weekly basis. Several researchers explicitly incorporated time in their analysis of personal relationships. Hill et al. (1976) found that breakups among dating couples varied at different points of the school year. Archer and Burleson (1980) found subjects' attraction to another (a videotape of a confederate) depended on whether the other subject revealed personal facts about himself either early or later in a series of topic discussions. As pointed out earlier, Milardo et al. (1983) examined changes in frequency and duration of interactions as a function of changes in relationship status. Although Baxter and Bullis (1986) also examined changes in relationship, these changes were assessed entirely through retrospective self-report. These retrospective accounts of change do not have as high extension as actual change measured across two points in time.

DISCUSSION

The extension and contextualization values of each study described in Table 7.1 are plotted in Fig. 7.3. The probability that the ongoing aspects of personal relationships (external validity of temporality) are represented increases as values increase along both dimensions. Thus, the research by Saegert et al. (1973) less likely represents the ongoing effects of mere exposure than the research by Milardo et al. (1983) represents the ongoing patterns of interaction between pair members and social networks. In other words and according to the present methods, the Milardo et al. design had more temporal validity than the Saegert et al. design. Although the nine studies are a limited sample, Fig. 7.3 suggests a general trend for personal relationship research to become more time sensitive from year to year. With further work on temporal scaling of relationship research, meta-analysts may be able to detect this and other types of trends. It is conceivable that research that relies entirely on self-report, and is low on contextualization, will yield varying results depending on degree of extension. For example, a comparison of retrospective accounts of turning points in relationships with actual change data would tell us something about the difference between perception of change and actual changes.

A systematic viewing of the temporal features of relationship research, such as the one suggested here, should help to increase our understanding of the relationship between nootemporality (psychological time) and sociotemporality (social time) (Fraser, 1987). Although a temporal scale may be helpful in examining and reviewing research, it should also be taken as a guide to planning research. Here it may be used with Kelly and McGrath's (1988) "S-B-O template," a guide for a more rigorous use of logic when conducting research that separates social units (S) from their behaviors (B) and their occasions (O). This last basic piece of information, occasions, is central for our understanding of time in planning social science research. Kelly and McGrath (1988) pointed out that certain types of complex (e.g., time series) designs are required to adequately interpret the meanings of such phenomena as level or slope differences within critical intervals. Through their recommendations and a wider understanding of temporal scale in relationships, researchers will be less forced, as were Festinger, Schacter, and Back, to use post-hoc analyses and explanations.

End Notes—Chapter 7

1. On process and structure. The understanding of process has long been a thorny problem for philosophers of science (e.g., Bateson, 1979; Whitehead, 1938). Whitehead distinguishes between individuals and forms of process, indicating that the "peculiarities of the individuals are reflected in the peculiarities of the common process which is their interconnection" (p. 98). Bateson (1979) distinguished between classification (form) and process as logical types that are categorically distinct, but that "structure may determine process and that, conversely, process may determine structure" (p. 196). In both these examples, a temporal pattern emerges as process determines structure or individuals and vice versa. It seems plausible to advance a model of relationships that attempts to classify these patterns as long as the resultant taxonomy does not dictate a view of relationships as stationary or determinate (i.e., as lacking in context). Developments in the area of contextualism in psychology (Rosnow & Georgoudi, 1986) may be helpful in specifying how social history and social time infuses our prevailing beliefs about PRs, which, in turn, shape our scientific classifications.

2. Recall that science is biased against wholeness. Discussion of scientific biases in this section can be best appreciated in context of the discussion of transpersonal intimacy and wholeness within previous chapters. Recall from chapter 2 that science cannot measure the whole of things (Bronowski, 1978). Chapter 3 also emphasized that the transpersonal form of intimacy (in time I see) required taking a long perspective. The discussion of chaos and living context (nurturing conditions) in chapter 4 described aspects of temporality that are independent of cause-and-effect phenomena (e.g., Ward, 1995). Most importantly, the previous chapter considered how multiple temporal contexts interface in the creation of meaning within intimate relations. Thus, the current listing of biases (e.g., individuocentric, methodological convenience, truncation of perspective, linearity) makes a compelling case that current research paradigms mitigate against a serious study of transpersonal or spiritual intimacy. A similar critique of science can be found in Berman (1988) and Schaef (1992). The current chapter, however, suggests that some methodological framework—the intercontextual model of temporal scale—may serve as a bridge between the limits of science and phenomena that underlie spiritual intimacy.

3. Temporal frame and temporal scale. It is interesting to note that in parallel to Kelly and McGrath's work, Duck and colleagues (Acitelli & Duck, 1987; Duck & Pond, 1989; Duck & Sants, 1983) suggest that people impose a temporal frame as a natural, rhetorical function in the accounts they give of their relationships. For Morton and Douglas (1981), this framing appears to be integral to the central task of mutual relationship definition, which is itself an ongoing process in developing personal relationships. Thus, it may be difficult to distinguish the "system time" of relationship definition from the narratives partners give to a researcher (i.e., in "experimental time"). The two are dynamically interrelated (if not one and the same). Because both experimenters and people impose a temporal frame, it should help researchers to know how their temporal framings capture, distort, facilitate, or inhibit the framings of couples.

4. Use of the terms outcome and criterion. The terms *outcome* and *criterion* are used with some caution because they imply some future "end-state" toward which a PR process may be directed or with which that process may be defined. I do not wish to build a linear, unidirectional assumption of time into the contextual model. However, I believe there are certain psychological and physiological states that are salient for the study of intimacy. These include emotions (happiness, sadness, anger, etc.), feelings of well-being and satisfaction, measures of physical health, and degree of commitment (feelings of certainty and stability about the relationship). I employ the term *outcomes* not to specify one particular outcome as critical, but as applying to a broad range of possible states. These could also be resources exchanged by partners (e.g., money, goods, information, services, status, and love; see Foa & Foa, 1971), or they could be qualities of intimacy—shifts in consciousness—discussed in chapter 2 (e.g., ongoingness, wholeness, willingness).

5. Contextual model and measurement theory. The basic assumptions of the contextual model are: (a) In reality, relationship is process, (b) process is only directly knowable through experience (i.e., the *intimate experience* described in earlier chapters), and (c) as such, the empirical measurement of process can only be approximated. These assumptions are compatible with measurement theory in the social sciences. For example, the domain-sampling approach (e.g., Ghiselli, Campbell, & Zedeck, 1981) would suggest that *processes of intimacy* represent a hypothetical domain that can only be imperfectly sampled. However, if we can adequately cover a full range of processes, then we can increase our ability to approximate the *true* variation in these intimate processes. The sentence-based descriptions reviewed in this section contain references to the relation between three temporal contexts. Consider the example, "new acquaintances, opening up sensitive topic areas that neither individual feels ready to discuss." Here we might hypothesize that the longer acquaintances know each other (a phase referent), the more likely they will choose topics of a more sensitive nature (a situation referent).

As I understand it, in an application of the domain sampling model, we would assume that there is a probabilistic relation between one event and another [e.g., between being a new acquaintance (measured by length of relationship) and the degree of sensitivity in a topic choice for discussion (measured through normative ratings of topics]. However, this probabilistic relationship between events from different contexts is not necessarily *dynamic*. It does not capture change from one moment to the next only the probability that, given certain conditions, certain events will occur. This "conditions-events' link is the domain the researcher would attempt to sample from. I propose a sentence-based unit for describing relationship across contexts only as a first step in capturing context (rather than dynamics). The domain-sampling approach may be helpful in assessing the reliability of measures that are able to assess multiple temporal contexts. However, in order to assess dynamics, the researcher would have to use sentence-based (multi-context) measures at multiple points in time.

6. Use of the term relata as compared with dyad. The term *dyad* has been used by social scientists to describe 2-person groups and emphasizes the two individuals in some interactive situation or functioning as a unit (e.g., Maguire, 1999). The term *relationship*, or *couple*, is often used in our every day language and emphasizes the unity or status of two individuals as a group already formed. Both these terms suffer from the problem of reification. By saying dyad, we see two separate individuals who may, at some point in the interaction, behave as a unit. By saying relationship, we see a single unit when, at many points in time, the partners behave independently. I prefer to use the term *relata* (from Whitehead) to connote a looser conception of a relationship (or to conceptualize individuals in a "loosely coupled" system), a relationship as the nexus of various states of flux across variable temporal contexts. Whitehead's (1929) idea of nexus, the togetherness of entities that have both spatial and temporal spread, would also have done except for the current emphasis on the temporal. Relata as much like the concept of "dharma" in Buddhist thought except with emphasis on relating of two individuals. A dharma is an independently existing distinct moment of existence that, in Buddhist philosophy, is the only true event (Sinha, 1983). Dharmas are simple, momentary, impersonal, mutually conditioned, and have no duration. Insight into the momentariness of phenomena—into dharma—is a basis for enlightenment. In the transpersonal form of intimacy described earlier, insight into the momentariness of relata (i.e., into our mutual conditionality, simplicity, and the deeply impersonal nature of our knowing each other) may also be a form of awakening.

7. Use of the term extension. Originally, I had used the term resolution instead of extension because it alludes to the idea of clarity or crispness in our picture of phenomena, not just how often we measure. Ted Huston (personal communication, 1990) suggested the term *extension* to more precisely convey that I am really describing the number of times or the frequency of points in which data are collected. I agree with Ted for the methodological focus of this chapter, although the relationship between the two ways of naming is important. I suspect that greater frequency of measurement implies greater familiarity with the phenomena, which implies greater clarity and resolution. Moreover, frequency or extension of measurement is probably only a necessary and not a sufficient condition for clarity: To have resolution requires some insight and care with the data (see Keller, 1983).

Current directions in relationship research may be summarized quickly. . . . Mesolevel theories that address person-situation interactions are not in great evidence, macrolevel theories tend to be ignored in psychology, and microlevel theories are almost nonexistent. (Berscheid, 1994, p. 119)

The overwhelming majority of studies examine the descriptive content of working models of attachment, whereas dynamic process-oriented questions are more rarely investigated. (Reis & Knee, 1996, p. 185)

THOUGHTS ON A NEW SCIENCE

- That we formulate or synthesize a theory that makes for a clearer and useful understanding of time as it shapes and shaped by intimate relations.

- That we understand how interactions, situations, and phases of a relationship weave together a pattern that provides opportunities for the transformation of persons and couples.

8

Theories of Personal Relationships and the Contextual Model

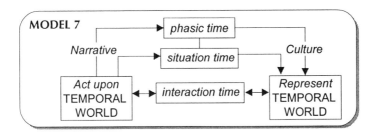

MODEL 7

Narrative — phasic time — Culture

situation time

Act upon TEMPORAL WORLD ←→ interaction time ←→ Represent TEMPORAL WORLD

THE PREVIOUS chapter suggested that a paradigm shift within the social sciences is taking place that will increase our understanding of human relationships in a more processual or time-sensitive manner. Chapter 7 prepared the groundwork for the theoretical analysis I attempt in this chapter. The current chapter applies the contextual model to a careful reading of 18 different theories that consider the role of time in personal relationships (PRs). It then synthesizes ideas from these theories into a model that articulates the relationships between interactional, situational, and phasic time. This chapter has two main objectives. First, it uses the tripartite model to show how existing theories can contribute to a more holistic, ongoing view of time in PRs. This holistic view—one that addresses the transpersonal aspects of personal relationships—is generally lacking in current theory. Second, it outlines a unified grammar or language of temporality in PRs; that is, it articulates some of the ways that the three contexts are woven together. As described in the first part of this book, it is this weaving of pattern across time that constitutes the intimate experience. Here we look at how scientific theory looks at different parts of this pattern.

The previous chapter reviewed issues of temporality that confront the social sciences in general and the field of personal relationships in particular. I tried to show that research and theory on personal relationships are not as sensitive to time as is possible. Researchers can respond to this problem by developing an interdisciplinary model that simultaneously views human relationships within three temporal contexts of increasingly greater width: interactions, situations, and phases. The interaction context focuses on the person-to-person interactions, and actions and perceptions that proceed over relatively short periods of time.

The situation context examines changes in relationships from situation to situation, and the coordination and exchange of psychological outcomes that occurs across situations. The phase context views the continuity of relationships within and across relatively long-term phases and the decisions couples make in moving from phase to phase. The current chapter applies this contextual model to an analysis of various theories about personal relationships just as the model was applied to research examples in the previous chapter.

TOWARD A UNIFIED GRAMMAR: ENRICHING THE MODEL WITH EXISTING THEORY

This section reviews models, theories, or perspectives (these terms here used interchangeably) of personal relationships that have included the dimension of time. Literature was chosen to provide variety within each of the three temporal contexts and to sample empirically oriented experimental models (e.g., microlevel models; Mettee & Aronson, 1974) as well as abstract, theoretically based propositions (e.g., macrolevel models; Kelley, 1979). The review represents the fields of social psychology (Altman & Taylor, 1973), communication studies (Argyle & Dean; 1965), family studies (Rodgers, 1987), and sociology (Davis, 1973) and spans over 35 years of theory (e.g., Kerckhoff & Davis, 1962, to Gottman & Silver, 1999). Using these general criteria, 18 perspectives are reviewed that highlight an array of temporal features from among current and past scientific conceptualizations of relationships. The purpose of this review is to integrate extant theory within the proposed contextual model. Hopefully, this integration will help to construct a grammar for translating between the "real" or "system" time of relationships and the methodological time researchers use when framing the flow of some relationship process. The review might increase researcher's awareness of biases that exist within present conceptualizations of relationships and perhaps cause them to cease their ignoring of macrolevel theories (see quote from Berscheid at start of this chapter) and investigate more process-oriented questions (as Reis & Knee suggested).

Method

In order to integrate theory with the tripartite contextual model, I first examined each model for its temporal aspects, giving a general description of the theory. Following this, I describe the temporal features of the model, the outcome or criterion state of each model, and the (implied) contextual aspects of each model. Table 8.2 (begins on p. 262) lists the models reviewed in this chapter (col. 1). I recommend first reading through the general descriptions (col. 2) of the table to get a sense of the range of ideas and to become familiar with the different names of the models. These descriptions are really thumbnail sketches often supported with some explanation in the following text.

General Description of Each Theory or Model

For the sake of organization, I categorize a PR theory or model within a single temporal context to which the theory primarily refers when explaining relationship process.[1] Table 8.2 lists six models that focus on interactions, four models that emphasize situations, and eight models that describe phases. Within each of these three categories there are models that focus on two temporal contexts (i.e., relationships are more than just communications, or more than just situations; e.g., Baxter, 1988) and most of the models allude to three temporal contexts. As happens in science, several independent theorists all work within a given framework. These frameworks are the equilibrium models of interaction (starting with Argyle & Dean, 1965), filter theories of mate selection (starting with Kerckhoff & Davis, 1962) and stage models of relationship dissolution (starting with Duck, 1982). Each of these theories is unique in their propositions about relationships; however, they are classified into these three categories in Table 8.2 because they identify the same premises about time (e.g., PRs obey laws of homeostasis).

Within each category, theories are listed in order of complexity. For example, the gain-loss model of interaction posits a minimum of only two points in time to explain the outcome of an interaction. In contrast, the communication perspective by Baxter (1988) describes several cycles of partner interaction as both a function of phase and cause of phase shift (i.e., partners have to interact with each other in certain ways if they are going to shift into a new phase of the relationship).

The second column of Table 8.2 gives a general description of each model. These highlight each model's temporal features and are not coherent summaries. They are best viewed as sketches, annotations to the theory, and as supplemental to the following narrative analysis. I have also, either in the table or the text, given some example of the type of relationship phenomena the theory or model describes.

Temporal Features of Each Model

Many theories of personal relationships describe (implicitly) the temporal features of shape, flow, structure, and order. There are a variety of temporal shapes (Kelly & McGrath, 1988; pp. 27, 81) that a causal and outcome event may take. These shapes vary in onset or acceleration, offset or deceleration, duration, cyclicity or in delay, and recurrent versus only happening once. For example, several researchers have described the temporal shape of passionate love. During the initial course of a relationship, passionate love is believed to have a quick onset and slow offset (e.g., Berscheid & Walster, 1974; p. 359). In the more articulate model reviewed here, passion "increases quickly but also peaks fairly rapidly . . . decreases . . . (and) reaches a more or less stable and habituated level" (Sternberg, 1986, p. 127). If one feels threatened with loss of the love and experiences withdrawal, Sternberg's model suggests that individuals may cycle through this sequence (accelerated increase → peaking → decreasing → plateau) recurrently. Outcome events also have variable shapes that may be either cyclical or delayed (e.g., after recognizing problems in a relationship, partners may show several cycles of repair and disengagement or breakups may occur immediately, Baxter, 1984). Some definitions and examples of these various temporal features are highlighted in Table 8.1.

TABLE 8.1

Characteristics of Temporal Features of Personal Relationships

Feature	Characteristics and some graphic examples
Change	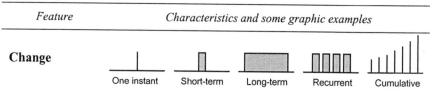

Changes in relationships can either be instantaneous, short term, or take a long time to (accumulate) affect the couple. They can be recurrent or occur only once. The effect of the change can be from one instant to the next or it can last for years (epochs). Change can also be a transition from one phase to another in the life cycle of the PR. Change can also accumulate (see "iteration" in previous chapters); each time a couple goes through a similar situation or process together they become more facile at resolving conflict or cultivating intimacy. Some theorists see change as continuous and some see it as having a limited duration (discontinuous); some see it as both—sometimes there is continuity and sometimes change has an abrupt quality.

Shape of causal process	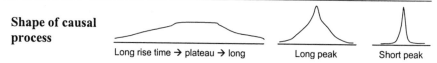

Many theorists give a central or primary role to a particular process or event that causes change in a relationship. This process has a temporal shape. This is sort of the "engine" that runs relationship development or moment-to-moment transitions. The cause can be an instant that interrupts the relationship flow, an (sudden or gradual) increase or decrease in information, a chain of events that culminate in a shift, or a phase that has a variable time to rise, a variable time to sustain itself, and a variable time to decay.

Order	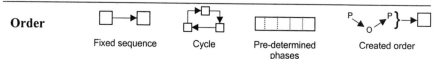

Some view PRs as showing a particular order to the flow of events while others see the order changing, and others see it as variable (sometimes there is an order and sometimes there is not). The order of events can be a particular series of comments (positive or negative appraisals: e.g., + - +; - - -; + + -): a communication sequence between Person and Other (P - O - P); a cycle of phases or filters that the couple passes through (e.g., express fear → listen → soothe → feel trust). The order may be a fixed, almost monolithic, set of preset stages that all couples pass through (e.g., attraction → interdependence → commitment). The order can also be created or emerge as a result of communication.

Continued

Table 8.1 (*Continued*)

Interval	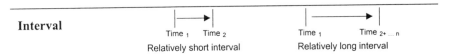

The interval of the PR phenomena may be restricted to a single discussion period or it may pertain to the whole life cycle of the relationship. It may also vary between these. For instance, an exchange of intimate sharing may happen from one moment to the next or it may take years (picking up the thread of an earlier conversation only after other events have transpired). Generally, models of interactive communication that focus on behavior specify a short interval (minutes), and models of psychological communication that focus on the state of the couple specify a variable interval.

Flow	

Flow pertains to any allusion in the model to how time may be experienced by partners. For some, time appears as a succession of critical events that somehow build on each other. For others, time has endurance—it continues in a smooth unabated fashion. Some see that partners feel that their relationship is headed in a forward direction, some in a backward direction, some both directions (bidirectional).

In addition to temporal shape, theories often contain conceptions of relationship change, that is, relationships change as a function of interaction, exchanges in a situation, or phase. Some theories suggest that relationships are always changing while others predict periods of change and stability. Unfortunately, theories do not always stipulate the nature of this change: whether change is continuous or discontinuous, whether it occurs in phases or on one occasion, or whether change is cumulative or cyclical. Still, ideas about change can usually be inferred from a careful reading of theory. McGrath and Kelly's (1986, p. 30) conceptualizations of temporal flow and temporal structure may be applied here.

McGrath and Kelly classify conceptions of the flow of time into four groups: unidirectional, bidirectional, recurrent, or developmental. Conceptions of temporal structure are also classified into four groups: successive, epochal, duration, transposable (relative). With regard to flow, PR theorists often imply that change occurs in *cyclical phases*, with either reversible patterns of recurrence or irreversible patterns of development, or in *uniform lines*, with either a reversible, bidirectional quality or an irreversible, unidirectional accumulation of events. With regard to structure, theorists often imply that change is experienced as *differentiated* with divisible epochs, or as *undifferentiated* with either a series of successive events or a uniform homogeneous duration. Unlike the contextual model proposed here,[2] none of the theories reviewed (or that I could find) appear to take time to be determined by the observer or transposable (relative) in the Einsteinian sense. In addition to conceptions of change, theories also contain reference to a specific order in which events may flow (e.g., attraction → interdependence → commitment, Scanzoni, 1979), but the interval of such phases is rarely specified.

Given authors' indefinite references to time, it is not always possible to discriminate these temporal features. If researchers are to be more sensitive to the temporal aspects of PRs, if they wish to translate theory into method, then they need more explicit guidelines for knowing when and for how long to sample causal and outcome events, when to sample for change, and what criteria are necessary for confirming that some hypothesized order of events has occurred or that the relationship has, in fact, "developed." There are some exceptions to the lack of explicit reference to time. Altman and Taylor provided specific accounts of rate change in how couples regulate privacy (e.g., slow acceleration versus fast) and Sternberg differentiated the temporal shapes of intimacy, commitment, and passion (for a recent review of this model, see Sternberg, 1998). Still, for both of these models the length of time of such features as onset, offset and duration are unspecified. The third column in Table 8.2 lists descriptions of temporal features to make these aspects of theory as explicit as possible (or, at least, to help us think about them more clearly). When there is not enough discussion of a feature to warrant an inference, that feature is not tabulated. Also, when a model conceives relationships as highly idiosyncratic—emphasizing the uniqueness of each relationship—then the feature is described as "variable."

Outcome or Criterion State of Each Model

An important aspect of the proposed contextual model is the criterion state or outcome of some temporal process. All the models reviewed attempt, in some manner, to understand or account for a particular psychological state vis à vis the relationship. These include: couple marital satisfaction, attraction, emotion, closeness, compatibility, intimacy, trust, termination of the relationship, interdependence, commitment, adaptation to divorce/remarriage, love, and mate selection. Some models view change as dialectic; thus, there is little homeostasis or stabilization within a relationship and no particular enduring state is identified (i.e., Altman et al., 1981; Baxter, 1988). In other models, the very existence of a personal relationship is itself the criterion state (Kelley, 1979) and for others so many states are described that it is difficult to focus on one without distorting the theory (Davis, 1973).

The contextual model, as a tool for interpreting and understanding, does not require the prediction of any particular state for its proof. An emphasis on some endpoint to be achieved imposes assumptions about the importance of some societal phase (e.g., success or failure) or assumptions about time as inertial and progressive. The model emphasizes *processes:* that occur within, that precede and follow, or that describe the temporal shape of these outcomes; it attempts to place emphasis on the understanding (rather than prediction) of trends or temporal patterns. The fourth column of Table 8.2 lists the central criterion or outcome state of each model and attempts to discern the temporal shape of this state as predicted by the theory.

Contextual Aspects of Each Model

The fifth and final column of Table 8.2 uses the language of the contextual model to reframe the theory. Due to the complexity of tripartite model, I have developed a figural shorthand. The interactional context is depicted as $[C_1]$, the situational as $[C_2]$, and the phasic as $[C_3]$. When models only allude to a specific context, these boxed figures are depicted with a dotted line. It should be stressed that these are my translations and are based on a revision of each theory as seen from the tripartite contextual model. Thus, the diagrams and narratives in this column are not, as such, summaries or formulations of the reviewed theories. Rather, they are interpretations of the theory in the light of temporality; these interpretations pay particular attention to any cross-contextual relationships alluded to within each of the 18 models. In the Table, interactions between the contexts are displayed with an arrow ($\rightarrow$). The following discussion gives a more complete account of each temporal context as has been construed by previous theorists and researchers.

THE TEMPORALITY OF PERSONAL RELATIONSHIP THEORIES

The following discussion examines personal relationship theories that explain relationships within each of the three temporal contexts. Within each context, I give a general description of each theory followed by an analysis of their temporal features and criterion states. These descriptions are brief and the reader should consult the original references for more detail on the theory. I then attempt to analyze these theories in terms of the temporal context model advanced in the previous chapter. The following analysis should be read in conjunction with Table 8.2. The table summarizes and supplements the text and graphically illustrates each theory as seen through the lens of the tripartite model.

Interactional–Sequential Time

General Description. The interaction models describe changes that occur as a function of a behavioral interaction between two individuals (review "General description" in col. 2, Table 8.2). The models deal with different relationship types: roles are either unspecified (Argyle & Dean, 1965; Mettee & Aronson, 1974), are intimate (e.g., Reis & Shaver, 1988), are married partners (e.g., Gottman, 1979), or are examined within the various phases of relationship development (e.g., Baxter, 1988). In the simplest model (Mettee & Aronson, 1974), the two individuals—subjects in an experiment—need not even have a face-to-face interaction. One subject is exposed to a minimum of two evaluative communications (e.g., praise, insult) from some other source and the subject's subsequent increase or decrease in attraction (liking) is assessed. In the most complex model (Baxter, 1988), the focus is on communication rather than sequence or structure of interaction. For example, couples are seen as communicating to control their level of closeness–distance (i.e., so that they do not feel either too close to each other or too far apart either). For Baxter (1988), this communication function shapes and is shaped by relationship phase: in earlier relationship phases, partners regulate their open disclosures in order to protect their vulnerability and maintain their autonomy. Later on, openness is regulated in order to maintain or repair the relationship and to maintain a level of predictability in the relationship (Baxter, 1988, p. 269).

Other models address the structure of single interaction episodes (i.e., transactions, Reis & Shaver, 1988; interchain sequences, Berscheid, 1983). The equilibrium (Argyle & Dean, 1965; Patterson, 1984) and intimacy (Reis & Shaver, 1988) models each contain a recursive feature. That is, at some point in the interaction, responsive feedback from Partner A to Partner B can change the level of the interaction toward either greater or lesser intimacy. Partners cycle through the interaction until some negotiated state of nonverbal and/or verbal intimacy is achieved. In contrast, in Berscheid's (1983) model, each partner causes the other partner's emotion. That is, they either interrupt or facilitate an already ongoing sequence of behaviors, thoughts, and actions. Interruption results in negative emotion whereas facilitation results in positive emotion. Partners are viewed as independent of and influencing the other's sequences of behavior. However, the amount of interconnections between the two partners defines the couple's "closeness" and the degree to which they facilitate each other defines the couple's "compatibility" (Berscheid, 1985).

Gottman (1979) gave couples various communication tasks in a controlled laboratory setting. He then analyzed their interactions to determine how communication patterns differ between satisfied versus troubled couples. Conditional probabilities were computed (i.e., for each sample, the probability that the husband will say x after the wife says y) and statistical summaries were derived among couples who were satisfied versus troubled. In contrast to the other deductive theories, Gottman's work is largely inductive and statistical. He extracted the temporal features of marital interactions using statistical analyses that identify certain regularities and cycles of interaction. The latest version of his model (Gottman & Silver, 1999) identifies interaction patterns that predict divorce.

Temporal Features and Outcome State. The following review highlights aspects of theory that describe specific temporal features of communications and interactions. The third and fourth columns in Table 8.2 review these features. (Refer again to Table 8.1 for an overview of temporal features.)

There are two empirical models, Aronson and Lindner's gain–loss model and Gottman's model of marital interaction, in which time is experimentally manipulated. As such, time's flow is controlled, successive, irreversible and linear. All changes or causes in the relationship are due to communication. Such change is instantaneous and assumed to have relatively immediate effects. This is largely due, perhaps, to the constraints of the laboratory session. However, certain trends of communication (Gottman) reveal cyclical properties: How one partner responds to another (feedback) depends on the discussion topic and couple type.

Generally speaking, Gottman showed that the husband will say x type of statements (e.g., disagree) after the wife says y type of statements (e.g., "mind reading") when the couple is in a distressed marriage and working on a conflict communication task. This finding is important for the contextual model because it shows that phasic characteristics of couples (whether they are distressed versus healthy) appear to interact with situational features at the exchange-situational level (i.e., whether they are working through a conflict versus a non-conflict task) in determining a communication sequence. The outcomes in these two models, attraction (Aronson & Lindner) and satisfaction (Gottman), appear to be static and relatively enduring over time. Change in the relationship is not a critical concept in either of these experimental models. Although the gain–loss model implies a discontinuity: strangers may become acquaintances or acquaintances may strengthen their bond only if the sequence of evaluation changes from negative (insult, blame) to positive (praise, affection).

Three additional theories may be labeled as either homeostatic or dialectic. Homeostatic theories suggest that partners will interact to help restore some sort of equilibrium in the relationship or to resist abrupt change. That is, couples are driven to achieve some balance like a thermostat reads the temperature to restore heat. Alternatively, dialectic theories suggest that couples communicate not only to achieve balance but also sometimes to facilitate change. Because of their homeostatic view of interaction, the equilibrium (Argyle & Dean, 1965) and intimacy (Reis & Shaver, 1988) models view time as recurrent and successive (i.e., the thermostat of communication keeps resetting itself over and over). In contrast, Baxter's dialectic view of phases suggests time is bidirectional and epochal (i.e., couples can endure periods of separation or togetherness for only so long). For Baxter, relationships are composed of basic contradictions; couples cycle between these contradictions as their relationship progresses from one phase to another.

For each of these three theories, the causal agent is recurrent (e.g., intimate gestures cause changes in conversation) and the outcome is cyclical. For example, how much partners disclose (an outcome) may first increase then decrease and increase again depending on the regulation of intimacy (a cause) in the interaction. In contrast to these models, Berscheid views interchain sequences as unidirectional and successive. The temporal shape of cause (e.g., interruption) and outcome (emotion) occurs all at once and is not maintained; that is, emotion subsides over time. (*text continues on p. 272*)

TABLE 8.2

THEORETICAL MODELS OF PERSONAL RELATIONSHIPS THAT CONSIDER TEMPORAL FACTORS

Title/Author	General description	Temporal features[1]	Outcome state	Contextual aspects
		Theories that focus on interaction sequences		
The Gain-Loss Model (Aronson & Linder, 1965; Mettee & Aronson, 1974; review)	Examines individual reactions to sequential switches or consistencies in others' affective appraisal of them. **Example:** Liking (+) at Time 1 (T_1) changes to not liking (-) at Time 2 (T_2). Subjects exposed to an increase in liking, - to +, will be more attracted to the appraiser than those exposed to a + to + sequence.	Cs-Causal shape: change in information (e.g., + to -) Os-Outcome shape: undifferentiated (not given) Ch-Change: unspecified O-Order: distinct appraisals F-Flow: successive, unidirectional Experimental time, independent episodes; Acts between T_1 and T_2 are mediators of attraction.	*Attraction* Most research has been conducted in stranger encounter situations in the laboratory; although the model refers to spousal interaction.	No face-to-face interaction but a $T_1 \rightarrow T_2$ sequence. Time is strictly linear. Experimental isolation of the $T_1 \rightarrow T_2$ effects shows that attraction occurs when information at T_2 replaces information from T_1. $\boxed{C_1}$
The Interchain Sequence Model (Berscheid, 1983, 1985)	Behavioral sequences (chains) of separate individuals influence (i.e., interrupt, facilitate, mesh with) each other to form interchain sequences. Partners' own chains proceed independently across time but affect and are affected by each other. **Example:** Os behavior at T_1 affects P at T_2 who then acts to interrupt Os behaviors between T_3 and T_4.	Cs: an instant (interruption) Os: variable (from chain to chain) Ch: short-term change O: distinct Person-Other-Person (P-O-P) chain of events F: successive, unidirectional, developmental Time is comprised of causal sequences of P-O interaction.	*Emotion, Closeness, and Compatibility* *Emotion* due to O interrupting P. *Closeness* defined as amount of connection between chains. *Compatibility* equals degree of interchain facilitation.	Focuses on interaction between partner (P or O) actions and "activities" (P-O-P behavioral chains). Chain sequences may facilitate or disrupt interdependence [C_2] and relational transition [C_3]. $\boxed{C_1}$ $\rightarrow$ $[C_3]$ / $[C_2]$

Equilibrium Models of Interaction			
(Argyle & Dean, 1965; Patterson, 1976, 1984)	Changes in some component of nonverbal behavior will result in a compensatory shift in another component in order to maintain a comfortable level of intimacy and regulate interaction. (Argyle & Dean). **Example:** An increase in distance causes an increase of eye contact. Typical behaviors occur at certain points in the give and take of conversation sequences. [Patterson] **Example:** At end of speaking turns, speakers decrease pitch or loudness. Conversational behavior is a function of equilibrium in intimacy. Thus, the regulation of interaction around some equilibrium point gives time cyclical (recurrent and recursive) properties.	Cs: recurrent instants Os: variable (recursive) Ch: cyclical O: P-O sequences F: recurrent, successive (i.e., P-O acts recur in succession)	*Optimal level of intimacy* [C₁] [C₃] diagram These models focus on conversational sequences [C₁]. Research suggests that relationship stage [C₃] (stranger vs. nonstranger) shapes the pattern of equilibrium (Argyle & Dean) and the reciprocity of intimacy (Patterson). Interactive behaviors serve different functions, they: provide information, regulate interactions, express intimacy, control behavior, present the self, manage affect, and provide services.
Intimacy as Interpersonal Process (Reis & Shaver, 1988)	A and B influence each other through a serial process: 1. A's motives, fears and goals → 2. A's disclosure → 3. B's motives → 4. B's interpretive filter → 5. B's response to A → 6. A's interpretive filter → 7. A's reaction to B; 8. Feedback from 7 to 1 and 2. Motives (1, 3) affect behavior (2, 5) and interpretation (4, 6). Links between 1 through 7 are a relationship system. **Example:** B validating A may help A become less fearful and subsequently respond more openly.	Cs: recurrent instants Os: cyclical (variable?) Ch: cumulative, progressive Int-Interval: variable F: recurrent, duration of intimacy (i.e., intimacy is process) The model emphasizes process and feedback cycles. Relationships are viewed as "deriving from but extending beyond . . . individual intimate episodes" (p. 383).	*Intimacy* [C₁] [C₃] diagram Feeling validated, cared for, enjoying the fostering of others' self: their insight and personal growth. Other outcome is development of an intimate relationship. Focuses on intimacy and the relationship between the intimate relationship episode [C₁] and the ongoing relationship [C₃]: "interaction-relationship system." This includes history, imagined future, commitment, social network, stability, conflict, and metaperspective on the relationship.

Continued

TABLE 8.2 *(Continued)*

Title/Author	General description	Temporal features[1]	Outcome state	Contextual aspects
Experimental Model of Marital Interaction (Gottman, 1979)	Accounts for patterns of interactions, with four components: degree of structure, positiveness, reciprocity, and dominance. Married couples discussions are analyzed within three phases: (1) agenda building, (2) arguing, (3) problem solving. Conditional probabilities of partner-to-partner exchanges discriminate distressed from satisfied couples. **Example:** Mind reading with negative emotion is followed by agreement (sarcasm) only for distressed couples.	Cs: recurrent chains (sequences) Os: enduring, static, epochal (i.e., troubled vs. satisfied) Ch: cyclic (i.e., repetitive) Int: bound by discussion topic O: sequence (P-0-P....) F: unidirectional, successive, linear Listening and validation acts as a feedback loop within a chain of behaviors. This creates some cycling of sequences.	*Marital satisfaction and divorce* This research discriminated distressed from nondistressed couples and has been used to predict divorce (Gottman & Silver, 1999) States of communication or syndromes (typical interaction patterns) are identified.	Focus is on conditional probabilities and trends in expressive behavior that discriminate patterns of interaction [C₁] between distressed and satisfied couples [C₂]. Topic of focus in the interaction [C₃] is manipulated (e.g., decision-making task vs. discussion).
Dialectical Perspective of Communication Strategies (Baxter, 1988)	Examines how three dialectics are managed in the process of relationship development: autonomy-connection (A-C); novelty-predictability (N-P); and openness-closedness (O-C). Communication strategies cycle between 2 poles. There are four phases within A-C. 1) A to C: inter-spersing novelty with routine, 2) A and C: conflict increases, 3) A-C synthesis, and 4) C to A: cycles of ambivalence-conflict-repair (**example in text**).	Cs: recurrent epochal Os: variable Ch: continuous Int: variable O: distinct epochs F: development, recurrent, successive Time is non-linear and cyclical with communication processes shaped by different poles of dialectics at different phases.	*Cyclical salience of dialectic poles:* Dialectical perspective has no static endpoint. However, dialectic poles become salient at different phases of relationship development. For example, sometimes novelty is more important than openness.	Communication [C₁] is viewed a strategic action within a dialectical dynamic ↔ that varies as a function of phase [C₃] and navigating these dynamics leads to qualitative shifts across these phases.

Theories that focus on situational exchanges

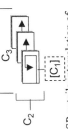

Triangular Theory of Love (Sternberg, 1986)	Three components of love vary in importance in short- vs. long-term relationships. Intimacy (I) increases from moderate to high importance; commitment (C) from low to high; passion (P) decreases from high to moderate. These changes are curvilinear. In successful relationships, I increases which leads to reduced uncertainty. Experienced C rises in an S-shaped curve. P increases, peaks rapidly and then habituates to an eventual stable level of arousal.	Cs: continuous Os: variable, curvilinear Ch: curvilinear, continuous Int: moderate F: variable across the 3 components Using the length of each side of a triangle to represent the love components, changes in each can be viewed simultaneously. These can be compared across time for two individuals in a relationship.	*Changes in each component of love are hypothesized to occur if relationships are to succeed.* Broadly stated, however, the theory attempts to account for relationship *satisfaction, success and failure.*	Focus is on moderate-term changes [C_2] within each love component (I, P, C) and how these modify relationship success [C_3]. Changes constitute qualitative shifts in relationship development but do not cause discrete transitions.
Social Penetration Theory (Altman & Taylor, 1973)	Social penetration (SP) is governed by rewards/costs, which are evaluated and forecasted so that subsequent interactions are chosen or terminated. Feedback leads to confirmation or revision of forecasts across interactions. Several postulates about time are: SP goes from superficial to intimate levels, SP rate varies as a function of rewards/costs. Model uses onion analogy with growth in intimacy occurring in breadth and depth.	Os: variable Ch: progressive F: unidirectional, successive Explicit psychological relationships between past (accumulation of interactions in memory), present (evaluation) and future (forecast). Eight prototype growth patterns are described.	*Intimacy* as well as trends in intimacy are central to the theory. Specific *changes* in breadth and depth are detailed. Different *rates* (slowdown and acceleration) of the relationship are detailed within 8 prototype patterns.	SP entails interrelation of present evaluation of interaction [C_1], forecasts of future interactions, and past history. Emphasis is on cross-interaction changes [C_2] as a function of outcomes. Mix of rewards/costs determine rate of development [C_3].

Continued

TABLE 8.2 (*Continued*)

Title/Author	General description	Temporal features¹	Outcome state	Contextual aspects
Dialectical Perspective of Social Penetration and Privacy Regulation (Altman et al., 1981)	Accumulation of processes beyond a threshold alters the relationship. Two dialectics—stability/change and openness/closedness (o–c)— cycle in frequency, amplitude, regularity, and duration. Short cycles of a dialectic may embed within longer cycles of another. Individuals are in/out of phase. **Example:** Early in relationship people engage in short, frequent, low stability bursts of o–c cycles which stabilize.	Cs: cyclic Os: variable Ch: cyclic Int: variable Ord: variable F: variable Concept of change, accumulation is central. Linear and cyclical processes account for crises, levels of intimacy, personal development, and timing of interactions.	The dialectical approach de-emphasizes homeostasis, stability, or consistency. There is no final state the model attempts to account for or is applied to.	C_2 C_1 C_3 O–c cycles ($\leftrightarrow$) of interaction [C_2], which occur in the context of relationship history [C_3] and determine the course ($\rightarrow$) of that history as well as the timing of specific interactions [C_1].
Interdependence in Personal Relationships (Kelley, 1979)	Social exchange entails transforming subjective outcomes to actual outcomes, where partners apply interaction rules and express dispositions. Interactions involve mutual transformation and communication, such that personalities are connected through time. **Example:** The "lovers quarrel" (exchange) permits each person to communicate (the disposition of) dependence and so strengthen the bond (mutual outcome).	Os: enduring disposition Ch: epochal F: subjective Transformation of the subjective (needs) to the objective (relationship), the current to the future is central. Time is not only cumulative, but qualitative shifts can occur through coordination. Dispositions are both derived from and control outcomes (conflicts, dilemmas). The two are dynamically interrelated.	*Personal relationship* is defined when a criterion level of interdependence is reached through transformation.	C_1 C_2 C_3 future state Interdependence is a function of interactions [C_2]. Interdependence entails applying internalized norms [C_3] to govern and transform the interaction $\rightarrow$. Transformations affect communication in a particular interaction [C_1].

Theories that focus on phases or transitions

Wheel theory of love (Reiss, 1960)	A continuous cycle of love with four phases: (a) rapport, (b) self-revelation, (c) mutual dependency, (d) personality need fulfillment, which leads to (a) again. Love is not a state but a process. Different types of love (romantic, sexual, rational) affects how one cycles through phases. **Example**: Romantic love entails cycling quickly through all four whereas sexual love may fixate on one way of revealing.	Time is circular.	*Love.* There is little discussion of static phenomena.	Focus is entirely on discrete stages [C_3] of love without reference to other temporal contexts.
Filter Theories of Mate Selection (Kerckhoff & Davis, 1962; Lewis, 1972; Murstein, 1970)	Mate selection entails a sequence of decisions about matching and complementarity of two partners. The decision points vary for the three theories but typically entail a sequence of fitting on (a) physical, stimulus characteristics (e.g., attractiveness), (b) empathic understanding and value similarity; (c) interpersonal roles (e.g., need complementarity). Each stage serves as a filter, usually before next stage can occur.	Cs: one-shot, maintained Os: continuous Ch: progressive, linear Ord: fixed Flow: successive, progressive, unidirectional Previous stages serving as necessary conditions for subsequent stages.	*Mate selection* (Kerckhoff & Davis). *Dyadic crystallization*, e.g., commitment, identity as a couple (Lewis). *Role performance* e.g., husband, wife (Murstein).	Focus is on discrete phases leading up to commitment. Each theory emphasizes role coordination as occurring later in the sequence. Relationships breakdown if various filters are not gone through, but breakdowns do not have distinct phases.

Continued

TABLE 8.2 (Continued)

Title/Author	General description	Temporal features[1]	Outcome state	Contextual aspects
Levels of Relatedness in Attraction (Levinger & Snoek, 1972)	Levels of relatedness: (0) zero contact, (1) awareness of other, (2) surface contact (some interaction), (3) mutuality (major interaction). Interaction, maintenance, evaluation, and attraction change from (0) to (3). Many forward (→) and backward (←) level changes are possible. Stage-like progressions are not necessary. Transitions are significant. **Example**: Attachment (2 → 3) may occur as circumstances move interactions beyond role requirements.	Cs: transition Os: at-once and maintained Ch: linear, epochal Flow: bidirectional, abstract Transition is central and probabilities of transition are viewed as higher across contingent levels (e.g., from 1 to 2) than non-contingent (e.g., from 1 to 3).	Nature of transition varies from level to level, from: 0 to 1, *approach* 1 to 2, *affiliation* 2 to 3, *attachment* 3 onward, *mutual development* (e.g., joint attitudes). Also, retrogressive transitions are accounted for.	 Change emphasized across levels. Development/deterioration are described across phases and mirror each other. Interactions/exchanges are not specified as part of the transitions, but circumstances and interactions are more likely at some levels than others.
ABCDE Model of Development & Change (Levinger, 1983)	Sequence: (A) Awareness; (B) Buildup; (C) Commitment; (D) Deterioration; (E) Ending. Not all go through all stages. The model focuses on transition. Buildup is gradual or stepwise. Decisions about compatibility are reversible. (B)-(C) transitions follow long sequence of interactions. (C) entails critical events (e.g., parenting). (C)-(D) entails responses to conflict. (D) can start in (B); (D)-(E) due to poor reward-cost balance, changes in self-concept (**example in text**).	Cs: phases, transitions Os: variable in onset, offset, duration, and cycles Ch: (dis) continuous Int: unspecified in phases but (A)-(E) is "long-term" Ord: variable but generally is ABCDE Flow: progressive, with recursion	*Person-Other interdependence* over time and related states for each phase. Positive examples are: (A) favorable impression; (B) compatibility; (C) coping, marital satisfaction; (D) increase standards in judgment of spouse; (E) healing.	 Focuses on transitions within phases [C_3] with a continuous loop conception of causality. Specific character of interactions (e.g., interchaining), outcomes, and situations (e.g., crises) [C_2] facilitate and are facilitated by (↔) phase.

Social Forces in Intimate Relationship Development & Change (Davis, 1973)	Facilitations and complications in internal/external social forces that help individuals construct intimacy. Forces are: probability (moving from strangers to acquaintances), con-gregation (e.g., cycles of copresence) communication (e.g., of intimacy), information, ecology, and inter-subjectivity. Maintenance-repair (Making up) and deterioration (Breaking up) forces are described. Time factors (e.g., synchrony of mood) are discussed in each phase. (**example in text**)	Cs: Social forces act at different times Os: variable in onset, offset, duration, and cycle Ch: continuous, organic Int: unspecified Ord: variable Flow: intimates determine With increasing intimacy, indivi-dual selves become organized temporally in new and joint ways. This organization is subject to social forces and requires maintenance.	Varies in each level, e.g., successful first encounter, increase in communication, familiarity, trust. Levels of commitment: exclude alternatives, common space and future. Complications: not scheduling a meeting, lack of time together, shared memories made salient during breakup.
			 Social forces come into play at different levels [C3]. One force [C2] deals with favors derived from interactions [C1] that help the person in transaction with the environment. Interactions [C1] and exchanges [C2] facilitate or complicate each force.
Social Exchange and Behavioral Interdependence (Scanzoni, 1979)	Progressive interdependence where actors increase/decrease involvement in accord with exchange principles (e.g., reciprocity). Stages are: I. Exploration (actors forego immediate in lieu of long-term rewards); II. Expansion of interlocking interests, central issues are negotiated (sex, contraception, coresidence); III. Commitment, issues of conflict become more important (**example in text**).	Cs: recurrent use of exchange principles Os: unspecified Ch: continuous, phasic Int: unspecified Ord: variable with recursion Flow: progressive Certain levels of interdependence necessary for behaviors to occur; e.g., minimum commitment required to manage conflict. Individualist interests decrease, collectivist interests increase from I to III.	*Interdependence* and change are the focus. Stage I: *maximum joint profit* and *trust* represents collective exchange norms. Stage II: *increases in rewards, and obligations.* Stage III: *high inputs* of a lengthy duration and consistent over time. C_3 — $\boxed{C_2}$ $\boxed{C_2}$ $\boxed{C_2}$ Exchanges [C2] are integral to the development of interdependence across relationship stage [C3] and increases in interdependence reinforce, mitigate, and potentiate exchanges at other stages.

Continued

TABLE 8.2 (*Continued*)

Title/Author	General description	Temporal features[1]	Outcome state	Contextual aspects
Sequential/ Process Models of Relationship Dissolution (Duck, 1982, 1984; Lee, 1984; Baxter, 1984)	Four phases for Duck: Intra-psychic search for justifying breakup (b) vs. repair (r). Negotiation of withdrawal vs. reconciliation; Social support for (b) vs. (r); and Grave-dressing and reformulation. Five parts of a sequence for Lee: Dissatisfaction, Exposure, Negotiation, Decision about termination, Changes executed. Baxter explored gradual vs. sudden onset of problems, rapid vs. protracted disengagement. All models include recursion in terms of (r) attempts at any point. Couples may cycle through a (b) vs. (r) sequence before reaching a final decision. **(examples in text)**.	Cs: dissatisfaction (continued) Os: exit decision (instant) Ch: (dis) continuous, phasic Int: variable Ord: variable, not all stages necessary Flow: progressive, bidirectional Lee described negotiational latency, overall time span of dissolution, "scale-downs" vs. "full-breaks," and resolution-termination consistency.	*Termination* vs. *Continuation* with *Repair* attempts Each model accounts for events that lead to breakups and so alludes to different rates and steps of dissolution (e.g., couples may not expose or negotiate dissatisfaction and exit directly after awareness of problems).	 Stages or trajectories in relationship breakup [C_3]. Models specify either interaction [C_1] or negotiation [C_2] as a possible step toward repair or reorganization. These interactions are viewed in terms of impact on dissolution.

| Family Reorganiz-ation after Separation/ Divorce/ Remarriage (SDR)

(Rodgers, 1987; McCubbin & Patterson, 1983) | Provides a "map" showing process of family reorganization across phases: 1. *Adjustment* to social, situational, and developmental stressors (resistance and coping); 2. *Accommodation with restructuring* (stressors reach crisis level, attempts at shared definition, agreed solution, system maintenance); and 3. *Accommodation with consolidation or "settling in"* to new level of binuclear family organization. If family unsuccessful at 1, then move to 2 or exhaustion. Consolidation also feeds back to increase restructuring. | Cs: recurrent adjustments to SDR
Os: variable in onset (the rest is unspecified)
Ch: continuous
Int: variable
Ord: relatively fixed
Flow: progressive, unidirectional

SDR is viewed not as events but as processes of organization and disorganization that comprise a critical life transition. | Degrees of *Bonadaptation/ Maladaptation* of new member to family (vice versa) and new family to community. |
Focus is on transition from a nuclear family to a binuclear family [C_3], which in the model, cannot occur without particular types of interaction [C_1] and various exchanges implying interdependence [C_2], (e.g., compromising). |

---

[1]Temporal features described in the table are Cs = shape of causal process, Os = shape of outcome process, Ch = nature of change, Int = duration of interval, Ord = order of events, Flow = flow of time. (Review Table 8.1 for a description of these temporal features.)

Although only a peripheral aspect of the intimacy model, change is viewed as a cumulative, progressive feature; that is, building intimacy leads to commitment. "When partners sense that they mutually foster these feelings (of being understood, validated), they become more aware that their relationship is intimate and typically become more committed to it " (Reis & Shaver, 1988; p. 385). In Baxter's model, interactions actively transform the relationship when, for example, "parties navigate this maze of (dialectical) contradictions and emerge with the desire to become interdependent beyond casual acquaintanceship" (Baxter, 1988, p. 264). Here, change is discontinuous, progressive and transformational; the entire relationship, not only its features, changes as a function of the interaction.

Contextual Aspects. The contextual model can uniquely depict each of the six interactional models. The simplest model, gain-loss theory, is only about an interaction sequence and so posits no explicit relationship with other contexts. As diagrammed in the final column of Table 8.2, only the interaction context $[C_1]$ is involved. The criterion state of attraction could be viewed as enduring over time (and so constitute a phase), but gain–loss theory does not situate this outcome in the broader context of relationship history; it is a strict experimental model. Although the interchain sequence model also focuses on interaction sequence; the criterion states of closeness and compatibility suggest that the meshing of interaction sequences does entail greater interdependence and relationship transition (a new phase). Importantly, Berscheid (1985) pointed out that compatible relationships are not necessarily enduring, enduring relationships are not necessarily compatible, and close relationships can not stay incompatible for very long (pp. 156–157). Endurance in the face of incompatibility depends on a variety of interchain characteristics; for example, couples will endure when partners must facilitate each other in order to complete certain sequences and plans. Thus, the continuation of a relationship—across situations and phases—is viewed as an effect rather than a cause of the interaction. As shown in Table 8.2, events in the interaction context $[C_1]$ may lead to changes in the situational context $[C_2;$ interdependence] and the phasic context $[C_3;$ relational transition].

In the equilibrium models, interaction is self-regulated, diagrammed as a self-reflective arrow pointing to $[C_1]$ in the Table. As such, interaction is restricted to interactional (rather than phasic or situational) time. Although Patterson was concerned with interaction and not relationship exchange he emphasizes that individuals vary in their "social control motives" (Patterson, 1984). That is, individuals control the intimacy level of their interactions, depending upon how much intimacy they want through their current exchanges. In a sense, the "thermostat" exists because of a deep desire for maintaining a certain preset level of intimacy rather than for achieving deeper intimacy. In addition, research (Argyle & Dean, 1965; Coutts & Schneider, 1976) indicates that the regulation of intimacy partially depends on stage of relationship (e.g., stranger versus friend dyads). Thus, situational $[C_2]$ and phasic $[C_3]$ time parameters are viewed as factors external to the interaction but which have an effect on its regulation or equilibrium.

The interpersonal process model (Reis & Shaver, 1988) views interaction within an "interaction-relationship system." In this system, phasic features of commitment and stability provide securities that foster intimate interactions. The focus of the model is less on this system and more on the process of intimacy as a self-regulated (i.e., homeostatic) interaction where partners reinforce each other's selves and modify each other's motives. Table 8.1 depicts the system as a bi-directional arrow between $[C_1]$ and $[C_3]$.

Gottman's (1979) experimental model manipulates phasic and situational aspects of time while examining interaction. Communicative sequences remain the unit of analysis $[C_1]$ while couples are given different types of communication tasks that, in effect, represent different types of interdependence or different situations $[C_2]$. Sometimes couples are required to discuss a conflictual aspect of the relationship; other times they are given an enjoyable puzzle to solve together. By giving these tasks to couples who are in stable or in unstable relationships, Gottman is controlling phasic parameters of temporal context $[C_3]$. The focus is on interactional time as it occurs within the context of controlled experimental time and also within the controlled contexts of situational time. Thus, no explicit relationship exists between phase, situation, and interaction; they seem to occur simultaneously. However, the recent version of his model (Gottman & Silver, 1999) suggests explicit causal connections between interaction $[C_1]$ and the outcome of relational stability or divorce $[C_3]$.

Baxter also examined how interactions might be regulated by and regulate the relational phase. The dynamics of communication and the relationship are mutually determinate and integral to each other. Couples will proceed from early stages, where the concern is moving from autonomy to connectedness, to later stages, where autonomy and connectedness are synthesized, only if the other dialectics are strategically communicated. For example, relationships will develop only if partners intersperse periods of predictability with novel interactions and periods of openness with privacy.

Exchange–Situational Time

General Description. The four theories in this section represent major theoretical attempts within the area of social psychology to understand affiliation within personal relationships. As such, they may be viewed as what McGuire (1980) called "guiding-idea theories" of affiliation. They view human action as initiated by active (vs. reactive) factors and motivated more by growth than by the desire to maintain equilibrium. They each implicitly view affiliation as directed toward an affective (vs. cognitive) end state to be established externally, that is, with others in their environment rather than toward changing some internal state. The process of commitment is integral, although not always explicit, in these models. This is because, by definition, relationships that move beyond a single interaction and have some continuity across situations require at least a modicum of commitment.[3] The theories describe how individuals both structure and respond to situations and how these actions are associated with certain outcomes (cf. affective, external, endstates, McGuire, 1980). These theories try to account for motivational and affective changes that occur between individuals as the relationship changes; be they changes in love (Sternberg, 1986), in self-disclosure (Altman & Taylor, 1973), in privacy regulation (Altman et al., 1981), or in motives as a function of social exchange (Kelley, 1979).

Changes may occur within a single interaction episode or in a relationship transition; the process or sequences of interaction or the stages of the relationship are only secondary aspects of these situational-exchange theories. From situation to situation, and within their ongoing personal relationships, individuals are motivated to balance rewards and costs (Altman & Taylor, 1973; Kelley, 1979), openness and closedness, stability and change (Altman et al., 1981). Individuals are also effected by the balancing of passion, intimacy, and commitment within themselves and with their partners (Sternberg, 1986).

Of the four models, the triangular theory of love (Sternberg, 1986) and social penetration theory (Altman & Taylor, 1973) tend to focus on changes that individuals experience as the relationship progresses. The direction of causality between experience and relationship is different in Sternberg's than in Altman and Taylor's model. For social penetration theory, how individuals experience relationship rewards/costs and how they forecast these will determine when, how, and whether there will be more self-disclosure (i.e., growth patterns in social penetration). Partners determine whether or not the relationship will deepen. In contrast, in the triangular model, the experienced course of love is a function (rather than a cause) of relationship duration. How the relationship proceeds determines partner experience. In the other models, the focus is on the state of the relationship itself, its cycles of openness-closedness, stability-change (Altman et al., 1981), or its degree of interdependence (Kelley, 1979). Changes in the relationship are linked less with individual experience and tied more to dyadic features: the degree of timing between partner's phases of openness or the coordination of outcomes between the partners.

In the triangular model, levels of passion, intimacy, and commitment may or may not be matched between the two partners. In general, satisfactory relationships are more matched than unsatisfactory relationships (Sternberg, 1986, p. 129), but because these three components change across time, it is likely that couples are rarely perfectly matched and they experience various lags in the type of love they feel for each other. In the severely mismatched example, one partner may be extremely more passionate, intimate, and committed. In the moderately mismatched example, both partners share equal intimacy but one is more committed and the other more intimate. By ascertaining match, Sternberg's model can account for dyadic aspects of love as these change through time.

Social penetration predicts eight prototypical growth patterns as a function of how partners remember past rewards, forecast future rewards, and currently assess the relationship. One example is the couple who has previously experienced large absolute rewards but who only foresees moderately positive ones in the context of a negatively assessed relationship. For this couple, the probable outcome of social penetration will likely show a "moderately rapid slowdown" (Altman & Taylor, 1973, Case 4a, p. 46). This contrasts with the rapid acceleration predicted for those who have had small costs in the past but who currently assess the relationship as positive (Case 7). Neither social penetration nor the triangular love models view change as a phasic or transitional phenomena; change appears to occur across situations as a function of experience, behavior, and motivation. Like all these situational models, time depends on the psychology of the actors (cf. "nootemporal"; Fraser, 1987).

In Kelley's interdependence model, two individuals have expectations about the outcomes to be received by interacting with each other in a certain situation. The rewards and costs available in the situation operate in connection with each partner's motives. Transformation occurs, in part, when partners coordinate their actions so that both of them are satisfied (i.e. they negotiate outcomes that meet each other's needs). In ongoing relationships, both partners will not always be equally satisfied with the outcome of a given interaction scenario. Rather, "outcomes are not reacted to one by one and in isolation, they are compared and cumulated over time" (Kelley, 1979, p. 19). Across situations, partners invoke various (competitive, common interest) rules through which conflict is mitigated and satisfactory interactions occur. Thus, relationship changes accumulate across situations as a function of the application of certain rules.

The use of social rules can also be found in other situation-exchange models. Argyle and colleagues (Argyle et al., 1981; Argyle & Henderson, 1985) described interaction rules that are used by partners to manage their relationships, and Morton and Douglas (1981) have theorized about the changes in rule usage (e.g., in the distribution of resources) that must occur in relationship growth. In the analysis of situational-exchange time, such rules play a critical part as couple's navigate from situation to situation, from activity to activity (e.g., being in bed together, going shopping, eating together), and from one relationship stage to another.[4] For example, showing emotional support and being faithful is a more central rule for spouses than dating couples and the latter pair places more emphasis on being punctual and respecting privacy (Argyle & Henderson, 1985). Other research has shown that husbands and wives budget their time both together and apart in a stereotypical or norm-governed fashion (Clarke et al., 1986). From Kelley's viewpoint, time budgeting and the application of such rules is determined or modified by the dispositions of the two individuals. If partner's can mutually apply these rules from situation to situation so that they satisfy each other (cf. "mutual relationship definition"; Morton & Douglas, 1981), then their personalities become connected through time, they achieve "dispositional interdependence."

Temporal Features and Outcome State. Several of the theories in this section specify how situational or psychological outcomes are shaped over time but they are less clear about the temporal shape of cause. Outcomes for the social penetration theories (Altman and colleagues) are quite variable across dyads due to differences in rates of development and in the dyadic management of openness-closedness. Changes of love—apparently viewed as both a cause and an outcome—in the triangular model is explicitly defined as a curvilinear function of time (see Sternberg, 1986, Figs. 2, 3, 4, pp. 126-127). If the causal agent of the situational theories is viewed as residing within the individual (i.e., motives, memories, expectations), then the temporal shape of these intrapersonal processes is unspecified. Temporal fluctuations in the need for intimacy (Altman & Taylor, 1973), interpersonal dispositions (Kelley, 1979), and the need for stability/novelty (Altman et al., 1981) are not explicitly described. However, the theory of privacy regulation assumes that individuals do not want intimacy all the time; intimacy is cyclical. We might also assume that social exchange is sometimes motivated by individualistic needs and sometimes by collectivistic needs, but Kelley does not elaborate on the specific changes of motives that propel relationship changes.

In most of the models, relationship change is viewed as continuous versus discontinuous. The concept of change is central to privacy regulation theory; dialectical tensions and pendulum swings between stability and change govern relationships. As such, relationship change is bi-directional and recurrent, so much so that there is no homeostasis and no final, criterion state is specified. This contrasts with Altman and Taylor's earlier model, where temporal flow is relatively unidirectional and successive. That is, levels of self-disclosure (social penetration) either accelerate or decelerate as a function of a series of past, present, and anticipated interactions. Sternberg also described continuous changes in each love component as the relationship proceeds; for instance, relationships "flag" when intimacy and commitment do not increase over time.

For Kelley, certain exchange problems recur within relationships because of either partner's incompatible dispositions or their self-orientation. There are times when "each person is able to help the other by 'giving' but has a preference not to do so, that is, to 'keep' " (p. 128). Successive transactions occur because this situation is complex; "strict reciprocity may be attainable only over a long time span" (p. 129). In this example, partners cycle through certain exchange patterns that depend on dispositional factors. This cycle may take a long time to result in a shift or transformation of the particular interpersonal situation. However, with compatible dispositions (e.g., both partners cooperating), it is possible that a qualitative shift will occur and that dispositions will become interdependent. This occurrence is viewed as indicating the beginning of a "personal relationship." As such, it represents a discontinuity from previous nondispositional interaction scenarios. Kelley does not specify how long it takes to form a personal relationship, but his emphasis on dispositional interdependence suggests that such relationships do not emerge instantaneously. He also indicates that relationships do not require interactions; they have a "psychological persistence" even when there are no behavioral interactions to sustain them.

Contextual Aspects. The four social psychological models describe changes in relationships as a function of psychological processes across interaction situations [C_2]. That is, relationships change according to how individuals define and behave in the situation separately and together. The models consider interactions and phases, but they do not describe either the specific content of interaction episodes or predict particular social transitions. For example, in the triangular theory, one component of love is commitment. As such, commitment may be related to the critical stable phase of relationship development as considered by many stage theorists (e.g., Scanzoni, 1979). Because changes in each component of love correspond to changes in the relationship ("success," "failure," "flagging"), the triangular model also attempts to account for phasic shifts in relationship development. This is depicted in Table 8.2 as each of the love components influencing (arrow) relationship change [C_3].

The other models only allude to some aspect of single interaction episodes. In social penetration, individuals assess the "immediately preceding interaction with regard to a personal–subjective standard of desirability" (Altman & Taylor, 1973, p. 36). In this way the model does account for a single interaction episode by assessing its subjective outcome but it does not attempt to describe processes that occur within sequential-interactional time. The emphasis is on how individuals evaluate the interpersonal situation [C_2] for its past (←), it's future (→), and the effect these evaluations have on increased or decreased intimacy [C_2]. The other models attempt to specify certain types of interactions. Altman et al's (1981) dialectical perspective hypothesizes that cycles of openness-closedness will have an effect on when specific types of interactions will occur but not how they will proceed. Table 8.2 depicts this cycle as bi-directional (←→). For Kelley, the dispositional level of the relationship limits the interaction by selecting among (different) possibilities of social exchange. Here, too, we see that the type of interaction scenario [C_1] is influenced by social exchange factors but, unlike the models of the previous section, the specific temporal course of the interaction is unspecified.

Both of Altman's models view relationship changes as occurring within the broader context of relationship history [C_3]. There is "the prediction of a *slowdown* in social penetration *at later stages* of a relationship" (Altman &

Taylor, 1973, italics added, p. 45) and dialectical patterns of privacy regulation both change with as well as determine the course of relationship history. For Kelley, the introduction of social-transitional time occurs through the application of social norms that determine exchange patterns. As noted earlier, there appears to be a different ordering of interaction rules for couples at different stages of their relationships (Argyle & Henderson, 1985). Although Kelley did not specifically refer to such stage differences, his emphasis on rules indicate that social exchanges do not occur in a vacuum. Rules, roles, and norms—aspects of social phase—have a direct effect on the transformation of an interpersonal situation. This is depicted in Table 8.2 as $[C_3]$ mediating the relationship between current $[C_{2,\ at\ Time\ 1}]$ and future $[C_{2,\ at\ Time\ 1\ +\ n}]$ level of interdependence.

Phasic–Transitional Time

General Description. The eight models reviewed in this section each specify stages or phases that relationships proceed through in a developmental or dissolution schema. These include successive but cyclic phases of love (Reiss, 1960), sequential filters toward mate selection, commitment and role performance (Kerckhoff & Davis, 1962; Lewis, 1972; Murstein, 1976), levels of relatedness in attraction (Levinger & Snoek, 1972), phases and transitions in development (Levinger, 1983), social forces in intimate relationships (M. S. Davis, 1973), stages in behavioral interdependence (Scanzoni, 1979), sequences in relationship dissolution or break-down (Baxter, 1984; Duck, 1982; L. Lee; 1984) and relationship repair (Duck, 1984), and phases of family reorganization after separation/ divorce/remarriage (McCubbin & Patterson, 1983; Rodgers, 1987).

In each of these models, a specific order of phases is outlined. Except for the filter theories, authors do not suggest that a strict progressive adherence to this order be followed. Relationships may fixate at one stage (e.g., only certain type of love; Reiss, 1960); they may skip a stage (e.g., quickly move from acquaintance to attachment; Levinger & Snoek, 1972). Moreover, changes that begin in one stage may not be fully realized until much later (e.g., obligations engendered early in attraction may only have meaning after a commitment; Scanzoni, 1979). In the filter theories, success at one stage is generally viewed as a prerequisite before progress can occur. Developmental theories range in the number of stages they posit, from three (exploration → expansion → commitment; Scanzoni, 1979) to six (perceiving similarities → achieving pair rapport → inducing self disclosure → role-taking → achieving interpersonal role-fit → achieving dyadic crystallization; Lewis, 1972).

Two of the three dissolution models (Baxter, 1984; Lee, 1984) are empirically derived and all three dissolution models indicate that repair and maintenance can modulate breakups. At early, compared to later, stages of dissolution, communication and negotiation have a greater possibility of feeding back to the relationship and either delaying or aborting a breakup. Using couples retrospective accounts of their breakups, Baxter developed a flow chart that traces seven interrelated (recursive) steps of disengagement. These are: the onset of relationship problems, the decision to exit the relationship, initiating unilateral decision actions, the initial reaction of the broken-up-with-party, ambivalence and repair scenarios, initiating bilateral dissolution action, and ambivalence and repair scenarios. Baxter described roughly seven basic trajectories of disengagement that couples take (e.g., ambivalent indirect, swift direct). Lee (1984), also using retrospective accounts, derived a common sequence in separation. This sequence is: (D) Discovery of dissatisfaction; (E) Exposure of discontent; (N) Negotiation, issues are discussed; (R) Resolution, a decision is reached; and (T) Transformation, actual changes occur. Lee delineated various "separation scenarios" that adequately account for a full range of dissolutional trajectories. There are omission formats in which certain stages are skipped (e.g., D-E-N-R-T, D-E-N-R-T), extended formats where certain stages are prolonged (e.g., D----E-N-R-T) and mixed formats made up of combinations of omission and extended formats (e.g., D-E-----N-R-T.) Although these two empirical models represent single research contributions, they are relevant to the contextual model because they describe discontinuities of stages in accounting for their data. This research also demonstrates that actual stages of breakup are highly variable across couples and do not necessarily follow a fixed order.

Like the other models in this section, Rodger's (1987) phasic model of family reorganization is based on a review of the research literature. This model is included because of the changing nature of the family (e.g., serial marriages; see Brody et al., 1988) and the importance of the family to our conceptions of marital development. It describes the transition from the ending of one relationship to the beginning of another. Rodger's model is relevant to all temporal contexts and relationship phases because it provides a theory for understanding the various events that occur between relationships (i.e., the interactions and situations between the last phase of the old and the first phase of the new).

Temporal Features and Outcome State. Reiss' is the only phasic model that does not view relationships as advancing toward some resolved level of mutuality, commitment, or adaptation. Couples are continually cycling through a series of love phases without a necessary linear progression. Reiss' exposition is otherwise too brief to justifiably extract other temporal features. In contrast to Reiss, the filter models neglect cycle and emphasize linear succession. In these models, the temporal shape of filters (which are both cause and outcome) are unspecified. The changes that occur between phases are more likely a gradual transition (especially for Lewis, 1973) rather than an abrupt, instantaneous shift. Unlike the other developmental models, filter theories have a relatively fixed order of occurrence.

In most filter models, time flow is something extraneous and abstract to the relationship; couples seem to "pass through" stages (e.g., "move a pair from one level to another"; Levinger & Snoek, 1972, p. 5; a "critical intersection is passed," Scanzoni, 1979, p. 78). In contrast, Davis' (1973) accent on symbolic interaction provides a view of couples as determining concretely their own temporality: "They bind their basic beings together . . . by losing their old selves in each other, by creating each other anew, and by attempting to immortalize their relationship" (p. 205). Levinger (1983) revised his conceptualization of flow from the levels of relatedness model (Levinger & Snoek, 1972) to the ABCDE model. Previously, he viewed time as reversible; pairs demonstrate progressive and retrogressive transitions across the same levels. More recently, transition is progressive across phases and deterioration is qualitatively different than mere regression to an earlier phase.

The precise temporal shape of causes and outcomes are not specified by most of models, but some underlying causes are influential. For Scanzoni (1979), different exchange principles operate across different phases of relationship development. However, there is an underlying and recurrent cycling of *reciprocity*: "Relationships are maintained when actors perform valued services for others, and visa versa; and also when these performances continue to generate *ongoing* feelings of moral obligations to reciprocate benefits received" (p. 64, italics added). For Davis (1973), different social forces— congregation, information—may become active at different points in intimate relationships, but once created, the relationship has its own continuous, persistent quality:

> Whatever instinctual, emotional, or rational considerations induce a pair of individuals to procreate an intimate relation, its processes shortly acquire an inertia or structure of their own apart from its motivating force; and whenever this original vitalizing psychological impulse dies away, those who once were intimates may find the vitiated sociological skeleton of their relationship to be difficult to dismantle. (p. 285)

The temporal facets in each of the dissolution models might be best construed as shaped by a recurrent contest between centripetal and centrifugal forces (Duck, 1988b), between the barriers to leaving the relationship and the relative attractiveness of alternatives. During dissolution, these forces operate continuously but, when certain levels of breakdown have occurred, disengagement can occur rapidly enough to be discontinuous (e.g., Baxter, 1984). Still, the language of dissolution models is so replete with many temporal allusions (latency, onset, offset, scale-downs) and the interaction of maintenance and repair strategies is so continuous (Duck, 1984), that dissolutional outcomes and the ordering of stages is highly variable across couples.[5] Models of family reorganization after separation/divorce/remarriage (SDR) also contain a complex array of continuous adjustment and readjustment patterns (outcome) to the changing family situation (cause). These SDR models (e.g., McCubbin & Patterson, 1983) describe adjustment to these changes as a precursor of adaptation/accommodation to the new family situation. The latter process involves a continuous cycling between crises → restructuring → consolidation until there is some stabilization of the new family unit.

   Contextual Aspects. The Wheel theory, Filter theories, and level of relatedness model each focus entirely on the phasic context, $[C_3]$. Levinger and Snoek (1972) are the most articulate about transitions between phases, shown as movement (→ or ←) within stages of $[C_3]$. Levinger's ABCDE model (1983) articulates these transitions even further within a "continuous loop conception" of causality. This is depicted through self-referential arrows (⇥ or ⇤)to $[C_3]$. Here partner interactions $[C_1]$ both affect and are effected by environmental, personal, and relational events (Kelley et al., 1983). Factors that influence feelings about the relationship favorably or unfavorably are reevaluated in the light of new events and changing causal conditions (Levinger, 1983, p. 329). Thus, present interactions and exchanges $[C_2]$ may lead to a psychological revision of earlier phases and "processes of deterioration . . . may originate in the buildup phase and extend through the ending of the relationship" (p. 349). With the interchain model as a guiding heuristic (Kelley et al., 1983), Levinger integrated all three temporal contexts through examples of how interactions and exchanges help shape phasic transition (e.g., renegotiation during deterioration) and how phase helps determine interaction (see Table 8.2). The following quote emphasizes such references to temporal context and illustrates this integration: "*Early* in a relationship, *interaction* is marked by uncertainly [*sic*] and a high probability of 'interruption'; *later* it is marked by relative security and stability. It is possible to mistake such tranquillity as implying emptiness or passivity. Thus, spouses may not fully appreciate the *degree of their dependence* on each other and so may *dream of greater excitement* elsewhere (p. 341, italics added).

   Davis' (1973) philemic theory shows stages $[C_3]$ that result from social forces and how couples, through their exchanges $[C_2]$, navigate these forces. Both interactions $[C_1]$ and exchanges $[C_2]$ are described as affecting each of these different social forces. For Davis, these forces cause social psychological changes within the self. These changes determine interactions that feedback to determine further changes in the self. This continuous, symbolic interaction serves to either facilitate or complicate the effects of each force on the development of the relationship. This is depicted in Table 8.2 by the influence of stage $[C_3]$ on interactions $[C_1]$ and exchanges $[C2]$, which then shape the relational stage $[C_3]$. In particular, Davis (1973) devoted one chapter to the favors—social exchanges—that intimates do for each other. The benefits accrued from such exchanges may be facilitative only in certain phases of intimacy:

> The closest of intimates are connected not merely by mutual benefits, but by mutual being. Consequently, their relationship cannot be adequately described in terms of the cost and value of the favors they give and receive. They would find the whole economic rhetoric used to describe lesser intimacies to be completely inappropriate for describing their own relationships. If the economics of intimacy constitutes the substructure of personal relations, for close friends, at least, it is a phenomenologically invisible one. Should it surface in their consciousness at all, they consider their relationship to be breaking down. (Davis, 1973, p.166)

Interestingly, it is precisely this economic rhetoric that Scanzoni (1979) employs to account for such phenomena as trust and commitment. Applying social exchange principles, Scanzoni (1979) described stages of behavioral interdependence, rather than of phenomenological closeness. He explained the emergence of trust as the belief, tested over time, that ones' partner is willing to cooperate toward the mutual benefit of both. When one fulfills and exceeds obligations, the other becomes "more willing to negotiate even more complex arrangements" that involve greater trust. This and other changes in interdependence $[C_2]$ are the central and continuous source of phasic change $[C_3]$ in Scanzoni's model. Stages, by definition, differ in interdependence.

The dissolution or breakdown and SDR models of phasic context view both interaction and exchange as peripheral to but highly influencing transition. Either interaction or exchange is necessary for adjustment in SDR. In Table 8.2, this is depicted as $[C_1]$-$[C_2]$ interfacing with $[C_3]$. Unless there is some negotiation of maintenance and repair $[C_1]$-$[C_2]$, breakdown $[C_3]$ is more likely within the dissolution models. In both models, negotiation plays an important part in transition, whether it is a transition toward termination or toward a new family life. This negotiation is an ongoing process where couples adjust, adapt, and reorganize in SDR. Such a process is necessary for the move from a nuclear to a binuclear family. In contrast, negotiation plays either a minimal or no role in "full-break," or rapid disengagement trajectories. In dissolution models, then, interaction is often seen as having an ameliorative (but not essential) impact on breakdown.

Summary

Time: the familiar stranger
—J. T. Fraser

It may be gathered from a review of Table 8.2 that it is possible to distinguish theories, models, and perspectives within a single temporal framework. In fact, each theory can be seen as a variation on temporal emphasis; some concerned more with the prediction of transitions, others more with changes in psychological outcomes. Admittedly, the description of each model in the tripartite distinction requires understanding them in broad terminology.

However, time is a slippery topic; my purpose was to move us toward greater clarity and specificity on temporal distinctions that otherwise lurk between the lines, that is, in theorist's use of terms like *development*, *change*, and *trend*.

The next section outlines a synthesis of the models reviewed. A unified model is proposed that attends specifically to the nature of the relations between each of the three temporal contexts. In several of the theories reviewed, authors did point out relations between each of the contexts. The last column of Table 8.2 highlights, in diagrammatic form, these relationships. The models put forward by Altman and colleagues (Altman & Taylor, 1973; Altman et al., 1981), and by Levinger (1983) probably consider the interrelations of interaction, situation, and phase more than any of the others. I expand on these ideas by developing a more explicit set of relationships. In providing this model, I hope to hint at some grammar of time in relationships, a grammar that may be more precise in its appreciation of relationship process.

TOWARD A UNIFIED MODEL OF TIME IN RELATIONSHIPS

> Partners in developing relationships must engage in calibration of the relationship (Watzlawick et al., 1967), establishing rules, norms, or principles by which the relationship is to operate as a unique system. . . . Mutuality of relationship definition requires that the two individuals agree about the redundancies characterizing their exchange, where the redundant configurations summarily define the relationship. (Morton & Douglas, 1981, pp. 24–25)

> A key conclusion in the general organizational life-cycle literature is its clear-eyed insistence that the social organizations lack any fixed developmental sequence (e.g., Kimberly, 1980). This conclusion leads to the view of development as transformation, looking at . . . changes in the social form of a particular dyad, without any necessary concern for the directionality of their sequence. Just as water can pass directly from any of its phases—vapor, liquid, solid—to any other, so a Richard Burton/Liz Taylor relationship can resemble a "random walk" alternation among a variety of social forms and two young children can be friends, rivals, or enemies on different days of the week. (McCall, 1988, p. 479)

Consider some ordinary questions sometimes asked about relationships. How is it that a single interaction between two people can seemingly change the course of a relationship? Why is it that some periods in a relationship are fraught with more conflict than others? How do some couples manage to stay "faithful" and married for 30, 40, sometimes 50 years, whereas others divorce within a month? Although personal relationship research has begun to answer some of these questions, they entail some recognition that time plays an important role in relationships, or at least, in our ordinary—common-sense—conceptions of those relationships. I have examined the contextual aspects of 18 different models or theories of personal relationships and have applied a temporal scale to nine representative studies. Together, these analyses point to subtleties and complexities in relationship processes that resist a straightforward and simple classification. The model proposed here is derived from the logic of systems theory (Berscheid, 1986; Bertalanffy, 1968). Specifically, I have attempted to synthesize the conceptual aspects of each model as diagrammed in the final column of Table 8.2. The reader is again encouraged to use Table 8.2 as a reference tool as each of these diagrams served as building blocks for the model proposed here.

A Coherent Grammar of Time in Relationships

The different terms we use to describe the temporal aspects of human relationships do not, in themselves, provide a view of these relationships as ongoing or as processual. Given the many biases outlined in chapter 7—individuocentric, methodological convenience, truncation of temporal perspective, and unexamined assumptions from the natural sciences—social scientists tend to study relationships as static, cause and effect, phenomena. To fully appreciate the ever-changing nature of personal relationships, we should clearly articulate—or at least hypothesize—the relationships between the processes that occur within relationships.

The hypothetical model presented (see Fig. 8.1) construes relationships as both acting on (cf. time shaping) and representing the temporal world; that is, the three temporal contexts that make up the temporal world. Similar to Bandura's (1977) notion of "reciprocal determinism," there is a mutually interactive process between couple behavior, their temporal environment, and their cognitive representation of that environment. More specifically, there are four proposed pathways through which this mutual interaction continually unfolds. (a) Through interaction sequences, couples allocate time (schedule, time-budget) so that future situations become predictable and salient; (b) through interaction sequences, couples talk about their relationship in ways that define and transform their history; (c) within and across situations, partners adapt to different roles and rules (routines) which in turn govern their interactions; also, different situations make certain outcomes salient and, consequently, arouse certain psychological motives when partners interact; (d) within and across phases, couples show different degrees of adherence to cultural norms (expectations concerning age and relationship type) and pace their interactions accordingly.[6]

Through time allocation and relationship talk, couples act on the temporal world. Through role adaptation and sociotemporal pacing, couples represent the temporal world. This process of action and representation occurs "contemporaneously" (Lewin, 1951); the temporal world is ever "present" and ongoing. In addition to these four main pathways of temporality, relationships have an organizational life cycle. Independent of any specific face-to-face interaction, or set of interactions, the phases and situations cohere. Paraphrasing earlier quotes, relationships have an "organizational persistence" (Kelley, 1979) even after long periods of absence, and couples may find the "vitiated organizational skeleton" (M. S. Davis, 1973) of their relationship continues on its own.

Actions on Temporal World of the Relationship

The model proposed here (see Fig. 8.1) assumes that relationships are inherently transformational. The actions partners take with regard to their relationship determine, to a large degree, their representations of the relationship (e.g., previous quotes of Morton & Douglas, and McCall; see also Duck & Sants, 1983). Whereas many of those actions occur while couples are together, they also occur while they are apart, that is, between interactions or between situations. However, when couples are together, specific interactions will influence those times when they are not together, times that exist in both the immediate and distant future. There are two special types of things that couples do in this regard: They allocate time to their lives together and apart through scheduling and time budgeting; and they talk about their relationship, try to understand each other and reach a mutual definition of where they have been, where they are going, and where they are (Harvey, Agostinelli, & Weber, 1989).

Couples do not always or frequently engage in direct talk about the relationship, per se. However, their otherwise routine communications (cf. "redundancies," Morton & Douglas, 1981) have the effect of creating some degree of consensus (cf. "metaperspective," Acitelli & Duck, 1987) about the status of their relationship. Through time allocation (McGrath, 1988) couples transform their future situation and exchanges. When they interact, partners

---

RESEARCH   REFLECTION   17

ACTING ON THE TEMPORAL WORLD

There is a special set of actions—called routine maintenance—through which couples stabilize their temporal world. Communication scientists (Dainton & Stafford, 1993) have developed a list of such behaviors and found some occur more frequently than others. The following list (shown in order with most common first) gives some examples. It is interesting that small talk (not as deep as openness) occurs less frequently. This suggests that the main way of acting on the temporal world occurs through meaningful communication, not just plain talk. How much do you engage in routine maintenance?

1. **Positivity** (I try to be upbeat, buy gifts, tell jokes, apologize, act politely).
2. **Openness** (I try to share my feelings, discuss problems we are having, give and get advice, listen without judging).
3. **Assurances** (I try to make her feel better, say "I love you," make future plans, am faithful).
4. **Sharing tasks/joint activities** (I cook dinner, provide financial support).
5. **Talk** (We get together to just talk, we talk about our day).

necessarily cue or signal if, when, and how they will interact again. By prioritizing certain situations over others, they are creating discriminative cues. For example, communications such as "I'll see you later tonight," "I really enjoyed the park on Sunday," and "I don't know when I'll be back" contain information that influences current and future interaction scenarios. Through narrative, couples may transform the transitions and forms of their relationship (e.g., lovers, friends, strangers).

It is important to stress that face-to-face interactions often do not include explicit verbal narration about the relationship (i.e., metacommunication or "this is what I think is happening in the relationship, what about you?"). Rather, the things that are not said—emotions, postures, gestures, and nonverbal aspects of the interaction—can communicate much about the state and, consequently, the phase of the relationship. Also, when talking ("talking things out") does not work, couple's experience emotion (see Berscheid, 1983; Buck, 1989), which in turn serves a language function. Through emotion, partners communicate to each other the "ongoingness" of their own successes and failures at relationship definition and time allocation (Staske, 1999). Responsiveness to these communications can lead to enhanced coordination of schedules and enhanced mutual definition.

Representation of the Temporal World of the Relationship

Couple actions on the temporal world of their relationship do not, however, operate in a vacuum. Both the biotemporal world of daily, monthly, and life cycle changes in partner physiology and the sociotemporal world of changing customs and habits signal to partners when certain relationship transactions are appropriate (cf. contextualization cues; Gumperz, 1982). Thus, biotemporal factors and sociotemporal pacing affect pair member's representation of their temporal world (e.g., cultural punctuation; Levine, 1988). Couple's have temporal representations about a variety of relational factors that are determined by culture and environment. Although these representations lie within the stories or accounts couples give of their relationships (Harvey et al. 1990; Sternberg, 1999), timings in the external world have an influence. Dating couples are more likely to breakup at certain points during the school year (Hill et al., 1976). Individuals in later stages of courtship, relative to individuals in the early stages of courtship, spend less time with their social network less often (Milardo, Johnson, & Huston, 1983). Women who did not adhere to either masculine norm (e.g., professional training by age 28) or feminine norm (e.g., having child by age 28) social clocks are shown to suffer a variety of psychological problems (Helson et al., 1984). Thus seasonal changes, network changes in courtship commitment, age-related norms, and other sociotemporal pacers all effect couple's temporal arrangement of their lives.

In tandem with these pacers, the situations that couples enter also effect their temporal representation. We have seen that partners' love feelings and their

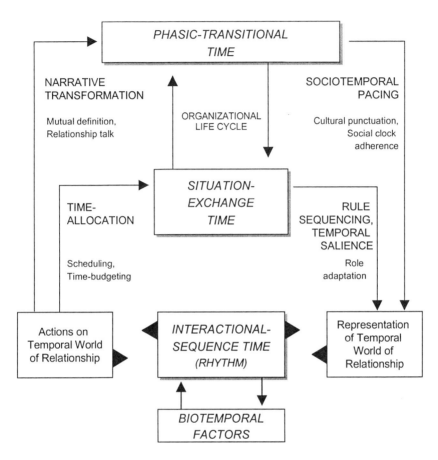

FIG. 8.1. Personal relationships calibrate across three temporal contexts.

interdependence changes, as do their needs for privacy and togetherness. In addition, situational changes effect pair members' temporal salience or the degree to which their thoughts about the relationship are relatively past, present, or future oriented (Werner & Haggard, 1985). For example, certain shared possessions and places trigger memories of the past, anticipation of partner's future behaviors in a situation can influence current behaviors toward one's mate, and partner's current satisfaction is determined by some synthesis of remembered, currently assessed, and future predicted rewards and costs. As the relationship itself becomes temporally salient, pair members represent it as having a continuous identity that outlives any particular interaction of the "contemporaneous" moment.

But representations of relationships do not proceed through memory and anticipation alone. This temporal salience also interacts with rules that individuals have to apply in carrying out their interactions. If the couple is to have a viable social relationship, possessing real and not just imagined continuity, then they must follow particular rules (cf. "interaction rituals," Goffman, 1967) within interactions and across situations. In other words, time allocation does not operate in a social vacuum. For example, one of the clearest interaction predictors of marital distress is the "self-summarizing syndrome" (Gottman et al., 1976) in which partners interrupt and mind-read, and generally give little indication that they want a dialogue. Thus, couples must forge certain rules or "redundant configurations" if they are to articulate a schema of their relationship as existing across situations. They may need to exercise "entry level" communication skills of soothing, nondefensive listening, and validation (Gottman, 1994b). As suggested by the "continuous loop" aspects of Fig. 8.1, this process (representation–interaction–narration) continues until couples are better able to allocate time and actively transform and give organization and coherence to their relationship.

Organizational Life Cycle

Theories suggest that relationships are entities that adapt to changes (Rodgers, 1987), respond to social forces (M. S. Davis, 1973), negotiate through stages (e.g., Duck, 1982, 1984), and are strategically communicated (Baxter, 1988). They are frameworks of "trust, stable expectations, and practices within which intimate interactions are more likely," and where mutual feelings of care, in turn, foster greater commitment to the relationship (Reis & Shaver, 1988). In short, relationships are organizations that exist apart from any set of interactions or situational exchanges. They have a life of their own. In the current model, the organizational life cycle arises from transactions between situation–exchange time and phasic–transitional time.

As couples coordinate outcomes and agree on a mutual definition, their interactions become increasingly liberated from the job of maintaining, repairing, scheduling or in short, organizing, their relationship. If they do not live in a fast-paced, future time-oriented culture, then this "freeing up" allows them more time to just be together. It is this time of being together for the sake of being together, which represents the durational, transcendental aspect of time that may be central to a spiritual understanding of human relationships. Few of the contemporary psychological theories reviewed (although see M. S. Davis, 1973) examine or incorporates this spiritual aspect of relationship time.

Organizational life cycle (McCall, 1988) represents the cyclical changes that occur as couples experience changes in each of the other four components in the model. Changes in scheduling and rule sequencing require couples to cycle through their interactions in search of rules, routines, roles, and habits. Changes in mutual relationship definition and sociotemporal pacing require couples to coordinate schedules in order to be together, "to talk" about these changes. These two cycles of change can account for the dialectical changes described in Baxter's (1988) and Altman et al.'s (1981) theories of relationship cycle. Openness–closedness and change–stability are simply manifestations of the organizational life cycle. Couples allocate psychological time apart (closedness) and together (openness) because of the varying requirements they have described in their mutual relationship definition. When interactions are liberated from organizational maintenance, then "things handle themselves." Interactions become more predictable, and the relationship is in a stable phase of its organizational cycle unless or until the laws of chaos take hold. Again, when there are changes in allocation, narration, pacing, rules, or salience, then the relationship experiences some instability until partners take action and re-erect their temporal world. Thus, there is a continuous cycling between action and representation, as indicated in Fig. 8.1.

Calibration

> Several years into my own marriage we went through a painful struggle lasting more than a year. We talked and sorted and tried new approaches, new agreements. The pain went on. His hopes vs. my fears. His fears vs. my trust. Each time the tension was close to snapping the cord that holds us together, one would back off, not caving in or giving up, but easing off, putting a little slack in the cord so we would have room to keep searching. Finally, a resolution began to emerge. By engaging in a discipline of time and listening and faith and love, we found an outcome that allowed each of us to feel more loved, more deeply understood, and more free to grow. (McBee, 1994, p. 8)

I now return to the quote by Morton and Douglas (1986) at the start of this section. Personal relationship researchers and theorists have begun to adapt a view of relationships as *transformational*. People's talk about relationships, whether it serves to frame the temporal duration of the relationship (Duck, 1994; Duck & Pond, 1989), or the navigational function of making it through a critical turning-point (Baxter & Bullis, 1986), has become a key variable in understanding time in personal relationships (also see Sternberg, 1999).

This transformational function of narrative links the current model with previous models of text (chap. 2), time shaping (chap. 4), script (chap. 5), and context (chap. 6). First, through talking about their relationship, couples can move from being "in their heads" (transcription) to actually changing the nature of their relationship and deepen their experience of intimacy (recall Quality 6, intimacy as the capacity to change). Second, talking—in the sense of planning and scheduling—shapes the couples future. Third, by talking in conscious and mindful ways, partners can examine the scripts that they project onto their partners (cf. imagos, Hendrix, 1992) and gain insight into archescripts. Finally, conversation helps couples to see their relationship in context and helps them navigate many contexts. Thus, a core aspect of interaction time—relationship talk and narrative—can impact relationship phase by transforming the couple.

However, as demonstrated by Fig. 8.1, this talk or narrative represents only one half of the equation, as it were. Recall from the discussion in chapter 7 of the "temporal initiative" that communication scientists tend to emphasize talk, social psychologists tend to emphasize person–situation interaction, and sociologists tend to emphasize organizational phenomena. A view of relationships that is sensitive to its processual nature would give equal emphasis to all of these factors (i.e., to the co-created and living context described in chap. 4). Each has different time lines that form a nexus in the ongoing relationship (cf. relata). Because humans are living beings and because they are constantly processing information from each of these contexts, this nexus is an active regulation of feedback and feed forward processes; it is a constant cycling between action and representation.

Morton and Douglas borrowed the term *calibration* from Watzlawick et al. (1967) in an allusion to these ongoing processes. *Webster's Ninth New Collegiate Dictionary* defines *calibrate* as "to standardize (as a measuring instrument) by determining the deviation from a standard so as to ascertain the proper correction factors."

According to the foregoing logic, *in time* relationships continually respond to behavioral (action) and representational differences and changes among its members. The entire process that I have sketched out may be viewed as a calibration of different temporal components. All temporal phenomena that arise as a function of two people coming together may be understood as a function of calibration in their relationship. If one measures a guided missile on it's trajectory toward a target, then the great majority of the time it is off-track. Mostly, it deviates and then responds to the deviation by over shooting the

---

RESEARCH   REFLECTION   18

CALIBRATION REQUIRES COMMUNICATION SKILLS

Communication scientists have developed a questionnaire that taps how partners calibrate relationships through communication skills (Burleson et al., 1996). Specifically, the *regulative skill* scale assesses whether one's partner has the ability to help one who has violated a norm—or deviated from a set of expectations—to fix the mistake effectively. Consider these items (adapted from Burleson et. al., 1996).

1. My partner helps me see why my actions broke a social rule or norm.
2. My partner makes me see how my mistakes hurt myself as well as other people.
3. My partner takes time to work through my mistakes with me.

hypothetical straight line it traverses. Importantly, that straight line is hypothetical. It does not exist. Rather, the reality is the moment-to-moment calibration around that straight line as the missile moves toward its goal. Like relationships, it somehow represents that hypothetical line and then acts in response.[7]

This ability to calibrate, to represent and act and represent and act, is what keeps the whole process moving with direction and organization. Patricia McBee noted "His hopes vs. my fears. His fears vs. my trust," as though describing this ongoing, back-and-forth calibration across strong emoti nal situations, which ultimately resulted in some deeper sense of intimacy.

Calibration is related to the transpersonal theme described in earlier chapters. In many personal accounts of satisfying and intimate marriages, individuals talk about the growing ability to "get along" with their partner, to work with, calibrate around, and ultimately transmute differences. This is the long-term or phasic aspect of calibration. For example, Borys (1991, pp. 112–113) wrote about his marriage: "We have been attracted to each other by our differences, and our differences have caused innumerable disagreements. Sometimes Susan's qualities have guided our growth, and at other times mine have led the way. But gradually, ever so gradually, we are absorbing what is best in each other and are becoming more whole." Bo Lozoff, (in Swift, 1996; p. 54) married for 30 years, talked about how this process takes time: "We were talking about the sacred journey and the point in marriage at which you've seen the other in every possible light, the very ugliest and worst and most evil, as well as the most divine and compassionate. There's no way to do that in a short time. . . . There is a gradual deepening and an enlightenment that come over time."

Maintenance of the organizational life cycle requires mutual relationship redefinitions and time re-allocation. These occur in response to changes in representations. These representations themselves are influenced by changing situational salience and sociotemporal pacers. Calibration is an ideal state that occurs when all of these processes are synchronized, when partner's schedules are synchronized; their definitions of the relationship are in agreement; they are keeping pace with their social clock; and they are managing the rules and roles of the relationship amidst changing psychological situations. Changes in any of these states leads to changes in all others. Because of the inherent complexity of all these "mechanisms," relationships can be subject to "chaotic attractors" and cycle through periods of upheaval and transformation very rapidly. Couple interaction is then required and it plays a pivotal role in attempts at recalibration.

At times, the relationship can become temporarily self-regulating and liberated through coordination of all four temporal components across the three temporal contexts. But living organisms, being what they are, do not "march forward with undisturbed poise" as Whitehead (1968) told us. In time, couples will either seek or, through situation and society, be forced to redefine their temporal worlds. And, perhaps after a certain point, couples may discern the conditions for intimacy to ripen without any additional effort on their part (cf. yüan). Thus, between chaos and structure and between time shaping and facilitative conditions, couples may learn to narrate, calibrate and transform their relationships in time.

End Notes—Chapter 8

1. Current review is not exhaustive. This review is not meant to be exhaustive and leaves out a number of theories that, it could be argued, may be more time-sensitive than the ones listed here. There are, for example, a number of theories that place major emphasis on interpersonal and marital communication (e.g., Berlo, 1960; Knapp, 1984) and theories about the family life cycle (e.g., Olson et al., 1983) that have not been considered here. The purpose of this study, however, is not a thorough review of the literature, but to provide enough examples in order to demonstrate how we can think about time in relationships in a new and different way. I do not assess the adequacy, viability, or parsimony of any of the models here. I only use them as examples for demonstration and application of the contextual framework developed throughout preceding chapters.

2. Extant theories focus on causality not conditionality. The current chapter, although focused on the empirical/scientific approach to time and intimacy, seeks to bring together ideas developed throughout the entire book, particularly chapter 4. For example, the theories reviewed tend to view time as either inherent in the stages couples go through (external cycles, external developments) (i.e., as reflecting temporal structure) or as created by the couple as a function of their actions (i.e., as reflecting time shaping). The theories define time in terms of causality. It will be recalled from chapter 4, that time can also be defined in terms of conditionality or nurturing conditions. In the broad model of temporal forces proposed in chapter 4, time is not only about structure and action but also about chaos and nurturing conditions. Many conditions are continually woven through the interplay of the four temporal forces. A review of the discussion of nurturing conditions and of chaos may be helpful. The 18 theories reviewed in this chapter do not contain any explicit reference to this conditionality. The theories here may be construed as "point attractor" or "periodic attractor" theories but not "strange or chaotic attractor" theories (see also p. 117).

3. Commitment. The importance of commitment for understanding time and intimacy has been described in previous models, especially in chapter 6. There we saw that we can make gradual and unconscious choices that commit us to unhealthy lines of action. The social psychological (situational–exchange) theories described in this chapter also focus on the process of commitment. In contrast, the phasic theories focus on commitment more as a given and its relative presence or absence as the defining characteristic of a stage or phase. Thus, we can see three broad distinctions in commitment. First, as a decision to follow—to make a choice—according to a certain sequence of behaviors without much attention to the ultimate consequences of those behaviors (chap. 6). Second, as a process that brings two individuals beyond just mere interaction into, at least, interacting across several situations (situation time). Finally, as a decision to make the relationship an entity, as through marriage (phasic time).

4. Rules. The reader may wish to refer to the more extended discussion on rules in chapter 4 (see Research Notes on Time Shaping) and chapter 6 (see particularly the section on

Temporality in Sociology). The fact that partners use rules in idiosyncratic fashion attests to the uniquely private aspects of intimacy. There comes a point for some when intimacy is defined by breaking the societal rules given to a couple and where they find their own unique (i.e., "dispositional" or personality determined) set of rules. Whether rules are inherited, idiosyncratic, fixed, or changeable, they play an important role in providing a context and helping couples to create meaning. Thus, "dispositional interdependence" is a term that reflects a point in which the weave of contexts has resulted in some discernible, interpersonal, and unique tapestry.

5. Relationship dissolution, chaos, and scripts. It is interesting that models of relationship breakup allow for great variability in the staging of those breakups. From the point of view of the temporal forces model (chap. 4), this supports the idea that chaos is a real force that couples strain to deal with and that, by definition, relationship dissolution may not conform to any neat set of stages. In fact, the view of deterioration in Levinger's stage model has been re-interpreted in the language of chaos theory (Baron, Amazeen, & Beek, 1994). From the point of view of the script model (chap. 5), individuals may have to summon and continually re-arrange a multitude of script elements in order to make sense of breakups (see Battaglia et al., 1998).

6. Four pathways of mutual interaction parallel with ideas in previous chapters. Each of these features relates to some aspect of models presented earlier. For example, the philemic effectiveness of relationship talk (Path b); that is, whether it really transforms the couple at deeper levels of intimacy, depends on their use of text (see chap. 2). Through time allocation (Path a) and relationship talk (Path b), couples essentially time shape (chap. 4). How couples adapt to rules, roles (Path c), and norms (Path d) represents the way relationship structure influences them (chap 4). The salience of situations (Path a), the arousal of particular motives (Path b) depends upon how overly scripted couples are (Chapter 5). These parallels are discussed in chapter 9.

7. On Calibration and Goffman's Interaction rituals. Many examples of calibration that occur in everyday conversation may also be found in the work of Goffman, especially in his book *Interaction Ritual* (1967). Whereas Goffman does not use the term *calibration*, many of his examples show how social situations are defined by the delicate give and take required to maintain organization in social interaction. For example, Goffman (1976) describes how talk keeps everyone from "saving face" in his essay on face work.

Thus when one person volunteers a message, thereby contributing what might easily be a threat to the ritual equilibrium, someone else present is obliged to show that the message has been received and that its content is acceptable to all concerned or can be easily countered. This acknowledging reply, of course, may contain a tactful rejection of the original communication, along with a request for modification. In such cases, several exchanges of messages may be required before the interchange is terminated on modified lines. The interchange comes to a close when it is possible to allow it to do so—that is, when everyone present has signified that he has been ritually appeased to a degree satisfactory to him. (p. 38)

Goffman is helpful reading for understanding the importance of talk and narrative as a calibrating function in relationships.

I swear by the time,
Everyone is in a state of loss,
Except for those who believe and do good and
join together in truth, patience, and constancy

—The Holy Qu'ran
(Chapter 103: Al-Asr; The Eventide)

⧗

The reason that we want life to mean something, that we
seek God or eternal life, is not merely that we are trying to
get away from an immediate experience of pain. Nor is it
for any such reason that we assume attitudes and roles as
habits of perpetual self-defense. The real problem does not
come from any momentary sensitivity to pain, but from our
marvelous powers of memory and foresight—in short from
our consciousness of time. (Watts, 1951, pp. 32–33).

9

Summary and Integration:
Toward a Transpersonal Science

I HAVE tried to delineate, in various ways and with seven different models, the relation between three main ideas: time, intimacy, and transpersonal experience. The task remains to summarize and integrate these models and ideas. Before integration, it will help to review the three main ideas as they have somewhat different definitions within each model.

TIME

Throughout, this book has explained how we can be more sensitive to the influence of time on intimate relationships as well as the influence of relationship on time. Because of the diverse perspectives used, my definition of time has varied across models. In Model 1 (chap. 2), time was experienced, framed, and understood differently depending on the *type of interaction* between two people (e.g., transaction vs. transformation). This first model developed the notion that personal interaction, through textual change, can actually create our experience of time; that is, interactions have a textual quality catalyzed by intimacy (e.g., ongoingness). In Model 2 (chap. 3), time was qualitatively and inherently different depending on the *type of relationship* in which intimacy was experienced. For example, learning about oneself requires knowing one's personal rhythms while a partnership entails journeying through time.

These two models focused more on the experience of time—whether experienced through interaction or through different types of relationship. In contrast, the next model (chap. 4) viewed relationships as themselves having different temporal features. These features are manifestations of temporal tendencies or forces (e.g., toward chaos or toward structure). Time was viewed across four quadrants of phasic tendencies. These temporal "forces" may or may not be external to the relationship, and relationships express or manifest them. Model 3 (chap. 4) introduced the idea that context—as nurturing condition—is itself a force or tendency rather than a logical abstraction. Thus, in reality, the abstract text of interaction described in Model 1 is never separate from the situation or context in which it unfolds. However, individuals bring to relationships their own idiosyncratic orientations toward text, or scripts.

These scripts are discussed in Model 4 (chap. 5) as cognitions that individuals embody within their personality and relationships. Here, time is

DIFFERENT PERSPECTIVES OF TIME ACROSS THE 7 MODELS

EXPERIENCED MOMENT TO MOMENT

Experience of time varies as interaction shifts in textual quality and is catalyzed by intimacy

1

EXPERIENCED THROUGH RELATION TYPE

Experience of time varies in different types of relationship

2

MANIFESTS QUALITIES OF RELATIONSHIP

Relationships are shaped by and manifest temporal qualities that can be observed

3

RELATED TO AS "OTHER"

Individuals "script" time with others through scripts, archescripts, and holoscripts

4

UNDERSTOOD THROUGH CONTEXT

Relationship events have meaning according to their place in different contexts

5

POSSESSES OBSERVABLE QUALITIES

Time in relationships has measurable qualities (e.g., length, sequence)

6

COUPLES RELATE TO TIME

Time is continuously acted on and represented within relationships

7

itself the "other" to which we relate as both individual and as partner. Time is not something experienced through interaction (Model 1), associated with relationship type (Model 2), or a feature of relationships (Model 3). In infancy and childhood, we learn (in healthy and not so healthy ways) to structure or give sequence to social time through scripts. Model 4 (chap. 5) attempts to show that these interpersonal or behavioral scripts are not simply conditioned by culture and environment, but are also informed by even deeper scripts called archescripts and holoscripts. To summarize ideas in Model 4, our relationship to time as "other" is informed by aspects of our personal experience and unique history (scripts), which are informed or shaped by how others in humanity's history have experienced time through human relationship (archescript). These archescripts are also determined and unified by the universal story (holoscript) alluded to in religion, cosmology, and mythology.

In Model 5 (chap. 6), the definition of time shifts to a less personal and more scientific perspective. The chapter focuses on the concept of temporal context and shows how relationships are made up of many such contexts. Intimacy, in the sense of knowing another, requires the ability to make sense of and give meaning to the other and to the relationship. Temporal context is the tool through which such meaning is ascribed. The chapter serves to also make distinctions between two epistemologies of time: as experienced through lover's knowing, and as used to measure and study personal relationships by scientists.

Model 6 (chap. 7) elaborates on the scientific use of temporal context and develops a schema for assessing methodological sensitivity to time. Unlike previous models, time here is seen purely as an objective matter. For example, it is studied as interval, length, sequence, and phase. Model 7 (chap. 8) continues to use the scientific view of time and examines how theories of personal relationships are sensitive to temporal context. Through an analysis of these theories, a new interdisciplinary model is developed that attempts to integrate three core temporal contexts: interaction, situation, and phase. Here time is something that couples both act on (through narrative and scheduling) and cognitively represent (through culture and pacing).

INTIMACY

Just as time has received different definitions throughout this book, so has the concept of intimacy. The phrase used in chapter 2, *intimacy as text*, conveys the use of text as a metaphor for the intimate process. Model 1 alluded to many different qualities of intimacy (ongoingness, wholeness, capacity to change, sensitivity to context) that text—by itself—reflects and mimics. As such, intimacy is a multidimensional phenomenon that we capture with language and poetry. It is itself defined through such language and poetry. Model 1 introduced a central paradox alluded to throughout the book. At one level, relational interactions use text to become intimate, but at another level intimacy is defined by the abandonment of this same text.

In Model 2, intimacy, like time, is defined by the type of relationship involved. Importantly, relationship intimacy, or co-journeying, is defined by sharing time and by how two individuals relate to, use, and record time. Intimacy is defined as two individuals being together through time. So here, time and intimacy are joined in definition. In Model 3, intimacy is also defined by one's relationship to time; specifically, the degree to which one is *present, flowing,* and attuned to *coincidence or synchronicity.* Although the previous models described qualities or definitions of intimacy, Model 3 discusses the capacity for intimacy. Implicit in the model are the notions that intimacy develops as one remains present and flowing while a myriad of temporal forces impinge on a relationship.

Model 4 defined intimacy as a process involving a conscious partnership:

> As a process, intimacy occurs as two or more individuals (a) recognize, communicate, and change their own addictive scripts—in short, they are willing to reveal character flaws or darker, more hidden aspects of their selves. In doing so, individuals (b) embrace how they unconsciously and mindlessly project latent scripts onto each other (archescript)—in short, they learn more about these hidden parts of their being and find a deep commonality (similarity or complementarity) to these parts.

DIFFERENT PERSPECTIVES OF
INTIMACY ACROSS THE 7 MODELS

QUALITIES EXPERIENCED VIA TEXT

Qualities of intimacy emerge as
we work through and
1 abandon text

EXPERIENCE VARIES ACROSS RELATION

Intimacy means different things
in different relationship
2 types (e.g., self, other, God)

CULTIVATED AS A CAPACITY (PRESENCE)

Awareness of temporality in
relationships requires presence,
flow, and synchroncity
3

CONSCIOUS PARTNERSHIP

Self-awareness of scripts is key to
(intra-, inter-, and trans-)
personal intimacy
4

COGNITION OF PATTERNS IN TIME

Intimacy is domain of both
scientists and lovers:
It entails "Knowing"
5

PHENOMENON TO BE STUDIED

The true study of intimacy
involves sensitivity to
temporal context
6

COUPLE RESPONSIVENESS TO CHANGE

Intimacy lies in how partners
respond to moment to
moment changes
7

Whereas Model 3 described intimacy as an individual capacity, Model 4 attempted to show how the various blocks to intimacy inevitably requires putting this capacity into action—that is, making an ongoing and concerted effort to uncover and relinquish ways in which one distorts or projects onto one's partner. Intimacy is the art of "embracing" these darker parts with one's partner. Model 5 takes a more objective or cognitive approach to defining intimacy. Intimacy involves the apprehension and comprehension of patterns that can only emerge in time and the use of context as an aid in this perception. Thus, like Model 2, intimacy and time were joined in definition. Model 2 (chap. 3) focused on the couple moving together through time. Model 5 (chap. 4) focused on the cognition of patterns that arise through this movement. Because the focus is on the perception of pattern, individuals both within as well as outside the relationship (scientists) are privy to this form of intimate knowing.

The final chapters elaborated on this last definition by exploring methodology for perceiving pattern (chap. 7) and by discussing how relationship theories of other authors take glimpses at pattern (chap. 8). The last model also offered a process model of personal relationships where relationships were seen as constantly changing in relation to the temporal world. Intimacy is shaped as couple's become more responsive when calibrating their relationships to change.

TRANSPERSONAL INTIMACY

Throughout this book, I have attempted to describe the spiritual side of intimacy. This idea is best summarized through the philosophers and poets (quoted earlier):

> *To care for one's neighbor more than oneself, to take on responsibility for the Other, . . . is to enter into a sacred rather than an ontological or epistemological history.* –Levinas

> *Self-transformation is precisely what life is, and human relationships, which are an extract of life, are the most changeable of all, rising and falling from minute to minute, and lovers are those in whose relationship and contact no one moment resembles another.* –Rilke

In essence, to know and be known by another, to care for another, requires greater and greater degrees of selflessness. Because relationships are ever-changing, one's attachment to self, to the way things are, are constantly put to the test. I have tried to describe how, through relationship, the spiritual element of life infiltrates our experience of intimacy and, conversely, how intimacy often gives us an important foundation for spirituality. This is one form of the time-intimacy equation described in the preface.

Chapter 2 explained how, as individuals let go of their preconceptions and scripts (text), they transcend differences between them and are able to weave a relationship together. Here, the transpersonal aspect of intimacy was defined as a progressive series of turning points through text; particularly from meaning (making sense of the other), to meeting (changed by and with the other), to flowing and detaching from outcomes. Chapter 3 defined the transpersonal aspect of intimacy more specifically in the realm of faith and spiritual connection to a higher power. However, this form of intimacy in one's life has radical implications and reverberations within one's more mundane relationships. Unlike chapter 2, transpersonal intimacy does not come in linear stages but can permeate all types of relationship.

The key ideas in chapter 4 that pertain to transpersonal intimacy were those of facilitative or nurturing conditions and time transcendence. Here, relationships were seen as possessing conditions or pre-potent tendencies for the creation of spiritual connection between two individuals. By learning how to slow down and listen, the chapter argued that individuals can develop sensitivity to and cultivate these conditions. In so doing, the relationship becomes a vehicle for the transcendence of time altogether. From a broader perspective, the entire chapter conceived of relationships as a vehicle for enlightenment. By paying attention, staying present to, and working with the myriad features—the pattern—of change, the relationship becomes a teacher of lessons in impermanence, compassion, vulnerability, and creativity.

ASPECTS OF TRANSPERSONAL INTIMACY IN THE 7 MODELS

LETTING GO (DETACHMENT) OF TEXT

Transcend separateness
through real-time dissolving
of pre-conceptions

1

FAITH

Having the faith that one will see
and understand events, and
situations (the "BIG" picture)

2

NURTURING CONDITIONS

Developing sensitivity to timing,
transitions, entrainment and
sharp awareness of yuän

3

SELF-OBSERVATION

Becoming aware of and letting
go of the "scripted self"

4

MYSTERY

Always knowing that there is the
unknown of the "other"

5

INTERRELATEDNESS (CONTEXTUALITY)

Empirically deduced
comprehension of the big
(multivariate) picture

6

INTERRELATEDNESS (CALIBRATION)

Harnessing calibration of action
upon and representation of
temporal world

7

Whereas chapter 4 showed how a personal study of change and relationship becomes a spiritual vehicle, chapter 5 explored how a personal study of one's own self (script) can reveal deeper meanings (archescript) to ordinary events. As individuals, we may work through relationship issues through dreams, journaling, and fascination with certain myths and stories. These various methods become paths for developing more personal understanding and insight into the bigger picture of relationship. In Model 4 (chap. 5), the transpersonal was conceived as connection to both the deep past of humanity and transcendent universal principles. Relationships, particularly their difficulties and problems, become vehicles for insight into this connectedness.

Chapter 6 dealt with the transpersonal theme by discussing how ways of knowing may or may not entail a spiritual sense or connectedness. This chapter noted Buber's distinction between the "I–It" and the "I–You" world, and mentioned that we can lose perspective by focusing on the empirical march of the "It-world" and neglect the true, the good, and the beautiful of the "You-world." Alternatively, we gain perspective by enriching the context of study to include both worlds, one unfolding in time, and one that, through the spiritual aspects of intimacy and the deeper, scientific commitment to mystery, transcends time. Here the transpersonal was seen as the world of mystery; relationships, whether we are participants or observers, will always entail an edge of "not knowing." There will always be something to be known. The question is whether we approach the process of knowing in a caring, connected, moral, and responsible way or whether we adopt a view that decomposes and fragments the world into mechanistic processes. The artful balance between the need for continuity and structure—for making things static—and the need for mystery and the unexpected is, in a sense, a spiritual discipline for both lovers and scientists. The remaining chapters developed the idea of connectedness in scientific knowing by introducing the perspective of connectedness across temporal frames (*intertemporality* or *contextualization*).

Chapter 7 addressed the importance of seeing the bigger picture by arguing for the need to conduct temporally sensitive research, that is, research tied less to a single temporal frame (e.g., the experiment) and referencing relationships across many contexts. Chapter 8, after reviewing theory, tried to show how this bigger picture is always happening in the moment-to-moment ways that couples respond to change and relate to time. Here

the metaphor of weaving is seen in a practical way: in order to carry out their relationships, partners must calibrate across different temporal contexts. They talk to each other, follows social rules and routines, schedule or budget time in accordance with different situations and phases.

These perspectives can also be viewed as different aspects of a transpersonal capacity (see Figure above). In addition to the seven perspectives summarized earlier, is the key factor of *presence*. Presence was discussed at length in chapter 4.

TOWARD INTEGRATION

In the modern world, in which we live mainly for the moment, it is easy to overlook the taste of the soul for a greater sense of time and a profound notion of community . . . Care of the soul is not a project of self-improvement nor a way of being released from the troubles and pains of human existence. It is not at all concerned with living properly or with emotional health. These are the concerns of temporal, heroic, Promethean life. Care of the soul touches another dimension, in no way separate from life, but not identical either with the problem solving that occupies so much of our consciousness. (Moore, 1992, pp. 302–304)

Just as the aforementioned summary shows many different definitions, I have
argued that relationships exist at many different levels. One way of simplifying
this discussion of "level" is to distinguish between deep and surface aspects of
relationships, and process and sequential aspects of relationships. (These
distinctions were also discussed in chap. 6.) The first distinction pertains to
notions of intimacy in that we become intimate as we move beyond a surface
knowledge to a deeper one. The second distinction pertains to notions of time in
that it may be understood as a series of discontinuous moments strung together
in a sequence of past–present–future, or it may be experienced as an ongoing
continuous process where the present flows in a seamless fashion in many
directions. As a way of integrating the previous models, I will argue that the
capacity to shift from surface to deep and from a sequential to processual view is
a transpersonal capacity. It is, in the language of Moore, a way of caring for
one's soul, of being able to deepen into our otherwise ordinary, linear
experiences. It requires the various characteristics and processes mentioned,
*Letting Go, Faith, Nurturing Conditions, Self-analysis, Mystery, connectedness
through Contextuality, connectedness through Calibration.* In effect, the
practice of these capacities constitutes a form of spiritual discipline.

These stated relationships summarize how the various models proposed
may be integrated into a single model. In simple form, this model appears as such:

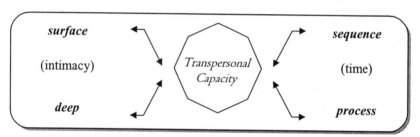

The capacity to translate back and forth between the mundane sequence of
events that unfold within a relationship and the deeper processes those events
reflect is one that requires a lifetime to develop and cultivate. For example, as
described in chapter 4, certain disruptive and chaotic events—those that most
test relationships—are also those that allow opportunities for transcendence.
Seen in another light, truly intimate relationships are the vehicle through which
the constant translation between surface sequences and deep processes most
often takes place. This translation occurs through language and text when we
move from understanding each other's meaning, to a deeper meeting, and
ultimately to flowing together (chap. 2). It occurs when we move from a
dialectic fixation or concern with whether the relationship is in one state or
another (e.g., stable vs. chaotic) to a simple awareness of intimacy as it arises
moment to moment (chap. 4).

The Relationship Between Surface Sequence and Deep Process

The description of surface sequence and deep process can be embellished with language from previous models. The surface sequence of relationships—the more direct and observable aspects—can be categorized into one of the three main temporal contexts and may be viewed as occurring predominantly in one of three time frames: interaction time, situation time, and phasic time. The deep process of intimacy—less observable by those outside the relationship but more directly felt by partners—can be stimulated or cultivated through one of three processes: transcendence both through and of text (chap. 2), development of faith (transpersonal/spiritual intimacy) (chap. 3), and understanding facilitative/nurturing conditions (chap. 4).

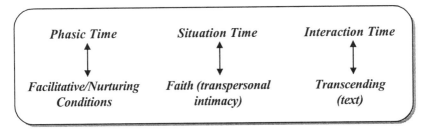

In fact, there may be tendencies for the three contexts and three processes to align with each other in systematic ways. A transpersonal science of intimacy would seek to examine these alignments in showing how human interaction ultimately has a spiritual purpose. In other terms, there may be a teleology to all interactions, situations, and phases; there is an underlying design and purpose that shapes these temporal aspects. A transpersonal science would examine how these patterns corresponded with partner's actual experiences of intimacy. The following are some initial thoughts describing the possible alignments between temporal frames and transpersonal experience.

Interaction Time. The process of communicating—speaking and seeking understanding—typically occurs and is measured across interaction sequences. This process has been previously defined through the textual metaphor and movement from transcription to transcendence. The observer who studies temporal aspects of interaction sequences may find it easier to measure acts of transcription and translation than acts of transformation. However, if interactions, particularly those that are intimate or that seek deeper intimacy, have a teleological or purposeful quality than the entire sequence may reveal an underlying organization or pattern in which specific transactions have a direction toward them. Studying such patterns may reveal what makes partners experience some interactions as more or less transformational and transcendent.

Situation Time. The social roles and types of relationships we encounter usually shape the development and decay of situations. Thus, it is more likely for there to be a discussion of spiritual topics between a religious leader and a church member from the same church than between a student and a high school teacher. The observer who studies temporal aspects of situations or how a couple transitions from one type of situation to another might examine patterns that develop over time. For example, a researcher may study how certain topics are approached or avoided or the degree of flow versus abruptness in the beginning and ending of certain situations. These patterns are likely to be determined by how much the individual or partner is fixated versus flexible in their view of intimacy. As described in chapter 3, individuals may have problems (disharmony) if intimacy is only understood or experienced within an interpersonal or romantic relationship and they neglect the individual/intrapersonal, faith/transpersonal, or societal/community types of intimate relationship. Researchers could explore whether certain patterns of exchanges will be shaped by these imbalances.

Phasic Time. The development and decay of phases is usually shaped by the longer term temporal forces of relationships. For intimacy, in particular, nurturing conditions has a premiere role in shaping phasic transitions (see Fig. 4.1). The observer who studies these transitions across many couples may begin to distinguish patterns that suggest nurturing conditions or more distal/secondary causes for couples in addition to the more directly observable and immediate proximal causes. For example, the life history of all couples often involves a "power struggle" phase or a "working through differences" period. This phase may be addressed in one interval of time or it may resurface periodically over time in intervals of varying duration. It is possible that those couples who address this phase directly have a different understanding of nurturing conditions. For example, they understand "right timing" or they know how to make smoother transitions. Studying such differences across couples may reveal how a couple's orientation toward nurturing conditions influences the long-term phases of their life together.

Scripts As a Way of Centering

Three key qualities of the transpersonal capacity are self-analysis and the capacities to, on one hand, see the bigger picture of how events are embedded within other events (contextuality) and, on the other hand, to realize the limits of our knowing and embrace the mystery of life. As shown in chapter 5, this capacity is facilitated through an analysis of script. In many ways, scripts play a pivotal role in the development of intimacy. They help us to know and they bring us to the edge of knowing. Just as I have shown parallels between the three time frames (interaction, situation, phase) and transpersonal capacities, so there are parallels between time frames and scripts.

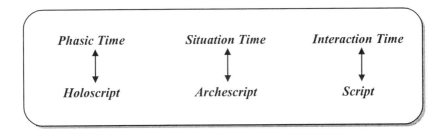

In this model, scripts tend to manifest in behavioral interactions, archescripts tend to be understood from analysis of situations, and holoscripts are most discernible over the longer term phases of intimate knowing. Leonard (1986) revealed how the inward archescripts of *Beauty and the Beast* informed her outward relationship. This helped prepare her for the deeper commitment of making a vow with her lover and entering into the mystery of life with him:

> The man I met was a man of depth and creativity, of introversion and fantasy, a man who knew the soul of the Beast of the woods . . . In our first year together we even lived in a rose-covered manor house, a magical place in the heart of the redwoods . . . But I was often afraid of this dark, mysterious, many-roomed house deep in the woods. For I still had Beauty's fear of the Beast, fear of his rage and masculine primal power. . . . In this relationship I now had to learn to consciously use the power of my inner Beast, the power of assertion that had previously been lost. . . . Both for the outer wedding of our potential marriage and the inner wedding with the divine, the Beast had to be faced, loved, and wed so the sacred union with the divine prince could occur. (pp. 184–185).

Leonard engaged in self-analysis to uncover scripts about her own lack of assertiveness and the fear of losing her independence. By so doing, she developed the courage to "face" the Beast and make the commitment to the long-term vow. In the previous quote, we see how the initial *situation* of living in the woods was symbolic of Beauty's entering into the domain of the Beast. The situation is understood (contextualized) through Leonard's application of the *Beauty and the Beast* metaphor (archescript). This helps her to face the deeper situation of her own psyche, and she was able to move into a new phase of her relationship through the vow. In a later chapter she described this process.

> We long for the eternal but it eludes us. Rilke believed that we should let the eternal come forth freely rather than try to gain it through possessing, a desire doomed to failure. We must learn to accept our finitude and live in its measure rather than vanish in longing for the infinite. The challenge in love is to learn the secret measure of loving in the human realm. We cannot project all meaning onto the gods or onto each other. We cannot possess another's soul. But we share the mystery. (p. 224)

The vow requires both accepting the limits of our own personal story and of opening up to the greater mystery. As I have tried to show, we may be led to a place in intimacy through our capacity to know (through text, through script). However, as we continue on this journey, especially the changes inevitably brought from living with another, those capacities may no longer serve us. We enter into a mystery and leave the past behind. In this way, true intimacy is continually renewed (recalibrated). Leonard (1986) quoted Rilke in making this point.

Is it not time that, in loving,
we freed ourselves from the loved one, and quivering, endured:
as the arrow endures the string, to become, in the gathering
   out-leap,
something more than itself? For staying is nowhere. (p. 225)

The ability to see one's own scripts (or projections, imago, distortions), to look deeper for their archetypal roots, may lead to the realization that every interaction and situation is brought about by multiple contextual factors (cf. destiny, karma, yüan). Relationship becomes a teacher, a mirror for enlightenment. There is the possibility then of detaching from the hubbub and the details of the particular interaction or situation and embrace the timelessness of being. Importantly, this is not an intellectual process. It requires living and *living with* rather than analyzing or reacting to, in any personal way, the ups and downs (the four forces and eight functions) of the relationship. Rather, as we embrace the "ongoingness" of the surface sequence ←→ deep process relationship, we simultaneously become part of and are constituted or defined by the story. In some mysterious way, the holoscript informs the phase of the relationship, just as our archescripts mold the situations we encounter, and our idiosyncratic scripts shape the occasion of our interaction.

CONCLUSION

The various threads outlined in this chapter may be summarized in a single schema (see Fig. 9.1 and also the appendix for an integration of the various RESEARCH REFLECTIONS). In the center of this model is the relationship as it arises moment to moment and is shaped by events occurring at surface and deep levels. Chapter 7 described how this relationship may be better labeled a *relata* than a relationship because of the tendency for the latter to be reified (see endnote 6 in chap. 7, p. 248). To clarify, relata is defined as individuals existing in a "loosely coupled" system, or within a nexus of various states of flux across variable temporal contexts. As such, it is not an entity, but a constant process of coming into being. To the degree that we are attached to a relationship, then to that same degree we cannot experience the deep process of intimacy; that is, text transcendence, transpersonal initmacy, and nurturing conditions. However, each of the models—by depicting relationships within temporal context—offers a map back from the surface to the deep.

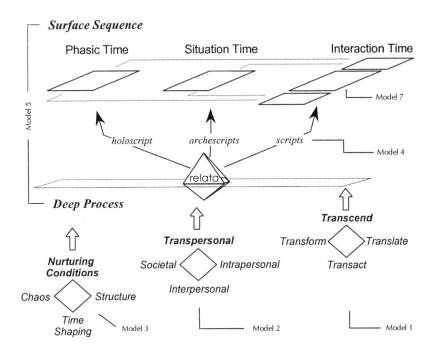

FIG. 9.1. Integration of the seven models.

As Fig. 9.1 attempts to show, many different aspects of time form a nexus in the relata. There is constant process and change and yet the "other" may still be there with us. Instead of focusing on time (i.e., memory of the past or plans for the future) but by resting in the moment together, it is possible to understand this coming into being. By integrating the various models in this book I hope to show, in a single frame, how any understanding of intimacy or of time must deal one with the other.

⧗

For thousands of years, couples have understood the deep process of time simply as they rest, walk, or talk with each other. After his wife Davy passed away and as part of his grieving, Vanauken (1980) spent much time recalling all the events of his life with her; something he called the "Illumination of the Past":

> But all the fulfillments were somehow, it seemed to me, incomplete, temporary, *hurried*. We wished to know, to savour, to sink in—into the heart of the experience—to possess it wholly. But there was never enough time; something still eluded us...

> And yet, after all, the clock is not always ticking. Sometimes it stops and then we are happiest. Sometimes—more precisely, some-not-times—we find "the still point of the turning world." All our most lovely moments perhaps are timeless. Certainly it was so for Davy and me. That very day when we sat on the wall and talked of time. (pp. 200-201)

Appendix:
Integrating the Research Reflections

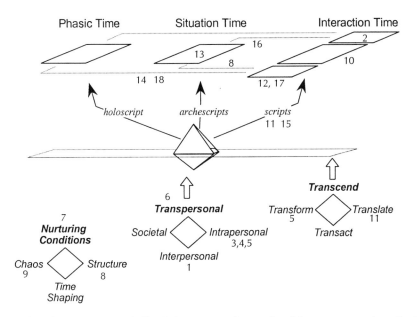

The above version of Fig. 9.1 suggests that each of the measures described in the 18 RESEARCH REFLECTIONS (RR) may be used to investigate the ideas put forward in this book. As can be seen in the figure, not every idea has a corresponding measure. I offer these questions to help stimulate further exploration.

- How does interpersonal intimacy (RR # 1) overlap with intrapersonal (3, 4, 5) and transpersonal (6) intimacy? Do partners differ in how they balance these as suggested by the self-rating scale in chapter 2 (see p. 81)?
- Does the capacity for being in the moment (presence, RR # 5) with a partner influence how much one hides family secrets or scripts (15)? Do these also influence the kinds of stories partners tell (12) about their relationship?
- Can couples be identified by whether they tend to be oriented toward nurturing conditions (7) versus form (8) or chaos (9)?
- Is it possible to use the different measures to explore the process of calibration within a couple? For example, do differences in morningness-eveningness (10) influence routine maintenance (17), or other communication processes (e.g., communication apprehension-14, regulation-18)? How do these processes, along with the resources partners exchange during the day (16), influence the stories (12) and metaphors (2) they use to describe their relationship?
- How are the above processes influenced by attachment style (11) or relationship with God (6)? For example, do insecurely attached partners structure their time (8) differently? Does having a partner with a more secure view of God change this?

References

Abbott, A. (1988). Transcending general linear reality. *Sociological Theory, 6* (Fall), 169–186.

Acitelli, L. K., Douvan, E., & Veroff, J. (1993). Perceptions of conflict in the first year of marriage: How important are similarity and understanding? *Journal of Social and Personal Relationships, 10*(1), 5–20.

Acitelli, L. K., & Duck, S. (1987). Intimacy as the proverbial elephant. In D. Perlman & S. Duck (Eds.), *Intimate relationships: Development, dynamics and deterioration* (pp. 297–308). Newbury Park, CA: Sage.

Acker, S. R. (1989). Designing communication systems for human systems: Values and assumptions of "Socially Open Architecture." In J. A. Anderson (Ed.), *Communication yearbook/12* (pp. 498–532). Newbury Park, CA: Sage.

Adamopoulos, J. (1991). The emergence of interpersonal behavior: Diachronic and cross-cultural processes in the evolution of intimacy. In S. Ting-Toomey & F. Korzenny (Eds.), *Cross-cultural interpersonal communication* (pp.155–170). Newbury Park, CA: Sage.

Adams, R. N. (1975). *Energy and structure.* Austin, TX: University of Texas Press.

Agudo, P. (1978). Intimacy with self vs. self-alienation. In A. Polcino (Ed.), *Intimacy: Issues of emotional loving in an age of stress for clergy and religious* (pp. 15–24). Whitinsville, MA: Affirmation Books.

Ainsworth, D. M. S., Blehar, M., Waters, E., & Wall, S. (1978). *Patterns of attachment.* Hillsdale, NJ: Lawrence Erlbaum Associates.

Allen, P. G. (1986). *The sacred hoop: Recovering the feminine in American Indian traditions.* Boston: Beacon Press.

Almaas, A. H. (1986). *Essence: The diamond approach to inner realization.* York Beach, ME: Samuel Weiser.

Almaas, A. H. (1987). *Diamond heart (Books One and Two).* Berkeley, CA: Diamond Books.

Altman, I., & Taylor, D. A. (1973). *Social penetration: The development of interpersonal relationships.* New York: Holt, Rinehart & Winston.

Altman, I., Vinsel, A., & Brown, B. (1981). Dialectic conceptions in social psychology: An application to social penetration and privacy regulation. In L. Berkowitz (Ed.), *Advances in experimental social psychology* (pp. 107–160). New York: Academic Press.

Amato, P. R., & Booth, A. (1997). *A generation at risk: Growing up in an era of family upheavel.* Cambridge, MA: Harvard University Press.

Amato, P. R., & Rogers, S. J. (1997). A longitudinal study of marital problems and subsequent divorce. *Journal of Marriage and the Family, 59*, 612–624.

Amazon.com (1999). Interpersonal relations [WWW document]. [http://www.amazon.com] [accessed November 1, 1999].

Amodeo, J., & Amodeo, K. (1986). *Being intimate: A guide to successful relationships.* New York: Arkana.

Antill, J. K. (1983). Sex role complementarity versus similarity in married couples. *Journal of Personality and Social Psychology, 45*, 145–155.

Archer, R., & Burleson, J. (1980). The effects of timing of self–disclosure on attraction and reciprocity. *Journal of Personality and Social Psychology, 38*, 120–130.

Argüelles, J. (1988). *Earth ascending.* Santa Fe, NM: Bear & Co.

Argyle, M. (1978). *The psychology of interpersonal behavior.* Middlesex, England: Penguin.

Argyle, M., & Dean, J. (1965). Eye-contact, distance and affiliation. *Sociometry, 28*, 289–304.

Argyle, M., Furnham, A., & Graham, J. A. (1981). *Social situations.* Cambridge, England: Cambridge University Press.

Argyle, M., & Henderson, M. (1985). *The anatomy of relationships: And the rules and skills needed to manage them successfully.* London: Heineman.

Arnold, C. L. (1992). An introduction to hierarchical linear models. *Measurement and Evaluation in Counseling and Development, 25,* 58–90.

Aron, A., & Aron, E. N. (1996). Self and self-expansion in relationships. In G .J. O. Fletcher & J. Fitness (Eds.), *Knowledge structures in close relationships: A social psychological approach* (pp. 325–344). Hillsdale, NJ: Lawrence Erlbaum Associates.

Aronson, E., & Linder, D. (1965). Gain and loss of esteem as determinants of interpersonal attractiveness. *Journal of Experimental and Social Psychology*, *1*, 156–171.

Aronson, E., & Mills, J. (1959). The effect of severity of initiation on liking for a group. *Journal of Abnormal and Social Psychology*, *59*, 177–181.

Auble, P. M., Franks, J. J., & Soraci, S. A., Jr. (1979). Effort toward comprehension: Elaboration or "aha!"? *Memory and Cognition*, *7*, 426–434.

Augustine Fellowship (1986). *Sex and love addicts anonymous*. Boston: The Augustine Fellowship.

Baert, P. (1992). *Time, self and social being: Temporality within a sociological context*. Brookfield, VT: Ashgate.

Baldwin, C. (1991). *Life's companion: Journal writing as a spiritual quest*. New York: Bantam.

Baldwin, M. W. (1995). Relational schemas and cognition in close relationships. *Journal of Social and Personal Relationships*, *12*, 547–552.

Ballonoff, P. (1974). *Genetics and social structure: Mathematical structuralism in population genetics and social theory*. Stroudsburg, PA: Dowden, Hutchinson & Ross.

Bandura, A. (1977). *Social learning theory*. Englewood Cliffs, NJ: Prentice-Hall.

Barlow, C. (1997). *Green space, green time: The way of science*. New York: Springer-Verlag.

Baron, R. M., & Boudreau, L. A. (1987). An ecological perspective on integrating personality and social psychology. *Journal of Personality and Social Psychology*, *53*, 1222–1228.

Barret, B., & Barzan, R. (1996). Spiritual experiences of gay men and lesbians. *Counseling and Values*, *41*(1), 4–15.

Barry, W. A. (1970). Marriage research and conflict: An integrative review. *Psychological Bulletin*, *73*, 41–54.

Barthes, R. (1978). *A lover's discourse: Fragments*. New York: Hill & Wang.

Bartholomew, K., & Horowitz, L. M. (1991). Attachment styles in young adults: A test of a four-category model. *Journal of Personality and Social Psychology*, *61*, 226–244.

Bateson, G. (1972). *Steps to an ecology of mind*. New York: Ballantine.

Bateson, G. (1979). *Mind and nature*. New York: Dutton.

Battaglia, D. M., Richard, F. D., Datteri, D. L., & Lord, C. G. (1998). Breaking up is (relatively) easy to do: A script for the dissolution of close relationships. *Journal of Social and Personal Relationships*, *15*(6), 829–845.

Baxter, L. (1984). Trajectories of relationship disengagement. *Journal of Social and Personal Relationships*, *1*(1), 49–74.

Baxter, L. (1992). Root metaphors in accounts of developing relationships. *Journal of Social and Personal Relationships*, *9*(2), 253–276.

Baxter, L. A. (1988). A dialectical perspective on communication strategies in relationship development. In S. Duck (Ed.), *Handbook of personal relationships: Theory, research, and interventions* (pp. 257–273). New York: Wiley.

Baxter, L. A. (1990). Dialectical contradictions in relationship development. *Journal of Social and Personal Relationships*, *7*(1), 69–88.

Baxter, L. A., & Bullis, C. (1986). Turning points in developing romantic relationships. *Human Communication Research*, *12*(4), 469–493.

Baxter, L. A., & Simon, E. P. (1993). Relationship maintenance strategies and dialectical contradictions in personal relationships. *Journal of Social and Personal Relationships*, *10*(2), 225–242.

Becker, E. (1973). *The denial of death*. New York: Free Press.

Belenky, M. F., Clinchy, B. M., Goldberger, N. R., & Tarule, J. M. (1986). *Women's ways of knowing*. New York: Basic Books.

Belitz, C., & Lundstrom, M. (1997). *The power of flow: Practical ways to transform your life with meaningful coincidences*. New York: Harmony Books.

Benjamin, J. (1988). *The bonds of love: Psychoanalysis, feminism, and the problem of domination*. New York: Pantheon.

Benson, P., & Spilka, B. (1973). God image as a function of self-esteem and locus of control. *Journal for the Scientific Study of Religion*, *12*, 297–310.

Berger, C. R. (1988). Uncertainty and information exchange in developing relationships. In S. Duck (Ed.), *Handbook of personal relationships: Theory, research, and interventions* (pp. 239–255). Chichester, England: Wiley.

Berger, P., & Kellner, H. (1964). Marriage and the construction of reality: An exercise in the microsociology of knowledge. *Diogenes*, *46*, 1–24.

Berger, P. L. (1980). *The heretical imperative: Contemporary possibilities of religious affirmation.* Garden City, KS: Anchor.

Bergmann, M. S. (1987). *The anatomy of loving.* New York: Ballantine.

Bergmann, W. (1992). The problem of time in sociology: An overview of the literature on the state of theory and research on the "Sociology of Time," 1900–1982. *Time & Society: An International Interdisciplinary Journal, 1*(1), 81–134.

Bergson, H. (1911). *Creative evolution.* London: Macmillan.

Berlo, D. (1960). *The process of communication.* New York: Holt, Rinehart & Winston.

Berman, M. (1988). *The reenchantment of the world.* Toronto: Bantam.

Berman, S., & Weiss, V. (1978). *Relationships.* New York: Hawthorn.

Berne, E. (1964). *Games people play.* New York: Grove Press.

Berne, E. (1976). *Beyond games and scripts.* New York: Grove Press.

Berry, W. (1985). Poetry and marriage: The use of old forms. In J. Welwood (Ed.), *Challenge of the heart: Love, sex, and intimacy in changing times* (pp. 170–172). Boston: Shambhala.

Berscheid, E. (1983). Emotion. In H. H. Kelley et al. (Eds.), *Close relationships* (pp. 110–168). New York: Freeman.

Berscheid, E. (1985). Compatibility, interdependence, and emotion. In W. Ickes (Ed.), *Compatible and incompatible relationships* (pp. 143–162). New York: Springer-Verlag.

Berscheid, E. (1986). Mea culpas and lamentations: Sir Francis, Sir Isaac, and the "slow progress" of soft psychology. In R. Gilmour & S. Duck (Eds.), *The emerging field of personal relationships* (pp. 267–286). Hillsdale, NJ: Lawrence Erlbaum Associates.

Berscheid, E. (1994). Interpersonal relationships. In L. W. Porter & M. R. Rosenzweig (Eds.), *Annual Review of Psychology* (pp. 79–129). Palo Alto, CA: Annual Reviews.

Berscheid, E., & Reis, H. T. (1998). Attraction and close relationship. In D. T. Gilbert, S. T. Fiske, & G. Lindzey (Eds.), *The handbook of social psychology* (Vol. 2, pp. 193–281). Boston: McGraw-Hill.

Berscheid, E., & Walster, E. (1974). A little bit about love. In T. H. Huston (Ed.), *Foundations of interpersonal attraction* (pp. 356–382). New York: Academic Press.

Bertalanffy, L. (1968). *General systems theory.* New York: Braziller.

Betcher, W. (1987). *Intimate play: Creating romance in everyday life.* New York: Viking Penguin.

Bettelheim, B. (1984). *Freud and man's soul.* New York: Random House.

Bianco, M. (1981). *The Velveteen rabbit, or, how toys become real;* illustrated by Michael Green. Philadelphia, Pa.: Running Press

Bilmes, J. (1986). *Discourse and behavior.* New York: Plenum.

Birdwhistell, R. L. (1970). *Kinesics & context: Essays on body motion communication.* Philadelphia: University of Pennsylvania Press.

Blau, P. (1975). *Approaches to the study of social structure.* New York: The Free Press.

Blumer, H. (1969). *Symbolic interactionism.* Englewood Cliffs, NJ: Prentice-Hall.

Blumstein, P., & Schwartz, P. (1983). *American couples: Money, sex, work.* New York: Simon & Schuster.

Bochner, A. P. (1976). Conceptual frontiers in the study of communication in families: An introduction to the literature. *Human Communications Research, 2,* 381–397.

Bohm, D. (1980). *Wholeness and the implicate order.* London: Routledge & Kegan Paul.

Bolen, J. S. (1984). *Goddesses in every woman: A new psychology of women.* New York: Harper (Colophon).

Bolig, R., Stein, P. J., & McKenry, P. C. (1984). The self-advertisement approach to dating: Male-female differences. *Family Relations, 33,* 587–592.

Bolton, R. (1979). *People skills.* New York: Touchstone.

Bond, M. J., & Feather, N. T. (1988). Some correlates of structure and purpose in the use of time. *Journal of Personality and Social Psychology, 55*(2), 321–329.

Bornstein, M. H. (1989). Sensitive periods in development: Structural characteristics and causal interpretations. *Psychological Bulletin, 105*(2), 179–197.

Borys, H. J. (1991). *The way of marriage: A journal of spiritual growth through conflict, love and sex.* Kirkland, WA: Purna Press.

Boszormenyi-Nagy, I. (1974). Ethical and practical implications of intergenerational family therapy. *Psychotherapy and Psychosomatics, 24,* 261–268.

Boszormenyi-Nagy, I., & f, G. (1973). *Invisible loyalties: Reciprocity in intergenerational family therapy.* New York: Harper & Row.

Boucouvalas, M. (1980). Transpersonal psychology: A working outline of the field. *Journal of Transpersonal Psychology, 12*(1), 37–46.

Bower, G. H., Black, J. B., & Turner, T. J. (1979). Scripts in memory for text. *Cognitive Psychology*, *11*, 177–220.

Bowlby, J. (1969). *Attachment and loss* (Vol. 1, Attachment). New York: Basic Books.

Bradbury, T. N., & Fincham, F. D. (1988). Individual difference variables in close relationships: A contextual model of marriage as an integrative framework. *Journal of Personality and Social Psychology*, *54*, 713–721.

Bradbury, T. N., & Fincham, F. D. (1989). Behavior and satisfaction in marriage: Prospective mediating processes. In C. Hendrick (Ed.), *Close relationships* (pp. 119–143). Newbury Park, CA: Sage.

Braiker, H. B., & Kelley, H. H. (1979). Conflict in the development of close relationships. In R. L. Burgess & T. L. Huston (Eds.), *Social exchange in developing relationships* (pp. 135–168). New York: Academic Press.

Branden, N. (1980). *The psychology of romantic love*. Los Angeles: Tarcher.

Braudel, F. (1969). *Ecrits sur l'histoire*. Paris: Flammarion.

Brehm, S., & Kassin, S. (1990). *Social psychology*. Boston: Houghton Mifflin.

Brehm, S. S. (1985). *Intimate relationships*. New York: Random House.

Brickman, P., Dunkel-Schetter, C., & Abbey, A. (1987). The development of commitment. In P. Brickman (Ed.), *Commitment, conflict, and caring* (pp. 145–221). Englewood Cliffs, NJ: Prentice-Hall.

Briggs, J., & Peat, F. D. (1989). *Turbulent mirror: An illustrated guide to chaos theory and the science of wholeness*. New York: Harper & Row.

Broderick, C. B. (1988). To arrive where we started: The field of family studies in the 1930s. *Journal of Marriage and the Family*, *50*, 569–584.

Brody, G. H., Neubaum, E. & Forehand, R. (1988). Serial marriage: A heuristic analysis of an emerging family form. *Psychological Bulletin*, *103*(2), 212–222.

Bronowski, J. (1962). The educated man in 1984. In P. C. Obler & H. A. Estrin (Eds.), *The new scientist: Essays on the methods and values of modern science* (pp. 143–154). Garden City, NY: Anchor.

Bronowski, J. (1978). *The origins of knowledge and imagination*. New Haven, CT: Yale University Press.

Brothers, J. (1994, June). Marriage is for loving. *Good Housekeeping*, p. 56.

Brown, J. R., & Rogers, L. E. (1991). Openness, uncertainty, and intimacy: An epistemological reformulation. In N. Coupland, H. Giles, & J. M. Wiemann (Eds.), *"Miscommunication" and problematic talk* (pp. 146–165). Newbury Park, CA: Sage.

Bruess, C. J., & Pearson, J. C. (1993). "Sweet pea" and "pussy cat": An examination of idiom use and marital satisfaction over the life cycle. *Journal of Social and Personal Relationships*, *10*(4), 609–616.

Buber, M. (1970). *I and Thou*. New York: Scribner's. (Original work published 1958).

Buck, R. (1989). Emotional communication in personal relationships: A developmental interactionist view. In C. Hendrick (Ed.), *Close relationships* (pp. 144–163). Newbury Park, CA: Sage.

Buhrmeister, D., Furman, W., Wittenberg, M. T., & Reis, H. T. (1988). Five domains of interpersonal competence in peer relationships. *Journal of Personality and Social Psychology*, *55*, 991–1008.

Bullough, V. L. (1976). *Sexual variance in society and history*. New York: Wiley.

Bumpass, L. L., & Sweet, J. A. (1991). The role of cohabitation in declining rates of marriage. *Journal of Marriage and the Family*, *53*, 913–927.

Burgess, R. L., & Huston, T. L. (Eds.). (1979). *Social exchange in developing relationships*. New York: Academic Press.

Burleson, B. R., Kunkel, A. W., Samter, W., & Werking, K. J. (1996). Men's and women's evaluations of communication skills in personal relationships: When sex differences make a difference—and when they don't. *Journal of Social and Personal Relationships*, *13*(2), 201–224.

Bush, B. J. (1978). I have called you by name. In A. Polcino (Ed.), *Intimacy: Issues of emotional loving in an age of stress for clergy and religious* (pp. 35–54). Whitinsville, MA: Affirmation Books.

Buss, D. M. (1987). Selection, evocation, manipulation. *Journal of Personality and Social Psychology*, *53*, 1214–1221.

Buss, D. M. (1989a). Conflict between the sexes: Strategic interference and the evocation of anger and upset. *Journal of Personality and Social Psychology*, *56*, 735–747.

Buss, D. M. (1989b). Sex differences in human mate preferences: Evolutionary hypotheses tested in 37 cultures. *Behavioral and Brain Sciences*, *12*, 1–49.

Buss, D. M., & Schmitt, D. (1993). Sexual strategies theory: An evolutionary perspective on human mating. *Psychological Review, 100*(2), 204–232.

Byrne, D., Ervin, C., & Lamberth, J. (1970). Continuity between the experimental study of attraction and real life computer dating. *Journal of Personality and Social Psychology, 16,* 157–165.

Cahn, D. C. (1990). Perceived understanding and interpersonal relationships. *Journal of Personal and Social Relationships, 7*(2), 231–244.

Cameron, C., Oskamp, S., & Sparks, W. (1977). Courtship American style: Newspaper ads. *Family Coordinator, 26,* 27–30.

Cameron, L., & Low, G. (1999). *Researching and applying metaphor.* Cambridge, England: Cambridge University Press.

Campbell, D. T., & Stanley, J. (1966). *Experimental and quasi-experimental designs for research.* Skokie, IL: Rand McNally.

Campbell, J. (1972). *Myths to live by.* Toronto: Bantam.

Capra, F. (1975). *The Tao of physics: An exploration of the parallels between modern physics and Eastern mysticism.* Boulder, CO: Shambhala.

Carkhuff, R. R. (1983). *The art of helping* (5th ed.). Amherst, MA: Human Resource Development Press.

Carlson, E., & Stinson, K. (1982). Motherhood, marriage timing, and marital stability: A research note. *Social Forces, 61,* 258–267.

Carlson, R. (1984). What's social about social psychology? Where's the person in personality research? *Journal of Personality and Social Psychology, 47*(6), 1304–1309.

Cate, R. M., & Lloyd, S. A. (1988). Courtship. In S. Duck (Ed.), *Handbook of personal relationships: Theory, research, and interventions* (pp. 409–428). New York: Wiley.

Chang, G. C. (1974). *The Buddhist teaching of totality.* University Park, PA: Penn State University Press.

Chang, H., & Holt, R. G. (1991). The concept of Yüan and Chinese interpersonal relationships. In S. Ting-Toomey & F. Korzenny (Eds.), *Cross-cultural interpersonal communication* (pp. 28–57). Newbury Park, CA: Sage.

Chapple, E. D. (1970). *Culture and biological man: Explorations in behavioral anthropology.* New York: Holt, Rinehart & Winston.

Cherlin, A. (1981). *Marriage, divorce, remarriage.* Cambridge, MA: Harvard University Press.

Cialdini, R. B. (1985). *Influence: Science and practice.* Glenview, IL: Scott, Foresman.

Clarke, D. D., Allen, C.M.B., & Salinas, M. (1986). Conjoint time-budgeting: Investigating behavioral accommodation in marriage. *Journal of Social and Personal Relationships, 3*(1), 53–71.

Clark, M. S., & Reis, H. T. (1988). Interpersonal processes in close relationships. *Annual Review of Psychology, 39,* 609–672.

Cline, R. J. (1989). The politics of intimacy: Costs and benefits determining disclosure intimacy in male-female dyads. *Journal of Social and Personal Relationships, 6,* 5–12.

Cole, T., & Leets, L. (1999). Attachment styles and intimate television viewing: Insecurely forming relationships in a parasocial way. *Journal of Social and Personal Relationships, 16,* 495–512.

Colegrave, S. (1979). *Uniting heaven and earth: A Jungian and Taoist exploration of the masculine and feminine in human consciousness.* Los Angeles: Tarcher.

Conville, R. L. (1991). *Relational transitions: The evolution of personal relationships.* New York: Praeger.

Cooper, D. A. (1992). *Silence, simplicity, and solitude: A guide for spiritual retreat.* New York: Bell Tower.

Cornett, C. E., & Cornett, C. F. (1980). *Bibliotherapy: The right book at the right time.* Bloomington, IN: Phi Delta Kappa Educational Foundation.

Cottle, T. J., & Klineberg, S. L. (1974). *The present of things future: Explorations of time in human experience.* New York: The Free Press.

Coutts, L. M., & Schneider, F. W. (1976). Affiliative conflict theory: An investigation of the intimacy equilibrium and compensation hypothesis. *Journal of Personality and Social Psychology, 34,* 1135–1142.

Cox, M. J., Paley, B., Burchinal, M., & Payne, C. C. (1999). Marital perceptions and interactions across the transition to parenthood. *Journal of Marriage and the Family, 61,* 611–625.

Crick, F. (1994). *The astonishing hypothesis: The scientific search for the soul.* New York: Touchstone.

Crohan, S. E. (1992). Marital happiness and spousal consensus on beliefs about marital conflict: A longitudinal investigation. *Journal of Social and Personal Relationships, 9*(1), 89–102.

Cronbach, L. N., & Furby, L. (1970). How we should measure "change"—or should we? *Psychological Bulletin, 74,* 68–80.

Csikszentmihalyi, M. (1990). *Flow: The psychology of optimal experience.* New York: Harper.

Cupach, W. R., & Spitzberg, B. H. (Eds.). (1994). *The dark side of close relationships.* Mahwah, NJ: Lawrence Erlbaum Associates.

Cutler, W. B. (1991). *Love cycles: The science of intimacy.* New York: Villard Books.

Cutler, W. B. (1999). *Women's responses to genital stimulation: Evidence for the functional role of timing* [WWW document]. [*http://www.athena-inst.com/inabis98.html*] [accessed April 2, 2000].

Dainton, M. & Stafford, L. (1993). Routine maintenance behaviors: A comparison of relationship type, partner similarity and sex differences. *.Journal of Social and Personal Relationships, 10,* 255-271.

Daly, J., & Kreiser, P. O. (1994). Affinity seeking. In J. A. Daly & J. M. Wiemann (Eds.), *Strategic interpersonal communication* (pp. 109–134). Hillsdale, NJ: Lawrence Erlbaum Associates.

Daly, K. J. (1996). *Families & time: Keeping pace in a hurried culture.* Thousand Oaks, CA: Sage.

Daly, M., & Wilson, M. (1983). *Sex, evolution, and behavior.* Boston: Willard Grant Press.

Davis, M. S. (1973). *Intimate relations.* New York: The Free Press.

Davison, T. (1995). *Trust the force: Change your life through attitudinal healing.* Northvale, NJ: Aronson.

de Beaugrande, R. (1982). Psychology and composition: Past, present, and future. In M. Nystrand (Ed.), *What writers know: The language, process, and structure of written discourse* (pp. 211–268). New York: Academic Press.

Demos, J., & Boocock, S. S. (Eds.). (1978). *Turning points: Historical and sociological essays on the family.* Chicago: University of Chicago Press.

Derlega, V., Metts, S., Petronio, S., & Margulis, S. T. (1993). *Self-disclosure.* Newbury Park, CA: Sage.

Deutsch, M., & Krauss, R. M. (1960). The effect of threat on interpersonal bargaining. *Journal of Abnormal and Social Psychology, 61,* 181–189.

Dickemann, M. (1981). Paternal confidence and dowry competition: A biocultural analysis of purdah. In R. D. Alexander & D. W. Tinkle (Eds.), *Natural selection and social behavior* (pp. 417–438). New York: Chiron Press.

Diez, M. E. (1984). Communicative competence: An interactive approach. In R. N Bostrom (Ed.), *Communication yearbook: 8* (pp. 56–79). Beverly Hills, CA: Sage.

Dimmitt, B. S. (2000, January). Angel for lost children. *Reader's Digest, 156,* 66.

Dindia, K., & Allen, M. (1992). Sex-differences in self-disclosure: A meta-analysis. *Psychological Bulletin, 112,* 106–124.

Dinnerstein, D. (1976). *The mermaid and the minotaur: Sexual arrangements and human malaise.* New York: Harper & Row.

Doob, L. W. (1971). *Patterning of time.* New Haven, CT: Yale University Press.

Dressler, D. M. (1973). Life adjustment of retired couples. *International Journal of Aging and Human Development, 4,* 335–349.

Drigotas, S. M., Rusbult, C. E., Wieselquist, J., & Whitton, S. W. (1999). Close partner as sculptor of the ideal self: Behavioral affirmation and the Michelangelo phenomenon. *Journal of Personality and Social Psychology, 77,* 294–323.

Driscoll, R., Davis, K. W., & Lipetz, M. E. (1972). Parental interference and romantic love. *Journal of Personality and Social Psychology, 24,* 1–10.

Duck, S. (Ed.). (1982). *Personal relationships 4: Dissolving personal relationships.* London: Academic Press.

Duck, S. (Ed.). (1984). *Personal relationships 5: Repairing personal relationships.* London: Academic Press.

Duck, S. (Ed.). (1988a). *Handbook of personal relationships: Theory, research, and interventions.* New York: Wiley.

Duck, S. (1988b). *Relating to others.* Chicago: Dorsey.

Duck, S. (Ed.). (1991). *Understanding relationships.* New York: Guilford.

Duck, S. (1994). *Meaningful relationships: Talking, sense, and relating.* Newbury Park, CA: Sage.

Duck, S., & Miell, D. E. (1986). Charting the development of personal relationships. In R. Gilmour & S. W. Duck (Eds.), *The emerging field of personal relationships* (pp. 133–143). Hillsdale, NJ: Lawrence Erlbaum Associates.

Duck, S., & Pond, K. (1989). Friends, Romans, Countrymen lend me your retrospections: Rhetoric and reality in personal relationships. In C. Hendrick (Ed.), *Close relationships* (pp.17–38). Newbury Park, CA: Sage.

Duck, S., & Sants, H. (1983). On the origin of the specious: Are personal relationships really interpersonal states? *Journal of Social and Clinical Psychology, 1*(1), 27–41.

Durkheim, E., & Mauss, M. (1963). *Primitive classification*. Chicago: University of Chicago Press.

Eckerman, C. O. (1993). Toddler's achievement of coordinated action with conspecifics: A dynamic systems perspective. In L. B. Smith & E. Thelen (Eds.), *A dynamic systems approach to development: Applications* (pp. 333–358). Cambridge, MA: MIT Press.

Eisler, R. (1987). *The chalice and the blade: Our history, our future*. San Francisco: Harper & Row.

Ellis, D. G. (1979). Relational control in two groups systems. *Communication Monographs, 46*, 153–166.

Ellis, D. G., Fisher, A. B., Drecksel, L., Hoch, D. D., & Werbel, W. S. (1979). *Rel/Com: A system for analyzing relational communication*. Unpublished coding manual, University of Utah, Salt Lake City.

Epstein, S. (1979). The stability of behavior: I. On predicting most of the people much of the time. *Journal of Personality and Social Psychology, 37*(7), 1097–1126.

Erikson, E. (1964). *Childhood and society*. New York: Norton.

Erkel, R. T. (1995). Time shifting. *The Family Therapy Networker, 19*(1), 32–39.

Estés, C. P. (1992). *Women who run with the wolves*. New York: Ballantine.

Evans, R. P. (1995). *The Christmas box*. New York: Simon & Schuster.

Faulconer, J. E., & Williams, R. N. (1985). Temporality in human action. *American Psychologist, 40*(11), 1179–1188.

Fassel, D. (1990). *Working ourselves to death: The high cost of workaholism & the rewards of recovery*. San Francisco: Harper.

Fehr, B., & Baldwin, M. (1996). Prototype and script analyses of laypeople's knowledge of anger. In G. J. O. Fletcher & J. Fitness (Eds.), *Knowledge structures in close relationships: A social psychological approach* (pp. 219–245). Hillsdale, NJ: Lawrence Erlbaum Associates.

Feinstein, D., & Krippner, S. (1988). *Personal mythology: The psychology of your evolving self*. Los Angeles: Tarcher.

Feng, D., Giarrusso, R., Bengtson, V. L., & Frye, N. (1999). Intergenerational transmission of marital quality and marital stability. *Journal of Marriage and the Family, 61*, 451–463.

Festinger, L. (1957). *A theory of cognitive dissonance*. Stanford, CA: Stanford University Press.

Festinger, L., Schacter, S., & Back, K. (1988). The ecological bases of friendship. In L. A. Peplau, D. O. Sears, S. E. Taylor, & J. L. Freedman (Eds.), *Readings in social psychology: Classic and contemporary contributions* (2nd ed., chap. 10). Englewood Cliffs, NJ: Prentice-Hall.

Fine, G. (1979). Small groups and culture creation: The idioculture of little league baseball teams. *American Sociological Review, 44*, 735–745.

Fisher, A. B. (1978). *Perspectives on human communication*. NewYork: Macmillan.

Fisher, M., & Stricker, G. (1982). *Intimacy*. New York: Plenum.

Fisher, W. R. (1992). Narration, reason, and community. In R. H. Brown (Ed.), *Writing the social text: Poetics and politics in social science discourse* (pp. 119–218). New York: de Gruyter.

Fiske, D. W. (1988). From inferred personalities toward personality in action. *Journal of Personality, 56*, 815–833.

Fiske, S. T., Pratto, F., & Pavelchak, M. A. (1983). Citizens' images of nuclear war: Contents and consequences. *Journal of Social Issues, 39*, 41–65.

Fletcher, G. J. O., & Fitness, J. (1996). *Knowledge structures in close relationships: A social psychological approach*. Mahwah, NJ: Lawrence Erlbaum Associates.

Foa, U. G., & Foa, F. B. (1971). Resource exchange: Toward a structural theory of interpersonal communication. In A. K. Siegman & B. Pope (Eds.), *Studies in dyadic communication* (pp. 291–325). New York: Pergamon.

Foot, H. C., Smith, J. R., & Chapman, A. J. (1979). Nonverbal expressions of intimacy in children. In M. Cook & G. Wilson (Eds.), *Love and attraction: An international conference* (pp. 131–136). Oxford, England: Pergamon.

Forman, F. J., & Sowton, C. (1989). *Taking our time: Feminist perspectives on temporality*. Oxford, England: Pergamon.

Forrester, J. (1992). In the beginning was repetition: On inversions and reversals in psychoanalytic time. *Time & Society: An International Interdisciplinary Journal, 1*(2), 287–300.

Foucault, M. (1972). *The archaeology of knowledge*. London: Tavistock.

Franz, von, M. L. (1981). *Puer aeternus*. Santa Monica, CA: Sigo.

Fraser, J. T. (1975). *Time, passion, and knowledge*. New York: Braziller.

Fraser, J. T. (1987). *Time: The familiar stranger*. Redmond, WA: Tempus.

Fraser, J. T., Lawrence, N., & Haber, F. C. (1986). *Time, science, and society in China and the West (The study of time V)*. Amherst: University of Massachusetts Press.

Frisbie, W. P., Opitz, W., & Kelly, W. R. (1985). Marital instability trends among Mexican Americans as compared to Blacks and Anglos: New evidence. *Social Science Quarterly, 66*, 587–601.

Fromm, E. (1976). *To have or to be?* New York: Harper & Row.

Fuller, J. A., & Warner, R. M. (2000). Family stressors as predictors of codependency. *Genetic, Social, and General Psychology Monographs, 126*(1), 5–22.

Funder, D., Parke, R. D., Tomlinson-Keasey, C., & Widaman, K. (Eds.). (1993). *Studying lives through time*. Washington, DC: American Psychological Association.

Gackenbach, J. (1998). *Psychology and the Internet: Intrapersonal, interpersonal, and transpersonal implications*. New York: Academic Press.

Gallagher, C. A., Maloney, G. A., Rousseau, M. F., & Wilczak, P. F. (1989). *Embodied in love: Sacramental spirituality and sexual intimacy*. New York: Crossroad.

Gardner, H. (1984). *Frames of mind: The theory of multiple intelligences*. London: Heineman.

Garfinkel, H. (1967). *Studies in ethnomethodology*. Englewood Cliffs, NJ: Prentice-Hall.

Garthoeffner, J. L., Henry, C., & Robinson, L. C. (1993). The modified interpersonal relationship scale: Reliability and validity. *Psychological Reports, 73*, 995–1004.

Geen, R. G. (1981). Behavioral and physiological reactions to observed violence: Effects of prior exposure to aggressive stimuli. *Journal of Personality and Social Psychology, 40*, 868–875.

Gerbner, G., Gross, L., Morgan, M., & Signorelli, N. (1986). Living with television: The dynamics of the cultivation process. In J. Bryant & D. Zillman (Eds.), *Perspectives on media effects* (pp. 17–40). Hillsdale, NJ: Lawrence Erlbaum Associates.

Gergen, K. J. (1973). Social psychology as history. *Journal of Personality and Social Psychology, 26*(2), 309–320.

Gergen, K. J. (1988). If persons are texts. In S. B. Messer, L. A. Sass, & R. L. Woolfolk (Eds.), *Hermeneutics and psychological theory* (pp. 28–51). New Brunswick, NJ: Rutgers University Press.

Gergen, K. J. (1992). *The saturated self: Dilemmas of identity in contemporary life*. New York: Basic Books.

Ghiselli, E. E., Campbell, J. P., & Zedeck, S. (1981). *Measurement theory for the behavioral sciences*. San Francisco: Freeman.

Giblin, P. (1989). Use of reading assignments in clinical practice. *American Journal of Family Therapy, 17*(3), 219.

Giddens, A. (1984). *The constitution of society*. Berkeley, CA: University of California Press.

Gioscia, V. (1971). On social time. In H. Yaker, H. Osmond, & F. Cheek (Eds.), *The future of time* (pp. 73–141). New York: Doubleday.

Gleick, J. (1999). *Faster: The acceleration of just about everything*. New York: Pantheon.

Godwin, D. D., & Scanzoni, J. (1989). Couple consensus during marital joint decision-making: A context, process, outcome model. *Journal of Marriage and the Family, 51*, 943–956.

Goffman, E. (1959). *The presentation of self in everyday life*. Garden City, NY: Doubleday.

Goffman, E. (1967). *Interaction ritual: Essays on face-to-face behavior*. New York: Pantheon.

Goffman, E. (1974). *Frame analysis*. Cambridge, MA: Harvard University Press.

Goldscheider, F. K., & DaVanzo, J. (1989). Pathways to independent living in early adulthood: Marriage, semiautonomy, and premarital residential independence. *Demography, 26*(4), 597–614.

Gollub, J. O. (1991). *The decade matrix*. Reading, MA: Addison-Wesley.

Gottman, J. M. (1979). *Marital interaction: Experimental investigations*. New York: Academic Press.

Gottman, J. M. (1982a). Emotional responsiveness in marital conversations. *Journal of Communication* (Summer), 108–120.

Gottman, J. M. (1982b). Temporal form: Toward a new language for describing relationships. *Journal of Marriage and the Family, 44*, 943–962.

Gottman, J. M. (1983). How children become friends. *Monographs of the Society for Research in Child Development, 48* (3, Serial No. 201).

Gottman, J. M. (1994a). *What predicts divorce? The relationship between marital processes and marital outcomes*. Hillsdale, NJ: Lawrence Erlbaum Associates.

Gottman, J. M. (1994b, May/June). Why marriages fail. *The Family Therapy Networker, 18*(3), 40–48.

Gottman, J. M., Markman, H. J., & Notarius, C. (1977). The topography of marital conflict: A sequential analysis of verbal and nonverbal behavior. *Journal of Marriage and the Family, 39*, 461–477.

Gottman, J. M., Notarius, C., Gonso, J., & Markman, H. J. (1976). *A couple's guide to communication*. Champaign, IL: Research Press.

Gottman, J. M., & Roy, A. K. (1987). *Sequential analysis: Temporal form in social interaction*. New York: Cambridge University Press.

Gottman, J. M., & Rushe, R. H. (1993). Special section: The analysis of change. *Journal of Consulting and Clinical Psychology, 61*(6), 907–983.

Gottman, J. M., & Silver, N. (1999). *The seven principles for making marriage work*. New York: Crown Publishers.

Goulding, R., & Goulding, M. (1987). Injunctions, decisions, and redecisions. *Transactional Analysis Journal, 6*(1), 41–48.

Gouldner, A. W. (1960). The norm of reciprocity: A preliminary statement. *American Sociological Review, 25*, 161–178.

Gray, J. (1992). *Men are from Mars, women are from Venus: A practical guide for improving communication and getting what you want in your relationships*. New York: HarperCollins.

Gross, S. (1992). Reading time—text, image, film. *Time & Society, 2*(1), 207–222.

Guerney, B. G., Jr. (Ed.). (1977). *Relationship enhancement: Skill training programs for therapy, problem prevention, and enrichment*. San Francisco: Jossey-Bass.

Gumperz, J. (1982). *Language and social identity*. New York: Cambridge University Press.

Gurvitch, G. (1964). *The spectrum of social time*. Dordrecht, Holland: D. Reidel.

Hacker, H. M. (1981). Blabbermouths and clams: Sex differences in self-disclosure in same-sex and cross-sex friendship dyads. *Psychology of Women Quarterly, 5*, 385–401.

Hagberg, J. O., & Guelich, R. A. (1989). The critical journey: Stages in the life of faith. Dallas, TX: Word Publications.

Hall, E. T. (1983). *The dance of life: The other dimension of time*. Garden City, NY: Doubleday.

Hannah, B. (1981). *Encounters with the soul: Active imagination as developed by C.G. Jung*. Santa Monica, CA: Sigo Press.

Harrison, A. A., & Saeed, L. (1977). Let's make a deal: An analysis of revelations and stipulations in lonely hearts advertisements. *Journal of Personality and Social Psychology, 35*, 257–264.

Hartup, W. W. (1979). Levels of analysis in the study of social interaction: An historical perspective. In M. E. Lamb, S. J. Suomi, & G. R. Stephenson (Eds.), *Social interaction analysis* (pp. 11–32). Madison: University of Wisconsin Press.

Harvey, J. H., Agostinelli, C., & Weber, A. L. (1989). Account making and formation of expectations about close relationships. *Review of Personality and Social Psychology, 10*, 39–62.

Harvey, J. H., Christensen, A., & McClintock, E. (1983). Research methods. In H. H. Kelley et al. (Eds.), *Close relationships* (pp. 449–485). New York: Freeman.

Harvey, J. H., Weber, A. L., & Orbuch, T. L. (1990). *Interpersonal accounts: A social psychological perspective*. Oxford: Basil Blackwell.

Haslam, N. (1995). Factor structure of social relationships: An examination of relational models and resource exchange theories. *Journal of Personal and Social Relationships, 12*(2), 217–227.

Hassel, D. J. (1985). *Searching the limits of love: An approach to the secular transcendent: God*. Chicago: Loyola University Press.

Hauerwas, S., & Burrell, D. (1989). From system to story: An alternative rationality. In S. Hauerwas & L. G. Jones (Eds.), *Why Narrative?* (pp.158–190) Indiana, IN: Notre Dame University Press.

Hayakawa, S. (1972). *Language and thought in action*. New York: Harcourt, Brace & Jovanovich.

Hayward, J. W. (1987). *Shifting worlds, changing minds: Where the sciences and Buddhism meet*. Boston: New Science Library.

Hazan, C., & Shaver, P. (1987). Romantic love conceptualized as an attachment process. *Journal of Personality and Social Psychology, 52*, 511–524.

Heald, C. (1987). *Intimacy with God: Pursuing a deeper experience of God through the Psalms (A devotional study)*. Colorado Springs, CO: NAV Press.

Heaton, T. B. (1991). Time related determinants of marital dissolution. *Journal of Marriage and the Family, 53*, 285–295.

Heidegger, M. (1962). *Being and time*. Translated by J. Macquarrie & E. Robinson. New York: Harper.

Heider, F. (1958). *The psychology of interpersonal relation*. New York: Wiley.

Helson, R., Mitchell, V., & Moane, G. (1984). Personality and patterns of adherence and nonadherence to the social clock. *Journal of Personality and Social Psychology, 46*(5), 1079–1096.

Hendrick, S. (1988). A generic measure of relationship satisfaction. *Journal of Marriage and the Family, 50*, 93–98.

Hendricks, G., & Hendricks, K. (1990). *Conscious loving: The journey to co-commitment.* New York: Bantam.

Hendrix, H. (1992). *Keeping the love you find: A guide for singles.* New York: Pocket Books.

Henry, J. (1971). *Pathways to madness.* New York: Random House.

Hetherington, E. M. (1976). Divorce, new relationships and sexual satisfaction. *Family Relations, 25*, 422–431.

Hewes, D. E., & Planalp, S. (1987). The individual's place in communication science. In C. R. Berger & S. H. Chaffee (Eds.), *Handbook of communication science* (pp. 146–183). Newbury Park, CA: Sage.

Hill, C. T., Peplau, L. A., & Rubin, Z. (1976). Breakups before marriage: The end of 103 affairs. *Journal of Social Issues, 32*(1), 147–168.

Hillman, J. (Ed.). (1979). *Puer papers.* Irving, TX: Spring Publications.

Hillman, J. (1985). *Anima: An anatomy of a personified notion.* Dallas, TX: Spring Publications.

Hillman, J., & Ventura, M. (1992). *We've had a hundred years of psychotherapy—and the world's getting worse.* San Francisco: Harper.

Hines, B. (1996). *God's whisper, creation's thunder: Echoes of ultimate reality in the new physics.* Brattleboro, VT: Threshold.

Hochman, D. (1994, March). Virtual relationships. *Us,* 33–37.

Hochschild, A. R. (1997). *The time bind: When work becomes home and home becomes work.* New York: Henry Holt.

Hollis, M. (1987). *The cunning of reason.* Cambridge, MA: Cambridge University Press.

Homans, G. (1961). *Social behavior: Its elementary forms.* New York: Harcourt, Brace, & World.

Hope and recovery: A twelve step guide for healing compulsive sexual behavior. (1987). Minneapolis, MN: CompCare Publishers.

Horne, J. A., & Ostberg, O. (1976). A self-assessment questionnaire to determine morningness-eveningness in human circadian rhythms. *International Journal of Chronobiology, 4*, 97–110.

Horney, K. (1942). *Self-analysis.* New York: Norton.

Howard, G. (1964). *The history of matrimonial institutions.* New York: Humanities Press. (Original work published 1904).

Huston, T. L. (1994). Courtship antecedents of marital satisfaction and love. In R. Erbver & R. Gilmour (Eds.), *Theoretical frameworks for personal relationships* (pp. 53–65). Hillsdale, NJ: Lawrence Erlbaum Associates.

Huston, T. L., & Levinger, G. (1978). Interpersonal attraction and relationships. In M. R. Rosenzweig & L. Porter (Eds.), *Annual Review of Psychology, 29* (pp. 115–156). Palo Alto, CA: Annual Reviews.

Huston, T. L., McHale, S., & Crouter, A. (1986). When the honeymoon's over: Changes in the marriage relationship over the first year. In R. Gilmour & S. Duck (Eds.), *The emerging field of personal relationships* (pp. 109–132). Hillsdale, NJ: Lawrence Erlbaum Associates.

Huston, T. L., & Robins, E. (1982). Conceptual and methodological issues in studying close relationships. *Journal of Marriage and the Family, 6*(1), 901–926.

Huston, T. L., Surra, C. A., Fitzgerald, N. M., & Cate, R. M. (1981). From courtship to marriage: Mate selection as an interpersonal process. In S. Duck & R. Gilmour (Eds.), *Personal relationships 2: Developing personal relationships* (pp. 53–88). London: Academic Press.

Hymes, D. (1972). Models of the interaction of language and social life. In J. Gumperz & D. Hymes (Eds.), *Directions in sociolinguistics: The ethnography of communication* (pp. 35–71). New York: Holt, Rinehart & Winston.

Hynes, A. H., & Wedl, L. C. (1990). Bibliotherapy: An interactive process in counseling older persons. *Mental Health Counseling, 12*(3), 288–302.

Ichazo, O. (1982). *Between metaphysics and protoanalysis: A theory for analyzing the human psyche.* New York: Arica Institute Press.

Ickes, W. (Ed.). (1985). *Compatible and incompatible relationships.* New York: Springer-Verlag.

Jamieson, L. (1998). *Intimacy: Personal relationships in modern societies.* Cambridge, England: Polity Press.

Janeway, E. (1981). *Powers of the weak.* New York: Morrow Quill.

Johnson, R. (1983). *We: Understanding the psychology of romantic love.* San Francisco: Harper & Row.

Johnson, S. (1991). *The ship that sailed into the living room: Sex and intimacy reconsidered.* Estancia, NM: Wildfire.

Jones, J. M. (1988). Cultural differences in temporal perspectives. In J. E. McGrath (Ed.), *The social psychology of time: New perspectives* (pp. 21–38). Newbury Park, CA: Sage.

Jung, C. G. (1921). Psychological types. In *Collected works of C.G. Jung, (Vol. 6).* Princeton, NJ: Princeton University Press.

Jung, C. G. (1963). *Memories, dreams, reflections.* New York: Vintage.

Jung, C. G. (1972). *Collected works of C.G. Jung* (R.F.C. Hull, trans.). Princeton, NJ: Princeton University Press.

Kahler, T. (1978). *Transactional analysis revisited.* Little Rock, AK: Human Development.

Kalupahama, D. J. (1975). *Causality: The central philosophy of Buddhism.* Honolulu, HI: University of Hawaii Press.

Kaminer, W. (1992). *I'm dysfunctional, your dysfunctional.* New York: Vintage.

Kaplan, A. (1964). *The conduct of inquiry: Methodology for behavioral science.* New York: Crowell.

Kaplan-William, S. (1991). *Dreamworking: A comprehensive guide to working with your dreams.* Olso, Norway: Journey Press.

Karpel, M. (1976). Individuation: From fusion to dialogue. *Family Process, 15,* 65–82.

Kast, V. (1986). *The nature of loving: Patterns of human relationship.* Wilmette, IL: Chiron.

Katz, S., & Liu, A. E. (1991). *The codependence conspiracy.* New York: Warner Books.

Kearl, M. C. (2000). *The times of our lives: Social encounters of the fourth dimension* [WWW document]. [www.trinity.edu/~mkearl/time.html] [accessed January 1, 2000].

Kearney, R. (1988). *The wake of the imagination.* Minneapolis: University of Minnesota Press.

Keller, C. (1986). *From a broken web: Separation, sexism, and self.* Boston: Beacon Press.

Keller, E. F. (1983). *A feeling for the organism.* New York: Freeman.

Keller, E. F. (1985). *Reflections on gender and science.* New Haven, CT: Yale University Press.

Kellerman, K., & Sleight, C. (1989). Coherence: A meaningful adhesive for discourse. In J. A. Anderson (Ed.), *Communication yearbook/12* (pp. 95–129). Newbury Park, CA: Sage.

Kelley, H. H. (1979). *Personal relationships: Their structures and processes.* New York: Wiley.

Kelley, H. H., Berscheid, E., Christensen, A., Harvey, J. H., Huston, T. L., Levinger, G., McClintock, E., Peplau, L. A., & Peterson, D. (1983). *Close relationships.* New York: Freeman.

Kelley, H. H., & Thibaut, J. W. (1978). *Interpersonal relations.* New York: Wiley .

Kelly, J. R., & McGrath, J. E. (1988). *On time and method.* Newbury Park, CA: Sage.

Kenny, D. A. (1988). The analysis of data from two-person relationships. In S. Duck, (Ed.) *Handbook of personal relationships: Theory, research, and interventions* (pp. 57–77). New York: Wiley.

Kenrick, D. T., & Keefe, R. C. (1988). *Gender differences in age criteria for a mate increase over the life span.* Manuscript submitted for publication.

Kenrick, D. T., & Simpson, D. (1996). *Evolutionary social psychology.* Mahwah, NJ: Lawrence Erlbaum Associates.

Kenrick, D. T., & Trost, M. R. (1989). A reproductive exchange model of heterosexual relationships: Putting proximate economics in ultimate perspective. In C. Hendrick (Ed.), *Close relationships* (pp. 92–118). Newbury Park, CA: Sage.

Kerckhoff, A. C., & Davis, K. E. (1962). Value consensus and need complementarily in mate selection. *American Sociological Review, 27,* 295–303.

Kerr, M., & Bowen, M. (1988). *Family evaluation.* New York: Norton.

Kiecolt-Glaser, J. K., Newton, T., Cacioppo, J. T., MacCallum, R. C., Glaser, R., & Malarkey, W. B. (1996). Marital conflict and endocrine function: Are men really more physiologically affected than women? *Journal of Consulting and Clinical Psychology, 64*(2), 324–332.

Kimberly, J. R. (Ed.). (1980). *The organizational life cycle: Issues in the creation, transformation, and decline of organizations.* San Francisco: Jossey-Bass.

Kincaid, D. L. (1987). *Communication theory: Eastern and Western perspectives.* San Diego, CA: Academic Press.

Kintner, E. (1969). *The letters of Robert Browning and Elizabeth Barrett Browning: 1845–1846* (2 vols.). Cambridge, MA: Harvard University Press.

Kirkpatrick, L. A. (1997). A longitudinal study of changes in religious belief and behavior as a function of individual differences in attachment style. *Journal for the Scientific Study of Religion, 36*(2): 207–217.

Kirkpatrick, L. A. (1998). God as a substitute attachment figure: A longitudinal study of adult attachment style and religious change in college students. *Personality and Social Psychology Bulletin, 24*(9), 961–973.

Kirkpatrick, L. A., & Shaver, P. R. (1992). An attachment-theoretical approach to romantic love and religious belief. *Personality and Social Psychology Bulletin, 18,* 266–275.

Kirkpatrick, L. A., Shillito, D. J., & Kellas, S. L. (1999). Loneliness, social support, and perceived relationships with God. *Journal of Social and Personal Relationships, 16,* 513–522.

Klinger, E. (1987). The interview questionnaire technique: Reliability and validity of a mixed idiographic-nomothetic measure of motivation. In J. N. Butcher & C. D. Spielberger (Eds.), *Advances in personality assessment* (Vol. 6, pp. 31–48). Hillsdale, NJ: Lawrence Erlbaum Associates.

Knapp, M. L. (1984). *Interpersonal communication and human relationships.* Newton, MA: Allyn & Bacon.

Knapp, M. L., Cody, M. J., & Reardon, K. K. (1987). Nonverbal signals. In C. R. Berger & S. H. Chaffee (Eds.), *Handbook of communication science* (pp. 385–415). Newbury Park, CA: Sage.

Knapp, R. H., & Garbutt, J. T. (1958). Time imagery and the achievement motive. *Journal of Personality, 26,* 426–434.

Knopf, J., & Seiler, M. (1991). *Inhibited sexual desire.* New York: Warner Books.

Knudson, R. M. (1985). Marital compatibility and mutual identity confirmation. In W. Ickes (Ed.), *Compatible and incompatible relationships* (pp. 233–252). New York: Springer-Verlag.

Kohler, J. (1975). *On the prehistory of marriage.* Chicago: University of Chicago Press.

Kornfield, J. (1993). *A path with heart: A guide through the perils and promises of spiritual life.* New York: Bantam.

Korzybski, A. (1958). *Science and sanity.* Lakeville, CT: International Non-Aristotelian Library Publishing.

Kövecses, Z. (1991). A linguist's quest for love. *Journal of Social and Personal Relationships, 8*(1), 78–98.

Kristeva, J. (1981). Women's time. *Signs, 4,* 13–35.

Kreckel, M. (1982). Communicative acts and shared knowledge: A conceptual framework and its empirical application. *Semiotica, 40,* 45–88.

Krueger, D. L., & Smith, P. (1982). Decision-making patterns of couples: A sequential analysis. *Journal of Communication* (Summer), 121–134.

Kuhn, T. S. (1970). *The structure of scientific revolutions.* Chicago: University of Chicago Press.

Kurdek, L. A. (1991). Marital stability and changes in marital quality in newlywed couples: A test of the contextual model. *Journal of Social and Personal Relationships, 8*(1), 27–48.

Kurdek, L .A. (1993). The allocation of household labor in gay, lesbian, and heterosexual married couples. *Journal of Social Issues, 49*(3), 127–140.

Laing, R. D. (1967). *The politics of experience.* New York: Ballantine.

Laing, R. D. (1969). *Self and others.* New York: Pantheon.

Laing, R. D., Phillipson, H., & Lee, A. R. (1966). *Interpersonal perception: A theory and a method of research.* New York: Springer.

Lamb, M. E., Suomi, S. J., & Stephenson, G. R. (Eds.). (1979). *Social interaction analysis.* Madison: University of Wisconsin Press.

Landy, F. J., Rastegary, H., Thayer, J., & Colvin, C. (1991). Time urgency: The construct and its measurement. *Journal of Applied Psychology, 76*(5), 644–657.

Langer, E. J. (1989). *Mindfulness.* Reading, MA: Addison-Wesley.

Lanham, R. A. (1992). *Revising prose* (3rd ed.*).* New York: Macmillan.

Lay, C. H. (1986). At last, my research article on procrastination. *Journal of Research in Personality, 20,* 474–495.

Lee, L. (1984). Sequences in separation: A framework for investigating endings of the personal (romantic) relationship. *Journal of Social and Personal Relationships, 1*(1), 49–74.

Lee, N. (1969). *The search for an abortionist.* Chicago: University of Chicago Press.

Leeds-Hurwitz, W. (1989). *Communication in everyday life.* Norwood, NJ: Ablex.

Lennard, H. L., & Bernstein, A. (1969). *Patterns in human interaction.* San Francisco: Jossey-Bass.

Leonard, L. (1986). *On the way to the wedding: Transforming the love relationship.* Boston: Shambhala.

Le Poire, B. A., Hallett, J., & Giles, H. (1998). Codependence: The paradoxical nature of the functional-afflicted relationship. In W. R. Cupach & B. H. Spitzberg (Eds.), *The dark side of close relationships* (pp. 153–176). Mahwah, NJ: Lawrence Erlbaum Associates.

Lerner, H. (1989). *The dance of intimacy.* New York: Harper & Row.

Levinas, E. (1987). *Time and other.* Pittsburgh: Duquense University Press.

Levine, R. V. (1988). The pace of life across cultures. In J. E. McGrath (Ed.), *The social psychology of time: New perspectives* (pp. 39–62). Newbury Park, CA: Sage.

Levine, R. V. (1988). Relearning to tell time. *American Demographics*, *20*(1), 20–25.

Levine, S. (1982). *Who dies?: An investigation of conscious living and conscious dying.* Garden City, NY: Doubleday.

Levine, S., & Levine, O. (1996). *Embracing the beloved: Relationship as a path of awakening.* Garden City, NY: Doubleday.

Levinger, G. (1976). A social psychological perspective on marital dissolution. *Journal of Social Issues*, *32*(1), 21–47.

Levinger, G. (1983). Development and change. In H. H. Kelley et al. (Eds.), *Close relationships* (pp. 315–359). New York: Freeman.

Levinger, G., Faunce, E. E., & Rands, M. (1976). [Interviews with spouses from "successful" marriages]. Unpublished raw data.

Levinger, G., & Rands, M. (1985). Compatibility in marriage and other close relationships. In W. Ickes (Ed.), *Compatible and incompatible relationships* (pp. 309–332). New York: Springer-Verlag.

Levinger, G., & Snoek, J. D. (1972). *Attraction in relationships: A new look at interpersonal attraction.* Morristown, NJ: General Learning Press.

Lévi-Strauss, C. (1963). *Totemism.* (R. Needham, trans.). Boston: Beacon Press.

Lewin, K. (1951). *Field theory in social science.* New York: Harper & Brothers.

Lewis, R. A. (1972). A developmental framework for the analysis of premarital dyadic formation. *Family Process, 11*, 17–48.

Lewis, R. A. (1973). A longitudinal test of a developmental framework for premarital dyadic formation. *Journal of Marriage and the Family*, *37*, 16–25.

Lips, H. (1997). *Sex and gender* (2nd ed.). Mountain View, CA: Mayfield.

Luborsky, L., Sackheim, H., & Christoph, P. (1979). The state conducive to momentary forgetting. In J. Kihlstrom & F. Evans (Eds.), *Functional disorders of memory* (pp. 325–353). Hillsdale, NJ: Lawrence Erlbaum Associates.

Luhmann, N. (1976). The future cannot begin. *Social Research*, *43*, 130–152.

Lynn, M., & Bolig, R. (1985). Personal advertisements: Sources of data about relationships. *Journal of Social and Personal Relationships*, *2*, 377–383.

Lyon, D., & Greenberg, J. (1991). Evidence of codependency in women with an alcoholic parent: Helping out Mr. Wrong. *Journal of Personality and Social Psychology*, *61*(3), 435–439.

MacKay, D. G. (1988). Under what conditions can theoretical psychology survive and prosper? *Psychological Review*, *95*(4), 559–565.

Maguire, M. C. (1999). Treating the dyad as the unit of analysis: A primer on three analytic approaches. *Journal of Marriage and the Family*, *61*, 213–224.

Mahler, M. (1968). *On human symbiosis and the vicissitudes of individuation.* New York: International Universities Press.

Malone, T. P., & Malone, P. T. (1987). *The art of intimacy.* New York: Prentice-Hall.

Mare, R. D. (1991). Five decades of educational assortative mating. *American Sociological Review*, *56*, 15–32.

Margulis, L., & Sagan, D. (1991). *Mystery dance: On the evolution of human sexuality.* New York: Summit.

Marini, M. M. (1978). The transition to adulthood: Sex differences in educational attainment and age at marriage. *American Sociological Review*, *43*, 483–507.

Marini, M. M. (1984a). Age and sequencing norms in the transition to adulthood. *Social Forces*, *63*(1), 229–244.

Marini, M. M. (1984b). The order of events in the transition to adulthood. *Sociology of Education*, *57*, 63–84.

Marini, M. M. (1984c). Women's educational attainment and the timing of entry into parenthood. *American Sociological Review*, *49*, 491–511.

Maslow, A. H. (1976). *Religion, values, and peak experiences.* New York: Penguin.

Masters, W. H., & Johnson, V. E. (1974). *The pleasure bond: A new look at sexuality and commitment.* Boston: Little, Brown.

Matoon, M. A. (1985). *Jungian psychology in perspective.* New York: The Free Press.

Matsuhashi, A. (1982). Explorations in the real-time production of written discourse. In M. Nystrand (Ed.), *What writers know: The language, process, and structure of written discourse* (pp. 269–290). New York: Academic Press.

Maturana, H. R., & Varela, F. J. (1980). *Autopoiesis and cognition: The realization of the living.* Boston: D. Reidel.

May, R. (1969). *Love and will*. New York: Norton.

Mazur, R. M. (1973). *The new intimacy: Open-ended marriage and alternative lifestyles*. Boston: Beacon Press.

McAdams, D. P. (1985). *Power, intimacy, and the life story: Personological inquiries into identity*. Chicago: Dorsey.

McAdams, D. P. (1989). *Intimacy: The need to be close*. New York: Doubleday.

McBee, P. (1994, July). Marriage as a spiritual discipline. *Friends Journal, 40*(7), 6–8.

McCall, G. J. (1988). The organizational life cycle of relationships. In S. Duck (Ed.), *Handbook of personal relationships: Theory, research, and interventions* (pp. 467–484). New York: Wiley.

McClintock, C. G., & Liebrand, W.B.G. (1988). Role of interdependence structure, individual value orientation, and another's strategy in social decision making: A transformational analysis. *Journal of Personality and Social Psychology, 55*, 396–409.

McGill, A. L. (1989). Context effects in judgments of causation. *Journal of Personality and Social Psychology, 57*, 189–200.

McGrath, J. E. (1988). *The social psychology of time: New perspectives*. Newbury Park, CA: Sage.

McGrath, J. E., & Kelly, J. R. (1986). *Time and human interaction*. New York: Guilford.

McCubbin, H. I., & Patterson, J. M. (1983). The family stress process: The double ABC model of adjustment and adaptation. In H. I. McCubbin, M. B. Sussman, & J. M. Patterson (Eds.), *Social stress and the family: Advances and developments in family stress theory and research* (pp. 7–37). New York: Haworth.

McGuire, W. J. (1980). The development of theory in social psychology. In R. Gilmour & S. Duck (Eds.), *The development of social psychology* (pp. 53–80). London: Academic Press.

McHugh, P. (1968). *Defining the situation: The organization of meaning in social interaction*. New York: Bobs-Merrill.

McLaughlin, S. D., Grady, W. R., Billy, J. O., Landale, N., & Winges, L. D. (1986). The effects of the sequencing of marriage and first birth during adolescence. *Family Planning Perspectives, 18*(1), 12–18.

Mead, G. H. (1934). *Mind, self, and society*. Chicago: University of Chicago Press.

Medina, J. J. (1996). *The clock of ages: Why we age—how we age—winding back the clock*. New York: Cambridge University Press.

Meichenbaum, D. (1988). What happens when the "brute data" of psychological inquiry are meanings: Nurturing a dialogue between hermeneutics and empiricism. In S. B. Messer, L. A. Sass, & R. L. Woolfolk (Eds.), *Hermeneutics and psychological theory* (pp. 116–130). New Brunswick, NJ: Rutgers University Press.

Merton, T. (1985). *Love and living*. (N. B. Stone & P. Hart, Eds.). New York: Farrar, Straus, & Giroux.

Mettee, D. R., & Aronson, E. (1974). Affective reactions to appraisal from others. In T. H. Huston (Ed.), *Foundations of interpersonal attraction* (pp. 236–284). New York: Academic Press.

Metzner, R. (1980). Ten classical metaphors of self-transformation. *Journal of Transpersonal Psychology, 12*(1), 47–62.

Michael, D. N. (1989). On thinking about the future. *Journal of Humanistic Psychology, 29*(1), 37–53.

Michaels, J. W., Acock, A. C., & Edwards, J. N. (1986). Social exchange and equity determinants of relationship commitment. *Journal of Social and Personal Relationships, 3*(2), 161–176.

Mickelson, K. D., Kessler, R. C., & Shaver, P. R. (1997). Adult attachment in a nationally representative sample. *Journal of Personality and Social Psychology, 73*(5), 1092–1106.

Microsoft. (1999). Telepresence [WWW document]. [http://www.research.microsoft.com/research /BARC/Telepresence/default.htm] [accessed October 30, 1999].

Miell, D., & Duck, S. (1986). Strategies in developing friendships. In V. J. Derlega & B. A. Winstead (Eds.), *Friendship and social interaction* (pp. 129–144). New York: Springer-Verlag.

Mikulincer, M., & Arad, D. (1999). Attachment working models and cognitive openness in close relationships: A test of chronic and temporary accessibility effects. *Journal of Personality and Social Psychology, 77*(4), 710–725.

Milardo, R. M., Johnson, M. P., & Huston, T. L. (1983). Developing close relationships: Changing patterns of interaction between pair members and social networks. *Journal of Personality and Social Psychology, 44*(5), 964–976.

Milgram, S. (1974). *Obedience to authority: An experimental view*. New York: Harper & Row.

Millar, F. E., & Rogers, L. E. (1976). A relational approach to interpersonal communication. In G. R. Miler (Ed.), *Explorations in interpersonal communication* (pp. 87–103). Beverly Hills, CA: Sage.

Mischel, W. (1968). *Personality and assessment*. New York: Wiley.

MIT Media Lab. (1999). Research on affective computing [WWW document]. [URL http://www.media.mit.edu/affect/AC_affect.html] [accessed October 30, 1999].

Modell, J., Furstenberg, F. F., Jr., & Hershberg, T. (1976). Social change and transitions to adulthood in historical perspective. *Journal of Family History*, *1*, 7–32.

Montgomery, B. (1993). Relationship maintenance versus relationship change: A dialectical dilemma. *Journal of Social and Personal Relationships*, *10*(2), 205–224.

Moore, T. (1992). *The care of the soul*. New York: HarperCollins.

Moore, T. (1994). *Soulmates*. New York: Harper & Row.

Moore-Ede, M. (1993). *The twenty-four-hour society: Understanding human limits in a world that never stops*. Reading, MA: Addison-Wesley.

Morgan, S. P., & Rindfuss, R. R. (1985). Marital disruption: Structural and temporal dimensions. *American Journal of Sociology*, *90*(5), 1055–1076.

Morton, T. L. (1978). Intimacy and reciprocity of exchange: A comparison of spouses and strangers. *Journal of Personality and Social Psychology*, *36*(1), 72–81.

Morton, T. L., & Douglas, M. A. (1981). Growth of relationships. In S. Duck & R. Gilmour (Eds.), *Personal relationships 2: Developing personal relationships* (pp. 3–26). London: Academic Press.

Müller, E. (1968). *Morphologische Poetik*. Germany: Tubingen: M. Niemeyer.

Murray, D. W. (1994). Poor suffering bastards: An anthropologist looks at illegitimacy. *Policy Review, 68*, 9–15.

Murray, H. A. (1938). *Explorations in personality*. New York: Oxford University Press.

Murstein, B. I. (1976). *Who will marry whom? Theories and research in marital choice*. New York: Springer.

Needleman, J. (1998). *Time and the soul*. New York: Currency/Doubleday.

Neubauer, A. C. (1992). Psychometric comparison of two circadian rhythm questionnaires and their relationship with personality. *Personality & Individual Differences*, *13*(2), 125–131.

Neumann, E. (1954). *The origins and history of consciousness* (Foreword by C. G. Jung). Princeton, NJ: Princeton University Press.

Neville, R. (1993). *Eternity and time's flow*. Albany: State University of New York Press.

Norton, A. J., & Moorman, J. E. (1987). Current trends in marriage and divorce among American women. *Journal of Marriage and the Family*, *49*, 3–14.

Nye, F. I. (1976). *Role structure and analysis of the family*. Beverly Hills, CA: Sage.

Nye, F. I. (1988). Fifty years of family research, 1937–1987. *Journal of Marriage and the Family*, *50*, 305–316.

Nystrand, M. (1982). *What writers know: The language, process, and structure of written discourse*. New York: Academic Press.

Oden, T. C. (1974). *Game free: A guide to the meaning of intimacy*. New York: Harper & Row.

Odin, S. (1982). *Process metaphysics and Hua-yen Buddhism: A critical study of cumulative penetration vs. interpenetration*. Albany: State University of New York Press.

Olson, D. H., McCubbin, H. I., Barnes, H. L., Larsen, A. S., Muxen, M. J., & Wilson, M. A. (Eds.). (1983). *Families, what makes them work?* Beverly Hills, CA: Sage.

Oostendorp, H., & Goldman, S. R. (1999). *The construction of mental representations during reading*. Hillsdale, NJ: Lawrence Erlbaum Associates.

Orbuch, T. L., Veroff, J., & Holmberg, D. (1991). *Memories of courtship in newlywed couples*. Unpublished manuscript, University of Michigan, Ann Arbor.

Orlock, C. (1993). *Inner time: The science of body clocks and what makes us tick*. New York: Birch Lane.

Orlofsky, J. L., Marcia, J. E., & Lesser, I. M. (1973). Ego identity status and intimacy versus isolation crisis of young adulthood. *Journal of Personality and Social Psychology*, *27*, 211–219.

Ornish, D. (1998). *Love & survival: The scientific basis for the healing power of intimacy*. New York: HarperCollins.

Ouspensky, P. D. (1973). *The psychology of man's possible evolution*. New York: Random House.

Pargament, K. I., Ensing, D. S., Falgut, K., Olsen, H., Reilly, B., Van Haitsma, K., & Warren, R. (1990). God help me (I): Religious coping efforts as predictors of the outcomes to significant life events. *American Journal of Community Psychology, 18*, 793–824.

Parks, M. R., & Adelman, M. B. (1983). Communication networks and the development of romantic relationships: An expansion of uncertainty theory. *Human Communication Research*, *10*(1), 55–79.

Parsons, T., Bales, R. F., & Shils, E. (1953). *Working papers in the theory of action*. New York: The Free Press.

Patterson, M. L. (1976). An arousal model of interpersonal intimacy. *Psychological Review*, *83*, 235–245.

Patterson, M. L. (1984). Intimacy, social control, and nonverbal involvement: A functional approach. In V. J. Derlega (Ed.), *Communication, intimacy and close relationships* (pp. 105–132). Orlando, FL: Academic Press.

Paul, G. L. (Ed.). (1987). Rational operations in residential treatment settings through ongoing assessment of client and staff functioning. In D. R. Peterson & D. B. Fishaman (Eds.), *Assessment for decision* (pp. 145–203). New Brunswick, NJ: Rutgers University Press.

Pearson, C. (1989). *The hero within: Six archetypes we live by.* San Francisco: Harper & Row.

Pearson, C. (1989). *Awakening the heroes within: Twelve archetypes to help us find ourselves and transform our world.* San Francisco: Harper & Row.

Peat, F. D. (1987). *Synchronicity: The bridge between mind and matter.* Toronto: Bantam.

Peele, S., & Brodsky, A. (1975). *Love and addiction.* New York: Taplinger.

Pepitone, A. (1981). Lessons from the history of social psychology. *American Psychologist, 36*(9), 972–985.

Petronio, S. (Ed.). (2000). *Balancing the secrets of private disclosures.* Hillsdale, NJ: Lawrence Erlbaum Associates.

Planalp, S., & Rivers, M. (1996). Changes in knowledge of personal relationships. In G.J.O. Fletcher & J. Fitness (Eds.), *Knowledge structures in close relationships: A social psychological approach* (pp. 299–324). Hillsdale, NJ: Lawrence Erlbaum Associates.

Powers, W. G., & Hutchinson, K. (1979). The measurement of communication apprehension in the marriage relationship. *Journal of Marriage and the Family, 41,* 80–95.

Prager, K. J. (1991). Intimacy status and couple conflict resolution. *Journal of Social and Personal Relationships, 8*(4), 505–526.

Prager, K. J. (1995). *The psychology of intimacy.* New York: Guilford.

Prather, H., & Prather, G. (1988). *A book for couples.* New York: Doubleday.

Priestly, J. B. (1964). *Man and time.* New York: Dell.

Prigogine, I., & Stengers, I. (1984). *Order out of chaos: Man's new dialogue with nature.* Toronto: Bantam.

Pruitt, D. G., & Rubin, J. Z. (1986). *Social conflict: Escalation, stalemates, and settlement.* New York: Random House.

Pryor, J. B., & Merluzzi, T. V. (1985). The role of expertise in processing social interaction scripts. *Journal of Experimental and Social Psychology, 21,* 362–379.

Putnam, R. (1995). Bowling alone: America's declining social capital. *Journal of Democracy, 6,* 65–78.

Quinn, R. E. (1996). *Deep change: Discovering the leader within.* San Francisco: Jossey-Bass.

Raudenbush, S. W., Brennan, R. T., & Barnett, R. C. (1995). A multivariate hierarchical model for studying psychological change within married couples. *Journal of Family Psychology, 9*(2), 161–174.

Raush, H. (1965). Interaction sequences. *Journal of Personality and Social Psychology,* 487–499.

Raush, H. (1972). Process and change—A Markov model for interaction. *Family Process,* 275–298.

Raush, H. L. (1981). Logical force, not quite logical people, and the pragmatics of change. *Communication, 6,* 99–116.

Rausch, H. L., Barry, W. A., Hertel, R. K., & Swain, M. (1974). *Communication, conflict and marriage.* San Francisco: Jossey-Bass.

Rechtschaffen, S. (1996). *Timeshifting: Creating more time to enjoy your life.* New York: Doubleday.

Register, L. M., & Henley, T. B. (1992). The phenomenology of intimacy. *Journal of Social and Personal Relationships, 9,* 467–481.

Reid, L. A. (1962). Religion, science and other modes of knowledge. In P. C. Obler & H. A. Estrin (Eds.), *The new scientist: Essays on the methods and values of modern science* (pp. 239–257). Garden City, NJ: Anchor.

Reilly, T., Atkison, G., & Waterhouse, J. (1997). *Biological rhythms and exercise.* New York: Oxford University Press.

Reis, H. T., & Knee, C. R. (1996). What we know, what we don't know, and what we need to know about relationship knowledge structures. In G.J.O. Fletcher & J. Fitness (Eds.), *Knowledge structures in close relationships: A social psychological approach* (pp. 169–191). Hillsdale, NJ: Lawrence Erlbaum Associates.

Reis, H. T., & Shaver, P. (1988). Intimacy as an interpersonal process. In S. Duck (Ed.), *Handbook of personal relationships: Theory, research, and interventions* (pp. 367–389). New York: Wiley.

Reiss, I. L. (1960). Toward a sociology of the heterosexual love relationship. *Marriage and Family Living, 22,* 139–145.

Reissman, C., Aron, A., & Bergen, M. R. (1993). Shared activities and marital satisfaction: Causal direction and self-expansion versus boredom. *Journal of Social and Personal Relationships, 10*(2), 243–254.

Ricouer, P. (1984). *Time and narrative* (Vol. 1). Chicago: University of Chicago Press.

Ricouer, P. (1985). *Time and narrative* (Vol. 2). Chicago: University of Chicago Press.

Rilke, R. M. (1985). Learning to love. In J. Welwood (Ed.), *Challenge of the heart: Love, sex and intimacy in changing times* (pp. 257–265). Boston: Shambhala.

Ring, K. (1967). Experimental social psychology: Some sober questions about some frivolous values. *Journal of Experimental Social Psychology, 3*, 113–123.

Ritterman, M. (1995). Stopping the clock. *The Family Therapy Networker, 19*(1), 44–51.

Robinson, J. P., & Godbey, G. (1997). *Time for life: The surprising ways Americans use their time.* University Park, PA: Pennsylvania State University.

Rodgers, R. H. (1987). Postmarital reorganization of family relationships. In D. Perlman & S. Duck (Eds.), *Intimate relationships: Development, dynamics, and deterioration* (pp. 239–268). Newbury Park, CA: Sage.

Rodgers, R. H., & Conrad, L. M. (1986). Courtship for remarriage: Influences on family reorganization after divorce. *Journal of Marriage and the Family, 48*, 767–775.

Rogers, L. E. (1972). *Dyadic systems and transactional communication in a family context.* Unpublished doctoral dissertation, Michigan State University, East Lansing.

Rosen, G. M. (1987). Self-help treatment books and the commercialization of psychotherapy. *American Psychologist, 42*(1), 46–51.

Rosnow, R. L. (1981). *Paradigms in transition: The methodology of social inquiry.* New York: Oxford University Press.

Rosnow, R. L., & Georgoudi, M. (Eds.). (1986). *Contextualism and understanding in behavioral science: Implications for research and theory.* New York: Praeger.

Roth, P. (1987). *Meaning and method in the social sciences.* Ithaca, NY: Cornell University.

Rowles, G. D. (1981). The surveillance zone as meaningful space for the aged. *The Gerontologist, 21*(3), 304–311.

Ruano, B. J., Bruce, J. D., & McDermott, M. M. (1969). Pilgrim's progress II: Recent trends and prospects in family research. *Journal of Marriage and the Family, 31*, 688–698.

Rubin, A. M. (1998). Personal involvement with the media. In J. S. Trent (Ed.), *Communication: Views from the helm for the twenty-first century* (pp. 257–263). Boston: Allyn & Bacon.

Rubin, Z. (1970). Measurement of romantic love. *Journal of Personality and Social Psychology, 16*, 265–273.

Ruble, D. N., Hackel, L. S., Fleming, A. S., & Stangor, C. (1988). Changes in the marital relationship during the transition to first time motherhood: Effects of violated expectations concerning division of household labor. *Journal of Personality and Social Psychology, 55*(1), 78–87.

Rule, B. G., Bisanz, G. L., & Kohn, M. (1985). Anatomy of a persuasion schema: Targets, goals, and strategies. *Journal of Personality and Social Psychology, 48*, 1127–1140.

Rusbult, C. E. (1983). A longitudinal test of the investment model: The development (and deterioration) of satisfaction and commitment in heterosexual involvements. *Journal of Personality and Social Psychology, 45*(1), 101–117.

Rusbult, C. E. (1987). Responses to dissatisfaction in close relationships: The exit-voice-loyalty-neglect model. In D. Perlman & S. Duck (Eds.), *Intimate relationships: Development, dynamics, and deterioration* (pp. 209–238). Newbury Park, CA: Sage.

Rusbult, C. E., & Buunk, B. P. (1993). Commitment processes in close relationships: An interdependence analysis. *Journal of Social and Personal Relationships, 10*, 175–204.

Rusbult, C. E., & Martz, J. (1992). *The decision to remain in an abusive relationship.* Unpublished manuscript, University of North Carolina, Chapel Hill.

Saegert, S., Zajonc, R. B., & Swapp, W. (1973). Exposure, context, and interpersonal attraction. *Journal of Personality and Social Psychology, 25*, 234–242.

Salzberg, S. (Speaker). (1993). *On delusion* (Cassette recording from 3 month retreat, October). Barre, MA: Insight Meditation Society.

Sanford, J. A. (1980). *The invisible partners: How the male and female in each of us affects our relationships.* New York: Paulist Press.

Sarnoff, I., & Sarnoff, S. (1989). *Love-centered marriage in a self-centered world.* New York: Hemisphere.

Saussure, de, F. (1959). *Course in general linguistics.* New York: McGraw-Hill.

Savory, A. (1988). *Holistic resource management.* Washington, DC: Island Press.

Scanzoni, J. (1979). Social exchange and behavioral interdependence. In R. L. Burgess & T. L. Huston (Eds.), *Social exchange in developing relationships* (pp. 61–98). New York: Academic Press.

Scanzoni, J. (1987). Families in the 1980s: Time to refocus our thinking. *Journal of Family Issues,* *8*(4), 394–421.

Scanzoni, J., Polonko, K., Teachman, J., & Thompson, L. (1989). *The sexual bond: Rethinking families and close relationships.* Newbury Park, CA: Sage.

Scarf, M. (1987). *Intimate partners: Patterns in love and marriage.* New York: Random House.

Schaef, A. W. (1987). *When society becomes an addict.* San Francisco: Harper & Row.

Schaef, A. W. (1989). *Escape from intimacy: The pseudo-relationship addictions.* San Francisco: Harper & Row.

Schaef, A. W. (1992). *Beyond therapy, beyond science: A new model for healing the whole person.* San Francisco: Harper & Row.

Scheflen, A. E. (1973). *Body language and social order: Communication as behavioral control.* Englewood Cliffs, NJ: Prentice-Hall.

Schlein, S., Guerney, B. G., Jr., & Stover, L. (1990). The interpersonal relationship scale. In J. Touliatos, B. F. Perlmutter, & M. A. Straus (Eds.), *Handbook of family measurement techniques* (p. 248). Newbury Park, CA: Sage.

Schnarch, D. M. (1991). *Constructing the sexual crucible: An integration of sexual and marital therapy.* New York: Norton.

Sears, D. O. (1986). College sophomores in the laboratory: Influences of a narrow data base on psychology's view of human nature. *Journal of Personality and Social Psychology, 51,* 515–530.

Servan-Schreiber, J. L. (1988). *The art of time.* Reading, MA: Addison-Wesley.

Sexton, R. E., & Sexton, V. S. (1982). Intimacy: A historical perspective. In M. Fisher & G. Stricker (Eds.), *Intimacy* (pp. 1–20). New York: Plenum.

Shackelford, T. K., & Buss, D. M. (1997). Cues to infidelity. *Personality and Social Psychology Bulletin, 10,* 1034–1045.

Sharabany, R. (1994). Intimate friendship scale: Conceptual underpinnings, psychometric properties and construct validity. *Journal of social and personal relationships, 11,* 449–469.

Sheehy, G. (1998). *Understanding men's passages: Discovering the new map of men's lives.* New York: Random House.

Shor, J., & Sanville, J. (1978). *Illusion in loving.* Los Angeles: Double Helix.

Shostrom, E. (1966). *Personal orientation inventory: An inventory for the measurement of self-actualization.* San Diego, CA: Educational and Industrial Testing Service.

Shrodes, C., & Russell, D. H. (1950). Contributions of research in bibliotherapy to the language-arts program *School Review, 58,* 335–342.

Sillars, A. L. (1985). Interpersonal perception in relationships. In W. Ickes (Ed.), *Compatible and incompatible relationships* (pp. 277–305). New York: Springer-Verlag.

Sillars, A. L., & Wilmot, W. W. (1994). Communication strategies in conflict and mediation. In J. A. Daly & J. M. Wiemann (Eds.), *Strategic interpersonal communication* (pp. 163–190). Hillsdale, NJ: Lawrence Erlbaum Associates.

Sills, J. (1987). *A fine romance: The passage from courtship to marriage.* New York: Ballantine.

Silverstein, J. L. (1992). The problem with in-laws. *Journal of Family Therapy, 14*(4), 399–412.

Simmel, G. (1907/1978). *The philosophy of money.* London: Routledge & Kegan Paul.

Simon, R. W. (1997). The meanings individuals attach to role identities and their implications for mental health. *Journal of Health and Social Behavior, 38,* 256–274.

Singer, J. (1972). *Boundaries of the soul.* Garden City, NY: Doubleday.

Singer, J. (1977). *Androgyny: Toward a new theory of sexuality.* Garden City, NY: Doubleday.

Sinha, B. M. (1983). *Time and temporality in Sâmkhya-Yoga and Abhidharma Buddhism.* New Delhi: Munshiram Manoharlal.

Slife, B. D. (1993). *Time and psychological explanation.* Albany: State University of New York Press.

Small, J. (1991). *Awakening in time: The journey from codependence to co-creation.* New York: Bantam.

Smolensky, M. H. (1992). Chronoepidemiology, chronobiology and epidemiology. In Y. Touitou & E. Haus (Eds.), *Biological rhythms in clinical and laboratory medicine* (pp. 659–672). Berlin: Springer-Verlag.

Snyder, M., & Ickes, W. (1985). Personality and social behavior. In G. Lindzey & E. Aronson (Eds.), *The handbook of social psychology* (3rd ed., Vol. 2, pp. 883–947). New York: Random House.

South, S. J., & Spitze, G. (1986). Determinants of divorce over the marital life course. *American Sociological Review, 51,* 583–590.

Spanier, G. B., Lewis, R. A., & Cole, C. L. (1975). Marital adjustment over the family life cycle: The issue of curvilinearity. *Journal of Marriage and the Family, 37*, 263–275.

Spencer, H. (1874/1976). *Principles of sociology* (Vols. 1–3). New York: D. Appleton & Co.

Sprey, J. (2000). Theorizing in family studies: Discovering process. *Journal of Marriage and the Family, 62*, 18–31.

Stanley, S. M., & Markman, H. J. (1992). Assessing commitment in personal relationships. *Journal of Marriage and the Family, 54*, 595–608.

Starhawk. (1979). *The spiral dance: A rebirth of the ancient religion of the great goddess.* San Francisco: Harper & Row.

Staske, S. (1999). Creating relational ties in talk: The collaborative construction of relational jealousy. *Symbolic Interaction, 22*, 213–246.

Stein, C. H., Bush, E. G., Ross, R. R., & Ward, M. (1992). Mine, yours and ours: A configural analysis of the networks of married couples in relation to marital satisfaction and individual well-being. *Journal of Social and Personal Relationships, 9*(3), 365–384.

Steiner, C. (1974). *Scripts people live.* New York: Grove Press.

Stephen, T. D. (1985). Fixed-sequence and circular-causal models of relationship development: Divergent views on the role of communication in intimacy. *Journal of Marriage and the Family, 45*, 955–963.

Stephens, L. (1996, December). Love line. *Utne Reader*, 49–57.

Sternberg, R. J. (1986). A triangular theory of love. *Psychological Review, 93*(2), 119–135.

Sternberg, R. J. (1988). *The triarchic mind: A new theory of human intelligence.* New York: Viking.

Sternberg, R. J. (1998). *Cupid's arrow: The course of love through time.* Cambridge, England: Cambridge University Press.

Sternberg, R. J. (1999). *Love is a story: A new theory of relationships.* New York: Oxford University Press.

Sternberg, R. J., & Hojjat, M. (1997). *Satisfaction in close relationships.* New York: Guilford.

Stinnet, N., Carter, L. M., & Montgomery, J. E. (1972). "Older persons" perceptions of their marriages. *Journal of Marriage and the Family, 34*, 665–670.

Stoll, C. S. (1974). *Female and male: Socialization, social roles, and social structure.* Dubuque, IA: Brown.

Strickland, L. H., Aboud, F. E., & Gergen, K. J. (Eds.). (1976). *Social psychology in transition.* New York: Plenum.

Surra, C. A., & Huston, T. L. (1987). Mate selection as a social transition. In D. Perlman & S. Duck (Eds.), *Intimate relationships: Development, dynamics, and deterioration* (pp. 88–120). Newbury Park, CA: Sage.

Swann, W. B., Langlois, J. H., Gilbert, L. A. (1998) *Sexism and stereotypes in modern society: The gender science of Janet Taylor Spence.* Washington, DC: American Psychological Association.

Swift, W. B. (1996, November/December). The work of oneness: How to make marriage a sacred union (Interview with Bo Lozoff). *Utne Reader*, 52–55, and 102.

Swensen, C. H., Eskew, R. W., & Kohlhepp, K. A. (1981). Stage of family life cycle, ego development, and the marriage relationship. *Journal of Marriage and the Family, 43*, 841–853.

Swensen, C. H., & Trahaug, G. (1985). Commitment and the long-term marriage relationship. *Journal of Marriage and the Family, 45*, 939–945.

Tannen, D. (1990). *You just don't understand.* New York: Ballantine.

Tart, C. (1983). *Transpersonal psychologies.* El Cerrito, CA: Psychological Processes.

Tart, C. (1987). *Waking up: Overcoming the obstacles to human potential.* Boston: New Science (Shambhala).

Tart, C. (1992). *Transpersonal psychologies: Perspectives on the mind from seven great spiritual traditions.* New York: Harper San Francisco.

Taylor, D. A., & Altman, I. (1966). Intimacy scaled stimuli for use I studies of interpersonal relations. *Psychological Reports, 19*, 729–730.

Teachman, J. D., & Polonko, K. A. (1990). Cohabitation and marital stability in the United States. *Social Forces, 69*, 207–220.

Tesch, S. A., & Whitbourne, S. K. (1982). Intimacy and identity status in young adults. *Journal of Personality and Social Psychology, 43*, 1041–1051.

Thibaut, J. W., & Kelley, H. H. (1959). *The social psychology of groups.* New York: Wiley.

Thomson, E., & Colella, U. (1992). Cohabitation and marital stability: Quality or commitment? *Journal of Marriage and the Family, 54*, 259–267.

Thomson, E., McLanahan, S. S., & Curtin, R. B. (1992). Family structure, gender, and parental socialization. *Journal of Marriage and the Family, 54*, 368–378.

Thornton, A., & Rodgers, W. L. (1987). The influence of individual and historical time on marital dissolution. *Demography, 24*(1), 1–22.

Ting-Toomey, S. (1983). An analysis of verbal communication patterns in high and low marital adjustment groups. *Human Communication Research, 9*(4), 306–319.

Tomkins, S. (1979). Script theory: Differential magnification of affects. In H. E. Howe & R. A. Dienstbier (Eds.), *Nebraska symposium on motivation* (pp. 201–236). Lincoln: University of Nebraska Press.

Touhey, J. C. (1972). Comparison of two dimensions of attitude similarity on heterosexual attraction. *Journal of Personality and Social Psychology, 23*, 8–10.

Tracy, K. (1998). Analyzing context: Framing the discussion. *Research on Language and Social Interaction, 31*(1), 1–28.

Trivers, R. L. (1972). Parental investment and sexual selection. In B. Campbell (Ed.), *Sexual selection and the descent of man* (pp. 146–179). Chicago: Aldine.

Trungpa, C. (1991). *Orderly chaos: The mandala principle.* Boston: Shambhala.

Tuckman, B. W. (1965). Developmental sequences in small groups. *Psychological Bulletin, 63*, 384–399.

Turner, J. H. (1988). *A theory of social interaction.* Stanford, CA: Stanford University Press.

Tzeng, O.C.S. (1993). *Measurement of love and intimate relations: Theories, scales, and applications for love development, maintenance, and dissolution.* Westport, CT: Praeger.

Vallacher, R. R., & Nowak, A. (1994). *Dynamical systems in social psychology.* San Diego, CA: Academic Press.

Vanauken, S. (1980). *A severe mercy.* San Francisco: Harper.

Vangelisti, A. L., & Caughlin, J. P. (1997). Revealing family secrets: The influence of topic, function, and relationships. *Journal of Personal and Social Relationships, 14*(5), 679–705.

Varga, T. A. (1998). Gender and gender role as related to intimacy, passion, commitment and sexual satisfaction. *Dissertation Abstracts International, 59* (2-B): 0916.

Ventura, M. (1995, April 16). Trapped in the time machine: A short history of how the nation got clocked. *Dallas Morning News,* pp. J1, J10.

Veroff, J., Sutherland, L., Chadiha, L., & Ortega, R. M. (1993). Newlyweds tell their stories: A narrative method for assessing marital experiences. *Journal of Social and Personal Relationships, 10*, 437–457.

Wachter, K., & Finch, C. E. (Eds.). (1997). *Between Zeus and the salmon: The biodemography of longevity.* Washington, DC: National Academy Press.

Wakefield, J. (1988). Hermeneutics and empiricism: Commentary on Donald Meichenbaum. In S. B. Messer, L. A. Sass, & R. L. Woolfolk (Eds.), *Hermeneutics and psychological theory* (pp. 131–148). New Brunswick, NJ: Rutgers University Press.

Ward, M. (1995). Butterflies and bifurcations: Can chaos theory contribute to our understanding of family systems? *Journal of Marriage and the Family, 57*, 629–638.

Warner, R. M. (1979). Periodic rhythms in conversational speech. *Language and Speech, 22*, 381–396.

Warner, R. M. (1988). Rhythm in social interaction. In J. E. McGrath (Ed.), *The social psychology of time* (pp. 63–88). Newbury Park, CA: Sage.

Warren, N. C. (1995). *The triumphant marriage: 100 extremely successful couples reveal their secrets.* Colorado Springs, CO: Focus on the Family.

Watts, A. (1951). *The wisdom of insecurity.* New York: Random House.

Watzlawick, P. (1976). *How real is real?: Confusion, disinformation, communication.* New York: Vintage.

Watzlawick, P., Beavin, J. J., & Jackson, D .D. (1967). *Pragmatics of human communication.* New York: Norton.

Watzlawick, P., Weakland, J. H., & Fisch, R. (1974). *Change: Principles of problem formation and problem resolution.* New York: Norton.

Weber, M. (1978). *Economy and society: An outline of interpretive sociology.* Berkeley, CA: University of California Press.

Wegner, D. M., Giuliano, & Hertel, P. T. (1985). Cognitive interdependence in close relationships. In W. Ickes (Ed.), *Compatible and incompatible relationships* (pp. 253–276). New York: Springer-Verlag.

Weinrich, H. (1964). *Tempus: Besprochene und erzählte welt.* Stuttgart: Kohlhammer.

Welwood, J. (1990). *Journey of the heart.* New York: HarperCollins.

Werner, C. M., Altman, I., & Brown, B. B. (1992). A transactional approach to interpersonal relations: Physical environment, social context, and temporal qualities. *Journal of Social and Personal Relationships, 9*, 297–323.

Werner, C. M., & Haggard, L. M. (1985). Temporal qualities of interpersonal relationships. In M. L. Knapp & G. R. Miller (Eds.), *Handbook of interpersonal communication* (pp. 59–99). Beverly Hills, CA: Sage.

Werner, E. E., & Smith, R. S. (1982). *Vulnerable but invincible: A longitudinal study of resilient children and youth.* New York: McGraw-Hill.

Wessman, A. E. (1973). Personality and the subjective experience of time. *Journal of Personality Assessment, 37*(2), 103–115.

Whitbourne, S. K., & Weinstock, C. (1979). *Adult development: The differentiation of experience.* New York: Holt, Rinehart & Winston.

Whitehead, A. N. (1929). *Process and reality: An essay in cosmology.* New York: Macmillan.

Whitehead, A. N. (1968). *Modes of thought.* New York: The Free Press.

Wilber, K. (1979). *No boundary: Eastern and Western approaches to personal growth.* Boston: New Science.

Williamson, M. (1994). *A return to love: Reflections on the principles of "A course in miracles."* New York: HarperPaperbacks.

Wilmot, W. W. (1987). *Dyadic communication* (3rd ed.). New York: Random House.

Wilner, W. (1982). Philosophical approaches to interpersonal intimacy. In M. Fisher & G. Stricker (Eds.), *Intimacy* (pp. 21–38). New York: Plenum.

Wolff, F. A. (1999). *The spiritual universe.* Portsmouth, NH: Moment Point Press.

Wood, J. (1993). Engendered relations: Interaction, caring, power, and responsibility in intimacy. In S. Duck (Ed.), *Social context and relationships* (pp. 26–54). Newbury Park, CA: Sage.

Worthington, E. L., Buston, B. G., & Hammonds, M. T. (1989). A component analysis of marriage enhancement: Information and treatment modality. *Journal of Counseling and Development, 67*(10), 555–560.

Wright, R. (1994, August). Our cheating hearts: Devotion and betrayal, marriage and divorce: How evolution shaped human love. *Time, 144*(7), 44–52.

Wu, Z. (1994). Remarriage in Canada: A social exchange perspective. *Journal of divorce and remarriage, 21*, 191–224.

Yaker, H., Osmond, H., & Cheek, F. (Eds.). (1971). *The future of time.* New York: Doubleday.

Yang, D. J. (2000, January 17). Craving your next Web fix: Internet addiction is no laughing matter. *U.S. News & World Report,* 41.

Yankelovich, D., & Barrett, W. (1970). *Ego and instinct.* New York: Vintage.

Young, K. S. (1998). *Caught in the net: How to recognize the signs of Internet addiction—and a winning strategy for recovery.* New York: Wiley.

Young, M. (1988). *The metronomic society: Natural rhythms and human timetables.* Cambridge, MA: Harvard University Press.

Young-Eisendrath, P. (1984). *Hags and heroes: A feminist approach to Jungian psychotherapy with couples.* Toronto: Inner City Books.

Yum, J. O. (1988). The impact of Confucianism on interpersonal relationships and communication in East Asia. *Communication Monographs, 55*, 374–388.

Zajonc, R. B. (1980). Cognition and social cognition: A historical perspective. In L. Festinger (Ed.), *Retrospections in social psychology* (pp. 180–204). New York: Oxford University Press.

Zeitlow, P. H., & Van Lear, C. A. (1991). Marriage duration and relational control: A study of developmental patterns. *Journal of Marriage and the Family, 53*, 773–785.

Zhu, S. H., & Pierce, J. P. (1995). A new scheduling method for time-limited counseling. *Professional Psychology: Research and Practice, 26*(6): 624–625.

Zerubavel, E. (1981). *Hidden rhythms: Schedules and calendars in social life.* Chicago: University of Chicago Press.

Zimbardo, P. (1985, March). Time in perspective. *Psychology Today,* 20–27.

Zweig, C., & Abrams, J. (Eds.). (1991). *Meeting the shadow: The hidden power of the dark side of human nature.* Los Angeles: Tarcher.

Author Index

Subject Index

About the Author

Joel B. Bennett is a researcher and consultant in the areas of employee well being, organizational health and stress, workplace culture, and employee training. He customizes employee focus groups, culture and benchmarking audits, and assessment centers to help guide positive organizational change. Clients include healthcare, the hospitality industry, federal and local government agencies, and community and academic organizations. He conducts workshops based on the ideas expressed in Time & Intimacy and is presently working on a follow-up manual that applies these ideas to daily living. Contact him at joel@timeandintimacy.com or j.bennett@tcu.edu. Dr. Bennett is on the staff of the Institute of Behavioral Research (www.ibr.tcu.edu; Texas Christian University) where he is responsible for the development and evaluation of a team-oriented training for substance abuse prevention. He has published research pertaining to substance abuse, violence, and other behavioral risks in the workplace as well as on factors that mitigate these risks (e.g., psychological presence, work group social health). Dr. Bennett also serves on the National Prevention Advisory Board for Magellan Behavioral Health, a subsidiary of Magellan Health Services.